MARY WOLLSTONECRAFT AND POLITICAL ECONOMY

Why was Wollstonecraft's landmark feminist work, the *Vindication of the Rights of Woman*, categorised as a work of political economy when it was first published?

Taking this question as a starting point, *Mary Wollstonecraft and Political Economy* gives a compelling new account of Wollstonecraft as critic of the material, moral, social, and psychological conditions of commercial modernity. Offering thorough analysis of Wollstonecraft's major writings – including her two *Vindications*, her novels, her history of the French Revolution, and her travel writing – this is the only book-length study to situate Wollstonecraft in the context of the political economic thought of her time. It shows Wollstonecraft as an economic as much as a political radical, whose critique of the emerging economic orthodoxies of her time anticipates later Romantic thinkers. *This title is part of the Flip it Open Programme and may also be available Open Access. Check our website Cambridge Core for details.*

CATHERINE PACKHAM is Professor of Eighteenth-Century Literature and Thought at the University of Sussex. She is the author of *Eighteenth-Century Vitalism: Bodies, Culture, Politics* (2012) and the co-editor of *Political Economy, Literature and the Formation of Knowledge, 1720–1850* (2018). She was the recipient of a Leverhulme Research Fellowship and has published widely on Wollstonecraft and eighteenth-century political economy.

CAMBRIDGE STUDIES IN ROMANTICISM

Founding Editor
Marilyn Butler, University of Oxford

General Editor
James Chandler, University of Chicago

Editorial Board
Claire Connolly, University College Cork
Paul Hamilton, University of London
Claudia Johnson, Princeton University
Essaka Joshua, University of Notre Dame
Nigel Leask, University of Glasgow
Alan Liu, University of California, Santa Barbara
Deidre Lynch, Harvard University
Jerome McGann, University of Virginia
David Simpson, University of California, Davis

This series aims to foster the best new work in one of the most challenging fields within English literary studies. From the early 1780s to the early 1830s, a formidable array of talented men and women took to literary composition, not just in poetry, which some of them famously transformed, but in many modes of writing. The expansion of publishing created new opportunities for writers, and the political stakes of what they wrote were raised again by what Wordsworth called those 'great national events' that were 'almost daily taking place': the French Revolution, the Napoleonic and American wars, urbanization, industrialization, religious revival, an expanded empire abroad, and the reform movement at home. This was an enormous ambition, even when it pretended otherwise. The relations between science, philosophy, religion, and literature were reworked in texts such as *Frankenstein* and *Biographia Literaria*; gender relations in *A Vindication of the Rights of Woman* and *Don Juan*; journalism by Cobbett and Hazlitt; and poetic form, content, and style by the Lake School and the Cockney School. Outside Shakespeare studies, probably no body of writing has produced such a wealth of commentary or done so much to shape the responses of modern criticism. This indeed is the period that saw the emergence of those notions of literature and of literary history, especially national literary history, on which modern scholarship in English has been founded.

The categories produced by Romanticism have also been challenged by recent historicist arguments. The task of the series is to engage both with a challenging corpus of Romantic writings and with the changing field of criticism they have helped to shape. As with other literary series published by Cambridge University Press, this one will represent the work of both younger and more established scholars on either side of the Atlantic and elsewhere.

See the end of the book for a complete list of published titles.

MARY WOLLSTONECRAFT AND POLITICAL ECONOMY

The Feminist Critique of Commercial Modernity

CATHERINE PACKHAM

University of Sussex

Shaftesbury Road, Cambridge CB2 8EA, United Kingdom

One Liberty Plaza, 20th Floor, New York, NY 10006, USA

477 Williamstown Road, Port Melbourne, VIC 3207, Australia

314–321, 3rd Floor, Plot 3, Splendor Forum, Jasola District Centre, New Delhi – 110025, India

103 Penang Road, #05-06/07, Visioncrest Commercial, Singapore 238467

Cambridge University Press is part of Cambridge University Press & Assessment, a department of the University of Cambridge.

We share the University's mission to contribute to society through the pursuit of education, learning and research at the highest international levels of excellence.

www.cambridge.org
Information on this title: www.cambridge.org/9781009395847

DOI: 10.1017/9781009395823

© Catherine Packham 2024

This work is in copyright. It is subject to statutory exceptions and to the provisions of relevant licensing agreements; with the exception of the Creative Commons version the link for which is provided below, no reproduction of any part of this work may take place without the written permission of Cambridge University Press.

An online version of this work is published at doi.org/10.1017/9781009395823 under a Creative Commons Open Access license CC-BY-NC 4.0 which permits re-use, distribution and reproduction in any medium for non-commercial purposes providing appropriate credit to the original work is given and any changes made are indicated. To view a copy of this license visit https://creativecommons.org/licenses/by-nc/4.0

All versions of this work may contain content reproduced under license from third parties.

Permission to reproduce this third-party content must be obtained from these third-parties directly.

When citing this work, please include a reference to the DOI 10.1017/9781009395823

First published 2024

A catalogue record for this publication is available from the British Library

A Cataloging-in-Publication data record for this book is available from the Library of Congress

ISBN 978-1-009-39584-7 Hardback

Cambridge University Press & Assessment has no responsibility for the persistence or accuracy of URLs for external or third-party internet websites referred to in this publication and does not guarantee that any content on such websites is, or will remain, accurate or appropriate.

Contents

List of Illustrations	*page* vi	
Acknowledgements	vii	
List of Abbreviations	x	
Introduction: Mary Wollstonecraft and Eighteenth-Century Political Economy	1	
1	Political Economy and Commercial Society in the 1790s	25
2	The Engagement with Burke: Contesting the 'Natural Course of Things'	50
3	Property, Passions, and Manners: Political Economy and the *Vindications*	76
4	Political Economy in Revolution: France, Free Commerce, and Wollstonecraft's History of the French Revolution	112
5	Property in Political Economy: Modernity, Individuation, and Literary Form	147
6	Credit and Credulity: Political Economy, Gender, and the Sentiments in *The Wrongs of Woman*	185
	Conclusion: Imagination, Futurity, and the Value of Things	215
Notes	225	
Bibliography	266	
Index	277	

Illustrations

2.1 'Don Dismallo'   *page* 73
4.1 James Gillray, 'The Sans Cullotes feeding Europe with
       the bread of liberty'   117
6.1 James Gillray, 'Political-Ravishment, or, The Old Lady
       of Threadneedle Street in Danger!'   189

Acknowledgements

This book has its origins in a question I asked myself back at the start of my career, when first teaching Wollstonecraft's *Vindication of the Rights of Woman* having recently completed a PhD on Adam Smith: namely, why was Wollstonecraft reading and quoting Smith in the early 1790s, and how might that alter how we think about her? My attempt to answer that question has taken me many years, and been much delayed, not least by other research projects and three years of administrative service as Head of English at the University of Sussex. Much support has also helped me along the way. A much-appreciated twelve-month Leverhulme Research Fellowship enabled me to lay the groundwork for the project and initiated a series of journal articles as I began to work out various arguments for the book. Some use is made of this earlier work in what follows, including in Chapter 2, which draws on parts of my article, 'Mediating Political Economy in Edmund Burke's *Reflections on the Revolution in France*', published in *Eighteenth Century: Theory and Interpretation* in 2019; a longer exert from '"The common grievance of the revolution": bread, the grain trade, and political economy in Wollstonecraft's *View of the French Revolution*', published in the *European Romantic Review* in 2014, appears in Chapter 4. I am grateful to the editors and publishers for permission to reprint it here. I gratefully acknowledge further support too, in the form of research leave from the School of English, which enabled me to bring the book to a conclusion. I have been able to present early versions of material at conferences and seminars at Oxford, Edinburgh, Southampton, Kings College London, Amsterdam, and Rotterdam, as well as here at Sussex; I am grateful for the invitations that enabled this and thank the audiences at each of these for the questions and responses that have helped to shape what follows. I also thank the sculptor Jenny Littlewood for the invitation to speak at the Royal Academy of Arts in London, to mark the display of her new bust of Wollstonecraft.

viii   *Acknowledgements*

As I have been labouring on this project, it has been wonderful to witness and participate in the current new wave of work on Wollstonecraft, from across the academic disciplines. I am grateful to have spoken on panels about Wollstonecraft alongside such experts as Eileen Hunt Botting and Julie Murray, and at Wollstonecraft events at which I learned much from Sandrine Bergès, Alan Coffee, Mary Fairclough, Daisy Hay, Laura Kirkley, Bee Rowlatt, Janet Todd, and others. I am sorry that Laura's new book on Wollstonecraft appeared in print too late for me to benefit from its insights and scholarship in this work. Emma Clery has done a vast amount to create a community of Wollstonecraft scholars and enthusiasts and to bring us together at memorable events at the Unitarian Chapel in Stoke Newington and St. Pancras Old Church: for this intellectual leadership and comradeship, and for her support of and interest in my work, I am immensely grateful. Amongst much else, these events have shown me the huge knowledge and appreciation of Wollstonecraft's work that exists beyond the boundaries of the academic world, and how much she is still looked to for insights and answers to the many pressing problems we face in today's world.

At the University of Sussex, I have benefited from being part of a community of outstandingly smart and dedicated colleagues. For support of many kinds as this research project developed, I would especially like to thank Peter Boxall, Mat Dimmock, Andrew Hadfield, Tom Healy, Lindsay Smith, and Pam Thurschwell. It has been a particular pleasure to debate Smith and political economy in many extended conversations with Richard Adelman; I thank him especially for his careful reading of most of the following chapters (and look forward to his own forthcoming new book). I am lucky at Sussex to work alongside two gifted eighteenth-century scholars, Andrea Haslanger and Emma Newport, and with a series of skilled doctoral students, past and present: Mike Rowland, Leah Edens, Matthew McConkey, Holly Weston, and Beth Watson. I also thank the wonderful students on my final-year undergraduate course, 'Special Author: Mary Wollstonecraft' and its successor, 'Wollstonecraft and After': your questioning intelligence and engagement continue to be one of the best parts of my job. Special thanks to the brilliant Kristi Hickle, Erika Mancini, Anna Stavrianakis, and Suzanne Tatham, for sharing (and allowing me to share) so much over the years: thoughtfulness, insight, and laughter, huge doses of unwavering solidarity, and (it has to be said) occasional leading questions. Beyond Sussex, John Whale and Peter de Bolla have both been important mentors, for whose early support I remain grateful. I thank Pete, as well as Mary Poovey, for attending as keynote

Acknowledgements ix

speakers a conference at Sussex in 2016 on 'Writing Political Economy, 1750-1850' organised by Richard Adelman and myself.

At Cambridge University Press, my thanks are due to Bethany Thomas and George Laver, for overseeing the book from proposal to print, and to series editor James Chandler. I also thank the Press's two anonymous readers for their insightful comments on the full manuscript, responding to which has helped me to make this a better book than it would otherwise have been. Remaining shortcomings and errors are of course my own.

Last but in no way least, thanks and huge love to my family, including my parents and siblings, and Kathleen Hebden, for so much support. I ended the acknowledgements of my first book by thanking Ed Hebden for his love, sanity, patience, and reassurance, and our daughters Miranda and Anna for showing me what there is to know about love, joy, and pride. The same is still true, but more so, so many years later. This book is for you.

Abbreviations

Frequently cited texts are referenced with the abbreviations below:

Works of Mary Wollstonecraft

All references are to *The Works of Mary Wollstonecraft*, ed. Janet Todd and Marilyn Butler, 7 vols (London: William Pickering, 1989).

HMV	*An Historical and Moral View of the Origin and Progress of the French Revolution; and the Effect it has Produced in Europe*, in *Works*, vol 6.
Mary	*Mary: A Fiction*, in *Works*, vol 1.
SND	*Letters Written during a Short Residence in Sweden, Norway, and Denmark,* in *Works*, vol 6.
VRM	*A Vindication of the Rights of Man*, in *Works*, vol 5.
VRW	*A Vindication of the Rights of Woman*, in *Works*, vol 5.
Works	*The Works of Mary Wollstonecraft*, ed. Janet Todd and Marilyn Butler, 7 vols (London: William Pickering, 1989).
WW	*The Wrongs of Woman: Or, Maria*, in *Works*, vol 1.

Other

AR	*Analytical Review: or, History of Literature* (London, May 1788–Dec 1798).
EPS	Adam Smith, *Essays on Philosophical Subjects*, ed. W. P. D. Wightman and J. C. Bryce (Oxford University Press, 1980).
ODNB	*Oxford Dictionary of National Biography*, www.oxforddnb .com.
Reflections	Edmund Burke, *Reflections on the Revolution in France*, ed. Connor Cruise O'Brien (London: Penguin, 1986).

TMS	Adam Smith, *The Theory of Moral Sentiments*, ed. D. D. Raphael and A. L. Macfie (Oxford University Press, 1976).
WN	Adam Smith, *An Inquiry into the Nature and Causes of the Wealth of Nations*, ed. R. H. Campbell and A. S. Skinner (Oxford University Press, 1979), 2 vols.

Introduction
Mary Wollstonecraft and Eighteenth-Century Political Economy

to commerce every thing must give way[1]

When Mary Wollstonecraft's *A Vindication of the Rights of Woman* was first published in 1792, it was classified by Joseph Johnson's *Analytical Review* (a periodical to which she herself contributed regularly) as a work of political economy.[2] This book takes its cue from this original – and overlooked – categorisation, to explore the relationship between Wollstonecraft and the political economic thought of her time, both in the *Vindication* and throughout the varied body of writing produced by her over the course of an extraordinary, if brief, writing career which lasted from the late 1780s to her untimely death, ten days after childbirth, aged 38 in 1797. Since then, the *Vindication*, Wollstonecraft's most well-known work, has been read in many ways – as a piece of political theory, as moral philosophical and religious writing, as a tract on education – and it is certainly all of these, and more. Little attempt has been made, however, to read it as a work of political economy, or to think seriously both about why it was so categorised, and what such a categorisation might mean for our understanding of Wollstonecraft's thinking and writing, both in this text and beyond. Relatively little attention has been paid to Wollstonecraft's relationship to the shifting and diverse body of thought named as 'political economy', even though Wollstonecraft was writing at a time when political economy and the nature and problems of commercial society were at the forefront of many radical writers' minds, and even though Adam Smith, author of *The Wealth of Nations* (1776), was, along with Jean-Jacques Rousseau, Catharine Macaulay, and the conduct writer John Gregory, one of the authorities with whom Wollstonecraft engages in the course of her work. Equally, Wollstonecraft's work as a whole has been approached through many of the disciplinary frames of the modern academy: literary criticism, intellectual history, the history of political thought, philosophy, feminist theory, and gender studies. Yet none of these fits her perfectly, able to do justice to the extraordinary range of her thinking and writing, or to provide an account of the recurring intellectual interests which, even across a markedly brief writing career, link Enlightenment philosophy and revolutionary politics, travel-writing and fiction, history writing, literary reviews, and an important essay on poetry. In particular, no existing monograph study on Wollstonecraft fully addresses what I argue in this book to be a crucial aspect of her intellectual formation: her persistent engagement, over the course of her career, with the emergent discourse of political economy, whose means of understanding and modelling human nature and human behaviour, as well as the relation of individuals to society and to morality, was becoming increasingly influential in the last decade of the eighteenth century, precisely the time of her writing.

What exactly was political economy in the last decade of the eighteenth century? Sylvana Tomaselli has observed that political economy in this period might address any of the following: money, bullion, national wealth, manufacturing, balance of trade, agriculture, consumption, population, war, taxation, tariffs, and levies. But equally, many of these were recurring concerns in policy debates which might be traced back to earlier periods: Tomaselli notes that the term 'political economy' was first coined in 1615 by Antoine de Montchrétien.[3] For Michel Foucault, eighteenth-century political economy was distinguished from an earlier 'classical analysis of wealth' by virtue of its innovative account of production, and the roles of the division of labour, capital, and the market.[4] Certainly, this period was one of self-consciously innovative thought addressing the area of human behaviour which we now identify as economic activity, but we need to be wary of retrospectively identifying eighteenth-century political economy through the language of present-day economics, a practice whose 'teleological straightjacket' can obscure the nature and specificity of the political economy of another time.[5] Descriptions of their endeavours by prominent thinkers in the field of eighteenth-century political economy are notable both for the capaciousness and ambition of what political economy might encompass and for the difference of its language from that of economics of today. At its heart was nothing less than understanding the shape and operation of society in its modern commercial form (and potentially also its reformation), and specifically how it met the needs, comforts, and even happiness of the population.[6] Here, then, was a project likely to interest Wollstonecraft, concerned as she is with the shape of human lives, and the limits on happiness, under the social conditions of commercial modernity.

Introduction 3

This 'science' of public happiness, as Anne Robert Jacques Turgot described it in a letter to Wollstonecraft's early mentor, Richard Price, included what we would recognise as economic concerns, but these were located within a broader field of political, moral, psychological, and historical study.[7] Tomaselli notes that Adam Smith's achievement, as the most notable political economic thinker of the age, took place within a set of questions which addressed 'substantial moral, political, historical, theological, psychological and epistemic issues' from which it should not be severed.[8] The context for such questions was the on-going attempt to understand what was perceived as the relatively novel, or emergent commercial society of the age, identified as quite distinct from older feudal models, or the slave-owning classical past. Commerce defined and shaped this modern present in ways which went far beyond its role in previous times: its growth was, Smith claimed in *The Wealth of Nations*, a 'revolution of the greatest importance to the publick happiness'.[9] Recognising this brought with it questions as to the best mode of political organisation for commercially oriented societies. Understanding commercial society also involved theorising human nature, its desires, motivations, and patterns of behaviour, and their cumulative expression and effects. It is for this reason that, above and beyond its particular modes of modelling economic activity, eighteenth-century political economy is understood as offering what Saree Makdisi describes as a 'narrative of organization': it was, as Clifford Siskin has noted, 'a primary site for the totalizing and rationalizing of the social', or (in James Thompson's words) 'the discourse that imagines or describes civil society and publicity'.[10] This perception that political economy provided the means for describing the lived conditions of commercial modernity is also present in words used by one of Smith's most astute contemporary readers, Thomas Pownall, former governor of Massachusetts, who welcomed *The Wealth of Nations* as offering above all else a 'system, that might fix some first principles in the most important of sciences, the knowledge of the human community'.[11] More than attending to matters of wealth production and financial administration, political economy can thus also be understood as the means by which the very nature of social existence and civil society in late eighteenth-century Britain was addressed and theorised. Here, this book claims, is the political economy with which Wollstonecraft engaged throughout her writing, in a struggle which included too, we shall see, an insistence that the very link between the organisation of wealth and its consequences for human lives was always in view.

If eighteenth-century political economy was a 'site for rationalizing the social', offering 'knowledge of the human community', our understanding of Wollstonecraft's engagement with it must recognise that she is involved in more than a critique of commerce or property ideology – although such moments in her writing are not difficult to identify. Equally, it is to do more than assert that her widely recognised political radicalism needs to be recognised as economic radicalism too. Certainly, such claims are part of what follows in the remaining chapters, but I am equally concerned to explore Wollstonecraft's engagement with late eighteenth-century political economic thought in its largest sense. I argue that Wollstonecraft's remarkably diverse body of work can be read as an ongoing effort to think through – and critique – the connected material, economic, moral, psychological, and social conditions of modern commercial contemporaneity. It thus constituted an early point of resistance to what political economy would very shortly become: a formalised, technical, and specialised science of wealth and finance detached from larger moral and political questions of human improvement and happiness. Engaging as she does with the writings and thought of Smith, Edmund Burke and others, precisely at the moment when certain political economic orthodoxies were forming, Wollstonecraft parries, counters, and debates, to offer political and moral critique of the world that commerce threatens to build, showing its human cost (not least to female lives), and arguing fiercely for alternative means of arriving at improvement, both at the individual and societal level, offering, further, an alternative vision of what improvement might indeed be.

Central to my argument is the recognition that, at the very time of Wollstonecraft's writing, during the political ferment of the revolutionary decade of the 1790s, political economy was itself in flux, as object of both political and discursive struggle. A 'protean' discourse, it was undergoing the various processes of organisation and systematisation by which a disciplinary field might be formed, but such processes took place under, and were marked by, all the pressures of a revolutionary age.[12] Thus, Dugald Stewart's heralding of Smith's achievement in this new 'science of politics' sought to defuse a charge of intellectual association with French revolutionaries by separating any potential political import of Smith's work from its economic doctrine.[13] This was a time of, on the one hand, increasing acceptance of Smith's work by a range of prominent politicians and thinkers, from Burke and William Pitt to Thomas Paine: evident, for instance, in its invocation in mid-1790s Parliamentary debates over poor relief. On the other hand, however, radical and revolutionary thinkers from many different perspectives were exploring ways of critiquing the increasing dominance of commerce in the 'marketplace' of society, and challenging political economy's accounts of human nature and behaviour, and

Introduction 5

of society and value. Such open debate was enabled by the lack of what Matthew Sangster has described as the 'professionalising discourses' which funnel texts to distinct, specialised audiences; yet, as he also notes, the state moved from the mid-1790s to close down sites of open, radical debate and dissent, a process which coincided with the increasing specialisation, and professionalisation, of political economic discussion.[14] One such site of non-disciplinary critique and dissent was Joseph Johnson's *Analytical Review*, which ceased publishing in December 1798, following Johnson's prosecution for treason. The *Analytical Review* reviewed a remarkably wide range of publications under the heading of 'political economy', as we shall see in the next chapter, and as already noted, described Wollstonecraft's second *Vindication* as one such work of political economy.

The year after Wollstonecraft's premature death, in 1797, the publication of Thomas Malthus's *Essay on the Principle of Population* marked a new phase of political economic thinking, which brought to the fore anxieties of resource capacity and population growth. Resistance to Malthus's perceivedly miserabilist arguments galvanised the opposition of many Romantic thinkers (including Robert Southey, Samuel Taylor Coleridge, and Thomas Carlyle) to political economy's 'dead science'; the imagination, the aesthetic, and culture were mobilised to counter political economy's apparently spiritless utilitarianism in a schism fundamental to modern thought.[15] But Wollstonecraft, from whom later Romantic thinkers learned so much, was already insisting on the role and value of imagination, sympathy, taste, and feeling before that later moment. She mobilised their associated literary forms (as well as political and philosophical writing) to closely track and critique a 'science of politics and finance' which, unlike her Romantic successors, she also recognised as among the most important of contemporary knowledge endeavours, concerned as it was, in her words, with the 'most important end of society, the comfort and independence of the people'.[16] In this sense, Wollstonecraft can be seen as an early resistor of the separation of the 'political' from the 'economic', and of economic from aesthetic value.[17] This book argues that Wollstonecraft's writings offer a unique perspective on the radical dialogue with political economic thought in the early and mid-1790s, one which recognised the power and importance of its analysis of commercial society whilst insisting that virtue, reason, and liberty should be central to improvement in the modern age. Political economy's failures on these fronts drew her strongest critique. The following chapters thus illuminate the discursive contests between opposing moral, cultural, economic, and political positions in the period immediately prior to both the formalising

6   Introduction

of political economy as a technical and disciplinary practice, and the hardening of Romantic opposition to it.

This study considers the major writings in Wollstonecraft's oeuvre, published from 1788 to 1798, within this context, presenting her as a radical thinker and writer who engaged and critiqued political economic thought at this crucial moment of political and intellectual flux. Approaching Wollstonecraft from the direction of the political economy of her time offers new insights into her writing and thinking, illuminating how her work has been informed by areas of thought whose relationship to Wollstonecraft is currently under considered, and showing how she contributes, in ways not previously noted, to the debates of her time. Wollstonecraft is shown drawing from, but also critiquing, key elements of Scottish philosophy and yoking that into radical thought on education, gender, morality, human nature, and the property system of modern society. I read her as engaging both explicitly and implicitly with the writings on such topics by Smith, Rousseau, Burke, and others, and show how concern with the problems and corruptions of commercial society, and the effects of wealth on the human personality and relations, and a restless search for some alternative, recurs across her career in writings of varying genres.

Such a perspective offers a new way of understanding the arc of Wollstonecraft's writing career, as it moves from fiction, through philosophical, political, and historical writing, to meditative travel letters and a return to the novel form. In each genre, I show Wollstonecraft repeatedly revisiting and recasting her overriding preoccupations and testing the potential of the new perspective offered by changed literary form. In this, writing itself is shown to be a crucial resource for engaging with the rise of a new discursive formation or knowledge practice. At the same time, I show how we can avoid choosing between Wollstonecraft the Enlightenment philosopher and Wollstonecraft the Romantic writer, by demonstrating how she may be approached as a crucial bridging figure between these two historical moments, who, by the time of her premature death, was increasingly confidently exploiting the resources of literary writing to counter the depredations of the commercial age, and the political economic thought that accompanied it.

The account of eighteenth-century political economy outlined above – a science of politics, happiness, and community – encompassed political and social thought which addressed society as a whole. Alongside such areas as education, morality, and personal behaviour, then, gender concerns might be understood to be within its remit. This was certainly the case in Wollstonecraft's revolutionary approach. If this book seeks to trouble

Introduction 7

the disciplinary boundaries of our own day, by attending to the historical emergence of the knowledge practices which gave rise to modern disciplinarity, it also offers a new take on Wollstonecraft's feminism by situating it within the larger project addressed by the book. Wollstonecraft's thinking about the situation of women is thus consistently approached as an aspect of her analysis of commercial modernity, within which women occupy a particular place. Whilst the 'miserable state' of her sex exemplifies the problems and failings of commercial society, for Wollstonecraft, their very abject status also means that they are uniquely placed to enact the very revolution of manners against property and history to which she urges them. Her return to the question of the 'wrongs of woman' in her final, unfinished novel, which combines close attention to the material, economic, affective, and psychological conditions of female lives, illustrates her perception of the connection between female lives, literary fiction, and the economic wrongs of her age.

***

One way to trace Wollstonecraft's relationship with the political economic thought of her day is to examine the few moments in her writing where she references Smith, the most prominent political economic authority in the 1790s.[18] Wollstonecraft was undoubtedly familiar with Smith's work, referencing both *The Theory of Moral Sentiments* (1759) and *The Wealth of Nations* in a number of her writings. She was also familiar with Rousseau, the leading counter-critic of European commercial modernity, and admired Montesquieu, an early theorist of commercial society. As this book shows in detail, Wollstonecraft's understanding of contemporary modernity stemmed from the theorisation of commercial society provided by the Scottish Enlightenment tradition of moral philosophy and conjectural history in which Smith worked. This combined two important elements: a post-Lockean, post-Newtonian empirical science of man and society, which, through David Hume and Smith, offered a theory of moral sensibility and sociality via sympathy; and a stadial history of the progress of human civilisation, which attended to the material and economic conditions of human society from early society onwards, and understood contemporary commercial modernity as civilisation's culminating stage.

Smith is most explicitly present in Wollstonecraft's work in her *A Vindication of the Rights of Woman*, where he is quoted, at times at considerable length, on four separate occasions. Described as a 'cool reasoner', Smith figures in the *Vindication* as a moral and philosophical authority whose thinking can both shore up Wollstonecraft's own arguments,

8

Introduction

but also be critiqued and extended. Thus, in perhaps Wollstonecraft's most famous use of Smith, his observation (from *The Theory of Moral Sentiments*), that wealthy or great men do not require virtue to receive public admiration, but rather attract it through the display of more superficial appearances and accomplishments, is extended by Wollstonecraft to women, in an analysis of the morally corrosive politics of display and self-objectification in 'the female world'.[19] But Wollstonecraft far from passively accepts Smith: she points to personal or cultural prejudice to question Smith's central theoretical construct of the impartial spectator, which grounds his account of moral judgement produced through multiple acts of social observation. She considers the implications of his thought for women, suggesting that 'it is not sufficient to view ourselves as we suppose that we are viewed by others': women are expected to surpass, not conform to, existing societal moral and behavioural ideals.[20] Rhetorically, the presence in her work of 'Dr. Smith', as she respectfully names him, helps to buttress Wollstonecraft's authority, but her ability to critique and extend his thinking signals a critical independence from him.

It is Smith the moralist, rather than Smith the theorist of commerce, with whom the *Vindication* engages most explicitly. As a guide to the complexity of her engagement with political economic thought then, these moments are something of a red herring. Smith is in fact a more complex, if less overt, presence elsewhere in Wollstonecraft's writing, including in her *Historical and Moral View of the French Revolution* (1794) and her *Letters Written During a Short Residence in Sweden, Norway and Denmark* (1796). Both works address, in markedly different ways, the problems and possible futures of modern European commercial society. *Short Residence*, as Chapter 5 further shows, draws extensively, although not uncritically, on a Smithian vocabulary and analysis, identifying 'improvements' of industry whilst also attacking the 'principle of convenience' imputed as the cause motivating economic activity. But the *Historical and Moral View*, the most understudied of Wollstonecraft's works, is probably the place where these issues are given the most comprehensive treatment. As Chapter 4 explores, this work – a philosophical or moral history in the Scottish Enlightenment tradition – weighs the progress and possibility of improvement and liberty against the early events of the French Revolution; and it also gives prominent space to the granting by the National Assembly of a free trade in grain. Liberating the grain trade was a key policy of the Girondin faction with whom Wollstonecraft associated during her stay in France between late 1792 and 1795; it was also a prominent measure in a Smithian enactment of 'natural liberty' in economic matters. Attention to the grain trade within her history shows how Wollstonecraft folds questions of economic liberty into a larger narrative of political liberty and improvement which, whilst anticipated in the early events of the Revolution, looked increasingly less likely by the time of her writing.

Given the attention to a prominent measure of economic liberty in this work, it is a surprise to find in its final pages a number of overt jibes at famous Smithian tenets, which articulate concerns over the 'destructive influence of commerce'.[21] The 'Dr Smith' whom the *Vindication* was happy to name becomes in *View* a pointedly anonymised 'celebrated writer', whose identity as the famous theorist of the division of labour nevertheless becomes clear as Wollstonecraft attacks his account (from the first chapter of *The Wealth of Nations*) of time being 'sauntered away, in going from one part of an employment to another', asserting instead that this is 'the very time that preserves the man from degenerating into a brute'.[22] The division of labour, indeed, 'renders the mind entirely inactive', she claims, and turns 'whole knots of men' into 'machines, to enable a keen speculator to become wealthy', and there is a further tilt at Smith in her claim that 'every noble principle of nature is eradicated by making a man pass his life in stretching wire, pointing a pin, heading a nail, or spreading a sheet of paper on a plain surface'.[23] Ironically, however, whilst such criticisms can clearly be read as criticisms of Smithian political economy, they not only reveal Wollstonecraft's thorough knowledge of Smith's work, but also repeat concerns which Smith himself had already articulated, and often in more powerful terms than Wollstonecraft. Smith's observation that the 'man whose whole life is spent in performing a few simple operations ... generally becomes as stupid and ignorant as it is possible for a human creature to become', and that 'this is the state into which the labouring poor ... the great body of the people, must necessarily fall, unless government takes some pains to prevent it', is arguably as powerful and disturbing as Wollstonecraft's own.[24] Similarly, Wollstonecraft's attack on the merchant who 'enters into speculations so closely bordering on fraudulency, that common straight forward minds can scarcely distinguish the devious art of selling any thing (*sic*) for a price far beyond that necessary to ensure a just profit, from sheer dishonesty, aggravated by hard-heartedness' recalls Smith's equally unflattering account of mercantile behaviour: 'People of the same trade seldom meet together [...] but the conversation ends in a conspiracy against the public, or in some contrivance to raise prices'.[25] Emma Rothschild has suggested that it was the 'most subversive parts of *The Wealth of Nations* and *Theory of Moral Sentiments* ... which inspired Wollstonecraft'.[26] But whilst Wollstonecraft repeats elements of Smith's critique – such as his worries about the social implications of the economic world he helped to bring into being – she does not, as he does, look to law and government for redress. For her, the remedy for the ills of the commercial world lay not in institutional reform or government action, but in the collective effects of individual moral reform. There exists no starker picture of the inadequacy of existing institutions to understand the oppressions suffered by, in this instance, women, from the legal and property systems of her day, than the judge's heartless response to Maria in the final pages of *The Wrongs of Woman*.[27] In Wollstonecraft's vision, the intersecting injustices produced by the emerging worlds of money, property, and labour are not easily remedied, the flaws of the new commercial world held starkly in relief.

Closing the *Historical and Moral View* with observations on commerce's 'destructive effects', Wollstonecraft's ostensible attack on Smithian principles repeats and at times reframes points originally made by Smith himself. A number of observations might be made here, beyond the immediate evidence of the extent to which Wollstonecraft was familiar with Smith's writing. Contextually, the tussle over Smith's reputation in the 1790s may help to explain why Wollstonecraft found it easier to conclude her work in cadences ostensibly critical of Smith. But arguably, a larger picture is suggested, both through the phrasings used, and in the omissions and silences which make up Wollstonecraft's depiction of Smith and her relation to it: a picture describing the mutual orientation of moral-critical discourses and political economic ones at a time of not only radical debate and political ferment, but marked discursive flux. Wollstonecraft's silent borrowing from Smith's own statements of the problematic consequences of the division of labour – her turning of his criticisms of the commercial system against him – occludes, to her rhetorical benefit, the extent to which theorists of political economy themselves worried about the social and moral implications of commercial society's pursuit of productive efficiency and wealth. Such an occlusion bolsters her own position as social and moral critic, but it also works to embed or bring into being a separation of political economic thought from moral, aesthetic, and literary critique, a separation later entrenched in Romantic characterisations of political economy as the 'Dismal Science'.[28] In 1794, we are not yet at that moment of full separation, but it is not far off, and Wollstonecraft's writing arguably anticipates its arrival. In her final paragraph, there is another unacknowledged debt to Smith's work, as Wollstonecraft deploys two crucially important metaphors which, if not deriving directly from Smith, are certainly used by him: the self-healing potential of the body politic, capable of working its own cure without intervention, and the capacity of the

Introduction

'philosophical eye' to overlook nature to discern the hidden causes of 'so many dreadful effects'.[29] If Wollstonecraft casts herself in this work as the historical critic offering a moral 'view' of modernity's unfolding events, it is clear the extent to which such a role is only made possible by inhabiting and repurposing political economy's own discourse.

***

It was not only her reading which informed Wollstonecraft's engagement with the political economy of her day, however. She was also a woman whose often economically precarious life is reflected in her thinking and writing. Born into a middle-class family in London in 1759, she witnessed her family's circumstances decline through the repeated failures of her father's various schemes of business. With little formal education, she experienced firsthand the limited employment options for women of her class (lady's companion, governess, schoolteacher) and the undesirability of all of them. She struggled with legal complexities to access money for family members, and sought, throughout her life, to support her siblings, or find secure establishments for them. She ran a school for a short period, before lack of funds forced it to close; during her affair with Gilbert Imlay, she anticipated emigrating to America and living on a farmstead with him and her sisters. All of this would have been part of, in Makdisi's term, her 'psychobiological modes of existence', themselves shaped in turn by larger social, political, economic, and cultural forces and contexts.[30] The psychic and affective experience of living as (for all but the final months of her life) an unmarried woman in a society whose primary principle of economic organisation was the possession of property by men arguably informs all of Wollstonecraft's writing, but is most evident in the autofictional elements of her novels as well as her travel writing. Neither the rich, but unhappily married protagonist of the early novel *Mary*, or Maria, the 'woman of sensibility' caught in a loveless marriage to the fraudster Venables in *The Wrongs of Woman*, reflect Wollstonecraft's life circumstances directly, but both speak to the affective experience of women caught in a 'machine of society' whose economic, social, property, and legal structures operate to disempower, exclude, and oppress them.[31]

Given these circumstances, the fact that Wollstonecraft managed to find her way to be a published writer of any kind is remarkable, and attests to formidable determination, intellect, and strength of character. Yet even as what she famously termed the 'first of a new genus' – a woman who sought to live 'in a comfortable way' by the pen – she was often in financial straits, in debt through most of her life.[32] Her career as a writer was defined by her

Introduction

professional relationship with publisher Joseph Johnson, who published her works: from the early educational works of the 1780s, and her first novel *Mary* (1788) to the *A Vindication of the Rights of Men* (1790) and the *A Vindication of the Rights of Woman* (1792), her *Historical and Moral View of the French Revolution* (1794), the *Short Residence in Sweden, Norway and Denmark* (1796), and the posthumous *The Wrongs of Woman* (1798). She also worked as a reviewer on Johnson's monthly periodical, the *Analytical Review*, and also (Janet Todd has suggested) as *de facto* editorial assistant on the same publication.[33] Wollstonecraft undoubtedly enjoyed a warmly supportive relationship with Johnson, who provided practical and emotional support, but the fact that she was often in debt, that Johnson loaned her money, and that working for him either as a reviewer, or as a writer of books which he published, was her main source of income means that the relationship was also structured by their relative positions of economic power and dependence.[34] If it is going too far to describe Wollstonecraft's relation to Johnson as that of an indentured writer, it is nevertheless true that her writing did not always come from a place of creative freedom but economic necessity.

What does it mean to be a penniless female writer who thinks about the economic conditions and structures of her day? Discharging 'all of my obligations of a pecuniary kind' was certainly one hope of Wollstonecraft's as she wrote her *Short Residence in Sweden, Norway and Denmark* (1796), a work which, whilst her 'most sustained attack upon modern commercial society', also (with an irony which Mary Favret has noted) gave her the 'financial independence she desired'.[35] For Favret, *Short Residence* is the 'work of an unmarried woman writer in need of money to support herself and her daughter', an 'enterprising writer' who, Ralph Wardle suggested, made 'capital … of what she had hitherto sought to conceal: her own personality'.[36] But whilst it is in this text that Wollstonecraft writes most explicitly about herself as a professional writer ('How few authors or artists have arrived at eminence who have not lived by their employment?'), an economic lens is not the only means of understanding Wollstonecraft's sense of the role of writing in her life.[37] Her late essay 'On Poetry' sketches the social role of the imaginative writer in entirely uneconomic terms, depicting the poet as conveying renewed and energised feeling in a modern age whose excess and sensationalism have wearied and desensitised the masses. The 'effusions of a vigorous mind', she asserts, 'will ever tell us how far the understanding has been enlarged by thought, and stored with knowledge'; 'profound thinking' mixed with 'reveries' offer affecting expressions of spontaneous feeling and deep understanding.[38] The imagination, with its

Introduction 13

links to virtue, and capacity for cohesion and unity, is the faculty through which a fractured modernity might begin to be mended. Although not a poet, this description might speak to Wollstonecraft's sense of her own resources and methods as a writer, and certainly suggests that she can articulate the role of imagination and writing in the commercial world in terms entirely distinct from the categorisations of labour offered by political economy.[39]

Wollstonecraft's writing is a reminder of how literary activity in this period doesn't always conform neatly to fixed categories. Stephen C. Behrendt has illuminated the 'discontinuities, the dissonances, the failure to "fit"' that characterised the 'literary landscape of Romantic-era Britain'.[40] It may be more useful to pay attention to the ways in which Wollstonecraft doesn't fit existing models of authorship or discipline, contemporary or otherwise, than to the ways that she does.[41] Miranda Burgess notes that the relative marginality of Wollstonecraft's position, largely outside formal systems of knowledge and excluded from many spheres of political economic debate, and further decentred as a woman writer, enables her to resist the 'economic-historical logic' of contemporary political economy.[42] But that outsider status also shapes the specific, writerly forms in which her resistance was manifested. Wollstonecraft's career originated in low-status contributions to print culture, compiling anthologies and educational works for children, and writing reviews, and that role as analytic, often caustic, reviewer informs the persona she adopts in responding to Burke's *Reflection on the French Revolution* in *A Vindication of the Rights of Man*, her first major work.[43] Writing like a critical reviewer enables Wollstonecraft to attend to and mobilise the very components of writing itself – including style, genre, persona, narrative, and the *ad hominem* attacks which Sangster has noted were newly commonplace in the periodical culture of the day – in the denunciation of Burkean political economy, as Chapter 2 shows in detail.[44] Our understanding of Wollstonecraft's take on political economy needs, then, to be informed by all this: by the particular situations which she experienced in her life and which conditioned her writing; and by attention to the consequent contexts, modes, styles, and genres of the writing she produced.

Wollstonecraft's is not always the voice of a philosopher; she rarely writes as a theorist or system maker, but as an observer, critic, thinker, and woman. By the same token, her views are not to be found in focused expositions or treatises, but are often conveyed through digressive discussion, or spread piecemeal across her writing. Each of her works is inflected with the particular concerns of its moment, differentiated as they are by the fast-moving political and personal events of the 1790s, a tumultuous decade on both fronts. At a time of conscious philosophical system-making, Wollstonecraft recognised how systems imprisoned women; she sought to disrupt them by whatever means necessary, and especially by mobilising different patterns of writing and thought against them.[45] Arguably, Wollstonecraft's expression of the psychic and affective experience of living as a woman in property society, in non-expert language, in literary writing, is a key part of her resistance to specialised disciplinary knowledge on such topics. If political economy collectively produced an account of the socioeconomic order and its functioning, including a role for women defined by their exclusion from property in a world in hoc to property, Wollstonecraft's writing, across a range of generic interventions, challenges such systematisations of the social whole. And equally, if political economic thinking attended to women by regarding their status as denoting the larger state of civilisational development, Wollstonecraft's innovation was to wrest 'woman' free of that symbolic role and to insist instead on the evidence of women's actual lived conditions in commercial modernity, using in part her own embodied experience to that end.[46]

***

Wollstonecraft's relationship to eighteenth-century political economy manifests in different configurations in each of her major works, coming in and out of focus across the highly varied writing of her short but productive career. At the same time, as the next chapter explores in detail, the term 'political economy' might name quite a diffuse set of questions and concerns. This included the defining debate of the time, on the moral status of commercial society, framed by Montesquieu and addressed in the Scottish philosophical tradition which Wollstonecraft knew well; as well as critiques of the mercantile system and its dependence on taxation, war, and empire; potential socioeconomic alternatives, including agrarian republicanism; and the role of property in commercial society.[47] Such questions, in fluid, on-going, interconnected debates, were an important part of the intellectual context in which Wollstonecraft was writing and thinking, as subsequent chapters demonstrate.

These debates preoccupied many of the philosophers and radical thinkers of Wollstonecraft's circle, yet few critics or historians have considered Wollstonecraft extensively in their light.[48] As Carol Kay has commented, any study of Wollstonecraft poses the problem or question of disciplinarity, and work on Wollstonecraft tends to follow the disciplinary divisions of our own time, reflected in the specialisms of modern scholarly subjects and institutional identities.[49] My exploration of Wollstonecraft through the lens of political economy deploys a term which arguably had more valency in her time than our own; this allows us to trace the shape of her thought through a perspective derived from her time, rather than ours. The fact that the political economy of her day does not always correlate to our own is in this sense a benefit: a difficulty worth grappling with for what it might reveal.[50] This book is not, therefore, an attempt to insert Wollstonecraft into a historical canon of late eighteenth-century thinkers and theorists on political economic matters; nor is it a work of intellectual history. Rather, in asserting that Wollstonecraft's engagement with a series of interconnected debates about the nature and future of commercial society was a crucial part of her intellectual preoccupations, it seeks to be as little confined by discourse or discipline as those debates – which ranged across works of moral philosophy, history writing, political tracts, travel letters, philosophical treatises, essays, and even fiction – themselves were. Whilst I read Wollstonecraft's writings against a series of broad and interconnected historical and intellectual contexts, I seek especially to attend to Wollstonecraft's texts as writing: not as records of 'flat' systems of thought but as complex, ambivalent, at times contradictory, and often engaging with multiple questions or trains of thought within a single text or textual passage or moment. It is this which adds to the richness, as well as the difficulty, of reading Wollstonecraft, and it entails attending in particular to questions of genre, style, language, and form – matters of textuality, in sum – alongside the content of her writing.

A further challenge to such a reading is posed by the recognition that, across her work as a whole, and even within particular texts, Wollstonecraft is not always complete or systematic. That is not to say that she is either eclectic or wilfully contradictory; rather, it is to suggest that to look for systematicity may not be the best approach to a thinker whose strengths and insight often rely on making links (at times leaps) between otherwise separate areas or patterns of thought, on working synchronously and connectively, and who worked in genres where digression or the conversational, episodic or anecdotal, would be tolerated or carry rhetorical weight.[51] System had its own history and fate in this period; it was also the focus of political attack, in its association with French revolutionary thought.[52] I offer a Wollstonecraft who works broadly and synthetically across and between traditions of debate and thought to produce strikingly original insights with powerful reach and significance, and to recast established patterns of thought, writing, and language in creative and innovative ways. It is certainly possible to find paradoxes within her oeuvre: to contrast, for instance, her reported admiration of the French communist Gracchus Babeuf, with her support for Girondist free grain trade; to note her admiration of the agrarian independence of farmers in northern Norway alongside, within the same text, her acceptance that economic progress brings freedom.[53] Rather than indict her for inconsistency, this book attends to the specific conditions and moments of her writing career, during the approximately ten years in which Wollstonecraft developed from a self-educated writer of tiny review pieces to a fully developed thinker of extraordinary power, maturity, and range, capable of working in multiple contexts and genres, and whose speed of development from one project to the next was often astonishing. Where else can we point to a writer who wrote two important philosophical polemics which shaped contemporary political debate, followed up with a ringside history of the most important European event of her day, then wrote a genre-breaking travelogue which anticipated and influenced the aesthetics of the next major literary movement, and finally set to work on a fiction which attempted to transform and rework the novel genre? Or to a thinker who is at once a moralist, a historian, a self-styled Enlightenment observer, a travel-writer and memoirist as well as a philosopher, social critic, political polemicist, and cultural theorist, who also moves increasingly in the direction of literary modes of production?[54] The range and breadth of Wollstonecraft's production are not without parallel – perhaps matching, in terms of capaciousness and variety (if not in terms of volume of output), the work of Rousseau, Voltaire, Diderot, or Coleridge – but the lives and careers of these formally educated men far outspanned the few short years of Wollstonecraft's writing life.

Crucial to my reading of Wollstonecraft is attention to the specificity of the kinds of writing she produced: travel writing, fiction, philosophical history, as well as two *Vindications* which combine philosophical writing with social criticism and political invective. Wollstonecraft refuses any attempt to contain her work within our contemporary disciplinary boundaries, and, whilst my title might be read (mistakenly) as an attempt to yoke her work to another field, that of political economy, the book rather seeks to read her *against* the historical emergence of political economy as a discipline. Disciplinary or discursive formation is not simply a passive background or context, however, but rather is often actively at stake, in play and under negotiation in her writing. Wollstonecraft repeatedly deployed writing of various kinds, in an age of proliferating print media, to contest the emerging patterns and verities of political economic discourse. Thus, as I argue in Chapter 2, not only is Wollstonecraft's much-studied response to Burke's *Reflections on the French Revolution* (1790) to be understood as

Introduction 17

a take-down of his defence of Whig political economy, but also as a tussle over its genre, in which the nature and purpose of writing itself are central. Ralph Cohen, pioneer in the study of the historical politics of genre, has shown how written form manifests larger social change; we know too how Wollstonecraft, a conscious innovator in writing and (through her review work) an acute and uncompromising critic of the writings of others, was critical of certain literary forms, such as the novel, because of their cultural baggage – associated as they were with particular modes of social forma-tion, identity, and behaviour (female identity, romance, and the marriage plot).[55] She was alert to the 'co-mingling and morphing of genre' which comprised the fluid and open conditions of late eighteenth-century print culture, and in which, as Wollstonecraft herself observed, patterns of lan-guage usage themselves slipped from printed text to spoken word, from 'essays into novels, and … into familiar letters and conversation'.[56] Part of the constant reinvention of Wollstonecraft's writing must then be under-stood as a restless seeking for an appropriate form adequate to the complex and shifting preoccupations she sought to address. What genre of writing could both do justice to the critique of commercial modernity and body forth the possibility of an alternative vision? How could writing itself be remade so that it might both document the oppressions of her age, and attack its political and economic structures, whilst striking forcefully at the affections of her readers and perhaps voicing too her own sufferings and wishes?

Something of this story about a Wollstonecraft caught between different modes or genres of literary performance is embedded in a well-established (even outmoded) dichotomy in secondary literature on Wollstonecraft which distinguishes between an early, rationalist Wollstonecraft and a later, more 'Romantic' one. Variations of this narrative appear in criticism which attempts to manage or mediate between apparent oppositions in early and late Wollstonecraft: between the critiques of sensibility present in *A Vindication of the Rights of Woman* and the invocations of sensibil-ity present in *A Short Residence,* or *The Wrongs of Woman*; or between a sex-averse, puritanical Wollstonecraft identified in the *Vindication*, and the sensuality at times present in her later writings.[57] Often these differ-ences are explained by evoking personal biography (Wollstonecraft's sex-ual maturation following her affair with Imlay) or some broader shift from the Enlightenment to the rise of Romanticism. This study situ-ates these evident differences – between Wollstonecraft the rationalist and the Wollstonecraft whose writing investigates and deploys feeling as part of her account of living in commercial modernity – within another, larger historical mapping, in which thinking and writing about feeling, once at the heart of the Enlightenment investigation into human nature, which gave birth to political economy, gets extruded from it at this time of discursive separation. Thus, the pre-disciplinary projects of the high Enlightenment (including the Scottish Enlightenment 'science of man') with their attempts to address ambitiously arching questions of human nature and society split into more local, fragmented, and separated discourses and textual practices, including both the literary ones now understood as marking the Romantic practice of 'Literature', and political economy itself. A story about the late-eighteenth century emergence of discipline, in short, brings with it one about the genres and textual spaces within which feeling gets written, as a concern with passion, affect, sympathy, and the rest is transferred from moral philosophy, and the political economy to which it gives birth, to literary writing at the century's end. This means that the consistent concern with sentiments and feeling in Wollstonecraft's texts is both an inheritance of that moral philosophical tradition and an attempt to redirect it. Wollstonecraft sought to use writing, and to mobilise feeling, as a means to politically agitate, shape public culture, and grapple with the emergent conditions of life in commercial society. Her reflection, in an aside in *A Vindication of the Rights of Men*, on the powers and limits of persuasive writing to alter fixed beliefs, is one indication of her self-awareness of this practice in her writing.[58]

The trajectory of Wollstonecraft's career, towards increasingly 'literary' modes of writing, can be read then not simply in terms of a Romantic turn to affect and lyric subjectivity, but as part of an experiment in the capacities and resources of writing to challenge the emergent conditions and structures of commercial society. A concern with expressive emotionality is present across her works, from the rhapsodies on sensibility and suffusions of religiosity in the early novel, *Mary*, or the fictional fragment 'Cave of Fancy' to the theory of poetic sentiment in 'On Poetry'. In one perspective, such concern with subjective emotionality might seem at odds with an engagement with political economy and the problems of commercial society, but what Daniel White terms 'affective spontaneity' or Mitzi Myers names an 'aesthetic of spontaneity' is an integral part of an examination of the affective and psychic conditions of commercial modernity.[59] That Wollstonecraft is looking beyond a rationalist solution to social and political problems becomes explicit by her last work, where rational argument falls on deaf ears in Maria's plea to the judge, and human feeling – whether that which binds Maria to Jemima and her daughter and saves her from death in one of the text's endings, or in the social sympathy enabled

Introduction 19

by sensibility at other moments in the text – is the only resource that remains in a broken world. Indeed, if, in choosing the genre of the novel, Wollstonecraft sought, as Godwin's *Caleb Williams* (1794) did, to use fiction to show 'things as they are', *The Wrongs of Woman* emerges not only as a demonstration of the effects of the existing organisation of property and wealth on female lives, not least through the institutions of marriage and law, but also as an account of the consequent social alienation of the feeling subject, and an attempt to mobilise readerly sentiments against it all.

Of course, Wollstonecraft was not alone in turning to affect, and its associated literary and aesthetic expressions, to confront and reform commercial society. Daniel White has shown how *The Enquirer* (1797) demonstrates Godwin co-opting a 'devotional language of sensibility' to construct a polite and progressive public culture.[60] Nor should we understand Wollstonecraft as wholly given over to a Romantic concern with interiority, affect, and subjectivity: *The Wrongs of Woman* (a work which, in its unfinished state, is only a third the length of what Wollstonecraft planned) is as fervently committed to exposing the material oppressions stemming from existing organisations of property and the law as it is to yoking those questions to explorations of sympathy, sensibility, subjective pleasure, and personal suffering. At the same time, Wollstonecraft's interest in sentimental subjectivity – in passions and affect as the grounds of human nature – shows how she is doing more than simply following the well-trodden path of moral critique of commercial culture, even whilst she often echoes the distaste of Rousseau, Price, Joseph Priestley, and others for contemporary luxury and manners. Her attitude to feeling in fact turns a theory of sentimental subjectivity which originates in Scottish thought *against* the property culture of that same tradition. In this way, she works with a fundamental contradiction inherent in Scottish philosophical thought: its attempt to reconcile an account of affective, sociable human nature with modern commercial society oriented to the production of wealth. Sensibility thus constitutes the means through which commercial modernity can be critiqued, beyond a mere critique of manners. As Wollstonecraft exclaims in Hamburg: 'to commerce everything must give way!'.[61] What might stop its path?

Wollstonecraft can in this way be seen as anticipating the Romantic valoration of subjective lyrical expression and the turn to art to reform corrupt modernity. As noted earlier, in retrospect, this mobilisation of the aesthetic (of art and feeling) against the market, and commercial society and values, is a deeply familiar one. It marks the split between an Enlightenment republic of letters, where 'literature' denotes 'writing' or knowledge, and the Romantic formulation of 'Literature', and its attendant split from 'Science' (as theorised by Wordsworth in the 'Preface' to the *Lyrical Ballads*, published within a few years of Wollstonecraft's death). Something of the fascination of reading Wollstonecraft lies in how she is situated uniquely at a hinge point where it was still possible to resist a split between these discourses, with their opposing narratives of value, and to imagine ways they might be yoked together to form the basis for an alternative future than the one which appeared to be coming into view. This, I argue, is what we might understand Wollstonecraft to be reaching towards, alongside her prescient insights into, in her eyes, the tragic unfolding of the next phase of Europe's commercial futurity and her warnings about the emerging aristocracy of commerce.[62] Her untimely death throws the hinge point where she is situated into particular relief, freeze-framing these questions in a way which might have become blurred or submerged had her life continued beyond 1797. My study shows how that abrupt cut-off uniquely foregrounds both the questions with which Wollstonecraft engaged and the experimental forms of writing and thinking with which she attempted to answer them.

***

This book contends that approaching Wollstonecraft's work from the perspective of the debate over commercial society offers a new way of understanding the shape of her thought, as well as appreciating anew the particular intellectual conditions from which it arose. It attends in close detail to Wollstonecraft's engagement with such debates, to show how she tracks, contests, borrows from, and counters them, in different ways and at repeated points throughout her career, through the different lens provided by each of her major works. The book proceeds chronologically, as the most effective way to tell the story of this engagement. The first chapter, *'Political Economy and Commercial Society in the 1790s'*, investigates how political economy was understood in Johnson's *Analytical Review*, to illuminate how its writings, its project, and potential was understood in Wollstonecraft's intellectual milieu. Political economy emerges as a heterogeneous discourse where political and moral ideas mixed with the economic, and where discussions of human nature, and human motivation, as well as of civil society, were often prominent. Writings reviewed as 'political economy' in the *Analytical Review* reveal how the term was used by radical and progressive thinkers as a means for collecting a range of critical perspectives on contemporary society, as well as setting out possible means of improvement. In the eyes of the *Analytical Review*, political economy offered the prospect of enacting reforms which might increase the happiness of ordinary people, and a means of critiquing existing injustices.

In Chapter 2, '*The Engagement with Burke: Contesting the "Natural Course of Thing"*', Wollstonecraft's *A Vindication of the Rights of Men* is read as staging not merely a political argument with Burke's *Reflections on the Revolution in France*, but a political economic one. I argue that in responding to Burke, Wollstonecraft carries forward the call for liberty which had occupied radicals in the 1780s onto new ground, to attack the very economic order on which late eighteenth-century society was founded. She exhumes the obscured economic substrata of Burke's work and exposes the oppressions and injustices of the socio-economic order which he sought to naturalise. Wollstonecraft's response resists the separation of political economic concerns from questions of liberty, equality, and happiness and asserts a human nature where sympathetic feeling for others should be used to reform human community, and to motivate political actions to sustain human happiness. Wollstonecraft shows how Burke weaponises 'specious' human feeling in defence of existing structures, and how, by making rhetorical art a device to serve political and economic order, he enacts an implicit hierarchy between political economy and human feeling. As we see in subsequent chapters, Wollstonecraft sought to mobilise authentic human feeling as an alternative ground of value across her career.

The next chapter, '*Property, Passions, and Manners: Political Economy and the* Vindications', shows that the 'revolution in manners' to which Wollstonecraft enjoins women in *A Vindication of the Rights of Woman* seeks to turn manners against political economy's property order. I show Wollstonecraft deploying a fully developed philosophical account of human nature to critique the culture, behaviour, psychology, and 'manners' of commercial society. Specifically, she counters the story of human motivation and effort deeply rooted in political economic discourse with an association of property with indolence, libertinism, and immorality. She articulates an alternative moral economy which links virtue to effort, labour, and exertion in the linked spheres of mind, manners, and morals. Closely associated with such efforts, the imagination is revealed as posing a fundamental challenge to Burkean political economy, as an independent power which frees the self from the subject relations of property order. This exertive economy of the human person in turn informs the demand for a social and political world where such efforts might be realised. Wollstonecraft's philosophy of human nature is thus not an abstraction from larger political questions but a crucial foundation

22   Introduction

for them. In calling for a 'revolution in manners' addressed especially to women, Wollstonecraft looks to a moral revolution against the forces of history, and calls on women to save commercial society from itself, and to save themselves from it. Political economy's separation of the public world of wealth acquisition from private affect and morality is thus rejected, and whilst the 'miserable' state of the female sex is an indictment of the commercial age, women are seen as best placed to enact its reformation.

Chapter 4, *'Political Economy in Revolution: France, Free Commerce, and Wollstonecraft's History of the French Revolution'*, turns to the work in which Wollstonecraft engages most explicitly with the political economic thought of her time, her *Historical and Moral View of the Origin and Progress of the French Revolution* (1794). It addresses in particular her treatment of the liberation of the grain trade in the early years of the Revolution. The political economy of grain was at the heart of Smith's new system of 'natural liberty', but it also pitted new ideas about market distribution against traditional ideas of moral economy and community. Wollstonecraft gives particular prominence to this issue in a narrative which explores the relationship between commercial and political liberty. The chapter also explores the larger intellectual and political context for such ideas, via Wollstonecraft's links with Girondin politicians, including Jacques Pierre Brissot, and hence the Shelburne circle of the 1780s, where support for free trade and moral political economy was nurtured in the years prior to the Revolution. A discussion of the involvement of Joel Barlow and Gilbert Imlay in provisioning the French Republic in the mid-1790s offers an alternative depiction of the realities of commerce during the revolutionary war and anticipates the hostility to commerce which comes to the fore in Wollstonecraft's later works.

We turn in Chapter 5, *'Property in Political Economy: Modernity, Individuation, and Literary Form'*, to address Wollstonecraft's engagement with narratives of property and property society in Smith and Rousseau, as reflected in her *Short Residence in Sweden, Norway and Denmark* (1796). Writing in the aftermath of the failure of the ideals of the French Revolution, property symbolises the necessary death of the property order of the *ancien régime*, but also stages questions of affective response and social relations, issues fundamental to political economy's own stories of social origin. Looming large in political economy's imaginary, the figure of property encapsulates and condenses the difficulties and ambivalences at the heart of late eighteenth-century modernity. Paying attention to property of many kinds, Wollstonecraft unfolds her critique of the contemporary political economic order and imagines alternatives to it, whether in

Introduction 23

the 'art of living' practised by 'the rational few' as witnessed in France, or in the independent, comfortable existence suggested by the farmstead or cottage.

The historical problem of commercial modernity, of which property is a visible sign, also poses questions of human personality and identity, given how the modern self is yoked to property, and individuated from others through property, especially in political economy's conjectural histories. Literary form emerges as a means through which these questions might be framed, and as a means of insisting on the 'something' more than individualism on which Wollstonecraft insists. Resisting the mediated social relations of market society's 'society of strangers', Wollstonecraft asks how the narrative of selfhood in the commercial age might be recast. Wollstonecraft's chosen epistolary form, and the unbounded, ongoing writing of self which takes place within it, troubles the finite culture of property and accumulation which she inhabits and traverses; meanwhile the novel, the form for her next piece of writing, is shown to counter the alienation, partiality, and social division which accompany the division of labour in modern commercial society.

The final chapter, '*Credit and Credulity: Political Economy, Gender, and the Sentiments in* The Wrongs of Woman', reads Wollstonecraft's unfinished novel, *The Wrongs of Woman* (1798), as an investigation into political economy's production of the credit economy and the gendered narrative of feeling which accompanied it. The chapter opens by discussing the Bank Restriction Act of 1797 as marking a crisis in the British credit system which made clear political economy's relation to affect: credit depends on moral relations and social belief. This crisis in credit enables a reading of Wollstonecraft's novel as investigating the relationship of affect, belief, and credulity to the world of economic activity. Adam Smith had attempted to regulate and suppress certain troubling and potentially disruptive forms of affect, including credulity and sensibility, which were feminised and relegated to the home, away from the public world of prudent self-interest. Through her protagonist, Maria, whose 'extreme credulity' paves the way for new forms of social feeling, Wollstonecraft rewrites the usual story of irrational femininity as the binary other to masculine rationality and reconsiders the credit which underwrites contemporary political economy. Wollstonecraft's story of the woman of sensibility demonstrates, and troubles, the mutual imbrication of financial and sexual economies in late eighteenth-century commercial society, whilst challenging both the affective economy of credit on which political economy rests and the system of gender which it brings with it. Wollstonecraft is thus shown to seek an alternative formulation of the relations between morality and commercial society – between affect and money – and to mobilise an alternative economy of social feeling to reform a selfish, sexualised world of commerce based on self-interest, by asking what else might circulate to social advantage.

In conclusion, I consider what lessons this reading of Wollstonecraft offers us today, at a time when orthodox economic thought is being challenged, not least by those addressing its links to climate change. Wollstonecraft's battles with political economic discourse, at the moment of its instantiation, pre-empt many of the criticisms levelled at economic thinking today, including ones which are especially urgent in the current context of planetary peril driven by the economic mantra of growth. Wollstonecraft's pity for the inhabitants of the earth in a future era of constrained resources illustrates how she anticipated the challenges we face today; her resistance to a culture of luxury and consumerism, and her assertion that the 'wants of nature' might be few, looks forward to attempts by today's heterodox economic thinkers to focus on sustainability and human wellbeing rather than ever-increasing GDP. Prominent in critiques of today's economic orthodoxies is the demand to recast the relationship between economics and imagination, to reconsider the relation between humanity and economic value, and to reintegrate culture and politics: to recast the economy so that it serves society, rather than extracting value from it. This suggests in turn the need to resist, or recast, the disciplinary separation of human knowledge, especially between the humanities and the social sciences, which has been in place since the early nineteenth century. As this book will show, it is precisely such a split that Wollstonecraft contested at the very outset of this economic journey, in her refusal to compartmentalise, in her commitment to a holistic view of human nature, and in her taking its impulses and behaviour as the grounds, the very conditions of possibility, for the reform and self-betterment of human lives and community.

CHAPTER I

Political Economy and Commercial Society in the 1790s

Question: what links the management of the silky-haired rabbit in Germany; the production of silk in France; the durability and worm resistance of ship timber; and considerations on isolating persons infected with smallpox? These confusingly heterodox topics are all subjects of works reviewed as works of political economy in Joseph Johnson's *Analytical Review: Or, History of Literature,* a monthly periodical whose publication, from May 1788 to December 1798, almost exactly corresponds with the span of Wollstonecraft's writing career.[1] Wollstonecraft had close links with Johnson, the *Analytical,* and its associated circle of thinkers.[2] Not only did she write perhaps as many as 400 or more reviews for the *Analytical Review,* she also acted (her biographer has suggested) as an editorial assistant to Johnson, continuing her involvement with the journal between and after her trips to France in 1792–1795, and her Scandinavian travels in 1795.[3] The periodical might therefore appear to be a good place to explore Wollstonecraft's understanding of political economy, but, at least initially, the picture is confusing. Thus, under the subheading of 'Political Economy', the *Analytical Review*'s 'Catalogue of books and pamphlets published in GB and Ireland in first 6 months of 1795' lists only one work that today would be recognised as belonging to that field, namely Turgot's *Reflections on the Formation and Distribution of Wealth.* Other works listed under 'political economy' address aspects of public administration, pertaining to the navy and the admiralty; one (to which we return later), by Samuel Crumpe, is on the employment of the poor; others address Church of England revenues and tithes. Yet a further group do not seem to fit even the broadest interpretation of the category of political economy at all, including Dyer's *Dissertation on Benevolence,* or Moser's *Reflection on Profane and Judicial Swearing.*[4]

One way of considering what 'political economy' might mean in the last decades of the eighteenth century would be to trace how the term was deployed by writers now recognised as key thinkers in the field. James

25

26 Political Economy and Commercial Society

Steuart's *Inquiry into the Principles of Political Oeconomy* (1767) gave the term some prominence. Steuart's spelling of 'oeconomy' recalls the origins of the word 'economy' in the Greek *oikos*, which referred to the provisioning of the household; Jean-Jacques Rousseau's 1755 article on 'Œconomy' for the *Encyclopédie*, later published as his *Discourse on Political Economy*, similarly begins with the household unit. Adam Smith's definition of political economy, on the other hand, takes as its focus not the social unit of the household but of the nation. For Smith, political economy aims 'to provide a plentiful revenue or subsistence for the people, or more properly to enable them to provide such a revenue or subsistence for themselves; and secondly to supply the state or commonwealth with a revenue sufficient for the publick services'.[5] But, whilst Smith contrasted his own system of 'natural liberty' with two other systems of political economy, the mercantile and the agricultural, he in fact used the term very sparingly.[6] Rather than understanding political economy to be a self-contained or formally defined field of inquiry in its own right, or indeed as the sole focus of his work, for Smith political economy was 'a branch of the science of the statesman or legislator', and as only one part of the larger inquiry in which he was engaged, which bridged moral philosophy, jurisprudence, conjectural history, and theories of law, justice, and government.[7]

Smith's sense of political economy as a 'branch of the science of the statesman' was perhaps enacted when he advised government ministers at the time of the War of American Independence, delaying the publication of *The Wealth of Nations* as a consequence. Winch has shown how the debate over America in the 1770s brought political economy into the heart of political discourse: on all sides, 'the medium of political economy [was used] to explore the most basic questions surrounding national identity'.[8] More than a narrow discussion of policy and legislation, it became a *'lingua franca'* for discussing the political dilemmas and possibilities faced by the new nation, encompassing 'more profound issues of a moral kind'.[9] Increasing recognition of the importance of trade and commerce to national prosperity on both sides of the Atlantic, and as fundamental to the emergent nature of what was recognised as modern commercial society, meant that political economic thought became newly influential as the means to understand the contemporary world in all its aspects: economic, but also social, moral, behavioural, and political. Something of this is conveyed in James Thompson's comparison of political economy with another emergent eighteenth-century mode of viewing the world, the novel: if the novel is 'that discourse that describes or imagines and so constructs privacy and domesticity, political economy is the discourse that imagines or describes civil society and publicity'.[10] It is a formulation that puts political economy at the heart of attempts to understand, and to improve, the political life and identity of the modern commercial nation and its people – and hence, given the range of commentary and viewpoints on such topics, casts it too as the ground for the hotly contested political debates of the time.

Historians of political economy, especially over the past thirty or so years, have taught us much about the growth and emergence of political economic thought at this time, but their enterprise runs the risk of using retrospective vision to render the field more coherent and unified than it may have felt at the time.[11] Reviewing works discussed as political economy in the *Analytical Review* offers a striking different picture of what political economy was understood to encompass at the time of Wollstonecraft's writing career. Political economy emerges as a heterogeneous and mixed discourse: a richly various confluence of political, moral, and economic ideas and writings, as well as emergent technical disciplinary principles, whose implications and possibilities were both evoked and hotly contested within the larger political debates of the time.[12] Far from fixed, technical, strictly defined, and inflexible, political economic thought was significantly 'protean'.[13] How was this new 'lingua franca' exploited by the radical and reformist thinkers associated with Johnson and his circle – and how might that have informed Wollstonecraft's writing?

Not only was political economy itself, as a set of interconnected political, economic, moral, and social concerns, loosely defined at this time. It also participated in a larger context of discursive flux and intellectual and political fights, in a decade in which late Enlightenment thought converged with 'the ideals of a republican and democratic revolution' whose possibilities – from modest reform to utopian social and political restructuring – were eventually vigorously repressed.[14] At one level, this is shown by the fate of Smithian political economy in the 1790s. Following his death in 1790, Smith's work was used by figures as different as Thomas Paine and Edmund Burke to quite divergent ends, whilst its foundation in property was rejected by others.[15] Fears that Smith's work would be linked, to its detriment, with French Revolutionary thought prompted Smith's biographer, Dugald Stewart, to defensively decouple its more technical economic principles and practices from larger political questions; he also emphasised Smith's work as 'speculative'.[16]

By the early years of the nineteenth century, political economy was gaining a foothold in educational institutions: Thomas Malthus was appointed as Professor of History and Political Economy in the East India College in Hertfordshire in 1805, and Stewart gave lectures on political economy at Edinburgh University in 1800. Yet it was still possible, in 1802, for Samuel Taylor Coleridge to describe political economy as 'a Science in its Infancy – indeed, Science, it is none'; or to call, a decade later, in 1812, for a 'genuine philosopher in Political Economy' to 'establish a system including the laws and the disturbing force of that miraculous machine of living Creatures, a Body Politic'.[17] Given this larger context of fierce political and intellectual contest, how did the thinkers associated with the *Analytical Review* deploy political economy to analyse and critique modern commercial society? What resources for understanding the moral, social, and political nature of late eighteenth-century commercial modernity did political economy offer radical thinkers of time, including Wollstonecraft? Greg Claeys has observed how the French Revolution debates of the 1790s led to a 'retreat' – except by ultra-radical and working-class writers – from a political language of rights, and the adoption of a different political language focused on the relationship of 'commerce, manners and civilisation'.[18] If for Smith, political economy is part of a 'science of politics', how would its 'lingua franca' be taken up by Johnson's circle, and how was Wollstonecraft situated in relation to that? We turn now to *Analytical Review* to explore this further.

Political Economy in the *Analytical Review*, 1788–1798

Published monthly from May 1788 to December 1798, the *Analytical Review* was a progressive, reformist publication co-founded by Thomas Christie and Johnson. Although Johnson has long been regarded as a 'radical' publisher, the elaboration of different strands of oppositionist thought in this period has enabled a more nuanced picture to emerge.[19] The politics of the *Analytical Review* have been characterised as seeking a 'middle course' between 'aristocracy and superstition' on the one hand and a blind admiration of 'equality and republicanism' on the other. It promoted liberty and independence, moderate Parliamentary reform, and a representative government; whilst 'resolutely middle class', it was 'sympathetic to the plight of the poor' but 'dryly intellectual' rather than 'emotionally populist'.[20] At the same time, many of those associated with Johnson were deeply involved in the political struggles of the day. By the late 1790s, the *Analytical Review* was running persistent criticism of the Pitt government. In 1798, Johnson was prosecuted for seditious libel, with a copy of the *Analytical Review* for September 1798 used as evidence at his trial, and he ceased publishing it that same year (although continuing to work as a publisher and bookseller).[21]

The *Analytical Review* had strong links to rational dissent: Johnson and Christie were both dissenters, and the campaign for the repeal of the Corporation and Test Acts was part of the context for the establishment of the journal.[22] The *Analytical Review* modelled the free and rational enquiry which was part of a conversational, collaborative, and rational-critical public sphere to which late eighteenth-century middle-class dissenting culture was committed.[23] Dissenters also 'dominated' commercial life, and political economy was on the curriculum in many dissenting academies, including some where leading dissenting intellectuals Joseph Priestley and Richard Price had previously taught.[24] Christie suggested that his new journal would be of interest to 'men engaged in active life and professional business ... who, though they may have an ardent love of knowledge ... are, however, too much involved in the necessary duties of their stations, to find leisure to peruse volumes in quarto and folio'.[25] Despite the ostensibly neutral language of late Enlightenment knowledge dissemination, it is clear that Christie's anticipated readers are the professional middle classes: readers with interests, in both senses of the term, in commercial and political economic matters.[26] At least some of the 'men engaged in active life and professional business' whom Christie envisaged reading his journal were likely to be dissenting merchants, traders, or other businessmen, and the journal might thus be expected to give reasonable space, alongside its other concerns, to commercial and economic topics.

References to commerce in the pages of the journal are indeed plentiful, and it offers much to illuminate how political economy was understood, and what concerns it addressed, for a particular segment of the reading public in the 1790s.[27] Although political economy does not appear in the list of topics covered by journal compiled by Johnson's biographer, numerous review articles were published under the descriptive section heading of 'politics and political economy', suggesting political economy had some recognition as a field or subfield of knowledge; references to 'commerce' and 'trade', meanwhile, were plentiful in the journal's indices.[28] Despite the apparent heterogeneity suggested by the works listed as 'political economy' at the start of this chapter, some sense of a coherent field of political economy does emerge. Some works, such as Voght's *Account of the Management of the Poor in Hamburgh (sic)*, explicitly announce themselves to be contributions to a 'branch' of political economy.[29] Others, whilst identified by the reviewer as on political economic subjects, present themselves either in more generalist ways (for instance, *Memoirs of the Society for the promotion of General Knowledge among the Citizens*) or with variant terms (such as *Considerations on Public Economy; wherein it's (sic) benefits are exemplified by historical Precedents*).[30] Still others, however, eschew the term: Thomas Percival's *Enquiry into the Principles and Limits of Taxation*, described itself as a contribution to a branch of moral and political philosophy.[31] Such evidence suggests that whilst there is an emergent sense of a field of political economic knowledge and practice, its boundaries are yet fluid, and it is not universally recognised, with the term being deployed in, to our eyes, both accurate and inaccurate ways. 'Political economy' clearly means different things for different individuals and is even open to redefinition for political ends. Thus, the *Analytical Review* reports the distinction made by Parliamentarian Henry Dundas, in a defence of the East India Company, between political economy, defined as the running of the polity, and commercial 'oeconomy': 'No writer upon political economy has as yet supposed that an extensive empire can be administered by a commercial association; and no writer on commercial oeconomy has as yet supposed, that trade ought to be shackled by an exclusive privilege'.[32] Such a differentiation of 'political' and 'commercial' economy insists on a separation that the composite term 'political economy' resists; it thus makes more difficult a consideration of the second objective detailed in Smith's definition of political economy: supplying the 'state or commonwealth with a revenue' for 'publick services'.[33]

Nevertheless, a recognisable sense of what we would now identify as the discipline of political economy can be discerned. A review of Crumpe's *Essay on the Best Means of Providing Employment for the People* in the *Analytical Review* for February 1795 hails a 'class of politicians', which 'made its appearance a few years ago in France, the members of which have been since known by the appellation of the "economists"': the physiocrat François Quesnay, as well as Turgot, Necker, and Smith are named in this context.[34] Wollstonecraft characterised the physiocrats in markedly similar terms in her *Historical and Moral View of the Origin and Progress of the French Revolution*, published later the same year. This 'class' of thinkers was international: many of the works reviewed as 'political economy' stemmed from France or elsewhere on the Continent, and their work is at times described as a 'science', as in the praise, in a review of a work on the *Government, Manners and Conditions in France anterior to the Revolution*, of Turgot as excelling in the 'science of political economy'.[35] Although at this time 'science' could still refer to knowledge in general, the depiction of political economy as a 'science' here might also acknowledge the occasional presence, in works reviewed under this heading, of mathematical approaches or statistical data, evident, for instance, in statistical tables or references to the work of Price.[36] Importantly, such factual methods do not preclude political economy from being understood as a form of moral knowledge, or as a way of putting benevolence into practice. Crumpe's reviewer describes the 'economist' 'class of politicians' as 'inspired' by the 'beneficient sentiments' of 'the present age', sentiments manifested in 'the attention now paid to whatever can alleviate the wants, subtract from the miseries, or increase the happiness of mankind'.[37]

The authority of their new 'science' enables economists to be distinguished from 'benevolent' but misguided princes, accounts of whose schemes 'of public utility' are also reviewed under the 'political economy' heading. These might include the 'benevolent endeavours of a good prince to promote the weal of his subjects' (review of *Discourses with Enlightened Citizens of the Country of Baden*) or the Bavarian Count of Rumford's various measures on poor relief (and innovations on chimney design).[38] Whilst their benevolence can, at times, have welcome effects, the reviewer of Voght's *An Account of the Management of the Poor in Hamburgh* approvingly quotes Voght's admonishment of instances where '[u]nthinking pity' has 'rashly stopped that natural course of things, by which want leads to labour, labour to comfort, the knowledge of comfort to industry, and to all those virtues, by which the toiling multitude so incalculably adds to the strength and happiness of a country'.[39] Evoking a 'natural course of things' which progresses from want to labour, comfort, and national prosperity, Voght uses a Smithian phrase which (as we shall see in Chapter 2) had been deployed too by Edmund Burke in his *Reflections on the Revolution in France*, published six years earlier. Its recurrence here signals the presence of a particularly Smithian political economic language, although one which, as we shall see, is adapted to different ends by some of its later users. Luckily, in this instance in Hamburg, benevolence is eventually guided into a 'proper channel', ensuring that poor relief is used as a 'spur' to 'industry' rather than 'sloth and profligacy'.[40] Employment schemes for the poor include making 'rope-yarn', an activity on which Wollstonecraft herself commented when visiting Hamburg. As we shall see in Chapter 4, Hamburg is for Wollstonecraft the epicentre of the immoral commercialism she denounces throughout her Scandinavian travels; and her sense that 'to commerce every thing must give way' is exemplified, literally, by her having to turn aside to 'make room for the rope-makers' as she walked by the river Elbe.[41] In what reads as an interpretative misstep by Wollstonecraft, the rope-making which for her exemplifies commerce overstepping its proper bounds, is, for the *Analytical Review*'s reviewer, a benevolent political economy attending to the poor through a 'proper channel'.

The sense of political economy – whether as a broad science of political administration, or as a narrower technique of finance, revenue, labour, and capital – as a new form of knowledge which will help to improve the human condition is echoed by Wollstonecraft herself in her *Historical and Moral View of the Origin and Progress of the French Revolution* (1794). The 'science of politics and finance' is at once 'the most important', as well as the 'most difficult of all human improvements': its difficulty stemming from its complex involvement in the 'passions, tempers, and manners of men and nations', its estimation of 'their wants, maladies, comforts, happiness, and misery', and its computing of 'the sum of good or evil flowing from social institutions'. Whilst it might 'advance' towards securing 'the sacred rights of every human creature', the steps by which it progresses are, she warns, bound to be slow.[42] This remarkable – and overlooked – passage sees Wollstonecraft putting a mixed language, combining references to a science of 'finance' and a methodology of 'estimating' and 'computing' human wants and needs, into the service of human happiness and perfection, with a final acknowledgement of 'sacred' human rights. Such a hybridised discourse helps us to see how Wollstonecraft herself, usually primarily understood as a political and moral writer, can also be read as a thinker on political economy as it was understood in her time. As her reference to the 'sum of good and evil flowing from social institutions' makes clear, virtue was, in Wollstonecraft's eyes, closely tied to the political, social, and economic organisation of society.

In September 1797 – the month of Wollstonecraft's death – the *Analytical Review* reviewed cleric and economist Robert Acklom Ingram's *Inquiry into the Present Condition of the Lower Classes and the Means of Improving It*: a work whose title could be taken to address precisely the 'wants, maladies, comforts, happiness, and misery' of the populace, which Wollstonecraft had associated with the new 'science of politics and finance'. Ingram's pamphlet, one of the first to make the case for the study of political economy in universities, argued that '[p]olitical science is so important to the interests of society, that it seems entitled to a much larger share of attention in education, than has hitherto been allowed it in our public schools'. His reviewer welcomed the work as a 'promising foretaste of the benefit which might be expected to accrue to society, if this subject were made a principal branch of academical instruction'.[43] Clearly, the *Analytical Review* supported such a programme, for the socially reformist benefits it might bring: Ingram's *Syllabus or Abstract of a System of Political Philosophy; to Which Is prefixed a Dissertation Recommending That the Study of Political Economy Be Encouraged in the Universities'* was reviewed in one of the last issues of the *Analytical,* for June 1799.[44] When, some twenty years later, Malthus set out to characterise the 'science of political economy' at the opening of his *Principles of Political Economy* (1820), he suggested that the subject bore a 'nearer resemblance to the science of morals and politics than to that of mathematics'.[45] Even as political economy began to gain an institutional foothold, beyond often short-lived dissenting academies, in schools and universities, then, the *Analytical Review* was not alone in regarding it as a field of study not wholly decoupled from either politics on the one hand or morality on the other: one that offered the means – perhaps the best means – to put the benevolent sentiments of the age into practice.

Debating Commercial Society in the 1790s: War, Debt, and the Possibility of Peace

Political economy reviews in the *Analytical Review* offer one picture of how political economy was understood in the 1790s and illuminate the nature of political economic debate among the liberal and progressive circle which produced and read the periodical. This is part of the context within which Wollstonecraft was thinking and writing; the questions and discussions which recur in its pages help us to understand some of the arguments – even some of the asides – which she makes in her work. If not often explicitly the focus of extended discussion, political economy reviews in the *Analytical Review* share in ongoing debates about the nature and shape of commercial society, its moral and social features, its dependence on a system of war and taxation, and its strengths and weaknesses; there is some discussion of alternative socio-economic models, and significant worry about the national debt produced by a commercial nation at almost perpetual war. More particular concerns include arguments about the organisation of property and inheritance, taxation, and related inequalities of wealth; persistent anxieties about moral standards in a supposedly luxurious manufacturing nation; and concerns about the state of the poor and modes of poor relief (a matter for Parliamentary debate in 1796 with Pitt's Poor Law Bill). As we now turn to give more detailed attention to the content of the *Analytical Review*, it is worth noting that in general, it is not possible to attribute its reviews to particular individuals: not only was anonymous reviewing usual practice in late eighteenth-century publishing, but some of the identifying signatures of contributors to the *Analytical Review* were shared among a number of individuals.[46] Rather than attempting to read these entries as the attributable opinions of individuals, or indeed following Cox and Galperin's suggestion of the *Analytical Review* 'communal' and 'jointly-created editorial voice', which may suggest more agreement and cohesion than actually existed, I read them as a collection of diverse voices contributing to on-going debate and national conversation.[47] In line with what Bugg has identified as Johnson's commitment to independent thought and 'open debate', the journal and the network behind it was a site of contest, divergent opinion, and lively difference.[48] For our purposes, tracing these debates not only helps contextualise Wollstonecraft's thinking but also illuminates important instances where her political economic thought, if it can be so termed, is striking different from the variegated progressivist consensus evidenced in the *Analytical Review*.

By far the most recurrent theme in the political economy reviews is concern about war, and the national debt and taxes which funded it. This is manifested both in the topics of the publications reviewed and in the commentary they receive from reviewers; it is present both where such issues are the main concern (such as an *Essay on the English National Credit*), and where they are contributory factors (the review of Sir Frederic Morton Eden's *State of the Poor*, for instance, claims poverty is caused by war and taxation).[49] Such debates go to the very heart of the nature of the modern British commercial nation, which defended and extended its commercial interests overseas through a 'funding system' of loans to the state from the public creditor first established in the 1690s. The innovative financial arrangements of the British 'fiscal-military state' led not only to the establishment of Britain as the pre-eminent global power, following defeat of its nearest rival, France, in the Seven Years War in 1763, but also to spiralling national debt, which, now larger than Britain had any likely means of paying off, was presented in the *Analytical Review* as a crippling and unsustainable burden.[50] Wollstonecraft's attack, in the *Vindication of the Rights of Woman*, on the 'present system of war', thus references and shares in a well-established critique of Britain's seemingly unsustainable cycle of debt, war, commerce, and empire, which many feared might end with the collapse of the nation state in its current form.[51] Rousseau's educational novel, *Emile* (1762), which of course Wollstonecraft knew, had predicted the collapse of Europe's commercial monarchies; Montesquieu, an early theorist of commercial society, also thought that Britain was on an unsustainable path; and David Hume had famously asserted that 'either the nation must destroy public credit, or public credit will destroy the nation'.[52] Two of dissent's foremost writers on political economy, Joseph Priestley and Richard Price, also warned of the precariousness of the British system. By the century's final decade, financial pressures of the war with France and intensified agitation for political reform reinvigorated such arguments: for

Debating Commercial Society in the 1790s 35

Tom Paine's *Decline and Fall of the English System of Finance* (1796), the inherent instability of the British finance system suggested the imminent collapse of Pitt's government.

Such concerns are readily evident in the pages of the *Analytical Review*: as, for instance, in the wide-ranging critique of the 'ruinous Consequences of the popular System of Taxation, War and Conquest', as the subtitle of one publication describes it.[53] Whilst a review of the report on the national debt, from the select committee on finance in March 1798, frames the topic as a relatively contained problem of finance, it is noted that the issue should concern the public due to both implications for taxation and the public nature of the debt, when 'half the nation' are 'venturing their all in the public funds'.[54] A more wide-ranging and polemical intervention is offered by William Morgan, nephew of Price, who aims to wake his readers from the 'delirium of unavailing conquests' by examining the effects of war on the nation's finances, vowing to address the self-interest of its audience, rather than its humanity, as the 'only means of awakening an effectual opposition to the present system'.[55] Morgan, an actuary, deployed financial data to strengthen his case, comparing debts contracted during the American war with those incurred in the ongoing war with France (including the infamous Imperial loans) to demonstrate 'the danger arising from a perpetual accumulation of new debts and taxes'.[56] Morgan's reviewer reports that, whilst we are told that the current war is being fought to defend 'all that is most important to property, social order and the religion of mankind', its huge expense, added to that of all the wars of the preceding century, threatens 'bankruptcy and ruin'. Wars, it is claimed, destroy, rather than improve, 'the property of the nation'.[57]

For the author of *Considerations on Public Economy*, reviewed in March 1796, Britain's 'enormous debts' were 'the only difficulty of serious magnitude this nation has at present to encounter'.[58] Opinion varied on how that 'difficulty' might be remedied. Patje's *Essay on the English National Credit*, discussed in the *Analytical Review* the following year, asserted that Britain would be saved by exploiting the 'untouched wealth' of England's 'waste lands': a comment that recalls Wollstonecraft's reference, in her *Vindication of the Rights of Men*, to the 'brown waste' of land lying unexploited.[59] Patje's confidence is not shared by his reviewer, however, who asks whether British 'precedency in manufactures and commerce' is 'equal to the excess of her public burdens'; Patje's assurance that British taxes are 'no heavy burden' is also strongly questioned: '*Every country where heavy taxes are collected is remarkable for an extreme inequality of wealth in it's (sic) inhabitants*'.[60] Discussion of national debt quickly opens into a larger critique of the political economic system. One strident example is a pamphlet by the American Joel Barlow, with whom Wollstonecraft had significant links: she was close to his wife Ruth, and Barlow was in France, as she was, in the mid-1790s, where (as we see in Chapter 4) he was involved in the same import activities as her lover Gilbert Imlay. Part I of Barlow's *Advice to the Privileged Orders in the Several States of Europe, Resulting from the Necessity and Propriety of a General Revolution in the Principles of Government*, published in 1792, was, like Wollstonecraft's first *Vindication*, one of many replies to Burke's *Reflections on Revolution*.[61] Part II, reviewed in the *Analytical Review* in September 1795, strongly links national debt, unfair taxes, and inequality in an attack on the funding system and the 'fraud' of taxation. Claiming that 'perpetual warfare' exists between governments, whose aim is only to increase revenue, and 'the great body of the people who labour', Barlow asserts that 'the art of administrating ... governments has been so to vary the means of seizing upon private property, as to bring the greatest possible quantity into the public coffers without exciting insurrections'.[62] Barlow approves of the French revolutionary state's seizing of church and emigrant property, anticipating that France's debts will thereby be 'nearly extinguished'.[63] The review's final sentence quotes Barlow's assertion that the nation's debts 'ought not' and 'will not, impede the progress of liberty', linking economic conditions with political freedom: a link explored too, as we shall see in Chapter 4, in Wollstonecraft's own history of the French Revolution, which had been published the previous year.

Property, and its rightful or wrongful ownership (by individuals, whose labour gives them property in its fruits, or by governments who wrongly 'seize upon private property'), figures large in Barlow's argument, as it does in a different way in both Wollstonecraft's *Vindications*. Attitudes to property, indeed, focus political differences in this period: Barlow's praise for revolutionary France's confiscation of ecclesiastical and aristocratic property directly opposes Burke's berating of the same act in his *Reflections on the Revolution in France* (1790): as we shall see in the next chapter, for Burke, this overturned the established, proper relationships of property, law, and government. As Barlow's pamphlet shows, an attack on governmental financial practices (debt, taxes, revenue, and expenditure) readily opens into, or is founded on, a larger attack on the basis or principles of government itself, and the forms of social and political order sustained by existing property organisations. Against Barlow's call for 'a general revolution in the Principles of Government', the *Analytical Review* elsewhere sets out the importance of property as the keystone of the British political and financial system, given commercial society's foundation on security of property ownership. This is the 'doctrine' offered by the 'Retrospect of the active World' published in the *Analytical Review* for July 1798, one of a periodic series of longer, anonymous, pieces that combined a survey of political events with analytical commentary.[64] Here the familiar pieces of an argument about war, debt, and property are cast in a new direction, to combine a long historical retrospect of Europe with a claim about the current revolutionary war and predictions about a global future in which 'an order of property and freedom' will secure the 'rights of men'. Here, as only occasionally in the pages of the *Analytical Review*, claims about political economic structures, orders and principles – including the funding system, and the public credit on which it relies – are strongly folded into an optimistic political narrative foretelling the global emergence on liberty.

As Burke had, the anonymous author of this piece deprecates the French revolutionary currency of the assignats: a 'sign of property' founded on the 'confiscation of the whole wealth of the ancient proprietors of France' as well as a 'fraud' on France's 'foreign creditors'.[65] The parallel with Burke, however, ends there, as the 'Retrospect' looks optimistically forward to a point beyond the French war, where European and other countries recognise their common need for liberty of government and security of finance. Property (and public credit as one form of property) and liberty are yoked together with the claim that the only way to achieve liberty for individuals and nations is through secure finance and property systems, backed by representative government. France's funding of its war, through the fraud of stolen property and purloining assets from conquered countries, is considered essentially unsustainable: France will not be free until 'her finance fall under … the protection of public credit'.[66] Property, this historical moment has made it possible to see, is what binds human society, its 'influence … on the great bond of civilisation' which earlier could not be understood, is now writ large, and in this way, the 'rights of men are to be protected only by protecting the rights of nations': only if the 'order of property, and the laws of public credit' are 'made sacred to all', can individuals and nations have 'any permanent prosperity'.[67] This is an argument that turns the political language of liberty and the rights of men in a new direction, folding it into a political economic discourse that subsumes liberty by making it dependent on security of property. In turn, 'an elective representation' is urged, not because this equates to a liberty in itself, but rather because it is only through 'solid government … fair representation, and legal taxation' that security of property and person can be found.[68] As we will see in Chapter 2, Wollstonecraft had offered a markedly different account of the relation of property and liberty in her *Vindication of the Rights of Men*, published eight years earlier: a mark of her distance from some of the political sentiments articulated in the *Analytical Review*.

The question of who wrote the 'Retrospect' is a tantalising one, but its faith in a peaceful and commercial future was not without precedent: Paine's *Rights of Man* had presented commerce as 'a pacific system' which could eliminate war.[69] Indeed, a circle of thinkers around Lord Shelburne (who was briefly Prime Minister from 1782 to 1783) had found in *The Wealth of Nations* the possibility of a cosmopolitan and peaceable free trade which might replace empire and the mercantilist system; the Eden Treaty of 1786, which sought to liberalise commercial relations between Britain and France, was the most substantive policy manifestation of such an approach.[70] Both Price and Priestley were part of Shelburne's circle, although the former retained significant reservations about the moral corruptions of trade and the extent to which it should be carried out. Earlier in the century too, the potential of commerce to secure peace between European countries otherwise caught in a seeming perpetual cycle of wars, whether over territorial conquest or disputed successions, had been mooted by Montesquieu; others, including Rousseau, contended on the contrary that commerce was a source of war. Whilst *The Wealth of Nations* offered a severe attack on British mercantilism (trade and foreign policy influenced by mercantile interests), Smith himself judged the full liberalisation of trade to be unachievable.[71] It was against a background of such bifurcated opinion on commerce, which carried, on the one side, the possibility of ushering in a new era of peace and prosperity, and, on the other, accusations of corruption and moral and social decay, that Wollstonecraft was writing. As we shall see when we turn in Chapter 4 to Wollstonecraft's history of her own historical moment, the possibility of human progress, understood as the advance of liberty and enlightenment, was in her eyes to be closely and complexly tied to that of economic freedom too – whilst progress on any of these fronts would not, she warned, be easy to achieve.

Problems in Political Economy: Property, Inequality, Luxury, and Poverty

In addition to reflecting – and contributing to – wide-ranging debate on the nature of commercial society, the *Analytical Review* also addressed a number of more particular issues under the heading of political economy. These included the problem of wealth inequality, understood to stem in part from current practices of property ownership and inheritance; anxieties

Problems in Political Economy

about luxury and social and moral decline, attributed to the development of a manufacturing and commercial economy; and, as we have already seen, concerns about poverty and the administration of poor relief. Whilst self-contained to some extent, discussion in each area often bled into others, illustrating how political economic writing at this time combined elements of economic, moral, social, and political thought. Such discussions help us to understand both Wollstonecraft's political and intellectual context, and the ways in which her engagement with such issues differed from many of her peers.

In both her *Vindications*, Wollstonecraft offered wide-ranging criticism of the established system of property ownership, tracing many of the ills and inequities of late eighteenth-century society to that cause. Similar concerns with property distribution, though less extensively traced, are present in the *Analytical Review*. The '*present state of property*', as one reviewer puts it, is upheld by laws which 'preserve property in large masses and prevent its (sic) distribution among all the members of wealthy families'.[72] This, along with the assertion that 'monopolists and capitalists' are 'exclusively favoured by the legislature' whilst labourers do not receive fair wage for industry, causes the reviewer to assert that entails (a privileged figure in Burke's *Reflections*), as well as monopolies, should be abolished. These claims are made by the reviewer of Sir Frederic Morton Eden's *State of the Poor*, reviewed across three issues of the *Analytical Review* from March to June 1797.[73] Discussion of the pressing current issue of poverty is thus readily linked to larger structuring causes in inequitable property organisation and the laws which preserve them. Describing the current poor laws as incompetent to their original purpose, the reviewer asserts that 'in a better constituted society, nothing of the kind would be at all necessary'. If, as we saw in the previous section, the so-called 'order of property' could be used to evoke a future defined by peaceable commerce, the 'present state of property' nevertheless evidenced many of the failings of existing property society, as currently organised. If *The Wealth of Nations* inspired some to imagine a 'polity based upon moderate gradations of wealth', property laws are clearly identified as interfering with its establishment.[74]

Robert Acklom Ingram, whose *Inquiry into the present condition of the lower classes and the means of improving it* prompted its reviewer to welcome the teaching of political economy in universities, similarly identifies a change in the laws of inheritance, as well as placing the burden of tax on landed property, as measures to address the 'unequal distribution of wealth'.[75] The perhaps somewhat abstract question of 'the condition of the lower classes' is given strikingly materialised form, and connected to a particular property form, in its association with cottages and their inhabitants, as it is for example by both Eden and Thomas Ruggles, in his *History of the Poor* (1793–1794).[76] For Ruggles, 'the crowded cottage', and for Eden, '[h]ovel[s] on the road-side' are poverty's visible signs. As we will see in Chapter 5, Wollstonecraft deploys the image of the cottage to condense questions of the viability and desirability of commercial modernity: it is for her an ambivalent sign both of commercial society's problems and limitations, and also of the possibility of an alternative to it. Eden and Ruggles both recommend enclosure of land to ensure efficient use and to prevent poverty's 'disfiguring' appearances. Wollstonecraft too, in her *Vindication of the Rights of Men*, asked why 'huge forests' were 'still allowed to stretch out with idle pomp' and why 'the industrious peasant' might not 'steal a farm from the heath', and she sketches a picture of a 'hut … far from the diseases and vices of cities' where 'chubby babes' and 'cheerful poultry' flourish.[77] A more abstract take on property and poverty is given in William Godwin's *Political Justice*, reviewed at length in August 1793, where the established system of property, and its unequal distribution, is denounced as leading to 'the spirit of oppression, the spirit of servility, and the spirit of fraud', all enemies of 'intellectual and moral improvement'.[78] Property, the very security of which was for Smith and Hume the foundation and precondition of commercial society, becomes, in Godwin's hands, the root source of the 'chief distributive injustices of commercial society'.[79] Property, it seems from the pages of the *Analytical Review*, attracted as wide and bifurcated a range of opinion, as commerce itself did.

Wollstonecraft's idealised image of the farm on the heath may be read as the flipside of a preoccupation with signs of luxury, or changes in behaviour and manners wrought by the speedy development of commercial society, which is periodically evident in the *Analytical Review*. A review of Sir John Sinclair's *Statistical Account of Scotland* evidences 'the progress of luxury' in commercially prosperous society through later dining times, wine drinking, and card playing.[80] Ruggles is more ambivalent: 'manufactures' are 'the boast, but destruction of the country', the cause of both 'national revenue', and 'general immorality and corruption'.[81] By contrast, part of Ingram's case for changing inheritance laws to address unequal distribution of wealth is that this would not simply alleviate poverty in itself, but 'excite' in 'the common people a desire of accumulation'; but he also attacks the 'increasing opulence in the higher classes', which he sees (as Rousseau did) as 'the result of continual subtraction from the comforts of the lower orders'.[82] His antipathy to 'opulence' recalls an older tradition of opposition to luxury, even whilst his concern to stoke 'a desire of accumulation' in the lower orders suggests Smith, commercial society's pre-eminent theorist. Anxiety about a society organised around commerce, and the production and consumption of manufactured goods, evidently persisted even as orthodox political economy gradually took root.[83]

Reviews in the *Analytical Review* also illuminate how political economic problems, such as those associated with poverty, were represented, framed, and perceived, including in affective and aesthetic terms. Even whilst Ruggles attributes the 'wretchedness of the labourer' to '*excessive civilization*', he suggests that it is sensibility – often itself seen as a sign of civilised refinement – which both registers such misery and suffers by it. Those who retreat from business to the country, he laments, so often have their sensibility wounded by seeing and hearing the 'misery of their fellow-creatures', that it is no wonder they 'desert their country mansions'. A conversation with the poor 'too often distresses humanity, and sends the hearer home dejected and dissatisfied'.[84] Ruggles operates a circular logic here: itself a marker of 'civilization', sensibility is wounded by the labourer's attempts to participate in the very refinements by which it is itself produced. Although a potential source of corruption, commercial civilisation nevertheless produces a sensibility which has at least some worth in its ability to register that very corruption. Its value, however, is undercut by an effete delicacy manifested in its tendency to depart poverty's scene: 'desert their country mansions'. This double-edged, self-wounding, sensibility is present at times in Wollstonecraft too, who famously hesitated to 'cultivate sensibility' in her daughter Fanny, 'lest, whilst I lend fresh blushes to the rose, I sharpen the thorns that will sound the breast I would fain guard'.[85] In Wollstonecraft's formulation, however, the potential 'thorns' to which sensibility might expose Fanny are due to the 'dependent and oppressed state of her sex'; the figure of vulnerable sensibility operates to critique an unjust world much more strongly than in Ruggles. Sensibility, indeed, is central to Wollstonecraft's periodic response to the problem of poverty, and more broadly is part of the armoury which she deploys to engage and counter the emergent discourse of political economy, and the way it approaches and frames its concerns. Both in her *Letters Written During a Short Residence in Sweden, Norway and Denmark* and in her final work, *The Wrongs of Woman*, Wollstonecraft mobilises sensibility as a form of social feeling capable of registering and responding to the suffering of others, and as manifesting an account of human nature to challenge that which political economy would construct. Rather than, as in Ruggles, connoting the vulnerability of excessive, self-wounding feeling, sensibility in Wollstonecraft often manifests a capacity for benevolent, humane, and philanthropic feeling for others, which operates at critical odds with a world where such affects, and the values they assert, are seemingly little regarded.

Aesthetic response offers another means for Wollstonecraft to register and evaluate the modern world which political economy is building, whilst also transmuting its terms. Daniel White has shown the importance of the image of the canal in dissenting writing where, in works such as Anna Letitia Barbauld's 'The Canal and the Brook' or her brother John Aikin's *Description of the Country from Thirty to Forty Miles round Manchester* (1795), it is a topographical mark of progress, showing how the advances of science, commerce, and utility might be combined with taste.[86] In the *Analytical*, the canal (or at times 'channel') is deployed as a metaphor to convey the effectiveness or otherwise of schemes to address problems in political economy: in the context of Hamburg poor relief, the legislator who attempts to improve the conditions of the poor without addressing poverty's fundamental causes is described as like 'one who diverts a stream from its original course, and now seeks to cut small canals to irrigate the original land which the diversion has now devastated'.[87] Here the irrigative figure of the canal is no longer celebrated as a sign of progress, but serves as a warning against legislative meddling uninformed by political economic knowledge. Wollstonecraft's account, in her *Letters from Sweden*, of visiting canal workings at Trolhaettae near Gothenburg, further transposes these terms, so that the 'grand proof of human industry' – the bustle and noise of workmen, the blowing up of rocks – is displaced by what are, for her, the more compelling 'wild scenes' and 'solitary sublimity' of the cascades and sterile crags at the same site. In such a context, the canal workings, 'great as they are termed, and little as they appear ... only resembled the insignificant sport of children'.[88]

The *Analytical Review*'s discussion of the condition of the poor – a pressing political topic in the mid-1790s, with Parliamentary debates over rising food prices, the cost of wages, and possible poor law reforms – reveals how more retrograde attitudes (moral anxiety about the corruption of luxury; a tendency to attribute poverty to character failings) come up against political economic discourse in its 'hardest' form: in particular, tables of statistical data comparing wages of labour to prices of provisions and population size.[89] The review of Ruggles' *History of the Poor* ends by quoting his disagreement with Smith's observations on the sufficiency of the wages of the labourer for his subsistence, asserting rising prices in relation to wages: '[h]ouse-rent, candles, shoes, butter, milk, and all sorts of butcher's meat have greatly increased in price, above the proportionable increase of labourer's wages; and even Dr. Adam Smith does not suppose all these luxuries'.[90]

The same crucial proportion between the price of labour and the cost of necessities is the foundation for Voght's *Account of the Management of the Poor in Hamburgh*; the review of Eden's *State of the Poor* also includes tables of prices of labour and provisions, as well as noting Richard Price's 'invaluable book on reversionary payments', and his observation that poor are more dependent on bread (hence corn) than in previous times. Such data are used to refute Eden's claim that the condition of the poor is improved; refuted too is the argument that the state of the poor is due to their improvidence, or that of their wives.[91] Such financial analysis enables a turn from moral condemnation of the poor to a political economic analysis of their motivation and behaviour: instead of poor relief and benevolence, labour should be enabled and stimulated, along with the 'desire of accumulation'.[92]

Detailed reflections on wages, and a comparison of the price of labour in Britain and France, also inform Arthur Young's *Travels During the Years 1787, 8 and 9*, which also expounds on the Smithian principle of the division of labour in relation to farming: larger farms for this reason will generate more profit for the farmer, and more wealth for the nation.[93] Such is Young's faith in agriculture, in fact, that his chapter on Manufacture concludes by asserting that agriculture alone, when thoroughly improved, 'is equal to the establishment and support of great national wealth, power, and felicity'.[94] There is no trace here either of the association of agricultural society with indolence, as mooted in Hume's essay 'Of Refinement in the Arts' (1741), or of the idealisation of agrarian virtue as a bulwark against mercantile corruption, to be found in Price's warning to the new American republic in his *Observations on the Importance of the American Revolution* (1785): rather, Young's defence of agriculture folds it almost entirely into the analytical terms of Smithian political economic discourse. Smith's own account of what he termed the 'unnatural and retrograde order' of European economic development had argued that the development of commerce had leap-frogged the capitalist development of agriculture which would more naturally have preceded it in the conjectural model of the four stages of economic development favoured by Scottish thinkers.[95] But Smith would not have agreed with Young (or indeed with the French physiocrats, who had theorised the primacy of agriculture) that agriculture had the strongest claim to become the basis of national wealth: for Smith, manufacturing offered better opportunities for division of labour, and hence growth, than agriculture.

A quite different vision of agriculture was implicit in the virtuous agrarianism which for some thinkers offered an appealing alternative to the perceivedly corrupt commercial order of war, tax, and empire. Price, for one, warning against the corruptions of trade, hoped that the new American republic would be populated by 'plain and honest farmers' rather than 'opulent and splendid merchants'.[96] This would be the best way to protect its 'simplicity of character' and 'manliness of spirit'; to prevent 'liberty and virtue' being 'swallowed up in the gulf of corruption'. His *Observations on the Importance of the American Revolution* (1784) had hailed

> the state of society in Connecticut and some others of the American provinces where the inhabitants consist … of an independent and hardy yeomanry, nearly all on a level, trained to arms, instructed in their rights, clothed in homespun, of simple manners, strangers to luxury, drawing plenty from the ground … protected by laws which (being their own will) cannot oppress, and by an equal government which, wanting lucrative places, cannot create corrupt canvassings and ambitious intrigue.[97]

The vision was of a principled, virtuous, agrarian existence, in a republic like those of ancient Greece and Rome, defined by simplicity, hard work, and plenty, and uncorrupted by commerce and war. Wollstonecraft, who planned at one point to retire with Gilbert Imlay to an American farm (albeit one purchased with the profits of his shady business activities), and who also sought to settle her brother on a farm in America, was not immune from its seductions. The figure of Darnford in *The Wrongs of Woman*, meanwhile, whose venality and moral failings come to a head during a short stay in America, embodied Wollstonecraft's later sense of how quickly the promise of America pursuing an alternative path from that of European commercialism had faded.

Conclusion

The picture of political economic thought in the period between 1788 and 1798 as represented in the *Analytical Review* is undoubtedly particular, in some ways eccentric and idiosyncratic, but it nevertheless has value. Most surveys of thought in this period tend to focus on voices which historical retrospect allows us to identify as major ones. The synchronic view offered by this chapter's exploration of political economy in Johnson's periodical allows such voices to jostle alongside more transient ones: both in the publications reviewed and in their anonymous reviewers. These have been worth attending to because of what they reveal about the nature of political economic thought at the time, which appears markedly diverse on at least two fronts: both in terms of the range of voices and opinions, which contribute to these debates, and in terms of the breadth of what political economy was understood to encompass at the time.

Conclusion

Political economy emerges from the pages of Johnson's periodical as a flexible and capacious area of inquiry, conscious of its relations with moral, social, philosophical, and even religious thought. It is equally capable of a more narrowly focused investigation of particular topics, perhaps pursued through relatively new forms of statistical or financial methods, or by marshalling various forms of data, such as on prices or wages, or war expenses. As a relatively undefined, or multiply defined knowledge practice, it was loose, open, and porous: capable of absorbing concerns from contiguous areas. Its inclusion in the *Analytical Review* attests to the editors' perception that it had a valuable contribution to make to the journal's founding aims: to 'advance the interests of science, of virtue and morality', as part of the 'genuine information in every department of Literature and Science' which the publication offered its readers.[98]

Jon Mee's assertion that conversation offers an important model for understanding Romantic discursivity is a suggestive way to think about the textual practice of the *Analytical*, which enabled its readers to participate in a conversation about political economic matters which was ongoing, fluid, and heterodox, and where thoughts on a topic in hand might just as easily be challenged and countered as confirmed and reiterated.[99] This is modelled through the format of the reviews themselves, which, by often giving generous space to quotation from the publication itself, interspersed with commentary or response from the reviewer, could become dialogic spaces (even without considering the responses of the reader, or any further conversations which the review itself might prompt). If Christie's initial plans for the journal anticipated its readers participating in 'diffusing' knowledge, the design of the periodical points to the potentially conversational basis for such diffusion.[100] As with any conversation, the intersecting debates in the political economy pages of the *Analytical Review* could span quite diametrically opposed positions (as we have seen in relation to both commerce and property); at the same time, the repetition of certain positions does suggest opinion settling around certain lines. Thus, Godwin's take on property, or Barlow's on taxation as 'fraud', each represent something of an outlier, although worth attending to as a marker of opinion in some quarters, or as demonstrating the destination of certain lines of argument, if taken to their full extent. At the same time, as with any conversation, the *Analytical Review* had a particular and recognisable tone. The journal's broadly positive attitude to commerce nevertheless harboured at times significant anxieties about some of its effects, whether on the national's moral or social fabric or on its labouring poor. Recognition of, at best, the potential of free trade to perhaps bring about a future era of peace and prosperity was balanced with at times stringent critique of existing forms of taxation, wealth inequality, and property laws. Political economy in the eyes of the *Analytical Review* offered both the prospect of enacting useful and benevolent reforms which might increase the happiness of ordinary people, and a means of critiquing perceived injustices or existing oppressions. Whilst, in one perspective, it might seek to mobilise a potentially problematic 'desire for accumulation' as a means for addressing social ills, on the other, its concern with the distribution of wealth, and the promotion of national prosperity, offered a potentially powerful means to ameliorate the living conditions of many.

How are we to understand Wollstonecraft in relation to this conversation about political economy? It seems unlikely, from the list drawn up by Todd and Marilyn Butler, and to the extent that authorship can be attributed, that Wollstonecraft herself authored any of the political economy reviews which have been discussed in this chapter.[101] She did review a biography of Paine, in which she commended his 'good sense' and the 'force' of his arguments; she also reviewed travel writings on America by the future Girondin leader, Jean-Pierre Brissot, although without commenting on the final volume devoted to commerce.[102] According to Todd and Butler, Wollstonecraft was also the author of a review giving fulsome praise to a proposal for a poll tax on the 'middling or trading class of people' to be used to relieve those who fall into 'penury and distress' due to failure in business; and of a further review condemning the employment of children in cotton factories in Manchester. 'Mistaken, indeed ... must be principles of that commercial system, whose wheels are oiled by infant sweat, and supine the government that allows any body of men to enrich themselves by preying on the vitals, physical and moral, of the rising generation!', she concludes.[103] As a contributor to the journal, even at times its editorial assistant, Wollstonecraft would have been familiar with the debates represented in its pages, and biography also speaks to her immersion in the radical and progressive circle around Johnson. Traces of certain well-trodden arguments from the *Analytical Review* recur in Wollstonecraft's writing: on occasion she appears to share with Price and Priestley a moral critique of commerce, or a distaste for luxury; her concern for the state of manners in commercial society, and the social consequences of the existing property order, is fundamental to her *Vindications*, as we see in the next chapters. But locating Wollstonecraft wholly within, or in relation to, certain traditions of political economic thought present us with a puzzle: her writing does not conform to the shape or contours of most, or all, political economic writing, but rather engages, but escapes and exceeds it. Whilst

Conclusion 47

marked by many of the debates which characterise late eighteenth-century political economy, her thinking rarely seeks to be confined by them, or to serve or answer them on their terms, but rather looks beyond their limits, often working cohesively to combine what we might class as political economic concerns with others.

Here it is worth considering the role of Wollstonecraft's gender, both in relation to her role at the *Analytical* and her perspective on emergent political economic thought. In terms of the former, scholars who have mapped Wollstonecraft's likely contributions to the journal suggest that her reviews focused on literary and educational publications, alongside the occasional scientific treatise. She reviewed novels, including by Charlotte Smith, as well as poetry, drama, travel writings, and sermons; she reviewed Olaudah Equiano's *Interesting Narrative*.[104] Although we cannot be certain, given the anonymity of its reviews, we may speculate that this division of labour in effect enacted a division of knowledge along gender lines: the 'soft' realm of literature, education, and culture, including the novels which Wollstonecraft so disparaged, assigned to a woman, with 'harder' political, commercial, and economic publications given to others. Considered from this perspective, even if it is a speculative one, the emergent field of political economic thought as presented in the *Analytical Review* appears as one in which a deeply political division of knowledge by gender has already taken place.

There are other ways of approaching the division of knowledge, however. Earlier in this chapter, we saw Coleridge assert that political economy should provide a means of elucidating the 'disturbing force of that miraculous machine of living Creatures, a Body Politic'. In a poet's eyes, the causal springs of action are just as much part of political economy as an analysis of labour, capital, and production; human motivation and emotion, and the behaviours, social customs, and moral codes connected to and consequent on them, should fall firmly within political economy's purview. This same realm of human passions and behaviour is precisely the concern of the literary and cultural publications assigned, as far as we can reconstruct from the *Analytical Review*'s anonymous pages, to Wollstonecraft for review. Here we have a way of approaching the 'puzzle', mentioned above, of Wollstonecraft's relation to the emergent field of political economic thought, by understanding it as a deep engagement which does not conform to the field's usual patterns and shape, but which refuses to disaggregate questions of human motivation and passions, of morals and manners, of customs and social codes, from practices of wealth, and organisations of labour and property. This is a refusal which runs counter to the gendered divisions of knowledge of her time, and which ensures that Wollstonecraft's engagement with political economy exceeds and transcends that emergent field.

Nor was this commitment to the world of human passion and behaviour simply for Wollstonecraft to be addressed by the literary and fictional writing, the 'trash' about which she was so often disparaging.[105] Miranda Burgess has argued that romance writing at this time was 'uniquely but diversely imbricated with political economy', and that it 'alternately competes with, supplements, and works with its readers to displace the contemporary philosophical and social debates of political economy', whilst remaining 'thoroughly invested in the questions political economy addresses'.[106] William Godwin, writing in the year of his marriage to Wollstonecraft, similarly offered 'romance' as the means to understand the 'machine of society'.[107] Wollstonecraft's final work, *The Wrongs of Woman*, drafted in the same year as Godwin's essay, suggests that she would agree, but whilst she wrote fiction at both ends of her writing career, she also described herself as a philosopher, and published works of history, politics, education, and travel writings. Her engagement with political economy, as a means of approaching and analysing the condition and problems of late eighteenth-century commercial society, would not be limited to fictional writing, but would extend its concern with the 'miraculous machine of living Creatures' to other writerly forms too. In so doing, she would resist the separation of human passions and experience, and their 'disturbing force', from an increasingly abstracted political economy. The generic range of her writing across her career, meanwhile, resists too a separation of writing into different genres or disciplines, whose distinct objects would address, in disconnected ways, abstracted and separated areas of human life and endeavour.

This book argues that approaching Wollstonecraft from the direction of the political economy of her time offers new insights to her writing and thinking, both in illuminating how her work has been informed by areas of thought whose relationship to Wollstonecraft is previously unconsidered, and in showing how she contributes, in ways not previously noted, to the debates of her time. Political economy in Wollstonecraft's time, as this chapter has shown, was very different from the subject delineated, for instance, in John Ramsay McCulloch's *The Literature of Political Economy*, published in 1845, some fifty years after her death. With its clear listing of the branches and subdivisions of political economy, McCulloch's work depicts a discipline whose field of expertise has been thoroughly organised – even flattened – in a way which contrasts dramatically with the joyfully heterodox, confused prolixity of the political economy reviews of the *Analytical Review*. Yet, as the remaining chapters of this book show, Wollstonecraft engages repeatedly with concerns later to be folded into McCulloch's taxonomy of political economic topics.[108] At times, that engagement is explicit and overt, even whilst little commented on by critics and historians; at others, it takes an awareness of the nature of late eighteenth-century political economy to understand that this is one of the fields to which she is responding. Thus, as we shall see in Chapter 4, Wollstonecraft's history of the French Revolution gives particular prominence to the fate of the grain trade in the early phases of the revolution, and links the freeing of the grain trade to the progress of liberty. Within Wollstonecraft's relatively small oeuvre, this frequently overlooked text has received little attention, and where it has been examined, critics tend to read it for a story about political revolution, not economic reform. The same is true for a far from overlooked text, Burke's *Reflections of the Revolution in France*, which prompted Wollstonecraft's first major work, *A Vindication of the Rights of Men*. As Chapter 2 shows, Burke deliberately disguises his fundamental preoccupation with a revolution in political economy by foregrounding a distracting theatrics for his reader's affective and sentimental entertainment, including the famous attack on Marie Antoinette's bedchamber. It is to Wollstonecraft's refusal to be distracted by the gothic 'romance' offered by Burke, and her disinterring instead, of Burke's defence of the existing political economic order of things, that we now turn.

CHAPTER 2

The Engagement with Burke
Contesting the 'Natural Course of Things'

Must we swear to secure property, and make assurance doubly sure, to give your perturbed spirit rest?[1]

The *Vindication of the Rights of Men*, published in November 1790, was the first major work of Wollstonecraft's career. An impassioned intervention into contemporary political debate, prompted by her reading of Edmund Burke's *Reflection on the Revolution in France* (also 1790), it marked a shift from Wollstonecraft's earlier educational publications. Her preface to the work relates that the *Vindication* was prompted by 'indignation ... roused' by her casual reading of Burke's *Reflections*.[2] But what exactly was it that she read in that dense and complex text which prompted her first major publication, a serious and impassioned work which is still studied today?

Scholarship readily offers a well-known story to answer that question, which approaches both Wollstonecraft and Burke's texts as marking the start of what Marilyn Butler termed the 'Revolution controversy': intense debates between British radicals and conservatives over the nature and significance of the French Revolution, whose early events were unfolding across the English channel.[3] Thus, whilst Wollstonecraft is understood to offer a 'rebuttal' of Burke's *Reflections*, Burke in turn is seen as responding to Richard Price's sermon, *A Discourse on the Love of Our Country* (delivered to the Revolution Society in late 1789 and published in January 1790), which fervently welcomed the early events of the French Revolution by seeing it as the latest manifestation of an 'ardor for liberty' sweeping from America to France to all of Europe.[4] The claim that Burke sat down 'immediately' to write the *Reflections* on reading Price's sermon recurs repeatedly in the historiographic literature, and Wollstonecraft's *Vindication* is at least partly understood as a reaction to a personal and political attack on her elderly friend Price, whose sermon she had already positively reviewed in Joseph Johnson's *Analytical Review*.[5] The 'Revolution controversy' story

50

thus offers a relatively close-focus context for reading these texts, which foregrounds the differing responses of its various protagonists to on-going events in France.

There are some problems with this reading, however. At first blush, Wollstonecraft's *Vindication* appears to deal little with liberty, or indeed with Price. Whilst she chastises Burke for an uncharitable attack on a venerable and religious old man, her work almost casually concedes the utopian nature of elements of Price's thoughts, and mounts what might be read as an almost nominal defence of liberty, which is treated so efficiently and briefly in the early stages of her text that it can hardly be taken as the real focus of her differences with her opponent. Equally, readers who look in the *Vindication* for the first salvo in a battle for 'the political rights that we now take for granted' will look in vain for very much developed thinking about rights at all, despite the foregrounding of that term in Wollstonecraft's title.[6] There is evidence which confuses the picture in relation to Burke's *Reflections* too. 'In reality', he wrote in a letter to Charles-Alexandre de Calonne, 'my Object was not France, in the first instance, but this Country'.[7] And, rather than an immediate reaction to Price, *Reflections* was likely meditated 'over a longer period' with the aim of 'discrediting' Lord Shelburne, patron of Price, Joseph Priestley, and other radical thinkers.[8] Writing privately during the period in which he was composing the *Reflections*, Burke states that whilst he 'intend[s] no controversy with Dr. Price or Lord Shelburne or any other of their set' he nevertheless means to 'set in a full View the danger from their wicked principles and their black hearts' and to 'do my best to expose them to the hatred, ridicule, and contempt of the whole world; as I shall always expose such, calumniators, hypocrites[,] sowers of sedition, and approvers of murder and all its Triumphs'.[9]

Burke had clashed with Shelburne and Price some years earlier, in the context of American colonists' struggles for independence, objecting to Price's definition of civil liberty as the absence of restraint: for Burke, this was 'destructive of all authority'.[10] Although his attack on Price's *Discourse on the Love of our Country* took place within the immediate context of revolutionary events in France, it is likely that Burke regarded his *Reflections* as fighting a new front in a well-established domestic battle over political liberty. He did so by defending the established British order, and, in particular, its very specific political economic settlement. In the process, he made use of the ways that the emergent discourse of political economy understood relations between individual subjects and the polity or nation in modern commercial society. In doing so, he opened a new front in ongoing battles over political liberty and happiness in a society increasingly recognised as, in the words of dissenting poet and essayist Anna Laetitia Barbauld, 'a great mart of commerce'.[11] Such battles now also became struggles over the extent to which the terms, concepts, and language of political economic discourse would be allowed to gain a foothold in contemporary political thought, and tests of strength of the various means of countering it.

Given this, this chapter reads Burke's *Reflections*, and Wollstonecraft's engagement with it, as a key moment in the ongoing reception and shaping of political economy in the early 1790s. It argues that Wollstonecraft's first *Vindication* is not simply to be regarded as a 'political disquisition' but as a political economic one: a direct challenge to the Whiggish political economy which Burke was trying to sure up.[12] In the version of political economy which informs Burke's *Reflections*, any nascent possibility of liberty and independence is threatened by the sacrifice of individual lives and happiness deemed necessary for the maintenance of commercial society's 'mart'. Given that the passage in Burke's text where this is most shockingly explicit was where Wollstonecraft trained her heaviest fire, such themes are likely to be central to the 'rousing' of her 'indignation' by his text. Further evidence of her attention to the relation of individuals to the social and political whole, and the consequences for both liberty and happiness, is apparent in her review of Catharine Macaulay's *Letters on Education* (1790), published in the *Analytical Review* in the same month that the *Vindication* appeared.[13] Wollstonecraft quoted at length Macaulay's exposure of a 'species of idolatry' in matters of government: making 'a deity of the society in its aggregate capacity', and sacrificing, 'to the real or imagined interests of this idol', the 'dearest interests of those individuals who formed the aggregate'. Such a reversal, Macaulay claimed, of the 'plain and reasonable proposition' that society was formed 'for the happiness of its citizens' placed such nations 'at war with the happiness of individuals'.[14] Wollstonecraft appeared to concur in her admonitions against the 'monstrous faith' of even 'civilized societies' who 'made a deity of their government, in whose high prerogative, they have buried all their natural rights'. Here was a powerful view of modern commercial society as an idolised 'aggregate' which failed to serve the rights, interests, or happiness of its individuals.

Defending the British order against such attacks entailed for Burke the justification of its very specific political economic settlement, characterised by historian J. G. A. Pocock as a Whig alliance between aristocratic government and commercial society.[15] In Burke's account, as we shall see, such a settlement sets out the very particular, but also delimited, liberty which may be enjoyed by its subjects: liberty of acquisition within the limits of what their labour might attain. Burke thus sought to counter political narratives which foregrounded liberty by defending the established Whig socio-political and economic order in, as Pocock says, the 'language and categories of political economy', to show the forms of liberty which that order already provides.[16] His opponents' rallying call of 'liberty' would thereby be derailed by changing the terms of the debate, and evoking a necessary submission to the 'natural course of things'.

This chapter shows how Wollstonecraft's engagement with Burke carries forward the call for liberty onto new ground by attacking the economic order on which late eighteenth-century society was founded.[17] Repeatedly critiquing the 'idol of property' around which Burke's text revolved, she shows how an economic order founded on property as currently organised produced a society which was oppressive, and an obstacle to liberty. In this line of attack, Wollstonecraft flushes out into the open an argument which, whilst only periodically explicit in Burke's text, is nevertheless deeply informative of it. Sarcastically reading Burke as the unsettled ghost in *Hamlet*, she asks: 'Must we swear to secure property, and make assurance doubly sure, to give your perturbed spirit rest?'[18] This exposure of Burke as governed – or haunted – by his allegiance to property shifts the ground of a political debate which Burke had hoped to hold on his terms, to expose the nature of the political economic settlement which his text defends, to explore the nature of life and liberty under that settlement, and to wrest the debate out beyond Burke's terms. Framed in this way, the liberty which Price had defended and theorised is no longer an abstract political or philosophical question; rather, it is referred to the specific material conditions of life, which are assessed against both the possibility of freedom, and the oppressions which are their consequence. That Wollstonecraft focuses on these issues in a text prompted by Burke's *Reflections* suggests that she finds such questions contained in some fashion in his text. Burke readily concedes that the order of property which he champions is 'unequal', but his argument runs far deeper than this.[19] As we shall see, the delimited form of liberty offered by Burke, the 'freedom of acquisition' whose rewards are not proportionate to the labour expended in its pursuit, is a function of a political economy whose defence requires the servile and miserable labour of one class whilst defining the idleness of another as part of a 'natural course of things'.[20] Wollstonecraft's *Vindication* exhumes the obscured economic substrata to Burke's work, and places centre stage the social, cultural and psychological consequences of the existing economic ordering of society, which Burke sought to both naturalise and make the object of affective bonds. The *Vindication* thus constitutes the next stage in an unfolding political campaign for liberty: an exposition of the oppressions stemming directly from the Whiggish property order which Burke's text obscurely defends.

In this reading, the *Vindication*'s motivating question might be taken as the following: in how many ways does the current economic order of things, in the 'present state of property' as the *Analytical Review* had it, impede the progress of liberty?[21] Its attack on the Whig property order is also invigorated with a more generalised sense of the corruptions of commerce and its erosions of the social fabric. As the next chapter shows, its analysis of the corruptions of wealth and the existing property order is continued in Wollstonecraft's second major work, the *Vindication of the Rights of Woman* (1792), where the call for a 'revolution in manners' turns a Burkean vocabulary of manners in a new direction, to reject the corrupt morals and manners which Wollstonecraft shows stem directly from the existing property order. The double move of the two *Vindications* is thus first, to flush out into the open the occluded defence of Whig political economy which Burke smuggles into his *Reflections* and to challenge its political oppressions, and then, in the second *Vindication*, to trace its consequences in the moral corruptions of the age, and map out a programme of moral and social reform via the education of women. In the process, the *Vindications* loudly and collectively challenge the norms of Whig political economy obscured, in Burke, by gothic drapery and sentimental veneration of established social and political structures. Against this, Wollstonecraft resists the separation of economic concerns from, on the one hand, questions of liberty, equality, oppression, and happiness, and, on the other, moral and social norms, and insists on the inextricable consequences which stem from the economic structures of society for all forms of social life, for morals and manners. The *Vindications* thus refused to countenance a political economy which, describing itself as the 'natural course of things', sought both to disaggregate an economic order from its political, and social consequences, and to drape itself in an ideology of sentimental attachment which operates against analytical inspection of what Burke would prefer his readers to leave unexamined.

Taking place as it does in written form, in a mode which closely tracks and refutes Burke's work whilst mobilising its own textual strategies, Wollstonecraft's challenge to Burkean political economy was not merely political but also discursive, generic, and linguistic. Part of this is evident in Wollstonecraft's rhetorical and stylistic differences with Burke. 'I shall be employed about things, not words!', Wollstonecraft stated in her second *Vindication*; Burke, meanwhile, 'was nothing if not a rhetorical strategist'.[22] Fundamentally at stake in their exchange was the nature, status, and even accessibility of political economic discourse itself, as Wollstonecraft responded to a text which sought to naturalise existing political and economic settlements whilst barely acknowledging this as its own strategy. The challenge of Wollstonecraft's response to Burke was not simply to address its politics, but also the discursive form taken by its political economic knowledge: its expression, style, and status, as well as its relationship with other forms of knowledge and modes of thinking and writing. At stake in their exchange is thus not only political economy as a theory of economic and socio-political behaviours, but also the very means by which political, social, and moral worlds might be known and represented in writing. A comparison of descriptive landscape writing – a mode long used to represent sociopolitical organisation – in Burke's *Reflections* and Wollstonecraft's *Vindication* shows how the relationship of political economic knowledge to the aesthetic and the affective, on the one hand, and to analytical reason and the imagination, on the other, is in play in these texts.

Political Economy and Landscape Description: Burke, Smith, and Wollstonecraft

Burke's *Reflections* and Wollstonecraft's *Vindication* share open, loose, even digressive modes of organisation. Whilst this has meant that the texts run the risk of being dismissed as disorganised or 'rambling and digressive', it also gave each author a remarkable flexibility in staging and framing their arguments.[23] The use of topographical writing in both texts is one sign of this discursive freedom. Both authors make periodic use of the landscape survey to bolster their arguments, but the nature and function of these passages are markedly different in each text, which yoke landscape writing to quite contrasting political economic ends.

A striking example in Burke's text occurs as he discusses French national prosperity in the period before the Revolution. Writing in 1769, years before the *Reflections*, Burke had perceived the state of the country's finances to be perilous, and even foreseen the Revolution itself: 'no man … who has considered [French] affairs with any degree of attention or information, but must hourly look for some extraordinary convulsion in that whole system; the effect of which on France, and even on all Europe, it is difficult to conjecture'.[24] Such knowledge is repressed from the *Reflections*, however, as Burke's defence of the French *ancien régime*

56 The Engagement with Burke

includes a flattering picture of the 'progressive improvement' of the country.[25] Orthodox political economic evidence is cited to support the claim that France enjoyed a 'very respectable degree of opulence': population growth (which for Smith correlated with national prosperity) and Necker's account of the *Administration of Finances of France* (1785), described as an 'accurate and interesting collection of facts relative to public economy and to political arithmetic'.[26] But Burke also produces the following extraordinary sentence:

> Indeed, when I consider the face of the kingdom of France; the multitude and opulence of her cities; the useful magnificence of her spacious high roads and bridges; the opportunity of her artificial canals and navigations opening the conveniences of maritime communication through a solid continent of so immense an extent; when I turn my eyes to the stupendous works of her ports and harbours, and to her whole naval apparatus, whether for war or trade; when I bring before my view the number of her fortifications, constructed with so bold and masterly a skill, and made and maintained at so prodigious a charge, presenting an armed front and impenetrable barrier to her enemies upon every side; when I recollect how very small a part of that extensive region is without cultivation, and to what complete perfection the culture of many of the best productions of the earth have been brought in France; when I reflect on the excellence of her manufactures and fabrics, second to none but ours, and in some particulars not second; when I contemplate the grand foundations of charity, public and private; when I survey the state of all the arts that beautify and polish life; when I reckon the men she has bled for extending her fame in war, her able statesmen, the multitude of her profound lawyers and theologians, her philosophers, her critics, her historians and antiquaries, her poets and her orators, sacred and profane, I behold in all this something which awes and commands the imagination, which checks the mind on the brink of precipitate and indiscriminate censure, and which demands that we should very seriously examine what and how great are the latent vices that could authorize us at once to level so spacious a fabric with the ground.[27]

Whilst the *Reflections'* digressive mode enables such a topographical excurse, the passage implicitly poses the question of the relation of this rhapsodic survey to earlier claims about French prosperity grounded in the authority of financial and political economic knowledge. A supplemental logic is in play, as though readerly affective engagement is needed to make good some unspoken inadequacy in his earlier assertions. Sublime awe (which 'commands' the imagination and 'checks the mind') is modelled as the response the survey should elicit from its reader, yet Burke is not himself so carried away that he is unable to issue a sharp condemnation of the 'vices' that would 'level' such a 'fabric' to the ground. The passage could

Political Economy and Landscape Description 57

be read as the cumulative statement, the apotheosis, of Burke's argument, but, with its dramatic shift of rhetorical gears, it might also be taken as somehow displacing what preceded it. Whilst the passage brings to a conclusion the preceding train of argument, it does so by both transcending and displacing it, offering a rhetorical moment which operates as a kind of alternative proof of the prosperity of France, which the Smithian gesture to population, or the evidence of Necker's financial accounting, could somehow not quite clinch.

Burke's turn to topography as – literally – the ground of his argument illustrates the repeated deployment in the *Reflections* of aestheticised reverie, which plays on the same modes of affective response and moralised sensation which he earlier theorised in his *Philosophical Enquiry into the Origin of Our Ideas of the Sublime and the Beautiful* (1757). Burke's survey of the material infrastructure which sustained French commerce also recalls the opening chapter of *The Wealth of Nations*, where Smith delineates the numerous forms of labour and trade which contribute to the creation of a worker's woollen coat. Smith's description of this 'homely production' moves from an initial survey of the 'joint labour' of the shepherd, the sorter of the wool, the dyer, the spinner, the weaver, and so on, through to the 'merchants and carriers' who provide the 'drugs' used by the dyer and the shears used by the shepherd. The passage ultimately describes, in tones almost as exhortative as Burke employs, the myriad interconnected forms of labour, transport, and commerce which sustain the production and circulation of goods in market society.[28] The discussion exemplifies the characteristic movement of Smith's text, from observation of individual acts and discrete behaviours, to the larger theorisation of an economic system of production and commerce.

Burke's *Reflections* also mediates between the particular and the general: between the material detail of human experience on the one hand, including particular experiences of history and affective and aesthetic sensation, and, on the other, a generalised system of political economy which it will describe and defend as 'the natural course of things'. There is a crucial difference, however. In Smith's opening chapter, attention to material things provides an entry point into the larger, theoretical supposition of an economic system. But whilst Burke's prospect view mimics a similar mode of political economic insight, the turn from observation of the material world to a developed economic understanding is stalled, as topographical survey halts in the face of the apparently overwhelming surface of things: rather than analysis of the cause or functioning of France's wealth, the affective response of 'awe' is offered. In Smithian epistemology, the imagination plays a crucial role in sketching the theorised 'chain' of connections by which observed objects, and their relations to others, might be explained.[29] In Burke, by contrast, the imagination is halted by an unnamed 'something', which 'commands' and 'checks' the mind, and which requires capitulation to the established political and economic system which has produced 'so spacious a fabric'. Burke's aesthetic reverie thus operates explicitly as the capitulation of reason, and as a block to economic analysis, and his own writing demonstrates what his text repeatedly asserts: that speculation is opposed to manners and sentiment – a claim which Wollstonecraft will strongly counter.

The aesthetic reverie which for Burke takes the place of economic analysis thus embodies his text's claim of the superiority of sentiment to speculation and reason. Such a claim is also embodied in Burke's resistance to any idea of 'digesting' the *Reflections* into 'a Systematic order', preferring to retain the generic fiction of his text as a conversational, gentlemanly letter to a friend.[30] His topographical survey of France bears comparison to the 'prospect view' theorised by John Barrell, which exemplifies the landed gentleman's privileged aesthetic and political oversight, unsullied by dogmatic particulars and interested details; it thus similarly enacts the 'gentlemanly' character of Burke's text.[31] That this topographical prospect culminates in a surrender to the established politico-social order – a veneration of the 'fabric' which others would lay to the ground – evidences the 'rhetorical strategy' which Hamilton detects beneath Burke's 'loose' gentlemanly style: the 'manners' of sentiment and feeling, enacted in the text, modelled by its authorial persona, operate as ideological cover for a supposedly natural political 'fabric'. The 'drapery' of Burke's highly rhetorical 'literary' writing, which addresses itself to the affective response of the reader, short-circuits the rational thought which Wollstonecraft repeatedly identifies as the proper grounds of the subject's relation to the world: as her second *Vindication* especially asserts, to be understood as a rational being is the ground of the liberty which is our right. This relation of reason and liberty is crucial for Wollstonecraft politically but also stylistically. This is shown in her own attention to landscape, which refuses the exhortative, rhapsodic prospect view of Burke for critical attention to particularity and detail. Wollstonecraft nevertheless also finds a place for reverie and imagination, not as a means to affirm what is, but as crucial tools for looking beyond the current organisation of things.

In contrast to Burke, for Wollstonecraft, it is the city which is the real test-case for gauging the nature and effects of late eighteenth-century commercial society. Horace Walpole, welcoming Burke's *Reflections*, hoped

Political Economy and Landscape Description 59

that Burke's 'foes' and their 'Amazonian allies' would 'return to Fleet Ditch' from which he suggested they had emerged; although he doesn't list her in their number, Walpole's association of Burke's opponents with the dirty corners of the city anticipates Wollstonecraft's deliberate attention to such spaces in her text.[32] The 'polis' which echoes in the term *political economy* recalls the city state which is the original political community in classical thinking, a community whose urban location is never really in focus in the Burkean landscape survey. Smith's definition of political economy – 'to provide a plentiful revenue or subsistence for the people, or more properly to enable them to provide such a revenue or subsistence for themselves; and … to supply the state or commonwealth with a revenue sufficient for the publick services' – similarly emphasises its purpose in provisioning (one way or the other) the needs of the community.[33] But in the last pages of the *Vindication*, Wollstonecraft sketches a cityscape which highlights a failure to meet the needs of the community in the commercial city of London, in a critical survey very different from those of Smith and Burke:

> In this great city, that proudly rears its head, and boasts of its population and commerce, how much misery lurks in pestilential corners, whilst idle mendicants assail, on every side, the man who hates to encourage imposters, or repress, with angry frown, the plaints of the poor! How many mechanics, by a flux of trade or fashion, lose their employment; whom misfortunes, not to be warded off, lead to the idleness that vitiates their character and renders them afterwards averse to honest labour! Where is the eye that marks these evils, more gigantic than any of the infringements of property, which you piously deprecate?[34]

Wollstonecraft's observations look past the Burkean 'boasts' of population and commerce to see, as in a Hogarthian visual satire, misery in 'pestilential corners', from 'idle mendicants', to complaining poverty, to the vitiation of character through unemployment, to (a little further on) 'the sick wretch, who can no longer earn the sour bread of unremitting labour', who 'steals to a ditch to bid the world a long good night', or lies, 'neglected' by 'mercenary attendants', in a hospital.[35] Her 'eye' which 'marks these evils' is capable of noting the particular details of lived historical experience, even when it is hidden in 'corners' or a 'ditch', but she is also quick to link such sights to their economic causes: the loss of employment due to fluxes 'of trade or fashion', the illness brought on by 'unremitting labour'.[36] These 'evils' are 'more gigantic than any of the infringements of property', which Burke 'piously deprecate[s]', she asserts, countering Burke's veneration of property with the alternative perspective of an 'eye' alert to the moral and social failings of the city. Like Burke's survey of pre-Revolutionary France, Wollstonecraft's view of London culminates in an affective turn, not to sublime 'awe' however, but with the suggestion that '[s]uch misery demands more than tears'. The 'pause' she takes to 'recollect' herself and 'smother the contempt I feel rising for your rhetorical flourishes and infantine sensibility' is represented by a double line of dashes, the typographical marking of such a necessary self-recollection.[37] Unlike Burke's rolling vision, contained within the multiple clauses of an endlessly expanded sentence, Wollstonecraft's survey is piecemeal, even fragmented, and its climax is not aesthetic surrender contained within and marked by syntactical cadences, but a self-made fracture in the 'fabric' of her text, which marks both horror at what has been witnessed, and contempt for a Burkean defence which would seek to justify it.

Wollstonecraft's puncturing of her text disrupts the smooth delivery of its descriptive acts; it reminds the reader of the historical particularity of the individual writing the text, who must 'pause' to gather herself, and, by extension, that of the text itself. By rupturing the readerly relationship to the text, the historically situated act of reading is also foregrounded; its author's need to 'recollect' herself to manage her emotional response to her words models the possibility that the reader, too, may have an affective response to the text, without prescriptively setting out what that response might be. For Marxist theorist Louis Althusser, descriptive acts ('a sort of philosophico-economic Phenomenology') underlie eighteenth-century political economy, central to its generation of a political economic knowledge which 'acts as if it were the description … [of] "*the world of needs*"'.[38] Through descriptive acts, in other words, political economy constructs a knowledge of civil society as a 'system of needs'.[39] The implicit claim of descriptive acts in political economic writing is to convey the reality of the world as it is, yet description constitutes a creative, constructive, persuasive act which seeks to elicit the consent of its reader, whether in Smith's account of the worker's coat, or in Burke's description of France.[40] Wollstonecraft's disrupting of her text breaks its bond of believability with its reader, and exposes its writerly nature, its situatedness, and the particularity of its perspective; rather than drawing its reader into crediting its description of the world, it frees the reader to believe or not, as personal judgement dictates. At the same time, her London cityscape shows how description can operate critically and dialogically to expose how a mode of knowledge which claims to understand the world as a system of needs fails to meet them. If Burke exhorts his reader to venerate a 'spacious' social fabric, Wollstonecraft describes what that fabric fails to provide,

Political Economy and Landscape Description   61

highlighting the failures of the promissory narrative underpinning commercial society. If description contributes to the construction (Smith) and defence (Burke) of political economy, in Wollstonecraft's hands it also enables a glimpse of some of its tragic effects.

Wollstonecraft admitted that 'Utopian reveries' at times informed Price's writings.[41] But she is not afraid to sketch alternative possible futures herself, although these are not the 'Arcadia[s] of fiction' to which, as she says, the imagination often turns, when 'revolt[ing]' from what 'is often … disgusting in the distresses of poverty'. Whether in her political treatises (as in the attack on 'stupid novelists' in the second *Vindication*) or in the prefaces to her fiction, she consistently and repeatedly attacks writing which lures the reader into artificial and unreal worlds, insisting instead on the responsibility of representation to depict the world as it is.[42] She attacks the attempt to turn from 'the distresses of poverty' in another landscape sketch, depicting a 'rich man' who 'builds a house' finished with 'art and taste', and surrounds it with 'sweeping pleasure-grounds, obelisks, temples, and elegant cottages, as *objects* for the eye', as well as (in a pointer to the source of such wealth in slave plantations) with trees grown 'to recreate the fancy of the planter'. Against such a vision, Wollstonecraft suggests that, if 'the heart was allowed to beat true to nature',

> decent farms would be scattered over the estate, and plenty smile around. Instead of the poor being subject to the griping hand of an avaricious steward, they would be watched over with fatherly solicitude, by the man whose duty and pleasure it was to guard their happiness, and shield from rapacity the beings who, by the sweat of their brow, exalted him above his fellows.[43]

This description, however, is presented in the subjunctive, as only a conditional possibility. Wollstonecraft cannot see, but only 'almost imagine' the paternal figure she depicts 'gathering blessings as he mounted the hill of life': so precarious is the vision that even imaginative sight is only partially achieved, and it struggles against a bracing alternative: the '[d]omination' which 'blasts all these prospects', whether in the form of the Acts of Enclosure which increase the 'property of the rich' and prevent 'the industrious peasant' from 'steal[ing] a farm from the heath', or laws of primogeniture, which prevent 'large estates' being 'divided into small farms'.[44] Wollstonecraft's sharp critique leavens a vision which might otherwise slip into the cloyingly nostalgic or the sentimental cliché (as the idealistic father-figure threatens to do); it maintains instead a descriptive opening where the imagination can depict not an impossible utopia, but an alternative reality which might just be possible. At this moment, we

62 The Engagement with Burke

are far from a more fully-fledged enactment of imagination's capacity to move beyond a description of what is, and figure forth what might be. But there is enough in these final pages of the first *Vindication* to suggest how the battle with the 'champion of property' will reach beyond rhetorical combat, and beyond the reason, understanding and knowledge which the second *Vindication* so vaunts, towards the capacity of the imagination to reach forward to what is not yet real, and figure forth new ways of thinking, being, and knowing.

The 'Natural Course of Things'

One presence detailed in the London cityscape at the end of Wollstonecraft's *Vindication* is an 'idle mendicant'. The term 'mendicant' might refer to a beggar, but more specifically, it could also refer to a monk seeking alms. This possibility recalls a crucial passage in Burke's *Reflections*: his response to the French revolutionary government's appropriation of monastic property to fund its new currency, the assignats.[45] The passage brings to the fore the particular nature of the politico-economic order which Burke is defending in the text, and especially its foundation on an alliance between property and commerce. Commentators on *Reflections* often note that Burke recognised that events in France 'menaced the Whig conception of government and society', but the specificity of this threat isn't always elaborated. Burke's response to the assignats, however, betrays a deep-seated anxiety about the potential effects of credit on which the Whig commercial property order itself relied.[46]

The most famous passages of *Reflections* include the sensationalised psycho-sexual drama of the attack on Marie Antoinette's bedchamber at Versailles, and the lament that 'the age of chivalry is gone', but revolutionary political economy is also given striking treatment:

> every thing human and divine sacrificed to the idol of public credit, and national bankruptcy the consequence; and to crown all, the paper securities of new, precarious, tottering power, the discredited paper securities of impoverished fraud, and beggared rapine, held out as a currency for the support of an empire, in lieu of the two great recognized species that represent the lasting, conventional credit of mankind, which disappeared and hid themselves in the earth from whence they came, when the principle of property, whose creatures and representatives they are, was systematically subverted.[47]

Burke's horror at the 'paper securities' of the assignats is of an overturned hierarchy: the gold and silver 'representatives' of property have been

The 'Natural Course of Things' 63

overthrown by the tottering 'idol' of public credit and its paper currency. Wollstonecraft did not directly respond to this passage, but her admired Macaulay did, and was perplexed as to why the new French paper currency so disturbed Burke, when it echoed what Britain's own financial revolution had established a century previously: a system in which government-backed credit circulated and was itself bought and sold.[48] Indeed, Burke himself had acknowledged, in his survey of France discussed in the previous section, that the British credit-based economy was a key factor in British economic superiority over France by the end of the eighteenth century.[49] The existence of such a system is occluded in Burke's would-be Shakespearean personification of value as gold and silver, creatures hiding in the ground. But the horror which the assignats elicit from Burke derives from their severing of the foundational link between value and property which Burke honours, as his own 'idol'. This founding bond of the Whig commercial order, between landed aristocracy and commerce, property and value, is dismantled by the assignats, offering a vision of credit operating uncontained by such constraints. Running through the passage, and perhaps seeping into the whole text, is horror at a political economy where land no longer determines value, and where property stimulates circulation and itself circulates. Underlying the passage is a recognition that the transmutation of a political economy founded on aristocratic property and commerce into one in thrall to the circulation of goods was already well under way in Britain too. Burke's horror at the assignats, his reaching for a retrograde language of money as gold, thus acts as cover for what his text will later concede: that the mobility of property, and the 'wheel of circulation' powered by servile labour which is its 'spring of action', is already an unchallengeable 'natural course of things'.[50]

Throughout *Reflections*, Burke makes extensive use of pejorative rhetoric to attack markets, and gives prominence by contrast to a faux-archaic discourse of chivalrous gallantry. This makes it difficult to perceive that his text is defending a Whig political economy in which property, including mobile property, is part of a system of government in which subordination and servile labour sustain the property system. George III apparently thanked Burke for speaking up for 'the cause of the Gentlemen', but as we shall see, what *Reflections* defends is not a gentlemanly system at all, but a labour economy in thrall to the circulation of goods.[51] The harsh outlines of what this means for 'the body of the people', and specifically for the possibility of liberty, are made clear in the *Reflections*' closing peroration, when an attack on the French revolutionary government (including the actions of Talleyrand, to whom Wollstonecraft was to dedicate her second

Vindication) broadens to outline what for Burke are the proper relations between 'acquisition', order, and government. It is evident that 'the power of acquisition on the part of the subject' is a rare and delimited form of liberty which is allowed to the subject as part of the maintenance of the order of the larger political whole. 'To be enabled to acquire' Burke states, 'the people ... must be tractable and obedient.... [They] must not find the principles of natural subordination by art rooted out of their minds. They must respect the property of which they cannot partake'. And finally, they

> must labour to obtain what by labour can be obtained; and when they find, as they commonly do, the success disproportioned to the endeavour, they must be taught their consolation in the final proportions of eternal justice. Of this consolation, whoever deprives them, deadens their industry, and strikes at the root of all acquisition as of all conservation.[52]

The theft (in Burke's eyes) of clerical property thus brings into relief his sense of a property order which subjects labour and mystifies 'the people'; it demonstrates too how a political economy of the production and circulation of goods sits at the heart of Burke's art of government. According to the 'principles of natural subordination', the people are yoked into a system of labour and acquisition whose 'success' is 'disproportioned to the endeavour', and where the only consolation is that promised after death. Liberty, the rallying cry of his opponents, can scarcely hope for a presence in Burke's vocabulary here, squeezed out as it is by the demands of a property system where labour and acquisition provide the defining grounds for subjecthood.

Wollstonecraft quoted this passage, and more, in the final pages of her *Vindication*, in contrast to her usual practice of confining references to Burke's text to her footnotes. She attacked its contempt for the poor, its 'tyrannic spirit' and 'factitious feelings', as well as its 'hard-hearted sophistry' and the 'specious humility' of its 'submission to the will of Heaven'.[53] Macaulay also singled it out for critique.[54] Against Burke's unspoken sense of the 'exclusive' right of the rich to pleasure, Wollstonecraft asserts the 'right' of the poor to 'more comfort than they at present enjoy', regardless of any consolations of the next world, and offers her vision, discussed above, of the 'decent farms' 'scattered over the estate' of the rich man, a vision which looks away from an economy founded on alienated labour and the circulation of goods, to agrarian contentment, a prospect which allures her a number of times in her writing, as later chapters will show. Yet Burke's commitment to the 'wheel of circulation' and the 'natural course of things', with the consequences they carry for those in 'innumerable servile … occupations' is even more explicit elsewhere in *Reflections*, in a crucial passage expounding on what was for Burke the deeply troubling appropriation of monastic property by the National Assembly.

Because, in his mind, monastic property stands for all landed property, Burke's argument involves what otherwise reads as an odd defence of the purported idleness of monastic life, through which he also justifies the idleness of a landed capitalist. This idleness, Burke says, 'is itself the spring of labour; this repose the spur to industry': a claim which rests on the assurance that the landowner's profits are properly reinvested.[55] In such terms, the idleness of the monks is fully justified; indeed, they are 'as usefully employed' as the 'many wretches' who are 'inevitably doomed' to work

> from dawn to dark in the innumerable servile, degrading, unseemly, unmanly, and often most unwholesome and pestiferous occupations, to which by the social œconomy so many wretches are inevitably doomed. If it were not generally pernicious to disturb the natural course of things, and to impede, in any degree, the great wheel of circulation which is turned by the strangely directed labour of these unhappy people, I should be infinitely more inclined forcibly to rescue them from their miserable industry, than violently to disturb the tranquil repose of monastic quietude […] no consideration, except the necessity of submitting to the yoke of luxury, and the despotism of fancy, who in their own imperious way will distribute the surplus product of the soil, can justify the toleration of such trades and employments in a well-regulated state.[56]

Burke's defence of monastic property (and all landed property) reveals much about the economic system (the 'natural course of things') which operates here as the grounds of nature and justice. That system, of extraordinarily unpleasant labour ('servile, degrading, unseemly, unmanly … unwholesome and pestiferous'), is justified by necessity and by utility – the phrase 'usefully employed' is repeated three times immediately prior to the quoted passage. As the experience of 'miserable industry' shows, human happiness is explicitly sacrificed to utility, a moment of ideological slippage which shows exactly why 'these unhappy people' cannot be rescued. But beyond utility lies something further. The drive or motor of utility is 'the yoke of luxury, and the despotism of fancy', to which it is necessary to submit, to maintain the 'great wheel of circulation' and 'distribute the surplus product of the soil'. In the earlier prospect view of the French nation, the imagination had enjoyed a kind of pleasurable aesthetic consumption of signs of French prosperity, but was still capable of being commanded, 'checked' on the 'brink' of 'indiscriminate censure' and required to respect the existing political 'fabric'. Here however, the tables are turned: now the imagination's authoritarian relation, despotic fancy, runs the show, requiring a necessary submission to its 'imperious ways', and its tyrannical demands for 'luxury' and consumption, more than a mere aesthetic pleasure which might be checked, will instead drive the wheel of circulation and the production of goods. Putative despot presiding imperiously over a consumer economy of goods, or useful scapegoat for the 'utility' of the 'social œconomy', fancy's supposedly irrefutable demands mean that many varieties of miserable labour must be tolerated even in a 'well-regulated state'.

Burke's overall tone here is of regretful capitulation to the unavoidable sacrifice of human lives: his is the sorrowful head-shaking and hand-wringing of the overseer of the 'great wheel of circulation', unavoidably complicit in a system of misery and unhappiness because its disturbance would be 'pernicious'. Unlike the plantation owner who has retired to the 'Arcadia' of his landscape garden, he is at least looking directly at what Howard Caygill has termed the 'violence of production', whose 'conflict' is otherwise 'relegated from civil society'.[57] Yet the gentlemanly persona of reasonably modulated regret merely clothes an underlying inflexibility, present in the language of necessity and fate which pervades the passage (the 'inevitable' 'doom' of the 'wretches'; the 'natural course of things'; submitting to the imperious 'yoke' and to 'despotism'.) And *that* fatalistic system, in turn, is presented in language which, as a would-be bolster to its authority, carries the mark of political economic discourse. Two of Burke's key phrases are directly borrowed from political economy's sourcebook, Smith's *The Wealth of Nations*, but the way these are used, to present labour's tragic predicament, caught in the wheel of circulation as in the wheel of fate, offers a picture quite absent in the Smithian source, which typically emphasises the motivation of the economic subject by describing labour as acting in its own self-interest, in pursuit of self-betterment. The phrase 'the natural course of things', on which Burke's by-standing apologia rests, is used at least eight times in *The Wealth of Nations*; it also appears in the prized 1755 manuscript in which Smith staked his claim to a theory of economic system precisely as allowing the 'natural course of things' to take place.[58] Crucially, however, Smith's argument against government intervention in the operation of trade and commerce never argued against regulation to prevent the forms of labour misery which Burke decries. By contrast, Smith was alert to the vulnerability of workers to cabals of merchants fixing the prices of labour or commodities, and he set out at length the responsibilities of government towards its subjects, which should include (anticipating Wollstonecraft) a system of national education. The phrase 'wheel of circulation' also appears in *The Wealth of Nations*, but it is used very precisely in a technical account of the circulation of money, not, as in Burke, to describe the circulation of goods as a figure for the economy in general.[59] In Burke, the phrase is abstract, general, and figural: a metaphor for political economy itself. Less descriptive and more imperative than in Smith, Burke's 'wheel of circulation' writes political economy as a tragedy, presenting the unstoppable production of goods as a wheel on which human lives are visibly broken.

Burke's weighing of 'servile, degrading … unwholesome and pestiferous occupations' against the 'useful employment' of 'lazy' monks 'no otherwise employed than by singing in the choir' recalls a passage in Smith's *Lectures on Jurisprudence* (from which much of his economic thinking grew), which similarly compares the labour of those in different social stations. Smith's survey runs from the 'luxury and ease and plenty' of the 'rich and opulent merchant', through to the clerks who do his business and the artisans who provide the commodities he enjoys, before arriving at the 'poor labourer' who 'supports the whole frame of society and furnishes the means of convenience and ease of all the rest', and who 'bears on his shoulders the whole of mankind'.[60] The comparison in Smith serves to emphasise the disparity between those at the hard end of the social division of labour and the comfort and convenience of those at the top; the passage as a whole is marked both by a recognition of the social and economic load carried by the workers, and an absence of the tones of regretful necessity that so marks Burke's writing. As Corey Robin points out, Burke's difference from Smith constitutes a fork in the ongoing development of political economy: where Smith is alert to how capital uses power (economic, legal) to extort more from labour, Burke overlooks labour in his late thoughts on value, instead linking value to free market mechanisms, and characterises capital, not labour, as the actuating principle behind 'the whole machine'.[61]

If property founds Burkean political economy (and can even be defended at its limit case, when provocatively associated with idle, singing monks), Wollstonecraft's response, as we see in Chapter 3, mobilised an alternative valoration of individual effort, extending a Smithian recognition of the economic value of labour into a moral, even aesthetic acknowledgement of effort, self-development, and improvement. In class terms, as Gary Kelly has argued, this can be read as a valoration of the meritocratic principles of the professional middle classes; in moral and religious terms, it describes the duty each individual should feel to act virtuously to emulate God; and it is related too to the effortful psychic strivings which, in aesthetic theory, accompany the sublime.[62] But Wollstonecraft's immediate response to Burke's condemnation of 'unhappy' multitudes to 'pestiferous' labour was clear. 'To suppose that, during the whole or part of its existence, the happiness of any individual is sacrificed to promote the welfare of ten, or ten thousand, other beings – is impious', she stated; the 'happiness of the whole must arise from the happiness of the constituent parts'.[63] Her words recall Macaulay's warning against making an 'idol' of the 'aggregate capacity' of the society, especially when this involved the sacrifice of 'those individuals who formed the aggregate', a reversal of the 'plain and reasonable' logic by which society is formed 'for the happiness of its citizens'.[64] Wollstonecraft's *Vindication of the Rights of Woman* would also repeatedly align the interests of private individuals and the state, which she sees as linked through virtue rather than the 'yoke' of luxury.

Wollstonecraft's attack on Burke's idolisation of the 'aggregate' over the happiness of individuals brings back into focus the human populace whose needs are foundational to political economy as defined by Smith. Indeed, her alternative account of human nature, and its capacity for happiness, is central to her countering of Burke's depiction of humanity yoked by necessity to labour through the despotism of its own desires. Attacking his 'endeavour to make unhappy men resigned to their fate' as the weak effort of 'short-sighted benevolence', she extoled instead a 'masculine god-like affection' which 'labour[s] to increase human happiness by extirpating error'. Instead of an ineffectual gospel of resignation, humanity should exert its powers in efforts to 'increase human happiness', in a task involving both 'enlightened understanding' and 'the impulse of feelings that Philosophy invigorates'. The very constitution of human nature directs us to such efforts, for 'the sight of distress, or an affecting narrative' produces a response of 'sympathetic emotion', and 'emotions that reason deepens' are 'justly terms the feelings of *humanity*'.[65] Differentiated from a 'vague' sensibility, it is in such 'active exertions of virtue' that our humanity (both our capacity for benevolence, and our identity as a species) consists.

This account of a human nature strongly characterised by a capacity for sympathetic feeling differs markedly from the despotic needs attributed to it by Burke. It illustrates Wollstonecraft's understanding of the relations between human nature and 'Philosophy', between the impulses of feeling which characterise humanity (in both senses) and the operations of reason and the understanding which ultimately should be used to build or reform human community. This is the account of human nature which should, she suggests, direct political actions towards human happiness; the contrast with Burke's capitulation to the 'natural course of things' is dramatic. As we will now see, Wollstonecraft returned to the condemnation of what she called Burke's 'system' in the final paragraphs of her text, denouncing its sacrifice of 'Nature and Reason' to 'authority', and drawing on the words of the blinded Gloucester in *King Lear* to suggest that 'the gods ... seem to kill us for their sport'.[66] The *Lear* reference makes explicit Wollstonecraft's grasp of the essentially tragic nature of Burkean political economy, in which individuals are passive sufferers of the forces of history, and contrasts with her own conviction of the capacity of reason and the feelings of humanity to work together in pursuit of human happiness. Caught between the two alternatives lies a struggle over the nature and purpose of writing itself, and its own relationship to human happiness, and to human fate.

Value, Feeling, and Writing

Wollstonecraft leaves the readers of her *Vindication* with words from Shakespeare's *King Lear* ringing in their ears: a tragedy which turns on the inequitable division of property within families, both in the initial unequal division of Lear's kingdom between his daughters, and in the subplot which motivates the illegitimate Edmund's attack on the inheritance of the legitimate Edgar. Property in *Lear* is the object of passions which tear families apart within and across generations, and which ultimately destabilise the nation. Such passions cause criminality, horrific injury, madness, and war; even Gloucester's insight that the 'the gods ... seem to kill us for their sport' comes at the cost of a blindness which also symbolically connotes his failure to see his illegitimate son with the same eyes as his legitimate heir. Frans de Bruyn has remarked that tragedy, the preeminent genre for writing the failure of the struggle for human happiness, is Burke's 'fundamental form'; Wollstonecraft's *Lear* reference suggests that she too recognises how the trope of tragedy works to naturalise political economy in the *Reflections*.[67] In this context, the 'wheel of circulation' which so determines the lives of workers recalls the wheel of fate which, as Ronald Paulson has shown, has been associated with tragedy since medieval times; Paulson further suggests that 'the basic mythos of tragedy' has always been used to 'keep mutability under control'.[68] The necessary turning of Burke's wheel of circulation also controls mutability, operating to resist and exclude its very possibility, even at the explicit price of human lives. But if the wheel of fortune connotes change as tragedy, the wheel of circulation announces the instantiation of a specific political economy which passes itself off, under the guise of the tragic, as fate or nature. Meanwhile, whilst classical decorum restricted tragedy to characters of high social rank, Burkean political economy enables tragedy to extend a more socially inclusive embrace. And where tragedy has been a genre used to narrate and understand change, and is thus often oriented to history or the past, here it is redeployed to colonise the future: the 'necessity of submitting to the yoke of luxury, and the despotism of fancy' seemingly refuting the possibility of future alternatives. Along with the familiarity of its outlines, and its elevated generic status, tragedy is thus useful for Burke's rhetorical strategy in *Reflections*: to elicit, and valorise, affective response from his reader, especially in relation to what he presents as the theatre of recent historical events. Burke's depiction of the subject's place in his 'system' can thus be maintained with the yoke of sentimental feeling and the tears so often elicited by the tragic unfolding of human fate.

Wollstonecraft's challenge to all this, however, is to suggest that the Burkean tragic 'system' reads the human predicament through the wrong generic lens, not least in its irreligious lack of optimism and the failure of its humanity. Her challenge to the 'tragedy' of Burkean political economy is thus also a resistance to a mode of knowledge which seeks to abstract a 'science' of wealth and prosperity away from a foundational concern with human happiness and well-being. In this context, it is helpful to recall John Guillory's account of the disciplinary history of political economy and its emergence from Scottish moral philosophy and the 'science of man' project. For Guillory, political economy's inability to 'solve the problem of the relation between the individual subject and market society' (a problem writ large in the 'necessary submission' to the 'wheel of circulation') provoked the discursive disaggregation of political economy from moral philosophy, as well as that of aesthetics, to which experiential questions of individual taste, sensation, and affect were relegated.[69] From this fracture stemmed two opposing discourses of value grounded, on the one hand, on systematised accounts of labour or the market, and on (variously more or less subjective) accounts of affect, on the other. Burke and Wollstonecraft's texts are situated prior to, or perhaps at the moment of, such a bifurcation between market and aesthetic value, at a time when, in Robin's words, 'the crucible of value' was 'heated to the highest degrees by the French Revolution'.[70] For Thompson, political economy's formation itself 'constitutes a gradual working through of this crisis' in value.[71] In this analysis, political economy is founded on a problem of form which brings with it a discursive break, from a conglomerated 'science of man' to a specialised mode of knowledge, one constituted by abstractions distilled from human experience, and from which, by the same token, the question of the human is alienated.

Value, Feeling, and Writing 71

Burke and Wollstonecraft both mobilise writing to address this crisis in value, though with enormously differing strategies. As we have seen, Burke mobilises sentiment, affect, and aesthetic and rhetorical effect to address the question of the individual's relation to the social order in market society, as reflected in various figures which recur in his text: the 'little platoon', the mortmain, the 'relation in blood'.[72] Equally, he seeks to use writing in general, including his own gentlemanly persona, as author of a letter to another gentleman, to fix value and opinion in the public sphere (even whilst, as in disavowal of such an ungentlemanly act, that intervention is presented as a personal, private communication). For Wollstonecraft, as her attention to the interstitial spaces of the commercial city – its ditches, hospital rooms, and 'pestilential corners' – suggests, the relation between the individual and the social whole in late eighteenth-century commercial society is one through which many can too easily fall, as the effects of poverty, unemployment, beggary, trade fluctuations, and illness attest. Burke's text obliges its reader to acquiesce in the silent fiction that the political tract she is reading is really a private letter: to read the text requires a concession to its strategies. This unspoken arrangement between text and reader echoes the uninterrogated historical settlements between authorities and subjects which the text itself presents. In her fierce, *ad hominem* attack on Burke in the early pages of her *Vindication*, Wollstonecraft refuses to acquiesce to such unreal social relations, repeatedly referring his textual persona back to his biographical person, using details from Burke's life and references to his Parliamentary speeches to challenge an authorial persona which would perhaps prefer, like Marie Antoinette herself, to hover 'just above the horizon' of such earthly specifics.[73] If one of Wollstonecraft's central contentions with Burke is that his version of market society is an affront to the common feelings of humanity, it makes sense to begin her exposition with the personal failings of the man from whom such an account stems. In contrast to Burke, Wollstonecraft's investment in the human is not stylistic or figural: it eschews aesthetic or rhetorical effect to directly and critically address the authorial person himself, as though to signal, amidst its 'crisis', that the human is her ground of value.

The problem of political economy's tragic instantiation in Burke – its sacrifice of humanity to circulation's 'great wheel' – is part of what Wollstonecraft's *Vindication*, which references *Lear* in its second last paragraph, and has 'God' as its final word, seeks to remedy. The human heart and human feeling are central to the solution, but so too is the reclaiming of form, writing, and representation, which collectively offer the possibility of redirecting human knowledge itself. As we shall see in later chapters, this problem was to preoccupy Wollstonecraft across her career. Her analysis of *Reflections* makes clear that the relationship between feeling and form, writing and humanity, has been fundamentally corrupted in Burke, and this schism goes to the heart of the political and cultural wrongs of the time, as well as to the fraud which he attempts on his readers. Thus, when Wollstonecraft asserts to Burke that for misery 'to reach your heart' it must 'have its cap and bells; your tears are reserved ... for the declamation of the theatre, or the downfall of queens', she is not simply accusing him of lack of feeling, but of reserving feeling, the mark of the human, for a formal and separate realm of aesthetic response, enacting a boundary between that and real life, so that, whilst the fall of the queen (rendered an artificial spectacle through the rhetorical constructions of his text) should, in his view, elicit a loud lament, the misery of multiple workers is justified through the complex and unchallengeable formulas of political economic arithmetic.[74] The satirical print *Don Dismallo Running the Literary Gantlet* (*sic*, Figure 2.1), published in late 1790, literalises and personalises Wollstonecraft's point here, showing Burke dressed in the costume of theatricality, wearing the cap of the jester or fool, whilst he 'runs the gauntlet' past various of his literary and political opponents, who are clothed, in striking contrast, in the ordinary dress of the day.[75] A similar accusation of compartmentalising, of separating artificially elicited sentiment from the real horrors of the world, recurs in Wollstonecraft's attack on colonial women – 'fair ladies' – who return to their sensibility novels to 'exercise their tender feelings' having just overseen the brutal whipping of their slaves.[76] And, as mentioned earlier, a distinction between fake, artificial feeling, such as she sees is cultivated by many novelists, and the authentic feeling of genius recurs in the prefatory matter to her own fiction, both *Mary* (which predates the *Vindications*) and the later *The Wrongs of Woman*. Her late essay, 'On Poetry', meanwhile, also turns on a distinction between artificial or fake sentiment and natural feeling.[77]

The attack on Burke as a purveyor and cultivator of false feeling is thus in line with what will become a recurring critique in Wollstonecraft's take on contemporary culture. Burke's text is especially invidious because of its author's evident strategizing of feeling: bending his reader's sentimental response to his rhetorical purpose to ensure that feeling bows (as the authorial persona does) to the wheel of circulation, and thus more broadly making the writing of human feeling subservient to the mediation of economic necessity. In this, Burke's text enacts a hierarchizing of the relative discourses of political economy and literary or aesthetic ones. Despite the foregrounding of many formal rhetorical and literary features in his text, its

Figure 2.1 'Don Dismallo'

repeated deployment of the figural, and its address to the affective response of its reader, such devices have no value in themselves, but are determined by their functional role in relation to Burke's defence of the 'natural course of things'. To read Burke's text for its literary art would be entirely to miss his point: rather, the literary, rhetorical, and aesthetic are deployed to 'beautify' the social and economic order, to gloss and drape Burke's political economic purpose. In her response to the *Reflections*, Macaulay denounces Burke's attempt to establish the 'happiness' of society on 'prejudice, opinion and the powers of the imagination'.[78] Wollstonecraft too calls her opponent out on this in the 'Advertisement' to the *Vindication*, but her vocabulary focuses more specifically on Burke's weaponising of affect, accusing him of presenting 'sophistical arguments' in the 'questionable shape of natural feelings', and of clothing his 'devious' thoughts in 'specious garb'.[79] 'Natural feelings' have been strategised, made an art or artifice or device, alienated from human life, the real contours of which Burke's text seeks to disguise, sentimentalise, or 'drape'. Against this, Wollstonecraft's prefatory note to the *Vindication* offers a mini-narrative of authentic feeling – her own – in a personal history of the origins of her response to Burke, which lie, indeed, in the growth of her own feeling. From turning the pages of Burke's text more 'for amusement than information', her 'indignation was roused', and the 'effusions of the moment' thus prompted, swelled to such a 'considerable size' that the idea of the *Vindication* was suggested.[80] Burke's strategy of securing his audience by mobilising 'specious' feeling has spectacularly misfired, at least in this case, a failure ensured by the strength of Wollstonecraft's own feelings and her confidence in them as grounds of judgement, and as authorising – compelling – her writing.

Despite the foregrounding of these themes in her 'Advertisement', few commentators on the *Vindication* have paid much attention to the fact that Wollstonecraft devoted significant space, at both ends of the text, to these questions of how we read, think, and feel, and to the mutual relations of wit and judgement, reason and fancy, understanding and the imagination. Such concerns are central to Wollstonecraft's challenging of Burke's mediation of political economic matters, because feeling, humanity, reason, imagination, and reading are all critical elements in the defence of the liberty and happiness which he threatens. Her remarks are thus more than an admonishment of Burke's style – 'pomp of words' thought it is.[81] Engaging with his text prompts her to consider the dangerous power of feeling, if disconnected from its proper roots in reason and understanding, and how readily written texts might play to that. Her remarks thus show that, beyond winning an argument with Burke, Wollstonecraft is thinking too about the obstacles which print culture (the tools of which she herself uses) faces in the hoped-for advance of reason. As well as challenging his political economic narrative, then, she reflects too on the strengths and weaknesses of the textual weapons they both use, and how writing and feeling might serve (or hinder) her. Soon after accusing Burke of needing '[m]isery' to be costumed in 'cap and bells' for it 'to reach your heart', she levels at him an aphorism taken from Rousseau's *Letter to d'Alembert on Theatre* (1758) which might well have served as an epigraph to her text, encapsulating as it does her perception of Burke's artful and immoral manipulations: '[t]he tears that are shed for fictitious sorrow are admirably adapted to make us proud of all the virtues which we do not possess'.[82] As Rousseau had in his *Letter*, an important discussion of the political role of spectacle in modern society, Wollstonecraft resists Burke's separation of the aesthetic and affective from political and economic life and asserts the possibility that feeling and happiness might not be alienated from, but reconciled with, the material conditions of human experience. Her own writing will seek to reintegrate feeling – not the 'mechanical instinctive sensations' but 'emotions that reason deepens, and justly terms the feelings of humanity' – into lived experience, rather than separate it out into a separate sphere of representation or signs.[83] At the same time, feeling – the gauge or measure of 'human happiness' or 'humanity' – can operate as a critique of oppressive laws and customs, and perhaps even generate a 'revolution in manners', especially among women, as we shall now see.

CHAPTER 3

Property, Passions, and Manners
Political Economy and the Vindications

sophistical arguments ... in the questionable shape of natural feelings[1]

Human passions, and their expression in writing, are central concerns for Wollstonecraft as she resists the would-be orthodoxies of late eighteenth-century political economic thinking. In the previous chapter, we saw how Wollstonecraft's critique of Burkean political economy involved an attempt to reclaim form, writing, and representation from their specious deployment by Burke. She rejected a textual practice which attempted to inculcate artificial feeling in its readers, exposing how such 'questionable ... natural feelings' were also deployed to assure readerly approval of, and complicity in, a political economy understood as the 'natural course of things' despite its costs in human lives and human happiness. This chapter discusses Wollstonecraft's concern with human passions further: by exploring her understanding of how they are deeply imbricated in existing social and political structures, and how they are key to its reform. Human feeling, in other words, is both central to the social order that political economy would construct, and to the work of challenging it. As we will see, in the *Vindication of the Rights of Men*, Wollstonecraft accuses the property order which Burke defends of corrupting human feeling by encouraging immorality, indolence, and libertinism. And her denouncement of the so-called 'manners' of commercial society is followed, in the *Vindication of the Rights of Woman*, by a call for a 'revolution in manners': a moral revolution by which women will save commercial society from itself, and save themselves from it.

Wollstonecraft's central critique of Burke's defence of property society in his *Reflections on the Revolution in France* is that his rationality has become separated from human feeling. It is appropriate, then, that the story of her response to the *Reflections*, given in the Advertisement at the start of her *Vindication of the Rights of Men*, tells of writing produced – impelled – by feeling. Wollstonecraft takes a bare twelve lines to offer a

76

mini-history of her authorship: the 'rousing' of her 'indignation' by the 'devious' and 'sophistical' *Reflections*, her 'effusions of the moment' finding expression on paper, and then in print. William Godwin's account, in his *Memoirs of the Author of A Vindication of the Rights of Woman*, similarly describes how, having read *Reflections*, Wollstonecraft 'seized her pen' in 'the full burst of indignation' and 'full of sentiments of liberty', sending early pages to the press even before the work was complete.[2] In these accounts, Wollstonecraft's authorship is almost an automatic, unwilled event, an inevitable expression of her sentiments. Feeling authorises the writer, in the fullest sense of the verb. Authorship is also, notably, something for which she has little time or space: she has no 'leisure' and no 'patience', for what must thus be a necessarily 'confined' writing. All of this is in stark contrast with the leisured production of Burke's text, which occupied most of the year preceding publication in November 1790, during which he also shared his work-in-progress with a few friends.[3]

The origin story of Wollstonecraft's first major work is appropriate to the ways in which the *Vindication* would level feeling against property. Enacting (if not announcing) her identity as a woman professional writer, 'the first of a new genus', the Advertisement is also notable for the terms in which Wollstonecraft narrates her entrance into the public sphere of contemporary print culture: into what remained, in the 1790s, of the Enlightenment republic of letters.[4] Those terms operate fiercely to contest and recast such a public print culture, including its nature, identity, and formation. In Jürgen Habermas's much-referenced account, the eighteenth-century public sphere was characterised by the use of critical reason in public debate and exchange, including print media, by private individuals, whose participation was enabled by the property ownership which, among other things, gave them leisure for such activity.[5] As Terry Eagleton notes, the public sphere was thus the expressive mode of property society, 'articulable only by those with the social interests which property generates', even if such interests were discussed through a veneer of apparent disinterest.[6] Although the eighteenth-century public sphere described by Habermas was undergoing significant transformation, even fragmentation, by the end of the century, Eagleton's terms illuminate the ideological nature of Burke's *Reflections*, which, as we saw in the previous chapter, sought to promote, in occluded fashion, the interests of property and property owners: the 'gentlemen' for attending to whose interests Burke was thanked by George III.[7] Burke's decision to pass his work off in what Wollstonecraft might term the 'specious garb' of a private letter from one gentleman to another only underlines, despite disavowing, his

Property, Passions, and Manners

desire to intervene in the public sphere of critical reason.[8] For her part, Wollstonecraft asserted that she knew 'not of any common nature or common relation amongst men but what results from reason', but her understanding of the 'reason' which binds human community was founded not on property, but on 'affections and passions': it is only the 'continuity of those relations that entitles us to the denomination of rational creatures'.[9] Reflecting on, and reasoning from, our passions and feelings is what differentiates mankind from beasts; this, properly, should provide the foundation for human community. Wollstonecraftian reason, as her Advertisement makes clear, originates in human feeling; the rationality of Burke's *Reflections*, as the previous chapter showed, turns on, and serves, property. Wollstonecraft's emphasis, in the *Vindication*'s origin story, on the motive power of feeling to mobilise and authorise her pen, thus constitutes a powerful attack on the very basis of the rationality which, according to Eagleton, was property society's expressive mode.

The insistence in the *Vindication*'s Advertisement that its author writes despite not having the time to write – despite having no leisure, and no patience – could not signal more clearly their exclusion from a property order of leisured gentlemen who dispassionately exercise reason in the public sphere. Wollstonecraft's disqualification by gender from that order was even clearer in the work's second edition, of December 1790, which bore her full name. Explicitly stated as not originating in leisure, her writing must therefore be understood as a form of work, a professional activity in some sense, announcing not disinterestedness but its opposite: the situated interestedness of the author, enacting some form of specialised knowledge and expertise.[10] In line with the Advertisement's emphasis on the authority of Wollstonecraft's feelings, one form of expert knowledge asserted in the first few pages of the *Vindication* is knowledge of human nature itself, demonstrated in the character analysis Wollstonecraft performs on Burke. Against the disinterested rationality of the property order, Wollstonecraft asserts knowledge of human character, behaviour, and virtue, and finds Burke to fall short. A fully developed philosophy of human nature – of the 'man' of her title – will be deployed in both her *Vindications* to counter a political economic discourse which Wollstonecraft reveals is in hock to property. This chapter shows how Wollstonecraft uses her account of human nature – of the roles of, and relationships between, passion and reason, enthusiasm and imagination – to challenge a Burkean (and Smithian) political economy whose view of human nature is simply to put it to work. The expertise in human nature which at one level informs her personal attack on Burke, at another enables a fully worked out critique of the culture, social behaviour, personal values, and psychological formations of commercial society: its so-called 'manners'.

Wollstonecraft's decision to open the first *Vindication* with a description of the context from which her writing was produced is thus in keeping with her concern with the manners of commercial society, as newly described and theorised by political economy. So too is her decision to foreground her writing as work, in addition to its emotional labour, in contrast to Burke, who would have the readers of his gentlemanly 'letter' believe that his writing was extrinsic to the world of work, even whilst that writing describes what he asserts are the laws conditioning the labour for others. Engaging as she does with Burke's account of political economy, the discourse of labour, it is only fitting that Wollstonecraft shows how writing participates in the world of work: how, rather than transcending it, writing is itself a form of labour, and one originating in, as well as recording and reflecting, the experience of the passions. As we shall see, in the first *Vindication*, Wollstonecraft wields her expertise in a reason founded on feeling to interrogate the values, culture, and manners of a property order defended by the leisured gentleman. This chapter shows how Wollstonecraft's critique of the contemporary property order in the first *Vindication* attacks property as a source of inequality, oppression, and injustice; it also shows how that analysis is continued in more detailed form in her second *Vindication*, the *Vindication of the Rights of Woman* (1792), in which the claims and values of political economic discourse are assessed not least by considering their implications for women. We begin by exploring how *A Vindication of the Rights of Men* responds to one of the most obvious manifestations of the political economy of Burke's *Reflections*: in Wollstonecraft's attack on Burke's veneration of property, and her unpacking of the multiple ills consequent on property's current forms.

A Vindication of the Rights of Men and the 'Sacred Majesty of Property'

Given her concern with property, the architectural metaphor with which Wollstonecraft asserts, early in *A Vindication of the Rights of Men*, that she will attack the 'foundation', not the 'superstructure', of Burke's opinions is wholly appropriate. We saw in the last chapter that the political economic argument in Burke's *Reflections* defends the existing Whig property regime in Britain, and attacks the French National Assembly's confiscation of church property to back its revolutionary currency, the assignats. But, unlike Catharine Macaulay, whose *Observations on the Reflections*

80 Property, Passions, and Manners

of the Right Hon. Edmund Burke (1790) offered an extended critique of Burke's economic argument, Wollstonecraft discusses neither the question of French national debt nor the establishment of the assignats nor the system of credit in general. Instead, the 'foundation' of her attack on Burke lies in identifying him as 'the champion of property, the adorer of the golden image which power has set up'.[11] And if Burke's outrage at the confiscation of church property chimes with his desire to defend property in general, so Wollstonecraft attacks an oppressive culture of property and power embodied by the French church. Where Burke sees French clergy as victims, Wollstonecraft depicts them as 'idle tyrants', indolent occupants of property which has been wrongfully seized in the past. Ecclesiastical property thus manifests the historical 'rapacity' of those who are also corruptly deferential to the nobility and court, whilst enjoying tithes which are a 'corner-stone of despotism'.[12] Wollstonecraft's institutional critique of the church is thus part of a wider assault on the injustices which all too frequently accrue to the existing property order, which underpins her discussion just as thoroughly as its defence motivates Burke's. Property, which sits at the heart of eighteenth-century political economy, and its social, moral, cultural, and psychological consequences, is thus central to Wollstonecraft's thinking from the very first pages of her *Vindication*.

Wollstonecraft's attack on property and its role in determining the 'order of society as it is at present regulated', as she puts it in her second *Vindication*, is wide-ranging and uncompromising.[13] As it is currently organised, she claims, the property order which Burke defends encapsulates everything which is on the wrong side of humanity, reflection, and reason. In particular, property and its veneration impedes liberty and virtue, and is oppressive and enslaving. Concern for property precedes and eclipses concern for freedom: 'Security of property! Behold, in a few words, the definition of English liberty'.[14] The defences offered by the 'champion' of property amount to a 'tyrant's plea', as numerous examples show.[15] Resistance to the abolishing of the slave trade demonstrates how laws protect or 'fence' property against justice. The pressing of working men into naval service means that the 'liberty of an honest mechanic … is often sacrificed to secure the property of the rich'. And farmers' property and crops are ruined by aristocratic hunters, protected by the game laws: thus 'industry [is] laid waste by unfeeling luxury'.[16] Such arguments, linking property to exploitation and oppression, counter Burke's claim that 'the great masses of property' form 'a natural rampart about the lesser properties in all their gradations'. They also mount a more radical argument than Macaulay, whose observation that all property owners have a shared interest in the law which secures wealth lacks the sense of searing injustice at the heart of Wollstonecraft's property vision.[17]

Wollstonecraft's attack on the Burkean property system also addresses its 'foundation' in the corruption of feeling. As she will explore in the second *Vindication*, a revolution in, and of, feeling is needed to restore society and put it 'on a more enlarged plan', but the social divisions currently enacted by the 'rampart' of property work against this, separating the classes by a 'wall' of envy and burying the 'sympathies of humanity' in 'the servile appellation of master'.[18] Such affective failings are identifiable in Burke himself. His sensibility is 'pampered'; his reason is the 'dupe' of his 'imagination'; and his heart is so 'sophisticated' that it is difficult for him to 'feel like a man': the National Assembly knows more of the human heart than he does.[19] Because Burke cannot participate in the 'common feelings of humanity', he views the poor simply as 'livestock' on an estate; the 'narrow circle' of his benevolence seeks only to perpetuate property in families, and indeed the rich in general step aside to 'avoid the loathsome sight of human misery'.[20] Lacking the 'natural feelings of humanity', Burke expounds instead an artificial aesthetico-sentimental order which takes the place of real pleasure and happiness. This is associated with specific property forms, and a preference for 'ideal regions of taste and elegance' such as the rich man's estate, built, as we saw in the previous chapter, to shield himself from seeing the poor.[21] This image of the enclosed landscape garden, offered at the end of the *Vindication*, picks up Wollstonecraft's depiction, at the beginning of the text, of Burke's writing itself as an 'airy edifice', a pagoda-like 'Chinese erection' or folly.[22] Both exhibit taste without purpose and without humanity, 'venerated', like property on its 'pedestal', without regard to moral virtues or political circumstances: aesthetic beauty in a moral vacuum. Had the French constitution been 'new modelled … by the lovers of elegance and beauty', it would have 'erected a fragile temporary building', instead of the possibility now offered of 'more virtue and happiness'.[23] Against Burke's 'spurious, sensual beauty', offered under the 'specious form of natural feeling', Wollstonecraft asserts an alternative moral order, founded on virtue, reason, and strength, to yield 'rational satisfaction'.[24] And as only liberty can provide the conditions in which virtue can flourish, Wollstonecraft returns a discussion often phrased by Burke in aesthetic terms back to a political argument, to reveal what is at stake in the property order which Burke would treat as an 'idol'.

Wollstonecraft traces the effects of the 'demon of property' not only in associated social and political injustices, but in the corruption of morals and (in the terminology of her time) manners.[25] Such corrosive effects are especially evident in families, where children are treated like slaves and 'demanded due homage' for the expected transferral of property through marriage or inheritance. Forced and arranged marriages, neglect of younger children and preference for older, a disinclination for early marriage, and hence harm to both male and female morals: all this is governed by the existing property order.[26] Wollstonecraft's early fiction, *Mary* (1788), offered a similar picture: its heroine is neglected until the death of her brother makes her heir to the family property, at which point she is hastily forced into a disastrous marriage arranged by her father 'over a bottle', whose chief aim is to nullify a counter-claim to the family estate. That the wedding ceremony takes place at the death-bed of her mother only underlines the ritual sacrifice of female lives to a male property order.[27] Property corrupts morals at another level too: closely linked to 'hereditary honours', it encourages excessive attention to rank, so that virtue is 'crushed by the iron hand of property' and substituted with class aspiration, as with the aping of the upper by the middle classes, who aim 'to procure respect on account of their property'.[28] Here, Wollstonecraft's sense that the attention given to rank and property has 'benumbed' the moral faculties like the 'torpedo's touch' counters the argument of Adam Smith's *The Theory of Moral Sentiments,* which contended that respect given to reputation upholds moral standards in commercial modernity.[29] By contrast, Wollstonecraft suggests that 'an immoderate desire to please … immerges … the soul in matter, till it becomes unable to mount on the wing of contemplation'.[30] This is why Europe's much-vaunted 'civilisation' – the 'golden age' mourned by Burke – is described as 'partial': because of the impediment posed to virtue, and hence to human potential and happiness, by hereditary property.

Attacking the 'foundation' of Burke's argument requires not only an assault on property, the 'idol' of Burke's text, but also the mobilising of a counter-discourse. Wollstonecraft enacts this in part through substituting alternative images for the Burkean idolisation of property on its 'pedestal', contrasting the fixity of idols with redistributive dissolution, and the solidity of property with more abstract and immaterial totems: labour, reason, effort, and mind.[31] Something of this is signalled in Wollstonecraft's revisiting of the metaphor of channels which runs through political economic writing from Adam Smith onwards, to recast the containment of wealth in the 'narrow channels' of church property into an image of natural redistribution: 'Can posterity be injured by individuals losing the chance of obtaining great wealth, without meriting it, by its being diverted from a narrow channel, and disembogued into the sea that affords clouds to water

Property and Idleness 83

all the land?'. Must we 'preserve the sacred majesty of Property inviolate'?[32] The 'mighty revolution in property' which Burke decries so vehemently is thus a natural dissolution; the National Assembly's appropriation of church property is simply a climactic 'disemboguing', which will redistribute wealth to all, just as clouds produce rain. A similar move beyond the negative confinement of physical property to something more abstract and transcendent appears in Wollstonecraft's depiction of the need for exercise of a human mind which too often 'gladly lets the spirit lie quiet in its gross tenement'; it is better improved through 'restless enquiries that hover on the boundary, or stretch over the dark abyss of uncertainty'. Such 'lively conjectures are the breezes that preserve the still lake from stagnating'.[33] Thought, the sign of our 'natural immortality' and 'the faint type of an immaterial energy', needs stimulation, otherwise, 'no longer bounding it knows not where, [it] is confined to the tenement'.[34] Property here is restricting and enervating, and opposed by more mobile and effortful, if immaterial and inchoate impulses. Such passages look back to the exhortative and enthusiastic 'effusions' of genius in *Mary*, and forward to the more explicit exposition of the virtues of self-exertion and self-improvement of the second *Vindication*. They also resist the confinement of value to the limits of property, as political economic discourse would have it, as well as disinterring and challenging an association of property with idleness and moral vacuity embedded deeply in political economic thought.

Property and Idleness in Political Economy

Wollstonecraft's critique of an aestheticised, feminised, and sexualised idleness in the eighteenth-century gender system – present both in her attack on Burke's idolisation of the passive, idle female body in *Reflections*, and in her second *Vindication*'s denouncement of Jean-Jacques Rousseau's depiction of female sexual passivity in his novel *Emile* (1762) – is well recognised by critics.[35] Sexualised notions of female indolence and languor were deeply embedded in eighteenth-century cultural discourse, including in Burke's *Philosophical Enquiry into the Origin of Our Ideas of the Sublime and The Beautiful* (1757). Wollstonecraft's depiction of such scenes as 'libertine' encapsulated her accusation of their political nihilism: the supposed natural weakness of the female body seemingly inevitably invited male predation, beyond any possibility of the social compact of consent.[36] Wollstonecraft's concern with idleness in a political economic context is much less recognised, however. In political economic thought, the supposedly originary idleness in human nature presents a foundational problem, concerned as it is with theorising the motivation for human effort and labour. Political economy was also troubled by the instance of the rentier or landlord, who lived idly, without working, and profiting from the labour of others. Wollstonecraft identified idleness as the pre-eminent moral failing of late eighteenth-century commercial society, and countered this by elaborating a moral economy of effort in the connected spheres of mind, manners, and morals, a valoration of individual exertion to counter the dangerous lassitude encouraged by the contemporary property system.[37]

We saw in the previous chapter how idleness unexpectedly accompanies Burke's defence of landed property in his assertion that the 'idleness' of the landed proprietor is 'itself the spring of labour; this repose the spur to industry'.[38] Although the context of Burke's remark makes clear that he is referring to surplus product or profit, this is presented as a characteristic or attribute of the proprietor himself, as the action (or inaction) of idleness and 'repose' which supposedly causes the labour of others. Burke's rhetoric collapses the difference between profit and proprietor, personalising a political economic discourse which otherwise tends to the abstract and reified. It also links the indolence of the proprietor and the labour of the worker in relations of cause and effect which offers a narrative of economic productivity seemingly as natural and inevitable as Rousseau's sexual scene of female passivity and male predation. Burke's naturalised economic narrative reinscribes on the economic front the familiar sexual binaries of passivity and activity, albeit at the expense of hinting at a feminine lassitude in the proprietor.

Burke's placement of idleness at the heart of economic production, as the supposed 'spring of labour', stems from his desire to defend landed property. The provocative oddness of his claim can be read as a mark of the contortions into which he is led in his attempt to reconcile the defence of landed property with an economic 'natural course of things' based on the production and circulation of mobile goods. But it is also symptomatic of the way in which the problem of idleness recurs within political economic thought itself. Burke's defence of the idle proprietor runs very close to David Hume's attack on the uselessness and inactivity of those living on public stock, in his 1752 essay denouncing the British system of public credit. Those who live on the profits of their stock, without any need to work, without any connection to society, and living in any part of the globe are depicted as sinking into 'the lethargy of a stupid and pampered luxury, without spirit, ambition or enjoyment'.[39] Idle, without social identity or responsibility, they undermine the natural bonds and activities which hold the state together, and thus encapsulate Hume's sense of the danger posed to the nation by public credit. Burke himself later weaponised idleness in an attack on the Duke of Bedford in his *Letter to a Noble Lord* (1796), in which he accrued to himself a language of labour and effort in contrast with the aristocratic idleness imputed to the Duke. The peculiar mobility of idleness in Burkean discourse, where is deployed both defensively and pejoratively, illustrates how Burke is 'caught in a vise' (*sic*) between loyalty to aristocratic rank and the desire to see his own labour recognised and rewarded; it illuminates too the strains placed on a Whig alliance of aristocratic landed property and commercial society, with growing recognition that commercial society was outgrowing the aristocratic context which had given it birth.[40] Such a perception lies behind the Burkean lament in *Reflections* at what he saw as a 'revolution in manners' – a phrase which Wollstonecraft picks up and repurposes in her second *Vindication*.

That idleness, as a supposed fundamental characteristic of human nature, posed a problem which political economy sought to resolve becomes clear if we backtrack briefly to the origins of political economic discourse in the Scottish science of man of the first half of the eighteenth century. This attempt to emulate the Newtonian science of nature through a philosophical investigation of human nature included investigations into the psychology of motivation. Thus, Hume's *Treatise of Human Nature* rejected the received philosophical wisdom that '[e]very rational creature … regulate[s] his actions by reason' and asserted that 'reason alone can never be a motive to any action of the will', opening the field to an exploration of the myriad ways in which passions inform and motivate human behaviour.[41] For a political economy which understands wealth as produced by labour, idleness and inactivity could not be countenanced: Hume's essay, 'The Stoic', argued that man must not allow his 'noble faculties to lie lethargic or idle', but is urged 'by necessity, to employ, on every emergence his utmost *art and industry*'.[42] Exactly how such a 'necessary' compulsion is impelled by the passions was theorised by Smith who, in a domestic tale of voluntary labour in *The Theory of Moral Sentiments*, suggested that a desire for 'conveniency' motivates effort in the present for benefits in the future:

> When a person comes into his chamber, and finds the chairs all standing in the middle of the room, he is angry with his servant, and rather than see them continue in that disorder, perhaps takes the trouble himself to set them all in their places with their backs to the wall. The whole propriety of this new situation arises from its superior conveniency in leaving the floor free and disengaged. To attain this conveniency he voluntarily puts himself to more trouble than all he could have suffered from the want of it; since

86 Property, Passions, and Manners

nothing was more easy, than to have set himself down upon one of them, which is probably what he does when his labour is over. What he wanted therefore, it seems, was not so much this conveniency, as that arrangement of things which promotes it. Yet it is this conveniency which ultimately recommends that arrangement, and bestows upon it the whole of its propriety and beauty.[43]

Smith's story about voluntary labour – a labour which is 'more trouble' than all we might suffer from 'the want of it' – demonstrates a thesis about the relationship between effort, convenience, and beauty which is capable of banishing the spectre of human idleness. Smith's chairs solve political economy's need to motivate a potentially idle humanity by positing a desire for 'convenience', a quality which resonates especially strongly with us, Smith suggests, because, more than simply being useful, it is beautiful. A similar appreciation of the conveniences presented by all manner of consumer objects – from watches to 'trinkets', 'toys', and 'baubles' – produces a culture of property with which we are essentially at one: even to the extent of suffering the inconveniences (such as the labour of having to tidy our furniture) which possession might entail.[44] The culture of property which the labour of commercial society produces and sustains – the world of goods sustained by the productive labour and the 'wheel of circulation' later extolled by Burke as the 'natural course of things' – is thus, in this story, an extension of our desire for convenience, a meeting through economic productivity of humanity's capacity to be connoisseurs. Later, in *Wealth of Nations*, Smith offered a broader version of this motivational principle, identifying a 'constant desire for self-betterment' as compelling labour.[45] Both accounts, however, illuminate how a narrative of motivation which is strong enough to overcome the pleasures of idleness is fundamental to political economic discourse.

The care with which Smith theorises the motivational passions which override idleness and underpin economic activity only underlines the oddness of Burke's attempt to reconcile the idleness of the landed proprietor with an otherwise mobile economy of productive labour. Wollstonecraft's attack on the late eighteenth-century property order turns all this on its head, however, by setting out a new relationship between property and idleness, and by critiquing the consequences for women of society founded on property. For Wollstonecraft, property occludes activity, industry, and virtue; idleness and indolence are not passive states which commercial modernity has overcome, but consequences of its economic and social organisation. And the argument is turned in women's direction, too, as we shall see, in Wollstonecraft's assertion that their desire to possess the

Labour, Effort, and Imagination 87

'property' of beauty draws them into a voluptuous, exotic world, where the business of pleasure replaces the industry of virtue.

A Vindication of the Nature of 'Man': Labour, Effort, Imagination

In identifying idleness as the fatal flaw in the social and moral order produced by the economic structures of her time, Wollstonecraft challenged contemporary political economic thought, and especially its account of economic value yoked to productive labour. In mounting such an attack on the contemporary property order, she writes large a moral anxiety about a political economy founded on property ownership which had accompanied the theorisation of commercial society from the first half of the eighteenth century. In Wollstonecraft, Hume's worries about the morally and socially corrosive nature of individuals living on the profits of public credit are generalised: the entire system of 'riches and hereditary honours' which is founded not merely on credit, but on property, is deemed socially, politically, and morally corrupt.[46] This fundamental element of Wollstonecraftian critique occurs repeatedly and in many forms through the pages of both *Vindications*. It is present, for instance, in her observation that the House of Commons is full of men of rank but not merit; the idleness of rank means that they lack the talents, virtue, and self-knowledge which are only 'unfolded by industry'.[47] The social effects of idleness are also thoroughly traced in her attention to manners in the second *Vindication*, where she notes how the idleness enabled by property plays itself out in sexualised powerplay in personal relations and in families: 'idleness has produced a mixture of gallantry and despotism into society', and men are 'slaves' of their mistresses whilst they 'tyrannize over their 'sisters, wives and daughters'.[48] The resonant picture of Mary's mother, in Wollstonecraft's pre-*Vindications* novel *Mary*, who sits idle on a sofa, a 'mere machine', gradually declining to death, crystallises the corrosive effects of idleness on women. Wollstonecraft returns to this image in her account of a 'weak woman of fashion' in the second *Vindication*, and it is difficult not to see her also informing the depiction of another indolent female perennial sofa-dweller and moral bystander, Lady Bertram in Jane Austen's *Mansfield Park* (1814), that later fictional exploration of the moral vacuity of property owners, their progeny, and their system of manners.[49] As we will see, it is precisely because women encapsulate the problem of idleness induced by the existing property system that they are so well positioned, in Wollstonecraft's eyes, to carry out the 'revolution in manners' to which she urges them.

The opposite of idleness, in both Wollstonecraft's *Vindications*, is virtue, associated with reason, duty, and the struggle of self-realisation. Talents, virtue, and knowledge are 'unfolded by industry', not inherited, as the Burkean property system would imply.[50] In a claim which chimes with Smithian political economy's founding of value on labour, and which clarifies that her attack on property is specifically on hereditary property and its associated rank and wealth, Wollstonecraft asserts that property in labour is the only property which 'nature' recognises: '[t]he only security of property that nature authorizes ... is, the right a man has to enjoy the acquisitions which his talents and industry have acquired'.[51] A nation or polity organised on such meritocratic principles, she suggests, would value ambition, not gaming, and love, not gallantry. Although she doesn't make the point, the principle of property in labour would have significant ramifications for women if, for instance, recognition of maternal labour, including breastfeeding, gave mothers legal ownership of their children; it would thus counter the existing legal right of fathers to remove children from their mothers, as Venables does in *The Wrongs of Woman*. The valoration of labour and the virtues which follow from it are also explicit in Wollstonecraft's remark that the poor don't need alms but 'employments calculated to give them habits of virtue' and her attack on the 'brown waste' of unused land when men want 'work'.[52]

Effort is valued by Wollstonecraft not because it generates wealth, but for its moral and social effects. In her motivational story, the 'springs which govern activity' place labour and effort at the heart of a moral economy of exertion, and her account of human nature is consistently preoccupied with its capacity for virtue, and the larger political and social conditions in which virtue might flourish.[53] For Burke, labour is hardly appealing: 'pestiferous' and 'unwholesome', it is a necessary burden carried out by the miserable majority in order to turn the 'great wheel of circulation'; its only value is economic, gained at the cost of human happiness and lives.[54] The mental and moral effort to which Wollstonecraft repeatedly exhorts her readers recasts labour in a different direction, to become an on-going effort to develop reason, knowledge, and virtue, and thus to contribute both to the improvement of the individual, and more broadly to the progress of civilisation itself. Countering Burke's 'natural course of things' thus necessitates resisting the confining of effort to a political economic category. Against a Burkean depiction of labour as abject and depersonalised, valued only for its economic effects, Wollstonecraft mobilises an expansive and wide-ranging exhortation of the activity of self-improvement, whose effects will range across the personal and social, moral, and political spheres.

Labour, Effort, and Imagination

Wollstonecraft's exposition of the need for, and nature of, this effort brings with it an account of her sense of the proper make-up of human nature, and the relations of its different capacities for feeling, reason, and imagination: part of an unapologetically 'metaphysical enquiry' that she ironically fears might 'derange' Burke's 'nervous system'.[55] It is a strategy which brings back into the heart of political philosophical discourse the human identity and personhood which is expunged or flattened in economic writing, where the reduction of 'labour' to an abstraction also reduces individuals to mere performers of operations, or labour functionaries. The labour or energy which Wollstonecraft values above all else is the immaterial activity of reason, which impels humankind beyond supine states of stasis and pleasure. Here, Wollstonecraft's argument about human nature is very different from the theories of labour motivation offered by Hume and Smith. Our very constitution, she asserts, once the 'first law' of self-preservation has been met, impels us beyond mere pleasure, to the 'exercise of our faculties' as 'the great end'. Our passions are 'necessary auxiliaries' of 'reason': they provide the motivating 'impulse', and enable us to gain 'not only … many ideas, but a habit of thinking'.[56] Without such impulses from our passions, thought, which is 'the faint type of an immaterial energy', is 'confined to the tenement'.[57] Property figures here as material constraint, as it does when Wollstonecraft reflects on the tendency of the human mind to too readily 'take opinions on trust' and 'gladly let the spirit lie quiet in its gross tenement'.[58] In contrast, mind is imaged in almost Biblical terms as a spirit hovering over the water when Wollstonecraft asserts that 'the most improving exercise of the mind … is the restless enquiries that hover on the boundary, or stretch over the dark abyss of uncertainty'.[59] Such rhetoric takes flight as Wollstonecraft asserts that her 'passions pursue objects that the imagination enlarges, till they become only a sublime idea that shrinks from the enquiry of sense, and mocks the experimental philosophers who would confine this spiritual phlogiston in their material crucibles'.[60] In such rhapsodic passages, rationality gives way to something transcendent, guided by the imagination to higher realms of perception, to grasp truths or insights akin to divine fire. Such a sublime endpoint to the efforts of passion to mobilise body and mind is in stark contrast to the submission of human nature to the world of work in political economic accounts of the 'springs of action'.

There is a danger, in these images, that mental effort disappears into the intangible or uncertain – the 'boundary', uncertainty's 'dark abyss', the inarticulable 'sublime idea' – towards which it is strongly compelled. Imagination, indeed, has a double-edged presence in the *Vindication*, where it is as just as likely to be object of attack – as in the denigration of Burke's 'lively imagination', the dangers of the 'vagaries of imagination', or the warning that a 'lively imagination is ever in danger of being betrayed into error by favourite opinions' – as it is to accompany reason.[61] It is therefore all the more important that, rather than being approached as separate functions, attention is paid to the correct relation which should exist between the elements of the human person: passion, reason, imagination.[62] Here, the proper combination is all. Thus, in the 'feelings of humanity' which distinguish 'active exertions of virtue' from 'vague declamation of sensibility', reason is presented as intimately connected with feeling, as deepening emotion and producing virtue.[63] Elsewhere, a sexual metaphor presents the 'feelings of the heart' as the 'sun of life' which impregnates an otherwise passive reason to create virtue.[64] Reason and reflection should thus motivate and accompany the 'auxiliary' of feeling, preventing against the dual dangers of vacuous and untested feeling, or unfeeling reason. The same balance is expressed in Wollstonecraft's characteristically wide-ranging style, which oscillates between sharp political critique and invective, and more effusive passages. Thus, a paean to the 'sublime ideas' pursed by the imagination follows quickly in the wake of an assertion that her 'fancy' never created 'a heaven on earth', in the same paragraph as the straight-forward assertion of the need to recognise the '*native* unalienable rights of men'.[65] The mixed economy of the human person, in which reason is informed by feeling and vice versa, is thus exemplified in the varied and flexible style of Wollstonecraft's writing.

The 'nervous exertions of morality' should properly be the output of this exertive human economy, but such efforts need to be made in a context where virtue is rewarded: that is, where merit, not rank, is recognised, a 'glorious change' which liberty might produce.[66] Such larger political questions are the context of Wollstonecraft's philosophy of human nature, and connect her work to the ongoing radical demand for liberty which, as we saw in the previous chapter, she shares with Richard Price, Catharine Macaulay, and others. Wollstonecraft's attention to the economy of the human person thus connects a radical tradition calling for political liberty with the analysis of human nature and individual subjectivity, whilst anticipating the further pursuit of liberty through the psychologised aesthetics of Romanticism. Liberty, the periodic rallying call of the *Vindication*, emerges as the definition of a context where human efforts towards virtue might flourish. It is illustrative of quite how closely integrated these different elements of Wollstonecraft's thinking are, that her account of thought as the 'faint type of an immaterial energy' occurs as part of an argument

Labour, Effort, and Imagination 91

attacking the practice of pressing men into naval service.[67] These apparently digressive trains of argument can make Wollstonecraft's text at times difficult to follow, but such moves show her repeatedly interrogating the claims of Burke's text and putting them through the machine of her own thinking. Wollstonecraft's account of human nature, and its valoration of mental and moral labour and effort, thus founds a politics which yokes together reason, improvement, and liberty to resist political economy's depredation of the human: her vindication of 'Rights' is firmly grounded on a developed theory of 'Man'. As the *Vindication of the Rights of Woman* will assert, society must be founded on the 'nature of man', not on prejudices; if political economy was similarly to be founded on the 'nature of man', Wollstonecraft suggests that it too should begin with knowledge of the human heart: with the motivation and effort which give virtue.[68]

Wollstonecraft's philosophy of human nature, and especially her mobilisation of an immaterial and transcendent imagination, is part of a fundamental challenge to Burkean discourse, which includes but reaches beyond a mere moral critique of political economy. In Wollstonecraft, the operation of mind, galvanised by feeling, is an elevated activity, an expression of the best of humanity. In giving a central role (alongside reason and feeling) to the imagination, Wollstonecraft celebrates a faculty which Burke feared as fundamentally at odds with the property order: an independent power that frees the self from the subject relations which for Burke were necessary to society's natural order. Alongside the moral exertions of our other faculties, Wollstonecraft elevates and mobilises the imagination against the property order: through its means, independent thought and subjectivity become capable of challenging the social bonds, ranks, and identities which for a thinker like Burke were part of a society naturally organised around property. Burke's fears, expressed in the *Reflections* and beyond, of 'electrick communication', of the supposed enthusiasm of men of letters, and of what Pocock terms 'decivilized intellect', are usually understood to refer to his opposition to a reformist Enlightenment culture of thought: the dangerous operation of mind separated from the protective context of pre-existing social structures.[69] Pocock's analysis of Burke's *Reflections* makes clear that Burke's fear of enthusiasm is related too to Hume's fear of credit and its consequent idleness, discussed above. Where Hume warned that idle proprietors were vulnerable to enthusiasm, so too are men of letters, in Burke's eyes: both are separated from the 'natural relations' and social bonds which property upholds. For Burke, upholding the social order allied to political economy entails a mental discipline, which Wollstonecraftian imagination wilfully transgresses, rejecting the subjection of mind to property relations. As her final work will explore, the imagination offers the possibility of alternative forms of social relation: thus, *The Wrongs of Woman* moves from early, Burkean fears of the enthusiastic mind 'left alone with its own creations' (an indictment of the fate of the female mind in property society) to the new social unit of Maria and Jemima, which dispenses with both men and property, and which is formed through imaginative sympathy.[70] If the problem remained of how such alternative social forms might be actualised, the imagination is nevertheless revealed as opposed to the property forms of commercial society, its liberation the elevation of an enthusiastic principle or power which commercial society long feared as a central threat.

Vindication of the Rights of Woman as Political Economy: Manners in Commercial Modernity

It is unusual in Wollstonecraft commentary for her two *Vindications* to be treated as linked.[71] The first page of the *Vindication of the Rights of Woman* describes the work as a 'treatise on female rights and manners', and it is this focus on 'manners' (a broad analytical category which denotes behavioural forms, customs, social organisation and lifestyle) which enables Wollstonecraft to extend and develop in the second *Vindication* the critique of the property order offered in the first.[72] Manners vocabulary makes an occasional appearance in the *Vindication of the Rights of Men*: for instance, in the claim that the 'partial' development of European civilization has refined 'manners at the expense of morals'.[73] But manners come centre stage in the second *Vindication*, including in the famous call, made a number of times, for a 'revolution in manners', which, in a rare typographical indulgence for Wollstonecraft, is placed in capitals in the final chapter.[74]

In offering a manners analysis, Wollstonecraft worked in the tradition of Scottish conjectural history: in its historical sociological perspective, social customs, including those pertaining to gender, are understood to vary according to different stages of economic development.[75] Conjectural history also understood the status and treatment of women to be indicative of the state of manners in any historical period. But where other historians measured the advance of manners by improvements in the social status and condition of women, Wollstonecraft's extended account of the 'miserable' state of the female sex is an indictment of both the reality and the self-image of the commercial age. It made clear the consequences for women of a hereditary property order whose deleterious effects on human

Manners in Commercial Modernity 93

nature, reason, and virtue were set out in her earlier work.[76] With women at the centre of her analysis, Wollstonecraft could offer a detailed account of the cultural and psychological formation of gender in the 'present order of property', linking gender strongly to existing economic structures and conditions.[77] The second *Vindication*'s language of manners thus shows how these two works are successive stages of an ongoing analysis, with the second *Vindication* developing the earlier text's critique of property into a fully worked out gender critique of the manners of the late eighteenth-century property order.

The progress from the first to the second *Vindication* also involves a call to intervene in the conditions of the historical present which both works analyse. If the first *Vindication* sees idleness as a consequence of property, the second seeks to turn manners *against* property, a revolution whose necessity is determined precisely by the effects of the property order on manners. This turning of manners against the property order of commercial society marks Wollstonecraft's departure from conjectural history, for in such a revolution, manners would no longer be the unforeseen and cumulative effect of economic change and social organisation but rather would seek to further extend the progress of society as described by the Scottish historians, beyond an age defined by commerce. This is to use manners as a lever to change historical process, and to reform the 'partial' civilisation of the commercial age. Wollstonecraft's 'revolution' would thus mark the point at which humankind was not determined by the unfolding of stadial history but instead stage a deliberate intervention in the material and psychological conditions of their lives. 'Self-creation' may appear a strong word for this process, but it is justified by some of the more exhortative passages of the *Vindication of the Rights of Woman*. Placed at the forefront of Wollstonecraft's manners analysis as they are, women are addressed as an important group of change-makers, a revolutionary vanguard, through whom individual moral improvement and social change might be brought about, to transform society under the banner of reason and virtue. Wollstonecraft's 'revolution' is thus an act of faith in the power of personal self-reform, and an experiment in how the cultivation of virtue by individuals might benefit the larger human community as a whole.[78]

Attending to Wollstonecraft's manners analysis also makes it possible to see how the second *Vindication* is not merely a treatise on female education (as it has often been read) but also as a work of political economy, as it was categorised by the *Analytical Review*.[79] Late eighteenth-century political economy was an outworking of conjectural history, which incorporated historical, sociological, and psychological analysis in its account of

94 Property, Passions, and Manners

the last of stadial history's four stages of social and economic development, the modern age of commerce. If Wollstonecraft's manners revolution was a call to intervene in the historical processes shaping the present, it was by the same token an attempt to resist the historical forces theorised by and underpinning political economy itself. If the determining 'springs of action' for Smith and others were a love of convenience, or a desire for self-betterment strong enough to motivate work, a 'revolution in manners' looks to manners as a counter to the expression of such forces informing the unfolding of human history, to offer a moral and social revolution against the forces of history themselves. And if the active subject theorised by political economy is male, women are the revolutionary agents of Wollstonecraft's manners revolution. The 'revolution in manners' is thus a rallying call for women to save commercial society from itself, and to save themselves from it.

Wollstonecraft's call for a manners revolution also marks her difference from commentators for whom a 'softening' or 'polishing' of manners provided the best means of accommodating virtue in a commercial society founded on the pursuit of wealth.[80] Bernard Mandeville's notorious provocation in *The Fable of the Bees* (1714) had suggested that 'private vice is public benefit', and Montesquieu's tale of the Troglodytes in his *Persian Letters* (1721) – to which we return in Chapter 5 – narrated the rise of commercial society, motivated by greed and desire for wealth, as involving an irrecoverable abandonment of an earlier virtuous pastoral existence. The 'sociological irony' of polite manners advocated by Hume and others was rejected by Wollstonecraft, in frequent denunciations of the separation of morals and manners, and calls for their urgent realignment.[81] More than once, the *Vindication of the Rights of Woman* asserts that private virtue can and must be generalised to generate public virtue: a rejection of the Mandevillean paradox of private vice-public virtue, just as her assertion that rational virtue must be the basis for individual action rejects the Smithian motivational principle of the pursuit of self-betterment.[82] In an essay 'Against Inconsistency in Our Expectations' which Wollstonecraft described as 'excellent', the writer and poet Anna Letitia Barbauld describes a choice between wealth or virtue: choose one or the other for your son, she advises, follow its path, but don't switch between them.[83] Wollstonecraft's praise for Barbauld's words suggests that she too believed that attempts to reconcile wealth and virtue through a show of fashionable, polite manners constituted a superficial skating over of a fundamental contradiction at the very foundation of her age.

Wollstonecraft's vehement linking of property with idleness and corruption in the first *Vindication* is the very antithesis of the argument that commercial society refines and polishes manners. As in her first *Vindication*, her argument in the second deploys a philosophical analysis of human nature, this time historically embedded to highlight the role of the passions as forces shaping the unfolding of human history. The second *Vindication*'s important opening chapter offers a condensed reading of the formation of European society through this lens, demonstrating her intellectual debt to conjectural history, but also showing how and where she differs from the story about the passions on which political economy is founded. By attending to the differences between the story that Wollstonecraft tells about the passions and their relation to reason and action (the 'springs of action'), and a Smithian narrative of the individual's affective motivation, we can see how her critique of political economy rests on an assertion that it is fundamentally at odds with 'the nature of man' on which society should be built.[84]

Wealth and the Passions in Commercial Society: Wollstonecraft versus Smith

Wollstonecraft's most famous work, the *Vindication of the Rights of Woman*, opens with a historical narrative of European civilisation from 'savagery' to 'monarchical government', announcing her account of 'woman' as specifically describing women in the current, commercial age. The 'wrongs' of contemporary women are thus from the outset understood through the conditions of the commercial age they inhabit. Wollstonecraft's mini-history bears comparison with the condensed history of Europe offered in book three of Smith's *Wealth of Nations*, where the rise of commerce is presented as a pivotal event in the formation of the modern age, breaking the hold of aristocratic power and contributing to the growth of knowledge. Wollstonecraft follows Smith's account to show commerce's role, alongside 'reason' and 'literature', in challenging the oppressive and corrupt power of kings.[85] But for Wollstonecraft, it is the passions which are ultimately the driving historical forces, and wealth, with its strong appeal to the passions, corrupts: her version of the 'wealth and virtue' problem discussed above. If the age of commerce is also the age of reason, the struggle between mind and passion which Wollstonecraft will suggest is constitutive of human nature is also historically embedded, with Janus-faced commerce linked to both reason and enlightenment on the one hand, and wealth and tyranny on the other. The opening of the mind associated with commercial society is thus in conflict with the passions drawn to the wealth which also accompanies it. The same historical forces are explored in more detail in Wollstonecraft's next work, and her only extended work of history, her *Historical and Moral View of the Origin and Progress of the French Revolution* (1794), but their outlines are evident here at the outset of her second *Vindication*.

The problem of wealth – a multi-faceted historical, political, and moral problem – thus dominates the *Vindication of the Rights of Woman*. It corrupts and perverts human nature, shown especially in Wollstonecraft's depiction of women, and it impedes the growth of the affections and sentiments on which a reformed civilisation might be built: 'vices and follies ... all proceed from a feculent stream of wealth that has muddied the pure rills of natural affection'.[86] As with her history of Europe, Wollstonecraft's account of the problem of wealth draws in part from Smith, but she adapts and extends his analysis. In *The Theory of Moral Sentiments*, Smith analyses the social effects of wealth by describing the power derived by kings from the visual display of their status. Wollstonecraft generalises this to depict the 'mass' in modern society craving the attention which wealth would give. Riches, alongside rank, 'dazzle' and bestow a 'pre-eminence' which many crave, eclipsing a proper concern with virtue.[87] Wealth and rank also provide a smoke screen behind which character hides, so that it becomes impossible for reputation to be founded on virtue: the 'drapery of situation hides the man, and makes him stalk in masquerade, dragging from one scene of dissipation to another the nerveless limbs that hang with stupid listlessness, and rolling round the vacant eye, which plainly tell us that there is no mind at home'.[88] This picture of a social world in hoc to a culture of display also speaks to the situation of women, for whom beauty is a rare and double-edged source of power, and who might also exploit – or be ruined by – reputation's shifting sands.

For Smith, social spectatorship (and the sense of being looked at by others) leads to the development of moral judgement; for him, it was possible for a virtuous reputation to be sustained and recognised in the eyes of social spectators. But Wollstonecraft's sense of the pervasive corruption of the artifice and 'masquerade' of the social world makes such an accommodation of virtue amidst the 'manners' of commercial modernity impossible. O'Brien has rightly observed that Wollstonecraft's attack on the 'partial' nature of contemporary European civilisation took aim at a culture of manners which encouraged individuals to internalise a 'socially ascribed' identity defined by their role or rank, at the expense of their moral identity.[89] For Wollstonecraft, this was too flimsy an account of virtue, and the notion of reputation, in particular, operated in especially insidious ways for women, too easily identified with the question of sexual 'virtue'. Her condemnation of the 'misery and disorder' of a theatrical society of empty display, with its 'jostling' of 'artificial fools', at times recalls Rousseau's rejection of modern society, but she has little time for Rousseau's response – a retreat to solitude – which is dispatched swiftly and thoroughly in the *Vindication*'s first chapter.[90] Rather, if our feelings respond to wealth and rank in a way which skews reputation and eclipses the possibility of virtue, we need to reform those feelings in order to then reform the 'partial' civilisation of modernity. The thorough social reform of the commercial age thus addresses the passions which are at its foundation.[91]

Wollstonecraft's concern with what she calls the 'mechanism' of our passions, the 'system of government which prevails in the moral world', is signalled in the image of the watchmaker used in a footnote to the first chapter of the *Vindication*: long associated with questions of the design and purpose of human nature.[92] For Wollstonecraft, the very existence of our feelings suggests they have a purpose: they were 'set in motion to improve our nature, of which they make a part, and render us capable of enjoying a more godlike portion of happiness'. The 'gracious fountain of life' gave us 'passions, and the power of reflecting' not to 'imbitter (sic) our days' but to lead us to happiness.[93] This is the moral lesson of the *Vindication*: that reflecting on our passions, and improving our nature will enable us to progress from self-love to sublime divine love, and thus attain, so far as is possible in this world, the 'happiness' which appears intermittently as a goal throughout the second *Vindication* (far more so than in the first). We must be careful, however, not to understand the 'happiness' at which we must aim, as merely what might be attained through 'moderation' and 'prudence', as if 'men were only born to form a circle of life and death'.[94] Rather, it is the 'natural course of things' to realise in old age, 'when an unwelcome knowledge of life produces almost a satiety of life', that (echoing Ecclesiasticus) 'all that is done under the sun is vanity': the 'awful close of the drama' draws near, with the imminent end of the 'first stage of existence'.[95] Whether consciously or not, Wollstonecraft echoes both Smith and Burke with her evocation of a 'natural course of things', a phrase used by both (as we saw in the previous chapter) to set out, although in significantly different ways, a 'natural course' defined by the productive activity of human labour. Wollstonecraft by contrast understands the 'natural course of things' to be the insights of old age into the vanity of life, including the error of understanding life's purpose as limited to the 'first stage of existence'. Nature, revealed by the wisdom of age, points us beyond the narrow 'circle of life and death' towards the 'immortality of the soul': the context in which our urgings towards a 'godlike portion of happiness' should be understood.

Smith too had attended to the end of life as a moment of retrospection in his own account of the workings of human nature. The story of the 'poor man's son' in *The Theory of Moral Sentiments* deploys the insights of age to explain the operation of our passions, and the actions which they 'set in motion'. But Smith's version of this is both more extended and more tragic than Wollstonecraft's. '[V]isited with ambition' by heaven 'in its anger', the poor man's son devotes his life to unrelenting labour in an attempt to attain the 'conveniences' which he sees enjoyed by the rich – the carriages, the accommodation, the servants – which he mistakenly thinks will bestow happiness. In pursuit of them, he 'sacrifices' throughout his life the 'real tranquillity' which 'is at all times in his power'. If, 'in the extremity of old age', he at last attains them, he finds them 'in no respect preferable to that humble security and contentment' which he had abandoned in their pursuit. Anticipating Wollstonecraft's sense of age as giving insight into life's vanities, but phrasing such insights rather more starkly, the poor man's son in old age realises that 'wealth and greatness are mere trinkets of frivolous utility, no more adapted for procuring ease of body or tranquillity of mind than the tweezer-cases of the lover of toys'. Power and riches now appear 'immense fabrics, which it requires the labour of a life to raise' which 'keep off the summer shower, not the winter storm' and which yet leave their possessor 'as much, and sometimes more exposed than before to anxiety, to fear, and to sorrow; to diseases, to danger, and to death'.[96]

The 'natural course' related in this sorry tale speaks, as in Wollstonecraft, to the misguided nature of worldly ambition; it points bracingly to the erroneous perception that 'power and riches' deliver happiness. Smith's fable echoes the description of the 'ever-busy civilised man' who 'sweats, scurries about … [and] toils until death', embodying the tragedy of futile modern existence, in the conclusion of Rousseau's *Discourse on the Origin of Inequality* (1755), but for Smith, this is not the end of the story.[97] Rather, he reflects that 'it is well that nature imposes upon us in this manner', for whilst it is a 'deception' to think that 'the pleasures of wealth and greatness' would be worth 'all the toil and anxiety which we are so apt to bestow' on them, this nevertheless 'rouses and keeps in continual motion the industry of mankind'. This motivating 'deception' of the passions, indeed, tills the ground, builds houses, and founds cities, and sustains 'all the sciences and arts, which ennoble and embellish human life'.[98] If in Burke's 'natural course', there is a 'necessary submission' to the 'wheel of circulation', in Smith that 'submission' is hard-wired into our nature by our passions: in a fundamental, even constitutive self-deception of 'nature', we are all the poor man's son, visited with ambition by heaven's

Wealth and the Passions in Commercial Society 99

anger. Whilst this is clearly tragic at the level of the individual, there are evidently significant economic and civilizational benefits. To the 'ironic' eye of the philosopher, able to see things play themselves out, this is an acceptable payoff. If Hume's 'sociological irony' accommodates morals to the manners of the commercial age, here is an 'economic' version of that irony: never mind the misery, look at the roads. It is that extra turn of the argument, the spinning of misery into the 'embellishments' of human life, that Wollstonecraft refuses.

If Smith looks beyond the old man's body, 'wasted with toil and diseases', to the 'deception' which 'keeps in continual motion the industry of mankind', Wollstonecraft insists instead on the 'unheard of misery' caused, for instance, by the pursuit of a cardinal's rank.[99] She resists a narrative of the 'springs of action' which has the tragic deception of human nature at the heart of its 'natural course of things'. If, for Smith, the passions produce as their unintended consequence the machinery or fabric of convenience writ large in human civilisation, happiness has been lost somewhere along the way, doubly displaced both by its deferral by labour, and the mistake or 'deception' that the objects or arrangements which deliver 'convenience' will provide pleasure or happiness. Wollstonecraft differs fundamentally from Smith both on the nature of the passions and the object of happiness. The feelings which in Smith compel us towards convenience with a seemingly inevitable determination are instead for Wollstonecraft part of God's plan for us to struggle with and improve ourselves; happiness is achieved not through possessions or convenience, but through improving our nature, and performing our duties.[100] This is why a strong claim about reforming our passions runs through the *Vindication of the Rights of Woman*, and here there is a payoff from the historical nature of her social analysis: we can reform our passions because they are themselves historically produced, not a permanent feature of human nature but a product of a corrupt and corrupting time. Such a reformation involves the individual turning herself – for in Wollstonecraft's account, the onus for such work falls to women – against the tendencies of her age, and against the very historical forces of her own formation. Such a critical orientation of the individual against her time is absent in Smith's account, as is a sense of the historicity of the motivational 'springs of action' which he presents. Certainly, in Smith, the passions are linked to the development of civilisation through each of its historical stages: thus the desire for convenience has supposedly caused everything which has 'changed the whole face of the globe', from the first cultivation of the ground to the more recent development of the 'sciences and arts'. Yet by virtue of its apparent omnipresence, the 'desire for convenience' appears an ahistorical force, consistently present in each stage of human progress. This overlooks the question of its origin: in Smith's account, the conveniences enjoyed by the rich need to already exist in order for them to be seen by others to motivate them to attain them for themselves. Smith's is thus a circular argument which renders transhistorical a sentiment which is arguably most obviously to the fore in commercial society, as is suggested in Smith's use of the language of consumer objects ('tweezer-cases', 'toys') for 'wealth and greatness'.[101]

From one perspective, Wollstonecraft's emphasis on reforming the passions could be read as a theological accommodation of a Smithian account of historical progress: whilst the passions of our nature impel civilisational progress, they also for her stage a God-given struggle which enables our self-improvement. Such an accommodation might appear to be implied in a passage in Chapter 5, where in a kind of dream-vision, Wollstonecraft sees 'the sons and daughters of men' playing out their roles as in a script written by Smith:

> I see the sons and daughters of men pursuing shadows, and anxiously wasting their powers to feed passions which have no adequate object – if the very excess of these blind impulses, pampered by that lying, yet constantly trusted guide, the imagination, did not, by preparing them for some other state, render short-sighted mortals wiser without their own concurrence; or, what comes to the same thing, when they were pursuing some imaginary present good.[102]

Here, not just the 'poor man's son', but, in a Blakean-formulation, all 'the sons and daughters of men' waste 'their powers' in pursuit of inadequate objects, impelled by a 'lying' imagination: Smith's necessarily 'deceptive' nature. '[V]iewing objects in this light', she continues, 'it would not be fanciful to imagine that this world was a stage on which a pantomime is daily performed for the amusement of superior beings'. The very same Shakespearean image used to condemn Burke's 'system' on the final page of the *Vindication of the Rights of Men* – the gods killing us 'for their sport' – returns to condemn a Smithian account of the 'constitution' of our 'nature' which makes us 'slaves' to 'hope and fear'.[103] At the same time, however, and like Smith, Wollstonecraft identifies an unintended consequence to this process: the 'excess' of passion prepares 'short-sighted mortals' for 'some other state', making them 'wiser' despite themselves. Her language is hedged and oblique, in a conditional formulation which approaches a double negative – 'no ... if ... did not' – and it is the 'adequacy' or otherwise of the 'object' which impels all this effort, which hangs in the syntactical balance. But the passage nevertheless points to some

Wealth and the Passions in Commercial Society 101

belated gaining of moral wisdom: some insight, perhaps, into the 'vanity of things' which she elsewhere notes is natural in the final stages of life. To return to the analogy of the watch, the very existence of the passions in our 'mechanism' evinces that they were 'set in motion' for a purpose: to 'improve our nature' and enable our attainment of a 'more godlike portion of happiness', not for our performance of a pantomime for the gods.[104]

Wollstonecraft's opposition to a Smithian narrative of our 'constitution' which makes us 'slaves … to hope and fear' emerges still more clearly from the larger context of this passage where, although ostensibly discussing Lord Chesterfield's advice to his son in his *Letters*, Smith appears still to be running through Wollstonecraft's mind. Attacking axioms 'made by men who have coolly seen mankind through the medium of books' and taking aim at the Smithian goal of securing 'ease and prosperity on earth', Wollstonecraft rejects the qualities of moderation and prudence which are central to *The Theory of Moral Sentiments*, especially in its outlining of a morality appropriate to the pursuit of self-interest fundamental to the commercial age.[105] In a jibe at Smith, or at his terminology at least, the pursuit of 'conveniences' is termed a mere 'vegetable life', in which the 'passions' and the 'powers of the soul' would be 'useless'.[106] The existence of the passions points, in Wollstonecraft's eyes, to our potential for more sublime virtue than sticking to 'the letter of the law'.[107] Asserting that 'the regulations (*sic*) of the passions is not, always, wisdom', and asking how they might 'gain sufficient strength to unfold the faculties', Wollstonecraft reflects that it is the very 'force of [men's] passions' which enables them to leap over 'the boundary that secures content' and strengthen their reasoning capacities, giving them 'superior judgement, and more fortitude than women'.[108] If 'going astray' enables men to 'enlarge their minds', the fruit of this, where moralists are concerned, would appear to be maxims which especially constrain and confine female minds and their affective natures. These are themes to which Wollstonecraft will return, especially in what was to be the final output of her career, *The Wrongs of Woman*, where, as we will see in my final chapter, the character of Venables embeds an extensive critique of Smithian prudence (called in the *Vindication* the 'cautious craft of ignorant self-love'). The turn to fiction, too, despite Wollstonecraft's earlier reservations about the novel form, will address the passions of the reader, offering an affective experience through which the boundaries of their experience might be 'overleaped' and their reasoning capacities unfolded. Given the tendency to associate such themes with the later end of her career, it is worth noting here in the *Vindication* the force of Wollstonecraft's insistence on the role of the passions in self-formation. Her counter-argument against a Smithian narrative in which the passions are yoked to economic benefit is thus neither the repressive rejection of the passions for rational self-correction nor the experiential narrowing of moderation and constraint exhorted by conduct books. She agrees with Smith that a 'common stream' of 'ambition, love, hope and fear' run through us all, but against him suggests that our reason can tell us that 'their present and most attractive promises are only lying dreams'. Yet we should not dampen our 'generous feeling' with the 'cold hand of circumspection'. The bestial passions of the Yahoos, and the passionless rationality of the Houyhnhnms, are equally unattractive models: it is through 'habits of reflection', attaining knowledge through fostering the passions, that we might improve ourselves, and what lies beyond us.[109]

Wollstonecraft's faith in the capacity of reason to reflect on the effects and consequences of the passions makes a strong contrast with the narrative of the passions on which Smithian political economy is founded. In Smith, an analysis of the passions founds a larger systematic account in which human labour is organised into systems of exchange, value, and wealth.[110] Smithian moral theory works upwards and outwards at dizzying speed, from one paragraph to the next, so that an argument about individual desire for convenience and self-betterment quickly becomes the inevitable cause of the larger economic system, such that it appears difficult to intervene in or unpack the one from the other. What 'boundary' has been 'overleaped' here, in the 'freer scope' enjoyed by the 'enlarged mind'? Wollstonecraft's quite different treatment of the passions opens up the possibility of escape from the story about wealth society that Smith offers, and sets the stage for the individual's moral struggle with conditions of the commercial age itself. For Wollstonecraft, the onus is on individuals to reflect on how the culture of riches, property, and rank of our time works on us to produce such passions as Smith describes, and to struggle against them. The possibility of rational self-interrogation against our 'mechanisms' shows that we need not be not ruled by the 'springs' of our nature but are capable of developing the reason, understanding, and self-knowledge which should properly be the basis of community and society itself, from the rational friendships between men and women which should constitute marriage, to the larger community of reason evoked in the first *Vindication*. To all of this, Wollstonecraft adds a call for social reform: a benevolent legislator should seek to 'make it the interest of each individual to be virtuous' and hence 'cement' public happiness on 'private virtue'.[111] This would mean working against our tendency to be swayed by riches, rank, and reputation not just at an individual level, but by

Wealth and the Passions in Commercial Society 103

organising society to minimise their effects, which, as the first *Vindication* demonstrated, include the moral and social corruptions consequent on property, rank, and dependence. In this way, 'an orderly whole is consolidated by the tendency of all the parts towards a common centre'.[112]

Wollstonecraft's commitment to understanding human nature as expressed and moulded by the character of the historical moment produces the constitutive problem or tension in her writing. If, as she says, 'hereditary power chokes the affections and nips reason in the bud', how are these very affections and reason to become the means through which we improve ourselves and our world?[113] The interposition of some additional force is needed to kick-start an alternative running of our mechanisms, to turn a vicious circle into a virtuous one. Within the economy of her text, this additional force is the exhortative power of her own voice, which ranges from philosophical argument to political invective, from sarcasm and irony to moral urging, from cultural denunciation to affective effusion: running the gamut of every possible tone to maximise the chances of working an effect on her reader. The question of where her own insight derives from – her capacity to trace the formation as well as the problems of her age – is not addressed (although as we have seen, there is at least one figuration of her insights as those of a dream or vision); like Smith, she enjoys the philosophical capacity for overview, insight, and connection despite being one of what she herself describes as the most abject of subjects, a woman. For some commentators, the combination of the nature and power of Wollstonecraft's rhetorical voice, and what is, in effect, her self-differentiation from the collective group of 'woman' which she addresses in her writing, has led to a characterisation of Wollstonecraft herself as 'masculine' in some way – despite both her famous 'wild wish' that differences of gender cease to be attended to, and her attack on the very characterisation of thinking women as 'masculine'. In her eyes, indeed, not even the men who 'have coolly seen mankind through the medium of books' have displayed any particular prowess in the acquisition of knowledge. Here is a voice, perhaps, which seeks to transcend the binaries of gender which might otherwise contain it.

As we saw earlier, and despite its counter-acting capacity to delude, the imagination offers the possibility of breaking out of the limits of knowledge marked by prejudice, historicity, and the inevitable impress of cultural formation. Whilst it is never suggested that we can simply imagine ourselves out of the problems of our time, the powers and capacity of the imagination are resources to which Wollstonecraft repeatedly returns. Combined with our historical experience, both collective and individual, it promises that the knowledge required for human improvement can be attained. The embodied experience of passionate existence, allied to proper reflection and the powers of reason, may thus generate imaginative insight. After all, it is in precisely such reflections on impassioned experience that Wollstonecraft's analytical voice originates: as the story of the Advertisement to the *Vindication of the Rights of Men* shows, her turn to authorship was impelled by the emotive experience of reading Burke. And as we shall now see, it is because women's experience in general is so marked by the commercial age – because women are so exposed to, and so particularly embody, the problems of commercial society – that it is to them that her rallying cry to turn that experience into knowledge and change is particularly addressed.

Property Redux: Women, Manners, and the Public Good

In conjectural history's manners tradition, the treatment and status of women were read as indicative of social progress (or its lack) from one epoch to the next. Wollstonecraft's focus in the *Vindication of the Rights of Woman* on the relationship between the 'manners of women' and the 'manners of the times' thus did not merely situate the problems of contemporary womanhood in the context of the property world of late eighteenth-century commercial society: it also used the former to critique the 'present modification of society', and to show how it might be reformed.[114] The picture she paints of things 'as they are at present organized' in civil government, from her observations of female manners, is a damning one.[115] Far from signalling the progress of the commercial age, women make clear its uneven development, embodying its 'partial' civilisation with their disturbing mix of the childlike (they 'lisp', they are like 'toys') and their sexual power games, or in the way their status (sexual and social) veers from object of veneration and elevation one moment, to abjection and obsolescence the next. Scurrying 'helter-skelter' around London in their carriages, reclining listlessly on their sofas, women do not connote progress but stasis, even arrested development: they thus pose the problem of history itself, of civilisation at once over- and underdeveloped.[116] The problems Wollstonecraft sees when she turns her attention to women are those of commercial society itself; hence her perception of a direct and unequivocal link between the status of women and human progress: 'till women are more rationally educated, the progress of human virtue and improvement in knowledge must receive continual checks'.[117]

Women, Manners, and the Public Good

Wollstonecraft was far from the first to approach women as a diagnostic or symbolic tool with which to explore eighteenth-century commercial modernity. Joseph Addison and Daniel Defoe, using the ambivalent but alluring figure of Lady Credit in the early years of the century, inaugurated a long tradition associating women with the troubling passions (desire, self-interest, avariciousness, and greed) of commercial society.[118] Lady Credit, in their allegory of the system of public credit, personified the nature of risk in an uncertain world; she was followed in the eighteenth-century economic and cultural imagination by a succession of female figures who embodied the enticements of commercial gain alongside anxiety about how such gain depended on the worst passions of human nature, and its deleterious social and moral effects.[119] Whilst he sidelined women from the main stage of economic and commercial activity, Hume's 'ironic' accommodation of morals to the manners of the commercial age was associated with the highly artificial figure of the *salonnière*, whose receipt of male gallantries and *politesse* helped to stabilise the passions of the commercial world, and to exemplify its supposed polish.[120] Such a figure was directly at odds with what Harriet Guest has described as 'the figure of insatiable feminine desire', projected 'out of itself' by the eighteenth-century 'discourse of commerce', as 'the image of its own amoralism', embodying the 'vices of commerce' as well as 'the radiance of the commodity'.[121] Even before Wollstonecraft's turn to the problem in her second *Vindication* then, 'woman' frequently named a central tension in eighteenth-century thinking about the morality of commerce, even whilst it was accompanied by a concern about the supposed demasculating effects of '*le doux commerce*' on men.[122]

The dominant metaphor for womanhood in the *Vindication* is the state of slavery and self-dispossession characterised by being the property of another. 'Woman' is thus the negative or inverse of the figure of the person imagined by a commercial modernity which is organised around gaining and owning property. In her reading of Hume's sceptical treatment of the problem of identity, Adela Pinch has noted how property objects and personal possessions might solve the problem of knowing the self, filling through a principle of contiguity the vacuum posed by the epistemological difficulty of securing self-identity. Possessions might 'provide a solid basis for the contingency of self by introducing a more properly proprietary category, such as property: the self may be a fiction, but its horses, carriages, and clothes are not'.[123] Where Hume sees the passions enacting a 'kind of person-ification', tying a 'bundle of perceptions' into a 'recognisable human form one can claim as our own', the same 'person-ification' might be performed by property objects.[124] If this is one way of understanding personhood in commercial modernity, however, it is not available to women. As the *Vindication* shows, women were largely excluded from or periphery to the world of ownership, whether understood as self-possession or possession of property (an analysis further developed in *The Wrongs of Woman*). The 'woman' of Wollstonecraft's title thus reveals enslavement and dispossession as the dark side of commercial modernity's defining concern with ownership and property culture.

Wollstonecraft sees enslavement in every context in which she considers women. '[E]very where' in a 'deplorable state', they are 'shackled' like slaves by the reputational requirement of propriety; they are slaves to the 'sensuality' of man; they endure 'slavish submission' to parents; they are even self-imprisoned in the 'gilt cage' of their beauty.[125] The figure of slavery operated throughout eighteenth-century political discourse as the opposite of the desired state of political liberty, but Wollstonecraft's comparison of women to 'poor African slaves ... subject to prejudices that brutalise' them references a more literal, explicit, form of slavery. The propriety which Rousseau and others recommend for women binds them in a kind of slavery and 'sweetens' the 'cup' of man just like the sugar produced by enslaved persons.[126] Codes of female propriety operate to control sexual behaviour and assure legitimacy in the male line of inheritance: a pointed parallel is thus drawn between two systems of male property ownership at home and in plantations overseas, perpetuated by reproduction on the one hand, and enslaved labour on the other, both sustained by the oppression, even 'brutaliz[ation]' of others.[127] At least for women, there is a route out: rational virtue and the settling of morality 'on a more solid basis' by recognising women as rational beings, without which woman will remain the 'slave of man'. The *Vindication*'s closing paragraphs nevertheless compare the sovereignty of fathers and husbands to that of Russian wife-beaters and Egyptian slave-masters.[128]

The *Vindication*'s larger narrative focuses on the state of 'woman' to show how a social order founded on wealth and hereditary property has stalled human progress. The attack on the property system familiar from the first *Vindication* returns powerfully in Chapter 9 of the second *Vindication* to show the 'pernicious effects which arise from the unnatural distinctions established in society', reiterating themes from the earlier *Vindication* but showing their effects on manners in more detail, especially in ways which relate to women. Property is thus a 'poisoned fountain' from which flow 'most of the evils and vices' present in the current 'modification' of society.[129] A version of Smith's parable of the poor man's son is

Women, Manners, and the Public Good

writ large to describe a domino-effect as the duties of the rich are done by deputies, leaving the rich to a life of idleness which others seek to emulate and attain, and so in 'the next rank … numerous scramblers for wealth sacrifice every thing to tread on their heels'.[130] The respect which virtue should receive is instead given to rank, and property becomes a false religion.[131] Whilst this is a general condemnation, such 'evils and vices' are particularised to illustrate their effects on women.[132] The claim that the system of property and rank impedes morality and humanity is illustrated by showing that female dependence produces vice; women can only be virtuous when independent from men, but dependence inculcates cunning, meanness, and selfishness. Indeed, Wollstonecraft asserts that riches are more destructive to women than men, as wealth enables some men to offer service as statesmen or soldiers, but no such public roles are available to women.[133] The importance of independence, meanwhile, which women lack, is underlined by Wollstonecraft's claim that it is both necessary for generosity and virtue, and associated with discharging the duties of one's station.[134] Female dependence on their property-owning fathers and husbands is thus an impediment to moral action.

The effects of the property system on female manners are addressed through three interconnected areas. Following Smith's account in *The Theory of Moral Sentiments* of the attention-economy centred on Louis XIV, Wollstonecraft argues that, deprived of other resources, women deploy beauty as a kind of property that bestows 'rank' and thus demands attention and bestows social power. Women thus exist as 'short-lived queens' rather than labouring to 'obtain the sober pleasures that arise from equality'.[135] Any apparent power is in fact dependence: 'were it not for mistaken notions of beauty, women would acquire sufficient [strength of body] to enable them to earn their own subsistence, the true definition of independence'.[136] Related to the issue of female social power is the question of female reputation, where, Wollstonecraft observes, 'attention … [is] turned to the show instead of the substance. A simple thing is thus made strangely complicated'.[137] Like the 'false respect' given to 'wealth and mere personal charms', that given to the mere 'show' of reputation blights the 'tender blossoms of affection and virtue'.[138]

Having shown the false respect given to beauty and the skewed operation of reputation, Wollstonecraft generalises her argument to associate women with what she sees as the voluptuousness of power and the indolence of wealth. Women luxuriate in the 'torrid zone' of pleasure alongside, in somewhat overheated rhetoric, the 'noisome reptiles and venomous serpents' who 'lurk under the rank herbage' of 'polished society', where 'there

108   Property, Passions, and Manners

is voluptuousness pampered by the still sultry air, which relaxes every good disposition before it ripens into virtue'.[139] On the 'rank soil' of wealth, idleness has generated 'swarms of summer insects that feed on putrefaction', and women, like men, are rendered weak and luxurious by the pleasures of wealth, becoming 'slaves to their persons', to 'glory in their subjection'.[140] Faux sexual mores also follow: 'so great is [women's] mental and bodily indolence, that till their body be strengthened and their understanding enlarged by active exertions, there is little reason to expect that modesty will take place of bashfulness'.[141] This association of hereditary property with idleness is familiar from the first *Vindication* ('what but habitual idleness can hereditary wealth and titles produce?' Wollstonecraft asked) but women are now among its 'unfortunate victims'. They 'seldom exert the locomotive faculty of body or mind; and, thus … are unable to discern in what true merit and happiness consist'.[142] Indolence not only prevents the exercising of one's faculties and performance of one's duty which in Wollstonecraft's eyes is necessary for the development of reason and virtue; it even prevents women from breastfeeding.[143] At the same time, women are also agents of arbitrary power and privilege, even tyranny. The 'weak woman of fashion' who lounges with 'self-complacency' on her sofa but insults an elderly and dependent petitioner is an 'irrational monster', like a lawless Roman emperor, or a Sybarite, 'dissolved in luxury'.[144] And as 'vicious or indolent people are always eager to profit by enforcing arbitrary privileges', such habits corrupt familial relationships, where rather than the natural affection which should exist, there is only a 'selfish respect for property'.[145] If 'every family is a state', to be founded on understanding and virtue, those in which property is the guiding principle are not just failures in moral and affective terms, but in a political sense too.[146]

Such language shows how Wollstonecraft's analysis of the situation of women bridges into her political economic critique. Lacking the force of any necessity which would stimulate and educate them, women are caught in 'negative supineness'.[147] As society is currently organised, 'what have women to do in society [is] … but to loiter with easy grace'.[148] For Wollstonecraft, happiness depends on the performance of duty, and whilst she implies that it is as wives and mothers that most women will fulfil their duties, she offers other examples of ways in which women might have active lives, including as shopkeepers, physicians, midwives or nurses, farm managers, or business women.[149] All this is neglected, however, as much by the women who neglect maternal duties for flattery, as by wealthy men for whom need does not provide the necessary impetus.[150] It is wholly significant that it is in Chapter 9's discussion of the effects of property that Wollstonecraft addresses the failure of society to enable women to be independent, active, and virtuous, for existing property society ensures that they have no way to make their private virtue contribute to the public good. Her perception that 'in order to render their private virtue a public benefit, [women] must have a civil existence in the State' is thus absolutely key.[151] Here in a nutshell is the thrust of the *Vindication*'s attack on the property order: it inhibits women by excluding them from 'civil existence'. That this claim lies at the heart of the *Vindication*'s argument explains why it was classified as a work of political economy by Joseph Johnson's *Analytical Review*. As both an attack on the manners produced by a system primarily organised by hereditary property and wealth, and the imagining of an improved version of human society, founded on reason, morality, and virtue, it presents an engagement with, and gender-based critique of, the discourse of political economy, which contests the exclusion of women from the sphere of rational action and civil participation, and looks to the constitution of human nature, as well as morality, for the proper foundation of society. As such, it chimes with Pocock's description of political economy in eighteenth-century Britain as a 'nascent social science of a remarkably new order, part of an enduring though increasingly historicized science of natural morality'.[152] Pocock's further claim that political economic discourse is also 'an ideological defence of the Whig ruling order' only underlines the political ramifications of Wollstonecraft's critical intervention, and how much is politically at stake in such 'nascent' knowledge forms.

The *Vindication*'s repeated exhortation of women to unfold their reason and virtue is thus about more than gender emancipation alone: their 'revolution' is the means by which the transformation of commercial modernity will be achieved. Gender is repeatedly mutually imbricated with larger civil and social improvement throughout the work, including often at the ends of chapters, where Wollstonecraft raises her eyes from the specificity of her attention to women to the larger vista within which her argument is located. Thus, Chapter 3 concludes by observing that 'wealth and female softness', which 'equally tend to debase mankind' are 'produced by the same cause': the present organisation of 'civil government'.[153] Wollstonecraft's attention to the cultural and psychological formation of female identity shows that gender is itself a product of the property order, an insight which perhaps explains both Wollstonecraft's profound disaffection for contemporary womanhood (so troubling to later feminist readers), and her 'wild wish' that 'the distinction of sex [is] confounded in society'.[154] If gender is historically constituted and enacted, as an effect and product of manners, then it too might be dismantled in any manners 'revolution'. What modern feminism recognises as gender liberation is an integral part of a larger vision for social and moral reform, a change in the 'very constitution of civil governments': a vision which depends on female reason and virtue for its first step.[155] The abjection of women in late eighteenth-century property society is the weak point through which the whole might be remodelled: if women might be newly considered 'rational creatures', and emancipated to virtuous participation in civil society, the whole edifice of property society might be reformed. Most vulnerable to property society's effects, women are rightly at the forefront of the possibility of change; they thus constitute, as observed earlier, a kind of revolutionary vanguard, although Wollstonecraft never phrases it quite this way. Women are thus both least best situated and also the key to future improvement of society as a whole: their very abjection makes them privileged potential agents of reform, through whom the change Wollstonecraft seeks in the 'manners of the times' might be brought about.[156]

Wollstonecraft's intervention in political economy is motivated not just by the indignation of political oppression and social injustice but also by faith.[157] To strive towards an improved world is not utopian dreaming, she insists; rather we are enjoined by God and by our God-given natures to improvement, to imitate his sublime virtues.[158] This faith-based perspective sits alongside, and runs parallel to, the historical and philosophical elements of Wollstonecraft's thinking. As we have seen in this chapter, Wollstonecraft's attention to our very natures – to our passions, our faculty of reflection, our capacity for reason – secures her argument. At present, she writes, 'the science of politics is in its infancy'; in its place '[b]rutal force has hitherto governed the world', and produced 'the present modification of society', in its 'corrupt state'.[159] A reform of manners – a change in the 'manners of the times' – and especially the separation of 'unchangeable morals from local manners', will change all this.[160] Directly critiquing contemporary manners, including those between the sexes, she extends political language to the sphere of human relations, identity formation, and individual affective experience. Just as the failure of modern morals can be shown in the social units (the family, the married couple) normally excluded from political economy's purview, so too would a manners reform transform not just these spheres, but recast the very relations between private virtue and the public state. In such a world, educated men and women would not be faithless; marriage would be based on affection; women would turn from the looking-glass to their children; men would not visit 'harlots', and mothers would not be coquets.[161] Crossing a manners analysis, with its attention to the minutiae and habits of psychological, affective, and social life, with a political language hostile to oppression and alert to 'legitimate rights', Wollstonecraft builds public virtue on the basis of private virtue, to reject the confinement of women 'to domestic concerns' and to contest political economy's separation of the public world of wealth acquisition from private affect and morality.[162] The 'truly benevolent legislator' will always endeavour 'to make it the interest of each individual to be virtuous', to make 'private virtue' the 'cement of public happiness', thus consolidating an 'orderly whole' by ensuring 'the tendency of all the parts towards a common centre'.[163] In the absence of such a legislator, 'public spirit must be nurtured by private virtue', a formula whose hope of reforming the public world with private morality nevertheless runs the risk of perpetuating their separation.[164] This then is the dream of Wollstonecraft's political economy: the establishment of a 'sound politics' which will diffuse liberty, in which men and women will become more virtuous, and the improvements which human nature itself suggests is possible will be realised.[165]

CHAPTER 4

Political Economy in Revolution
France, Free Commerce, and Wollstonecraft's History of the French Revolution

Sometime in the early months of March 1792, shortly after the publication of her *Vindication of the Rights of Woman*, Wollstonecraft hosted Charles Maurice de Talleyrand-Périogord, leading player in the French Revolution, in her London lodgings. Drinking tea, and also wine, from tea cups, Wollstonecraft and her visitor must have had much to discuss.[1] Talleyrand, to whom Wollstonecraft dedicated the *Vindication*, was the author of a 216-page Report on Public Education submitted to the French National Assembly in September 1791. Calling for both boys and girls to be educated, he nevertheless described a 'differentiated instruction' for girls, appropriate for their exclusion from the political world: the National Assembly's Declaration of Rights (1789) only recognised men over the age of 25 as citizens, preventing women's participation in the political sphere.[2] Talleyrand's argument was grounded in a claim about female bodies, whose delicacy, he suggested, showed that sexual difference is the will of nature: precisely the arguments, as presented by Rousseau, that Wollstonecraft rejected in the *Vindication*.[3] Just as she had in her dedication – whose purpose was less to praise Talleyrand than to bring her work to his attention – Wollstonecraft no doubt challenged her visitor on these views during his London visit.

But other topics, too, must have engaged their attention, given ongoing events taking place across the channel, and Wollstonecraft's status, evidenced by her *Vindication of the Rights of Men*, as an early supporter of the Revolution. Talleyrand was in London for three months from January to March 1792 on a specific diplomatic mission. In October 1789, as the then Bishop of Autun, and supported by Mirabeau, he had proposed that the National Assembly confiscate church property in order to meet national debts: a key move in the establishment of the French revolutionary currency, the assignats, and a measure which, as we have seen, provoked Burke's deepest fears about the revolution in political economy taking place in France.[4] The assignats were at the heart of plans by the Girondin minister of finance, Etienne Clavière, to establish a new, moral political economy, but were rapidly losing value; hence Talleyrand's visit to London, where, carrying letters for Lord Grenville, the foreign secretary, he sought to establish a commercial and political alliance with Britain. In a proposed extension of the Eden Treaty of 1786, which had sought to establish commerce between Britain and France 'on the basis of reciprocity and mutual convenience ... by discounting ... prohibitions and prohibitory duties', Britain was offered free trade with France's colonies in exchange for loans to bolster the assignat.[5] Hopes of such an alliance fell by July that year. As Chapters 2 and 3 have shown, Wollstonecraft's engagement, in both her *Vindications*, was with a British political economy seen through the writings of Burke and Smith, where commercial society is understood through the lens of stadial history, and where anxieties are expressed less about the nation's political structures than about commerce's moral effects. As we have seen, Wollstonecraft's manners 'revolution' looked to private virtue to align individual lives with the public sphere and thus cement the female 'civil existence in the state' which the French Declaration of Rights had just denied. Both *Vindications* resisted the formalisation of political economic discourse as a specialised science of finance detached from larger questions of human improvement and happiness, and instead debated the significance of wealth and commercial modernity in the larger contexts of human improvement, marked by the progress of virtue, reason, and liberty. The presence of the revolutionary legislator Tallyrand in Wollstonecraft's lodgings, drinking from her tea cups, suggests the possibility of a larger horizon, and different perspectives, from which to broach these questions.

By the end of 1792, Wollstonecraft was herself in France, where she was to stay until April 1795. Here she mixed with British radicals supportive of the early phases of the revolution, as well as French reformists and intellectuals; she met the American Gilbert Imlay, gave birth to his daughter, Fanny, and wrote *An Historical and Moral View of the Origin and Progress of the French Revolution*, which Johnson published in 1794. France offered Wollstonecraft a new vista for contemplating political economy, human improvement, and liberty (that recurring theme of the *Vindications*) amidst the galvanising and shocking context of revolutionary politics. Political economic debate here must have appeared less abstract, more particular, and practical, offering the tantalising possibility for theoretical positions to be put immediately into action in the fast-moving arena of the revolution. One issue in particular loomed large: the establishment of free trade in grain, a measure earlier attempted by Turgot, which continued to be supported by the Girondist politicians with whom she and other British radicals mixed, and whose (albeit temporary) achievement Wollstonecraft was to place at the heart of her historical narrative of the revolution. The question of a free grain trade linked the turmoil of revolutionary France with political economic thought, in France and Britain, as the politicians of the day sought to enact – or resist – tenets developed by the French physiocratic thinkers who had also influenced Smith. The stakes in this debate could not be higher, in a country where large parts of the populace spent half their income on bread, where famine was far from unknown, and where in 1789 the annual average price of corn was the highest of the previous thirty years.[6] The issue also tested attitudes to property, as the rights of property owners were pitted against the rights of the poor to subsistence, as upheld in traditional ideas of community and justice. The debate over free trade in grain, beyond pointing to the market as a solution to stockpiling and tariffs, thus posed fundamental questions about property and community, and about the extent or limits of property rights, which were the foundation of eighteenth-century political economy. A debate posing a traditional 'moral economy' against emergent political economy was also perceived to be about liberty: liberty of trade, but also the civil and political freedoms which many saw at the heart of the Revolutionary struggle.

Here then was a new canvas on which Wollstonecraft might continue to trace her story about human progress, and the role of reason and knowledge in the improvement of society and the advance of liberty. And, unusually among contemporary accounts of the early events of the Revolution, the historical narrative which she was to write in 1793–1794 singles out the grain trade, and demands for bread, for particular attention. Wollstonecraft's *Historical and Moral View of the French Revolution* (1794) situated those questions of human improvement alongside an account of the growth of knowledge in the fields of political economy, government, and finance, in which the Physiocrats are singled out for particular praise. Her narrative of revolutionary events, from the calling of the Estates General, to the march on Versailles of 5 October 1789 also gives prominence to the liberation of the grain trade by the King on that occasion, under pressure from the mob and from the National Assembly. Hers is a history which attends to the experiment in free trade as a crucial part of its revolutionary narrative, presenting economic liberation, human improvement, and political liberty as complexly interconnected. But it is one, too, whose attempt to keep faith in improvement via growth in knowledge must acknowledge that the one measure of economic liberty it narrates is achieved in part through the actions of an unapologetically named 'mob': the possibility, then, that change may arrive not only through the gradual progress of enlightenment but through ignorance and the ill-informed passion of 'enthusiasm'. Here then is a test for a 'philosophic eye' which seeks to continue to read revolution as the advance of liberty, and which is still committed to the analytic category of 'manners' to determine the pace and possibility of change, even in the face of what it can also see as corruption, vanity, degeneracy, and self-regard. Even the women whose potential as revolutionary subjects motivated Wollstonecraft's previous work are more complex agents of revolutionary change in her *View of the French Revolution*: freer and more spirited than their British counterparts, but, she fears, easily manipulated by aristocratic counter-revolutionary plots in ways they fail to comprehend. In some ways Wollstonecraft's most ambitious and carefully crafted work, and certainly her most overlooked, *View* also risks being her most contradictory one, which repeatedly negotiates between an ideal account of the gradualist unfolding of human progress, and the chaotic history which it actually narrates, which verges on the anarchy of the immediate moment in which Wollstonecraft was writing.[7]

Wollstonecraft's relationship to the events she narrated, as the philosophical historian of revolution, was not entirely disinterested or impersonal. Even as she celebrated free trade in grain, Imlay planned its import, alongside other commodities such as soap and iron, into France: this was the business which, as Wollstonecraft's letters to him from this time lament, so frequently caused his absence from her and their daughter.[8] Until the collapse of their relationship, Wollstonecraft's hopes for the future were invested in the proceeds of that trade, the profits of which were, she anticipated, to be used to buy a farmstead in America, on which she, Imlay, and Fanny would settle. Such possibilities, perhaps, coloured the rosy-hued view of husbandry and agrarianism which occasionally make an appearance in *View*, where their supposed virtue, domesticity, and simple manners are opposed to the potential corruptions of commerce, especially where speculators and extreme accumulations of wealth are involved. But even in the present, the trade in grain made Wollstonecraft's existence in France possible, as funds from Johnson were received via bills sent through the London merchants Turnbull, Forbes and Co, traders in flour, for whom Johnson's co-founder of the *Analytical Review*, Thomas Christie, was a Paris agent.[9] Until autumn 1793, when the French authorities tightened up, firms such as Turnbull's were able to get flour into France, despite the British blockade, often in a three-way play with American firms; their mutual connection with Christie thus gave Johnson a way to get money to Wollstonecraft, as is evidenced by a Wollstonecraft bill requiring Johnson to pay Turnbull £50 for money received from Christie as Turnbull's agent.[10] In the penultimate chapter of her *View*, Wollstonecraft's 'philosophical eye' traces the journey of Louis XVI and his family from Versailles to Paris, captured by the 'mob', and she notes he is preceded by 'forty or fifty loads of wheat and flour', whose symbolic freedom was thus the flipside of his own imminent incarceration.[11] Perhaps she silently noted too, how her own personal liberty, and the improvement and happiness which she sought in the future, were similarly yoked to the fate of grain, which was already indirectly enabling, and which might further provision, what she sought in her own life. On the transport of grain depended, indeed, her very work as a writer and circulator of knowledge, on whose gradual increase she believed the possibility of an improved future for humankind rested.

The Experiment in a Free Grain Trade

The central role played by bread in the cultural imaginary of revolution is evident in a print by the British print satirist James Gillray, published in mid-January 1793, as Wollstonecraft settled into her new surroundings in Paris (Figure 4.1). Entitled 'The Sans Cullotes feeding Europe with the bread of liberty', it depicted, in each of its corners, representatives of European countries (Holland, Germany and Prussia, Italy, and Savoy) having the bread of liberty thrust at them on weapons or at gunpoint, whilst their pockets are picked, or they are otherwise threatened, by thin and raggedly dressed Sans Cullotes. In the centre, John Bull is similarly being force-fed liberty's bread by the opposition politicians Charles James Fox and Richard Brinsley Sheridan, sartorially associated with the revolutionary Sans Cullotes through their red bonnets of liberty and their lack of legwear. Gillray's image literalises violent revolutionary liberty as bread, but it also plays on the material needs often driving political unrest, at a time of bad harvests, high food prices, and hunger. Savi Munjal has observed that hunger was also frequently associated with a lower-class thirst for knowledge, or perhaps with the misfeeding of that hunger with (as in a 1795 Coleridge lecture) 'poison, not food; rage, not liberty': themes which Wollstonecraft would develop.[12] The scarcity of bread, real or manufactured, recurs in Wollstonecraft's history of the early events of the French Revolution, but whilst Wollstonecraft notes the presence of physical hunger, acting on the knowledge which to her mind will bring about human improvement is too often blocked by degeneracy in morals, corruption in government, and excessive refinement in manners.

The Experiment in Free Grain

Figure 4.1 James Gillray, 'The Sans Cullotes feeding Europe with the bread of liberty'

Bread, and the grain from which it is produced, was also freighted with significance in contemporary political economic discourse, as it had been from at least the 1760s.[13] Wollstonecraft's history foregrounds the sanctioning, by the French National Assembly in August 1789, of the free circulation of grain, 'which had been obstructed by the ancient forms, so opposite to the true principles of political economy', but this action was preceded by decades of political economic debate.[14] In the very first chapter of her history, Wollstonecraft singles out 'the profound treatise of the humane M. Quesnai' as producing 'the sect of the *economists*', but whilst she describes the physiocrats as the 'first champions for civil liberty' who fought against the 'despotism' and oppression of 'enormous and iniquitous taxes', her truncated and telescoped narrative conveys neither the context, detail, and complexity of the emergence of physiocratic thought in France, nor the significant backlash to those free trade reforms which were made or the counter-arguments it met.[15] François Quesnay's physiocratic doctrines emerged as France regrouped following its defeat by Britain at the end of the Seven Years War in 1763, part of a conscious and deliberate attempt to map a different course of national economic development from the British model of international commerce funded by state-backed credit and military conflict.[16] Quesnay argued that agriculture offered an alternative source of economic growth and showed how productivity would be boosted if the grain trade was freed from the numerous forms of regulation and tariffs under which it laboured in France. Smith, who met Quesnay during his time in France from 1764 to 1766, was strongly influenced by physiocratic arguments; he paid tribute to Quesnay in the *Wealth of Nations*, and at one point intended to dedicate the work to him.[17] As Emma Rothschild observes, 'the political economy of food has been an emblem, at least since the 1760s' of what Smith was to describe as the 'obvious and simple system of natural liberty', a system which was also accused of 'heartlessness' by those who preferred a so-called moral economy, in which authorities oversaw food distribution, especially in times of shortage.[18]

Attempts to establish a free commerce in grain throughout France took place whilst Anne Robert Jacques Turgot, whom Wollstonecraft lavishes with praise, was Controller-General of Finances from 1774 to 1776.[19] Similar measures which Turgot had introduced as an official in the province of Limousin in the early years of the decade had mitigated the effects of famine in the region, but attempts to replicate them at the national level, coinciding as they did with bad harvests and political opposition, were perceived to be too radical, and Turgot was forced from office.[20] Wollstonecraft praises Turgot's 'enlightened administration': it offered France 'a glimpse of freedom, which, streaking the horizon of despotism, only served to render the contrast more striking'. But little detail is offered in her highly metaphorical, as well as personalised, account:

> Eager to correct abuses, equally impolitic and cruel, this most excellent man, suffering his clear judgment to be clouded by his zeal, roused the nest of wasps, that rioted on the honey of industry in the sunshine of court favour; and he was obliged to retire from the office, which he so worthily filled. Disappointed in his noble plan of freeing France from the fangs of despotism ... he has nevertheless greatly contributed to produce that revolution in opinion, which, perhaps, alone can overturn the empire of tyranny.[21]

Turgot's failure is attributed in part to character, in part to court opposition, but Wollstonecraft nevertheless associates him with a 'revolution in opinion' which she hopes may 'overturn the empire of tyranny'. Although she gives no detail of either the economic nature of his reforms or their contentious nature (her account contextualises his ministry within a struggle against tax burdens, rather than the attempt to deregulate grain trade), Turgot is clearly a figurehead in the revolutionary 'opinion' which will 'overturn' despotism and 'tyranny'.

But if this early discussion of Turgot eschews explicit comment on his economic policies, elsewhere, and indeed throughout *View*, Wollstonecraft presents the growth of political economic thought as not merely an exemplar, but the outstanding achievement of the Enlightenment progress of reason and knowledge, strongly linked with liberty and human progress. She praises a 'confederacy of philosophers' for drawing 'the attentions of the nation to the principles of political and civil government', and the *Encyclopédie* is noted principally for 'disseminating those truths in the economy of finance, which, perhaps, they would not have sufficient courage separately to have produced'.[22] This is a striking, arguably skewed account of the *Encyclopédie* project, which sought to turn knowledge in many fields away from philosophical abstraction and into the 'workshop' of practice. Nevertheless, referring to the physiocrats in the fashion of her time as 'the economists', she asserts that they carried 'away the palm from their opponents, showed that the prosperity of a state depends on the freedom of industry; that talents should be permitted to find their level; that the unshackling of commerce is the only secret to render it flourishing, and answer more effectually the ends for which it is politically necessary; and that the imposts should be laid upon the surplus remaining, after the husbandman has been reimbursed for his labour and expenses'.[23] Such a 'novel and enlightened system', she suggests, 'so just and simple', could not 'fail to produce a great effect on the minds of frenchmen': simplicity is repeatedly recommended throughout *View* for matters of government and policy, to enable their comprehension by the public, and boost political understanding. And she goes on to attack the 'many vexatious taxes' of the French government, which 'enervated the exertions of unprivileged persons, stagnating the live stream of trade' and were 'almost insuperable impediments in the way of the improvements of industry'. Such taxes were not merely economic impediments to 'the improvements of industry', however, but were also 'extremely teasing inconveniences to every private man, who could not travel from one place to another without being stopped at barriers, and searched by officers of different descriptions … the abridgement of liberty was not more grievous in it's (*sic*) pecuniary consequences, than in the personal mortification of being compelled to observe regulations as troublesome as they were at variance with sound policy'.[24] Such aligning of impediments to personal freedom of movement with regulatory impediments to commerce and industry indicates how Wollstonecraft's understanding of the economic freedoms advocated by physiocratic doctrine was, in her mind, part of a larger philosophy of liberty whose achievement, or otherwise, might be experienced in everyday life. In this context, her suppression, in the earlier account of Turgot's reforms, of their economic detail points to how she folds the story of economic liberty into a narrative of political freedom, resisting the separation of economic measures from the broad sweep of human progress and improvement in which, in her eyes, they are properly imbedded.

Such a sense of the role and place of economic reform is suggested too by Wollstonecraft's presentation of the liberation of the grain trade within a larger political narrative. For her, it is not only an important part of that political struggle, but also, alongside the Declaration of Rights, one of the few achievements of the early revolutionary period: one which (although *View* does not relate this) was however to be short-lived.[25] As the full title of her work emphasises, Wollstonecraft's is a 'historical and moral view' of the French Revolution: within which economic measures may be placed, but against which they will also be judged. Wollstonecraft's yoking of economic reforms into an overarching narrative of liberty is in line too with the approach of the Girondin revolutionaries, who were ascendant during the early period of her time in France, until their fall in June 1793, and with whom she and many other British revolutionary sympathisers mixed. As Rothschild comments, '[t]o see economic freedom as a component of revolutionary freedom was indeed one of the distinguishing principles of Girondin policy'.[26]

In telling the story of economic liberation as part of political freedom, Wollstonecraft was going against the grain of more conservative political forces in the mid-1790s. As Rothschild relates, this period saw a separation take place between notions of liberty in the economic sphere and in political life. In Edinburgh in 1793, Smith's disciple and biographer Dugald Stewart made precisely such a distinction to disentangle Smith's work, with its arguments for economic freedoms, from the accusation of political revolutionary overtones or sentiments: whilst safeguarding Smith's work from political attack, the move also contributed to the establishment of political economy as a distinct, technocratic analysis separated from broader political questions pertaining to human society.[27] In Paris, as Rothschild states, this bifurcation of economic and political liberties took a rather different form: for the Jacobins who came to power following the fall of the Girondins in June 1793, a commitment to revolutionary freedom did not bring with it a continued faith in the economic freedoms for which Condorcet and others had argued. Indeed, fixed food prices, the so-called 'maximum', were a key demand of the Sans Cullotes, who agitated

The Experiment in Free Grain 121

for the removal of the Girondins. Rothschild relates an anecdote from the abbé Morellet, a second-generation physiocrat, and acquaintance and translator of Smith, who was denounced to the authorities in September 1793 as part of a crackdown on suspected opponents to the government.[28] This led to an exchange with his denouncer on the question of the freedom of commerce, which he related in his *Memoirs*:

> Do you not think that freedom is the only means of preventing famines and high prices for subsistence grains? Is it not the case, I added slyly, that freedom is always good, and good for everything? I saw that my praise of freedom embarrassed him, and that he did not dare to argue with it. All in good time, he said to me. But today, the anxieties are too great, and one cannot speak of that sort of freedom.[29]

For Robert Darnton, this exchange represents a confrontation 'between the Revolution and the Enlightenment'. But it also encapsulates the fate of the free trade doctrine in the age of Revolution – politically sensitive, potentially inflammatory – just at the time when Wollstonecraft placed the liberation of grain at the heart of her history.[30]

Morellet's interrogation took place as Wollstonecraft, living with her newborn daughter in the seclusion of the countryside just north of Paris, worked on her own account of the French Revolution. Writing about the achievements of the physiocrats, she claims that the publication of their work in the 'abstract work' of the *Encyclopédie* enabled them to elude the 'dangerous vigilance of absolute ministers', and thus disseminate 'those truths in the economy of finance' which they otherwise would not have had courage to separately publish, or which 'if they had … would most probably have been suppressed'.[31] Wollstonecraft's biographers have commented on the dangerous nature of her writing a history of the Revolution, whilst in France during the reign of Robespierre's Terror. Helen Maria Williams, who was herself imprisoned at this time, advised Wollstonecraft to burn her manuscript. What has been less clearly articulated is precisely the nature of the threat that Wollstonecraft's *View* might have posed. Yet beneath its reading of the early years of the Revolution as part of humanity's long progress towards freedom is an insistence on economic liberty, including the specific policy of a free grain trade, as a central plank of that freedom. By the time that she was working on her history, many of Wollstonecraft's Girondin associates and sympathisers had been removed from power or imprisoned; in October 1793, the Girondin deputies were guillotined, an event which produced in her an 'intolerable' anguish which she described to William Godwin 'more than once' in later years.[32] Jacobin doctrine, as Morellet's anecdote relates, was in the ascendency, and those who held different views risked being denounced, and potential death. Just as the physiocrats on whom she lavishes praise smuggled their 'truths' in the *Encyclopédie* to evade detection, was Wollstonecraft also hiding a dangerous sympathy for Girondin free trade doctrines, within the pages of a 'Historical and Moral' progress of the Revolution?

Free Commerce, Peace, and Liberty in the 1780s

It is certainly possible to trace Wollstonecraft's links – direct and indirect, personal, political, and intellectual – with an international network of philosophers, politicians, and thinkers who supported the establishment of free commerce as part of a wider political vision, from at least the 1780s and into the early years of the 1790s. As Richard Whatmore has shown, many such figures, including Morellet himself, had links to the British politician William Petty, Lord Shelburne, but the group also reached across both the Atlantic and the English Channel.[33] Some of the connections dated from the time of Adam Smith's visit to France, in 1764–1766, when he met Turgot, Morellet, and other physiocratic thinkers; others became protagonists in the early dramas of the French Revolution and had their actions or speeches related in Wollstonecraft's *View*.[34] Collectively, this network of thinkers and their interconnected ideas and writings illuminates the immediate prehistory and context for both the presentation of economic liberty and free trade in Wollstonecraft's *View* and the issue of the free trade in grain in France in the early 1790s. Above all, it points to the great importance placed on free commerce as part of a larger transformation of international relations, which it was possible to imagine in the years between the American and French Revolutions. This new international order, which Shelburne anticipated, would replace a mercantilist competition between nations, fuelled by war, with free trade and political reform. From one perspective, the short-lived Eden Treaty (1786), which sought more liberalised trade between Britain and France, was the only tangible political outcome of such thinking; this was what Tallyrand, emissary of the Girondist party, was seeking to extend during his visit to London in the early months of 1792. From another perspective, however, the writing and thinking of this extensive network mark an important stage of progressive political thought in the years immediately preceding the French Revolution and illuminate what was at stake for some of its protagonists.

The nature and thinking of this pro-free commerce network can be shown by mapping the connections between various members of the

Free Commerce, Peace, and Liberty in the 1780s   123

Shelburne circle in the mid-1780s. The circle included Morellet, who had met Shelburne in Paris in 1771, and to whom, as well as to Smith, Shelburne attributed his 'first imbibing' the 'application of the principle of the liberty of trade to diverse questions of political economy'.[35] Shelburne later gave Morellet a copy of Smith's *The Wealth of Nations* on its publication in 1776. As a Secretary of State in Rockingham's ministry, and later briefly in 1782–1783 as head of his own administration, Shelburne saw the opportunity to establish a 'general freedom of commerce' whose first steps would be an alliance with France 'for free trade and political reform'.[36] Morellet was involved in the negotiations towards the Eden Treaty from 1782; his work on this was considered significant enough by Shelburne to warrant an annual pension.[37] Also in Shelburne's orbit was Wollstonecraft's early mentor Richard Price, whose 1776 pamphlet, *Observations on the Nature of Civil Liberty*, summarised Shelburne's views on the conflict with America and the possibilities for peace, and Shelburne continued to instruct Price, his 'dear friend', to inculcate 'these principles', and to 'dedicate your whole time, to cry down war throughout the whole world', in 1786.[38] The context for this exhortation was the publication in 1786 of Condorcet's *Life of Turgot*, later translated into English by Shelburne's close friend and secretary Benjamin Vaughan; Turgot's plan, outlined in that work and promulgated too by Concorcet, was to unite nations in peace under shared principles of 'law, commerce, morality and politics'.[39] Three years later, Price's *Discourse on the Love of Our Country* (1789), the work that prompted Burke's *Reflections on the Revolution in France*, listed Turgot, alongside Montesquieu and Fénelon, in a pantheon of scholars who promoted knowledge of rights and civil government:

> Our first concern as lovers of our country must be to enlighten it. [...] Happy is the scholar or philosopher who at the close of life can reflect that he has made this use of his learning and abilities, but happier far must he be if, at the same time, he has reason to believe he has been successful and actually contributed by his instructions to disseminate among his fellow-creatures just notions of themselves, of their rights, of religion, and the nature and end of civil government. Such were Milton, Locke, Sidney, Hoadly, etc. in this country, such were Montesquieu, Fenelon, Turgot, etc. in France. They sowed a seed which has since taken root and is now growing up to a glorious harvest.[40]

Price here offers a very particular canon of Enlightenment thinkers. Some are notable for their association with liberty (the republican Milton) or political thought (Locke, Algernon Sidney, and Benjamin Hoadly), but Montesquieu, Fénelon, and Turgot would be recognised as contributing to the branch of civil government that was coming to be known as political economy. Price's presentation of such a tradition was echoed, with slightly different terminology, in Wollstonecraft's *View*. There, she described the 'science of politics and finance' as 'the most important, and most difficult of all human improvements', but one which would eventually advance 'to that state of perfection necessary to secure the sacred rights of every human creature'.[41] Although neither Price nor Wollstonecraft here refer explicitly to 'political economy', both are characterising, and praising, practitioners of knowledge, which would later come to be named by that term.

Another figure in contact with Shelburne and British radicals in the mid-1780s was the French noble Honoré-Gabriel Riquetti de Mirabeau, who was to figure prominently in the early events of the French Revolution, and whose speeches to the National Assembly are included in Wollstonecraft's *View*, where they provide what almost amounts to a case study in the powers and dangers of political eloquence. Carrying a letter of recommendation from Benjamin Franklin, whom he knew in Paris, and who was also 'fascinated by the possibility of establishing a perpetual peace', Mirabeau visited Shelburne in London in 1784, and through him met Price; Morellet was also visiting Shelburne at this time.[42] As Price was to, Mirabeau also linked Turgot with Fénelon in his *Considérations sur l'Ordre de Cincinnatus* (1784), a work written under the encouragement of Franklin and which warned the new American republic against oppression by a newly emergent aristocratic class (Wollstonecraft later also warned of a new aristocracy of wealth). The alternative to this was 'political liberty, religious liberty, liberty of commerce and of industry'.[43] Included in the publication, to further expound on this vision, was a letter sent by Turgot to Price in 1778, responding to his *Observations on the Nature of Civil Liberty*, as well as an abstract of Price's own *Observations on the Importance of the American Revolution and the Means of Making It a Benefit to the World* (1784). As Whatmore comments, '[t]hese texts reiterated the pacific message of the Shelburne circle that European politics could be saved from political immorality by freeing trade and collapsing the mercantile systems of monopoly, which fuelled war or raised the prospect of debt-induced bankruptcies'.[44] If Europe is the immediate concern, however, America also figured prominently as the motivating ground of all three texts, and as a site onto which both political ideals and anxieties were projected. The new American republic was at once hailed as a land of liberty as yet free of the political and mercantile corruptions under which Europe laboured, addressed as the imagined site of further political improvement, and the recipient of warnings about the dangers certain forms of commerce represent to its liberty.

Free Commerce, Peace, and Liberty in the 1780s 125

All three of these notes are sounded in Turgot's letter to Price of 1778, which also explores the connections between, in Mirabeau's words, 'political liberty, religious liberty, liberty of commerce and of industry'. Reflecting on America's constitution, Turgot warns of the danger that the still only loosely confederated states will replicate the European 'jealousy of trade', the rivalry between nations which so marks European affairs. '[S]till involved in the mist of European delusions', some of the states do not perceive that 'the law of a perfect liberty of commerce is a necessary consequence of the right of property', but where that 'sacred principle of considering freedom of commerce as a consequence of the right of property is adopted, all imaginary interests of commerce vanish. All imaginary interests of possessing more or less territory vanish'.[45] Free commerce, a 'necessary consequence of the right of property', thus magically causes territorial disputes and competition between neighbours to disappear. In line with these sentiments, in Turgot's preliminary remarks, he attacks the 'system of monopoly and exclusion which is in vogue with all your political writers upon commerce, except Mr. Adam Smith and Dean Tucker', and comments on how Britain, which has been so successful in the natural sciences, 'could remain so far inferior to itself in the most important of all science, that of public happiness'.[46] Wollstonecraft similarly, in *View*, characterised the sciences of government and finance as among the most important of contemporary knowledge endeavours, linked, as with Turgot, to public happiness. Price reprinted Turgot's Letter in his *Observations on the Importance of the American Revolution* which, whilst having less to say that Turgot on the specifics of free trade, offered a paean to the simple life of the independent yeomen of Connecticut. This appealing depiction of the virtuous manners of the independent husbandman, as exemplified in American settlers, was to be reiterated in the writings of Girondin revolutionaries, and yoked to their vision of a republic of free and moral commerce. It was not a vision, however, which survived the fall of the Girondins in mid-1793, and it depended on the success of the revolutionary assignats, which were already suffering devaluation in late 1792, when Wollstonecraft arrived in Paris.

Price's praise for an America defined by an industrious, independent, and frugal farmer class is strikingly similar to the picture offered in *Letters from an American Farmer* (1782) by Turgot's distant relative, J. Hector St. John de Crèvecœur, which was published only a few years before Price's *Observations*. Crèvecœur, who by 1795 was living in Altona, outside Hamburg, was later to entertain Wollstonecraft as she came to the end of her Scandinavian travels in mid-1795; she notes that he is an acquaintance

126   Political Economy in Revolution

of Imlay's.[47] By this point, Hamburg was a thriving centre for merchants and shipping, including those who, like Imlay and his associate Joel Barlow, were running the British naval blockade of France. Wollstonecraft's *Short Residence in Sweden, Norway and Denmark* records her exchanging with her dinner companion declamations against the merchants of Hamburg who have made vast fortunes from these wars between nations. 'Why, madam', she records Crèvecœur remarking, 'you will not meet with a man who has any calf to his leg; body and soul, muscles and heart, are equally shrivelled up by a thirst of gain. There is nothing generous even in their youthful passions; profit is their only stimulus, and calculations the sole employment of their faculties'. For her part, the more she saw of 'the manners of Hamburg, the more was I confirmed in my opinion relative to the baleful effect of extensive speculations on the moral character … A man ceases to love humanity, and then individuals, as he advances in the chase after wealth'.[48] It is difficult not to read Crèvecœur and Wollstonecraft's dinner observations as marking the death-knell of Turgot and Shelburne's dream of an international order defined by peace and free commerce.

Wollstonecraft and the Girondins: Free Commerce, Manners, and Republican Political Economy

Price and Crévecour were not alone in idealising the supposedly simple manners of America in the second half of the 1780s. In the *Analytical Review* for September 1791, Wollstonecraft discussed *Nouveau Voyage Dans Les Etats-Unites de L'Amerique Septentrionale* (translated as *Travels in the United States of North America*) by the Girondin leader Jacques Pierre Brissot, a work which had first appeared in 1788. Brissot, she asserts, 'writes like an enlightened citizen of the world', with a 'zeal for liberty' which 'appears to arise from the purest moral principles, and most expansive humanity'. Brissot, she reports, travelled to America to 'observe men who had just recovered their freedom', and he reflects that the French, who 'have also obtained our liberty, and have now only to learn of the Americans the art of preserving it', the 'secret' of which 'will be found in their manners, or rather morals'. Brissot's motto, 'without morals, one can gain liberty but not keep it', suggests the 'absolute necessity' of securing these 'in order to settle liberty on a firm basis'. Wollstonecraft gives a few details from his book which exemplify the 'simplicity' observable in the 'manners of every class' in America, including in the 'innocent frankness' of American women, and the friendly relations which exist between the sexes, which contrast with the gallantry and coquetry, or 'sensual

Wollstonecraft and the Girondins

effeminacy', of 'European manners'. The 'artificial polish' of the manners of the rich in France contrasts with the 'purity of morals' which still 'prevails in America', where 'domestic comfort' appears on every side to 'glad the benevolent heart', and 'industry and content ... gave a smiling aspect to the neat cottages that nestled in the most solitary wilds'. In Brissot's writing, America emerges as a country where 'his favourite theories received life by being introduced into practice', a land of 'liberty, independence, and equality'.[49] By the time that Wollstonecraft wrote her review of his work in late 1791, Brissot was at the head of the Girondin party in the French National Assembly, where, with allies and associates who included Etienne Clavière, Condorcet, Thomas Paine, and (until his death in 1791, Mirabeau), he attempted to establish a regime of free trade, and moralised political economy, to promote 'frugality, industriousness and the growth of republican manners'.[50] The republican manners sketched in Price's *Observations* on America, reiterated in Brissot's work on America, and approved in her review by Wollstonecraft, were central to this vision.[51] These ideals were deep-seated: writing his memoirs in prison, in the months between his arrest in June 1793 and his execution the following October, Brissot states that if he could have chosen his place of birth, it would have been 'under the simple and rustic roof of an american (*sic*) husbandman. That is the occupation which would have made me proud'.[52]

All this was still ahead, however, when Brissot wrote *Nouveau Voyage* in 1788. Long a political radical, and longstanding critic of the French *ancien régime*, in his *Memoirs* Brissot attributes a step-change in his political education to Clavière, a prominent member of the Genevan représantants party, exiled from his home since the failure of the Genevan popular revolution against the aristocratic oligarchy in 1782, which the French had assisted in repressing.[53] Many représantants had links to the Shelburne circle, and to Mirabeau, whose writings, like Brissot's, would also promulgate Clavière's vision: indeed, before taking French citizenship and developing his own political ambitions, Clavière had anticipated that it would be through Mirabeau that his ideas would have influence. Political societies also promoted Clavière's politics, including the Société Gallo-Américane, founded in 1787, which sought to replicate American republicanism in Europe. Crèvecœur, who was in Paris that year, having issued a greatly expanded edition of his *Letters from an American Farmer*, provided information about America to the group and was an active member, as was Thomas Paine.[54] It was replaced the following year by the Société Française des Amis des Noirs, to attack the mercantilism associated with France's finance minister, Necker, and to argue for free trade. Members included Brissot, Clavière, Talleyrand, Condorcet, Morellet, and Dupont de Nemours, who had been secretary to Turgot during his time as minister, and who makes periodic appearances in Wollstonecraft's *View*.[55] As the society's name suggests, Clavière also opposed slavery, which he argued went against the system of liberty which he understood himself to be bringing about. Such activities enabled leading figures in what was to become the Gironde party to develop and articulate their political beliefs. Clavière served as Minister of Finance from 1792 to the fall of the Girondins in June 1793, but he struggled with the depreciating value of the assignats which were central to his political aims. It was as a last-ditch attempt to establish an alliance with Britain to shore up the assignats that Tallyrand was sent to London in early 1792, where he also met Wollstonecraft. When, in January 1793, in the first weeks of her stay in France, Wollstonecraft watched Louis XVI travel to the guillotine, it was in a coach supplied by Clavière.

The fullest exposition of the proto-Girondin reform policy appears in *De la France* (1787), initially published Brissot's name, although with an acknowledged 'debt' to Clavière's 'commercial philosophy'.[56] Arguing for an alliance between France and America to counter Britain's failing mercantile empire, it praised the morally sound life of America and criticised the unnatural growth of the French 'aristocratic' market focused on the production of luxury goods for the wealthy. America exemplified the possibility of a moral political economy, by showing how wealth might be linked to virtue. Public credit and commerce were thought both to depend on, and inculcate, trust and virtue (similar arguments had been made by Paine and Price): commerce helped to forge and sustain sociable relations between individuals, and to build trust, and hence to build the conditions for confidence in public credit. Brissot and Clavière even argued that Britain's defeat by the American colonists in 1776 was due to superior American virtue. Rousseau had previously linked the freedom of a state with the virtue of its people, as expressed in its manners; although, unremittingly hostile to commerce, he would never, as Clavière does, link wealth and virtue.[57] However, crucially, wealth was not to become excessive, as this would undermine virtue and produce inequality; commerce was rather to be used to weaken the old aristocratic order. As Girondin finance minister, Clavière looked to the assignats to create a new, more equitable social order of the moderately wealthy, a 'citizen body of moderate property owners'; in 1789, he had also proposed the melting down of gold and silver luxury goods to increase coinage and extend wealth.[58] As Brissot wrote in his *Memoirs*, Clavière's 'philosophy of commerce' sought to free commerce in order to achieve the 'prosperity of a free people': a 'moral' and 'revolutionary' political economy.[59]

This new regime of moderate wealth and republican morals was conveyed both in accounts of the idealised manners of the Americans, who were showing the way, and in the critique of existing French manners. The French aristocratic consumption of luxury goods skewed the national character and corrupted the passions: the French were shallow, pleasure-seeking, and flippant, devoted to 'frivolous arts', to 'luxury', the 'art of pleasing women, and the relaxation of manners'. Their love of frivolous entertainment was exemplified in the popularity of *The Marriage of Figaro*.[60] In contrast, the life of the American husbandman was 'more virtuous, more free & more happy', in an account praised by Thomas Jefferson in a letter to Brissot.[61] Wollstonecraft also was to foreground morals and manners in her *View*, which offered critical commentary on French habits of living, modes of conversation, and dedication to what is termed the 'art of living'. Indeed, Wollstonecraft attributed the disintegration of the revolution to the weakness and frivolity of the national character, in terms which echo the analysis of Brissot and Clavière. For her, the French character was the site of a conflict between 'folly, selfishness, madness, treachery … and depraved manners' on the one hand, and, on the other, a spirit of liberty released by advancing political and philosophical knowledge. Her attempt to balance such tensions produces an account which differentiates between the 'uncontaminated mass of the French nation', and higher orders 'embruted' by 'servility and voluptuousness', but the most significant historical agency is ultimately located in a 'mob' whose representation is deeply conflicted.[62]

The attention to manners and the French national character in *View* may reflect the concerns of a proposed series of letters on 'the Present Character of the French Nation' envisaged by Wollstonecraft to be the fruit of her French stay, of which only one survives (it may be the only one written). Published by Godwin after her death and written in February 1793, only a few weeks into her time in France, the 'Letter on the Present Character of the French Nation' describes Parisians as superficial lovers of pleasure, dedicated to trivial pastimes and fleeting pleasures. France is 'probably the most superficial [nation] in the world', its people the 'most sensual'. In Paris in particular, the 'soul of Epicurus has long been at work to root out the simple emotions of the heart', such that 'simplicity of manners' is banished by 'the selfish enjoyments of the senses'. Presenting her account as an investigation into the 'stage of civilization in which I find the French', as well as the 'circumstances which have produced its identity', she notes that the 'government' fostered the sensual indulgences which have so marked the Parisians, and anticipates 'the good effects of the revolution', although she is aware these will be 'last felt' in the capital. Her faith in a 'theory of a more perfect state', a 'cherished opinion' that 'strong virtues might exist with the polished manners produced by the progress of civilisation', is however threatened by a 'fear' that vice is a dominant cause of what she sees. Human nature itself, indeed, appears to be altered, such that she doubts '[w]hether a nation can go back to the purity of manners which has hitherto been maintained unsullied only by the keen air of poverty, when, emasculated by pleasure, the luxuries of prosperity are become the wants of nature'. Luxury has become a 'want of nature', a naturalised need, and the possibility of a return to simplicity has receded.

Although *View* would later champion the liberty of commerce as exemplified in a free grain trade, in this Letter, Wollstonecraft appears less convinced of the ameliorative effects of commerce, free or otherwise. The Girondin attempt to create a new social order through commerce might lie behind her observation that a 'narrow principle of commerce ... seems every where to be shoving aside *the point of honour* of the *noblesse*'. As her review of Brissot's *American Travels* had noted, 'honour' is the 'prime virtue in a monarchy', and Wollstonecraft can hardly have mourned its demotion, nor that of the '*noblesse*'. But, perhaps as yet unconvinced by the Girondin sympathisers with whom she would mix during her time in Paris, she suggests that 'little is to be expected from the narrow principle of commerce' which is driving such change in values. And the letter ends with an uncompromising attack on the new political regime, personified in the image of the 'cold calculator' devoted to the art of self-management, who considers his 'fellow-creatures merely as machines of pleasure' and whose 'excess' of 'depravation' preserves him where other 'more respectable' figures fall into traps.[63] There is an echo here of Smith's attack on the 'man of system', incorporated into the last edition of his *The Theory of Moral Sentiments* in 1790, and widely understood as his response to the French Revolution. The 'dregs of the old system', she fears, have remained to 'corrupt the new', and every 'petty municipal officer ... stalks like a cock on a dunghill'.

For whatever reason, Wollstonecraft's Letter was never published in her lifetime, and when she returns to manners in her history of the French Revolution, which she was to start writing in the next few months, her attitude has shifted significantly. The finely honed philosophical despair of the Letter gives way to a narrative in which there is still space for optimism. This is expressed most markedly in the sense that the achievements of the French Enlightenment, especially in the 'science of government', central to public happiness, have helped to disseminate a spirit of liberty, as well as to assemble the practical knowledge needed to achieve reform. Whilst she laments the anarchy of the mob, and fears a descent into chaos,

View retains faith – unlike the 'Letter' – in the possibility of gradualist improvement. What had changed in the short space of time between completing the earlier text, and embarking on the second?

Biography offers some possible answers to this question.[64] Arriving in Paris in mid-December 1792, Wollstonecraft spent her first few weeks in relative seclusion in a near-empty house, mixing little, and nursing both a cold and the emotional aftermath of rejection by the artist Henry Fuseli of her advances back home (an event which in part motivated her desire to leave London). After a period of time, however, Wollstonecraft started mixing with a British expatriate community in Paris which Todd reports was 'embedded in French political life' and 'attached to the faction in power in the Convention, the Girondins'.[65] Wollstonecraft also spent considerable time with Thomas Christie, co-founder of the *Analytical Review*, who had extended stays in Paris between 1789 and August 1793, and who was part of Thomas Paine's select circle, where Brissot also was a regular visitor.[66] According to Todd, Christie was 'deep in politics'; he had been asked by the National Assembly to work on the English version of the proposed polyglot edition of the new constitution, but her association with Christie aside, Wollstonecraft would have met many of the political movers and thinkers of the time, as Todd asserts, at 'salons and dinners' in Paris.[67] Paine and Turgot's disciple and biographer Condorcet, who was also part of these circles, were involved in committees concerned with land reform; Gary Kelly notes that reform of the centralised economic controls of *ancien régime* would have been frequently discussed 'among the business-minded denizens of Christie's Paris salon'.[68] As an agent to the flour merchants, Turnbull, Forbes, and Co, Christie would have had an interest in economic arguments around the grain trade; food provision was in any case one of the main political issues of the day, with grain prices and proclamations, debates, and votes relating to it reported in newspapers.[69] Wollstonecraft would thus have been immersed in social groups made up of Girondin allies and sympathisers, quickly becoming familiar with their preoccupations and the shape of their political thinking. She also could not have failed to experience the febrile political climate of Paris itself, where the availability and price of bread were hot political issues; she may even have witnessed bread riots.[70] This period only lasted for a few short months, however, as in June 1793, the Girondin deputies were arrested and imprisoned under pressure from the Jacobin clubs and demand for the establishment of fixed food prices. At this point, the group of English expats gradually disbanded, especially given the increased level of threat to foreigners following Britain's declaration of war on France in early 1793.

One of those whom Wollstonecraft met in Paris at Christie's house, in April 1793, was of course Gilbert Imlay, whose daughter Fanny she gave birth to in May 1794. It is through the lens of the affair with Imlay that Wollstonecraft's attitude to commerce is often presented: her surviving letters to him, sent during his frequent absences on business, lament that he is 'embruted by trade' and famously attack his 'money-getting face'.[71] The story often told of her hostile attitude to commerce is thus frequently intertwined with that of the gradual breaking down of their relationship, as documented by the seventy or so letters from Wollstonecraft to Imlay from this period (Imlay's letters to Wollstonecraft do not survive). Beyond this, however, the figure of Imlay enables us to plot in more detail Wollstonecraft's exposure to political and commercial affairs in revolutionary France, as well as further links to the Girondins. In the first instance, when Wollstonecraft first met Imlay in April 1793, he was involved in pitching directly to Brissot a scheme whereby through the intervention of an agent provocateur, the new French republic would be able to regain possession of New Orleans and Louisiana from the Spanish. By this point, Brissot had become convinced of the need for France to use war against its enemies to defend the revolution; the Louisiana territory would provide valuable resources. This proposal also brought Imlay into contact with Crèvecœur's son-in-law, the Girondin foreign affairs official, Louis Guillaume Otto. In the event, neither Imlay's scheme, nor those of others making similar proposals (including one submitted by Joel Barlow in November 1793) came to anything. Imlay's involvement, repeatedly pursing the scheme, under Brissot's encouragement, however, illustrates the close and fluid links between the expatriate English and American community of Girondin supporters in Paris, and figures at the very heart of the Girondin administration.[72]

When it became clear that the Louisiana scheme was to fall through, Imlay turned to the project for which he is better known: importing goods into revolutionary France against the British naval blockade, the activity in which he was involved whilst Wollstonecraft was writing her *View*, and which caused the lamentations against his preoccupation with business in the Wollstonecraft-Imlay letters. This was also the reason for Wollstonecraft's trip to Scandinavia in summer 1795, in pursuit of a ship connected to Imlay's business, and the silver it carried as payment for goods, which had gone missing. Whilst it is impossible to reconstruct Imlay's affairs with any certainty, not least due to the secrecy it required, Imlay's biographer Wil Verhoeven has suggested that between 1794 and 1795 Imlay worked either for or alongside his compatriot Barlow in some

Wollstonecraft and the Girondins 133

way, and that Barlow was one of the lynch-pins in the extensive network of American traders importing goods into revolutionary France.[73] Although this activity postdates the fall of the Girondin administration, stemming from Barlow's winning of an importation contract from Robespierre's government in December 1793, Barlow again illustrates the links between Wollstonecraft and her circle and Brissot, the figure at the heart of the Girondin regime. Barlow had made a 'haphazard', 'unfaithful, careless and inaccurate' translation of Brissot's American *Travels*, which, published in February 1792, cannot have been the edition which Wollstonecraft reviewed for the *Analytical Review*.[74] And even after Brissot's death, Barlow was again keeping the flame alive, publishing a translation of the last, revised, edition of Brissot and Clavière's *The Commerce of America with Europe; particularly with France and Great-Britain*, prefaced by a biographical sketch which included his eyewitness account of Brissot's execution.[75] The *Analytical Review* also continued to commemorate Brissot, remembering him in 1794 as a 'celebrated legislator', 'one of the ablest' and 'most virtuous supporters of the French Revolution'; and in a long review of Helen Maria Williams' *Letters Containing a Sketch of the Politics of France from the 31st May 1793 till the 28th of July 1794*, it quoted her praise of the fallen Girondins as 'illustrious martyrs' whose names should be remembered with those of 'Sydney, Russell and Hampden', linking them into a pantheon of fighters for 'the liberties of their country' which, as in Price's *Discourse on the Love of Our Country*, reached back to the English civil war.[76] Neither Brissot nor Clavière are mentioned in Wollstonecraft's *View*, although Mirabeau, who had died well before Wollstonecraft started work on her history, makes regular appearances in the work, and there are obvious reasons, relating to the nature of the political climate in France when she was writing the work in 1793–1794, why Wollstonecraft may have considered it prudent to omit their names from the historical record. Their absence there, however, should not obscure the many clear links between Wollstonecraft and the Girondin circle, and their policy of free commerce as part of a 'system of liberty' and republican manners was to have a central place in her historical narrative.

We saw at the start of this section that the idealisation of the simple manners of American settlers was part of the ideological vision of those who became the Girondin revolutionaries, and the buying and selling of American land is an activity which again links to Imlay and Barlow. Imlay's hugely popular *Topographical Description of the Western Territory of North America* (1792) fed the appetite of a European reading public avid to soak up its depiction of 'a transatlantic asylum of perfect equality and pastoral bliss', a vision also offered in his novel *The Emigrants* (1793).[77] Imlay's European adventure, then, was in part funded by selling a dream of America to the British. Prior to setting up in the importation business, Barlow, to whom Wollstonecraft remained cool, despite a close friendship with his wife, was involved in selling such a dream even more explicitly to the French. As Verhoeven details, Barlow had first come to France through his involvement in a scheme of questionable legality, in which as an agent of the obscure Scioto Association, Barlow sold American land to would-be French emigrants, who arrived in Ohio only to discover that the land which they thought they had bought was not theirs, and that the promised town of Gallipolis was a meagre settlement of log cabins.[78] Brissot, Clavière, and Wollstonecraft all anticipated, with varying degrees of certainty, emigrating to a new life in the States: Brissot oversaw a land purchase there on behalf of Clavière, in the years immediately prior to the Revolution, and was planning to settle in Philadelphia when the events of 1789 brought him back to France; Wollstonecraft, as mentioned above, anticipated settling with Imlay and her sisters on an American farm, on the profits of Imlay's business. There is a marked contrast between such dreams, both personal and political, and the dirty reality of the business dealings (whether Barlow's land scheme, or the importation business), which might facilitate them. For Wollstonecraft, who died in childbirth in 1797, Brissot who was guillotined in 1793, and Clavière, who stabbed himself in the heart in prison, the day before his trial, the dream of life in America would never become a reality. But in Spring 1794, however, as Wollstonecraft was completing her *View* and preparing for the birth of her daughter, Barlow moved to Hamburg, the 'honey-pot' centre of north European war trade, where in a year he amassed a fortune in his import business.[79] He later returned to the States and, in 1807, moved into a mansion on the banks of Rock Creek, between Washington and Georgetown.

Wollstonecraft's History of the Revolution: The Grain Trade, Political Will, and The Mob

Wollstonecraft's 'Letter on the Present Character of the French Nation' shows the centrality of 'manners' to her first attempt to understand the early years of the French Revolution. This attention to manners, present also in her earlier *Vindication of the Rights of Woman*, was carried forward into her major work of this period, the *Historical and Moral View of the Origin and Progress of the French Revolution*. Wollstonecraft's attention to the failings of the French national character – the 'headstrong' French are

Wollstonecraft's History of the Revolution 135

condemned for their vanity and theatricality, for their 'fatal presumption', despite their 'polished manners' – enables her to explain in part why the progress of knowledge by French Enlightenment philosophers has not yet succeeded in bringing about political improvement.[80] If, as she claims in her Preface, the Revolution was the 'natural consequence of intellectual improvement, gradually proceeding to perfection', and 'sincerity of principles' is 'hastening the overthrow of the tremendous empire of superstition and hypocrisy', she also needs to explain why such processes have been so impeded as events on the ground would suggest.[81] A focus on manners enables her to show the effects of political structures on human personality and behaviour, both before and during the Revolution. The French character is shown to have been corrupted by the *ancien régime*: by the tyranny and oppression of the monarchy and the court, and by laws which were overly complex and impeded understanding. Hence the character failings which were evident in the behaviour of many of those who played leading parts in the National Assembly, where vanity, enthusiasm, pride, and ignorance were all in play, preventing the straight-forward achievement of political economic reform: 'ignorance and audacity have triumphed, merely because there were not found those brilliant talents, which, pursuing the straight forward line of political economy, arrest, as it were, the suffrage of every well disposed citizen'.[82]

Wollstonecraft finds it all too easy to show the difficulties of political economic reform in this context. Narrating the failure of the Assembly to take measures to address France's deficit during Necker's time as Finance Minister, Wollstonecraft suggests that an 'able, bold minister, who possessed the confidence of the nation' might have proposed confiscating property and using it as security for a loan to serve the nation's needs and service its existing debt. Such a measure was of course later taken, with the confiscation of church and emigrant property, but Wollstonecraft's point is that it took 'the eloquence of Mirabeau', with its play on human passions, to achieve, whereas reason alone 'would have done the business', and 'men, attending to their own interest, would have promoted the public good, without having their heads turned giddy by romantic flights of heroism'.[83] Reason, and specifically reason in the guise of informed and sensible judgement about political economy, would have made the vagaries of eloquence, dependent on arousing emotional response in its listeners, unnecessary. The significance of this particular issue is underlined by Wollstonecraft's comments earlier in the discussion, on the importance of governments being regular in their demands for taxes: 'the manner of levying taxes is of the highest importance to political economy, and the happiness of individuals', and she argues, in line with physiocratic doctrine, that taxes should be laid on 'land, the mother of every production'.[84] The episode presents physiocratic political economic principles as the best means of achieving happiness and justice, ideally achieved through a version of reason which, given that it can depend on individuals looking after their own interest, bypasses the potential danger of oratorical appeals to passion. All of this, however, is expressed in the subjunctive: what ought to happen, not what actually has. The impediment to the enactment of the kinds of measures which are necessary to the 'happiness of individuals' is not the absence of knowledge, but failures of character. If political economic reform is hamstrung by the inadequacy of the characters of the time, how will it be achieved?

Wollstonecraft's *View* is thus at once a historical narrative of revolutionary events up to October 1789, and a philosophical account of obstacles preventing the unfolding of liberty, in which political economic knowledge plays a central part. Where Price's 'Discourse on the Love of Our Country' looked to 'civil government' for improvements in liberty, Wollstonecraft asserts that improvements in the human condition would ideally follow from progress in the sciences of 'politics and finance', the 'most importance, and most difficult of all human improvements'.[85] Her description of what sounds like a 'science' of political economy makes clear how, far from being an abstract or technocratic endeavour, it directly addresses the consequences for human happiness of governmental acts and policies, as well as taking its cue from human need and from human nature. It thus 'involves the passions, tempers, and manners of men and nations, estimates their wants, maladies, comforts, happiness, and misery, and computes the sum of good or evil flowing from social institutions'. Fully developed, such a project will 'secure the sacred rights of every human creature', the goal which Wollstonecraft has been invoking throughout all her major writings to this point. Its progress, however, is 'retarded' by the 'vanity and weakness of men': a restatement of the problem of the impeding of knowledge by manners, which risks humanity being caught in a vicious circle of political tyranny and ignorance.[86] How then is liberty to be gained and rights secured, in a country where corruption's effects are systematic and structural? In a rare positive remark on Britain, Wollstonecraft suggests (as Brissot and Clavière had, following book three of Smith's *Wealth of Nations*) that dissemination of knowledge, and hence liberty, follows the growth of commerce and the development of a mercantile middle class, but here agricultural and aristocratic France lags behind.[87] If the growth of knowledge and liberty is associated with commerce, here is another reason for free commerce, another justification for freeing the grain trade in particular. There is then much riding on the politics of the grain trade which her narrative traces, which thus carries a symbolic as well as practical significance. But how to kick-start this liberating process, given the existing constraints?

These concerns set the stage for the climactic events of Wollstonecraft's history, described in the last of its five books: the march on Versailles of 5 October 1789 and, importantly, the King's granting of the free circulation of grain. Wollstonecraft, who sees that the 'science of politics and finance' could secure the 'wants, comforts and happiness' of all, would want to read such an act as the expression of the growth of knowledge and the spirit of liberty. But instead it is presented as produced by a complex, ambivalent concatenation of events, involving a 'mob' which has quite possibly been manipulated by court counter-revolutionary conspirators, suspected of spreading rumours of a bread shortage in order to provoke the protestors in a way that would then justify a crackdown. Wollstonecraft's willingness to contemplate such court conspiracies is shared with other revolutionary sympathisers: many believed that 'court factions would stop at nothing to contain political opponents – even conspiring to storm or starve Paris'.[88] But her attention to the role of the mob also means that the act of liberation, the freeing of the grain trade, is produced at least in part by mob pressure, not enlightened knowledge; it thus threatens the very model of historical causation which otherwise sustains both her narrative and her hopes for the future. A theory of the growth of knowledge advancing political emancipation is thus challenged by the reality of actual events. Wollstonecraft's history thus tells the story of the liberation of the grain trade as an episode in the ongoing unfolding of liberty, whilst at the same time placing the 'scarcity of bread', 'the common grievance of the revolution', at the heart of a problem of historical causation and impeded political will.[89]

Wollstonecraft's 'moral and historical' account of the Revolution thus views bread in more than a purely economic light: the scarcity of bread is at the heart of a case study of political will, political knowledge, and the relations between the people, their representatives in the National Assembly, and the King. The possible liberation of the grain trade, a step on the path to broader political liberty, depends on its outcome. But whilst the Versailles chapter ends with an extended discussion of the 'will of the people', which is 'supreme' in theory, but which, 'in the infancy of society, and during the advancement of the science of political liberty' should be somewhat checked by 'the progress of that science', the events

Wollstonecraft relates represent precisely the opposite: the achievement of an act of economic liberalisation, as well as Louis's ratification of the Declaration of Rights, under pressure from an ignorant mob.[90] Whilst both of these measures had been well in train at the moment of the march on Versailles, it was only the arrival of the mob which caused Louis to concede both. And, as Wollstonecraft makes clear, the Parisian mob's will, far from being founded on knowledge, is both readily moulded, and a function of material neediness:

> A scarcity of bread, the common grievance of the revolution, aggravated the vague fears of the Parisians, and made the people so desperate, that it was not difficult to persuade them to undertake any enterprize; and the torrent of resentment and enthusiasm required only to be directed to a point to carry every thing before it. Liberty was the constant watch word; though few knew in what it consisted.[91]

Physical vulnerability has turned the mob into political playthings, an observation which is later echoed in the King's eventual submission to political demands under the threat of his own vulnerability. As Wollstonecraft says elsewhere, 'comforts' are needed for other improvements to follow, so bread's absence is indicative too of the general problem of the impeded political knowledge of the people. But the mob's desire for bread also prompts the philosopher-historian to meditate on motivation in general, and on how fermented passions motivate a populace towards an ultimately unknown goal:

> It seems, indeed, to be necessary, that every species of enthusiasm should be fermented by ignorance to carry it to any height. Mystery alone gives full play to the imagination, men pursuing with ardour objects indistinctly seen or understood, because each man shapes them to his taste, and looks for something beyond even his own conception, when he is unable to form a just idea.[92]

Here the possibility that Wollstonecraft contemplated in the account of the National Assembly's financial management discussed earlier, that trusting to 'reason' and men 'attending to their own interest' would be sufficient, appears unreachably remote.[93] The alternative depiction of motivation presented here is distinctly double-edged. On the one hand, enthusiasm fermented by ignorance hardly amounts to an ideal Enlightenment prescription for historical or political change. On the other hand, given the obstacles to actions founded on existing political economic knowledge which she has already described, pursuing 'with ardour objects indistinctly seen or understood' would appear to be the inevitable condition of all

Wollstonecraft's History of the Revolution 139

seeking political improvements. In their need for bread, the Parisians might thus exemplify the human condition in relation to political improvement, in general: experiencing need and desire, but lacking the knowledge to attain their goal, they are spurred on by fermented passion. Of course, the potential outcome of such process might be the anarchy into which Wollstonecraft fears that France has tipped at the time of her writing; her insistence that improvement follows the gradual advance of knowledge is an attempt to contain such dangerous, potentially excessive, passions. Yet her depiction of the eager pursuit of objects playing in the imagination, just beyond conception, seems to concede that there is something compelling about the involvement of the passions in political and philosophical pursuits, as the sublime phrasing indicates, and to suggest, too, that the imagination might step in to bridge the gaps which are beyond the reach of reason and knowledge. As Burke had observed in his *Philosophical Enquiry into the Origin of Our Ideas of the Sublime and the Beautiful* (1757), we are moved by obscurity and the unknown. Cast in the pejorative form of the unruly mob, the embodiment of an inchoate force of desire, passion, and frenzy, what the imagination represents here must clearly be kept at bay. Yet its potential to resolve, transform, and recast the difficulty and obstacles in the way of human self-betterment would be one of the themes of Wollstonecraft's next work, her *Short Residence in Sweden, Norway and Denmark*.

At this moment in her historical narrative, however, the political stasis of early October 1789, a moment of suspense amidst revolutionary fervour, is broken by action generated by the absence of bread (or fears of its scarcity), and an act of economic liberation follows. At this moment, as Wollstonecraft relates, the National Assembly was awaiting the King's sanctioning of the Declaration of Rights, as well as his approval of their freeing of the grain trade. Aware of his tendency to 'subterfuge' and 'profound dissimulation', it can do nothing to address the central obstacle which he represents until the mob effect action. Wollstonecraft's own account, bound to its nature as philosophical history, is arguably impinged or blocked too; however, much her 'philosophical eye' can see the need for the progress of the 'science of liberty', her 'duty' as a historian, as she says at the end of the chapter, is to 'record truth'.[94] Faithfulness to the historical record means that a 'philosophical' truth, the 'truth' of political knowledge, embodied in arguments for free trade, can't be fully articulated. Not only the Parisians, then, but the National Assembly and Wollstonecraft too are caught up in an impeded economy, where the circulation of knowledge, provision, and improvement is blocked, and in which liberalisation is needed on all fronts. It is the actions of the mob, putatively motivated by an absence of bread, whether real or not, which mobilise historical action, springing the trap of suspension which has been placed on both events and Wollstonecraft's narrative, though bringing in train problems which foreshadow those of the Terror.

Carefully examined, Wollstonecraft's account of the Versailles events reveals a certain narratorial sleight of hand, which, without explicitly saying so, and in however compromised a way, shows the role of the mob in securing a free grain trade. This is a result which, given her earlier, ambivalent, meditation on the productive power of enthusiasm, offers the best possible outcome to the mobilisation of an ignorant, manipulated rabble. In a significant moment in Wollstonecraft's narrative, an unnamed 'orator' acts as the representative of the people, and voices their 'grievances' to the National Assembly, asking for a 'continual provision of subsistence'; he also notes the people's concern over the delay in the formation of the constitution – a factor which, having been lamented lengthily by Wollstonecraft herself in the previous chapter, adds to his authority. According to a republican tradition of rhetoric, such a speech in the public space of the Assembly could be construed as an important moment of the political self-affirmation of the people.[95] The Assembly's response to his speech is that a free trade in grain has been requested from the King. Whilst Wollstonecraft maintains her orator's anonymity, other accounts name him as Stanislas Maillard, a key figure in the storming of the Bastille. Wollstonecraft's suppression of his identity as a political actor gives him further authority: unsullied with a political past, unburdened by an individual identity, he is merely and straightforwardly a representative of the people. In her account, the orator behaves with dignity when reprimanded for calumny against the clergy; and the extended account offered in the *New Annual Register*, which Wollstonecraft used as one source for her work, of the riotous behaviour of women at the Assembly (occupying the president's chair, drinking, interrupting business) is entirely absent.[96] For Wollstonecraft's reader, this moment might then be read as a rare but exemplary instance of direct communication between the people and their representatives, and one in which, given the Assembly's response, the demands of the people are met by the politicians. But such a reading is only possible if the compromised character and origins of the mob are repressed. Here, Wollstonecraft aids her reader, by earlier asserting that, on arrival at Versailles, unarmed women went to the Assembly, whilst the armed proceeded to the palace. If the mob, via their orator, here appears to enact an exemplary moment of popular petitioning, it is only by forgetting the other reading which shadows this one: of the political efficacy of combined ignorance and physical threat.

With its scene of massed, starving protestors demanding subsistence, Wollstonecraft's Versailles chapter asks to be read in relation to E. P. Thompson's 'moral economy': the responsibility of authorities to oversee grain supplies to ensure provision for the populace in conditions of extremis. It is precisely such a 'moral economy' which would be overturned by the establishment of a free grain trade.[97] Other critics have read what can appear as authorial high-handedness in Wollstonecraft's harsh characterisation of the mob, as ignorance about the operation of such a moral economy as Thompson outlines.[98] But popular protests – food riots – were far from uncommon in eighteenth-century Britain, and Wollstonecraft, whose father was briefly, if unsuccessfully, a farmer, might be expected to have been familiar with this context.[99] In fact, what Wollstonecraft represents in this episode is both a crowd making precisely such demands for subsistence, and the incorporation or transition of those demands into quite a different economic register. Whilst the mob's orator asks, in exactly the terms of the 'moral economy', for a 'continual provision of subsistence', he is answered by an assurance about free grain trade. The same exchange is repeated when a delegation of women petitions the King directly on the same matter, and he responds by sanctioning a free grain trade. In each case, the petitioners appear to believe that their request has been directly granted, when in fact this might be far from being the case: the women, for instance, kiss Louis' hand and return to their peers exultant at his charm and condescension. Where, in previous decades, attempts to establish a free grain trade in France ran into trouble because of their very evident departure from a moral economy provision, Wollstonecraft arguably narrates the establishment of a free grain trade under the cover of compliance with a request for such a provision and shows how a free grain trade is greeted as a moral provision.

This management of the transition between a moral economy and free trade shows one means of bridging ignorance and knowledge, superstition and enlightenment. If the mobilised, petitioning mob is ignorant and enthusiastic, they are met by a National Assembly which, on this matter at least, is already enlightened. Suspended between ignorance and enlightenment, the people can only ask for bread in the old language of feudal provision, but they are met by a new language of free trade. Bread too, as a political object, is suspended between two directions, both looking back to an era of feudal provision and forward to an era of free trade. The political protests, petitions, concessions, and even violence accompanying the arrival of that era, meanwhile, also usefully distract from the detail of what many of Wollstonecraft's readers may well have perceived as the rare (and, as it would turn out, temporary) achievement, amidst the revolutionary turmoil, of a welcome measure of economic reform.[100] But if some form of economic liberalisation is achieved here, the political will of the people is curiously sidelined. On the one hand, their political voice is justified, in that their demands brought about the conditions within which the King was made to act. But on the other, they prove easily duped and manipulated, as they fail to see that what they are granted does not exactly equate to what they demanded. Wollstonecraft's case study of popular political will is thus, at the same time, an examination of mass ignorance. In an insight quite as ironic as her earlier observation on the motive power of ignorance had promised, Wollstonecraft shows how popular political will, so compromised by enthusiasm, proves a sideshow – whilst also being efficacious – to the real political work of establishing economic liberty.

Beyond the Grain Trade: Commerce and the Future of Improvement

Wollstonecraft's decision to highlight the declaration of a liberalised grain trade in October 1789 is unusual among historians of the early phases of the French Revolution. Other accounts of the events at Versailles, including those likely to be known to her, offer what are otherwise similar narratives of events without mentioning the measure: it is absent from Thomas Christie's *Letters on the Revolution of France* (1791), Thomas Paine's *Rights of Man* (1791), Burke's *Reflections*, and Rabaut Saint-Étienne's *History of the Revolution of France* (1792). The conservative *Annual Register*, which draws on Saint-Étienne, makes great play of the bread shortages, but depicts the King not, as in Wollstonecraft, sanctioning the 'decree, relative to the free circulation of grain', but rather, in significantly different terms, ordering 'the immediate supply of Paris with provisions'.[101] In these other accounts, 5 October is significant only for the march on Versailles which preceded the attack on the royal bedchamber of the following night: the event which, since Burke's *Reflections*, was established in the mind of the British reading public as the most resonant emblem of the Revolution itself.

As we have seen in Wollstonecraft's account, the liberation of the grain trade is more than an attempt at economic reform: it marks a larger effort to yoke a chaotic narrative of revolution to that of improvement, and economic and political liberty. By giving special attention to political measures taken to liberate the grain trade, Wollstonecraft finds a way of co-opting

Commerce and the Future of Improvement

the often chaotic narrative of revolution, with all its vulnerabilities to historical accidents and contingencies, to that of reform and improvement, and uniting, if fleetingly, economic and political liberty. In doing so, like the physiocratic economists whom she praises, she disseminates a doctrine of free trade in another form and preserves the improved knowledge of enlightenment even within a historical document of violence and anarchy. As well as a history, then, her work can also be read as a test case in the possibilities for, and fate of, 'improvement', as suggested by 'moral view' of 'progress' announced in her work's full title. Its concern with the grain trade is thus in many ways quite distinct from the debate which was shortly to come to the fore in Britain in 1795–1796 (immediately after *View*'s publication in 1794), when a period of acute grain scarcity prompted political debate over legislative intervention in the domestic market for grain, part of larger discussions over poverty and poor relief.[102] Smith's arguments were used by both sides in these exchanges, in an episode which did much to establish the authority of Smithian political economy at a time when the future direction of political economic thinking was still in flux.[103]

Wollstonecraft's account of the liberation of the grain trade is a case study in the difficulty of bringing about the changes which would further the causes of liberty and human happiness: for her, the ultimate ends of political economy. Like much else which gets underway in the Revolution, however, the 'science of politics and finance', in which she invests such hopes, is far from being in a 'state of perfection'. Like many things in Wollstonecraft's revolutionary history, commerce is at a historical hiatus, suspended, like the mob itself, between two possible futures, of improvement or degeneration, liberty or oppression. At stake too is the relationship between philosophical history, Enlightenment's genre of human progress and improvement, and the new discourse of political economy. On the one hand, a new 'science of finance' might be seen, like philosophical history itself, as a narrative of improvement: the declaration on the grain trade might then be considered, as Wollstonecraft's staging invites, as of comparable importance to the Declaration of Rights itself. But on the other, criticisms which emerge in the last pages of *View* over other elements of political economic thinking suggest that the future of commerce as revealed by political economy may threaten or overturn progress itself. Arguably, Wollstonecraft's very foregrounding of an act of economic liberalisation presents an undecided generic question regarding the relation of the new economic science to the philosophical history from which it emerged, and hence poses too the question of the relation of political economy to morality, and of commerce to narratives of virtue and improvement. This is a dilemma reflected even in the very form of Wollstonecraft's narrative, which wants to present the liberalisation of the grain trade as the culmination of popular political protest, but is thwarted by the possibility that the popular movement is itself motivated by the plots of aristocrats. It is only through release from such aristocratic conspiracies that new possibilities for history and a meritocratic political economy can emerge. The establishment of political economy's narrative of equitable provision via the market thus risks being thwarted by excessive, tyrannical ambition on the one hand, and the all-too-malleable passions aroused by immediate material need, on the other.

The difficulties of integrating economic improvement into philosophical history's narrative of human progress come to the fore in *View*'s final chapter. An increasing foregrounding of political economic questions in its final pages seems to acknowledge that the future of improvement, if it doesn't lie in revolution, is bound up with the progress of both commerce and a 'science of politics and finance', already announced as 'the most important, and most difficult of all human improvements'.[104] For Scottish philosophical history, commerce brings improvement in manners, knowledge, and hence liberty, but, as Smith himself was aware, the division of labour, keystone of the fully articulated capitalist system of economic production, caused members of 'the labouring poor' to become 'as stupid and ignorant as it is possible for a human creature to become'; their 'dexterity' at their particular trade is acquired 'at the expense of ... intellectual, social, and martial virtues'.[105] Wollstonecraft repeats Smith's worry that the division of labour debases 'whole knots of men' who are, 'turned into machines', with 'every noble principle of nature ... eradicated by making a man pass his life in stretching wire, pointing a pin, heading a nail, or spreading a sheet of paper on a plain surface'.[106] Where Smith looks to education to mitigate these effects, Wollstonecraft shows how this arrangement enables 'a keen speculator to become wealthy', attacking the debasement of the lower classes in the process of giving 'convenience' to the 'luxury' of the upper classes, in a 'cast-like division'.[107] And countering Smith's critique of the time wasted by the worker who 'saunters' from one task to another, she asserts that '[t]he time which, a celebrated writer says, is sauntered away, in going from one part of an employment to another, is the very time that preserves the man from degenerating into a brute'.[108] As these comments make clear, the division of labour which Smith placed at the heart of his political economy causes commerce to threaten the virtuous cycle of enlightenment, and the very narrative of enlightened improvement. But Wollstonecraft also aims her fire more broadly, beyond the specific doctrines of Smithian political economy. She is critical of the merchant who 'enters into speculation so closely bordering on fraudulence, that common straight forward minds can scarcely distinguish the devious art of selling any thing for a price far beyond that necessary to ensure a just profit, from sheer dishonesty, aggravated by hard-heartedness, when it is to take advantage of the necessities of the indigent'.[109] The 'necessities of the indigent' invites her reader to consider her remarks in the context of the grain trade, and to reflect whether it might be an opportunity for such profiteering, or a guard against it. Above all, Wollstonecraft warns against the 'destructive influence of commerce' when it is carried on by men made 'eager by overgrown riches to partake of the respect paid to the nobility'. The worst effect of commerce, she asserts, in an echo of other radical writers of the time, is that it 'produces an aristocracy of wealth, which degrades mankind', so that 'savageness' is exchanged for 'tame servility, instead of acquiring the urbanity of improved reason'.[110]

Alongside her praise of the physiocrats, then, Wollstonecraft retains significant reservations about what Imlay, in his *Topographical Description*, termed 'aggrandized commerce'.[111] Periodically in *View*, she offers a glimpse of her favoured alternative: moderate agrarianism, defined by ideals of husbandry, domesticity and contentment, and independent living on the land. It is a vision that looks back to Price's praise of the independent farmers of Connecticut, refracted by Crevecoeur's *Letters from an American Farmer*, but on which, as we shall see in Chapter 5, Wollstonecraft puts her own stamp. At the same time, even whilst *View* represents her closest extended engagement with political economic thinking, little attention is paid to areas of policy other than the grain trade: the issues of the French national debt and the confiscation of church property are only relatively briefly addressed, and the assignats are unmentioned.[112] The specific nature of these omissions, as much as the criticisms of the final chapter, tell us much about Wollstonecraft's understanding of what political economy might be: a way of addressing the needs and wants of humankind so as to address 'the most important end of society, the comfort and independence of the people'.[113] This is a formulation which asks for a return to the territory of manners: how might the political organisation and administration of society and commerce be such that an 'independent and comfortable situation' might be attainable by the many, if not all? In this context, it is a telling indictment of the French, for Wollstonecraft, that they had 'no word in their vocabulary to express *comfort* – that state of existence, in which reason renders serene and useful the days, which passion would only cheat with flying dreams of happiness'.[114] In a glance at Burke, whom as we saw in Chapter 1, yoked a defence of monastic life to the 'toleration' of 'trades and employments' which were recognised as 'servile, degrading, unseemly, unmanly, and often most unwholesome and pestiferous occupations', Wollstonecraft comments that 'whilst lazy friars are driven out of their cells as stagnate bodies that corrupt society, it may admit of a doubt whether large work-shops do not contain men equally tending to impede that gradual progress of improvement, which leads to the perfection of reason, and the establishment of rational equality'.[115] '[A]ll associations of men render them sensual, and consequently selfish', she comments: the quest remains for a way of life, aside from monastic stagnation or the dehumanisation of the factory, which might secure rational improvement, independence, and comfort.

At the very start of *View*, in her Preface, Wollstonecraft attempts to distinguish between the 'uncontaminated mass of the French Nation', whose response to the flowering of Enlightenment philosophy prompted the overthrow of tyranny, and a specific class of people, more closely associated with monarchy and aristocracy, who were corrupted by 'servility and voluptuousness'.[116] Yet the presence and actions of an 'uncontaminated mass' prove elusive over the subsequent pages, which, whether in the complex presentation of the mob, or in the self-regarding and often ignorant National Assembly, too often show only evidence for failures of circumstances or character. The remarks of Wollstonecraft's final chapter suggest that the subject in political economy is similarly embruted, to use a Wollstonecraftian word: by the division of labour, by factory life, by the pursuit of wealth, by moral decline and by mental decay. Rather than a historical progress, we appear to have come full circle: or rather, still to be struggling to imagine the shape of an alternative future which will release us from the trap of the present. As the next chapter will argue, Wollstonecraft's attempt to sketch such alternatives, beyond the ruins of revolutionary hopes, and outside the remit too of a political economy whose future direction she deprecates, will return to the possibility of comfort, domesticity, and independence, in a vision of agricultural independence, and in a territory mapped out by manners. For Brissot and Clavière, a moral political economy had always been about manners and sentiments, and liberty was preserved through manners and morals. These, increasingly linked to a vocabulary of comfort and happiness, and a turn to domesticity as a context for both, are what Wollstonecraft rescued from the collapse of revolutionary ideals, as her quest continued for the conditions in which political improvement might be realised.

CHAPTER 5

Property in Political Economy
Modernity, Individuation, and Literary Form

How silent is now Versailles![1]

Part-way through her *Historical and Moral View of the French Revolution* (1794), Wollstonecraft describes a 'pensive wanderer' visiting the now-abandoned palace of Versailles. Mounting its 'sumptuous stair-case' and reflecting on the 'nothingness of grandeur', the visitor reflects that 'this was the palace of the great king', an 'abode of magnificence' which now only inspires 'pity'. Shifting back into narratorial mode, Wollstonecraft recounts the 'eagerness' with which she described the attack on the Bastille, which 'tumbled into heaps of ruins' the 'walls that seemed to mock the resistless force of time'. The fall of that particular 'temple of despotism' speaks too to the collapse of the power of court and monarchy located at Versailles, a substitutive logic which is perhaps necessary, given that Versailles's palace still stands. Yet, running counter to the would-be implications of such images of ruin, Wollstonecraft goes on to comment that 'despotism' still stands in the current era of 'licentious freedom', and she looks in vain for a 'change of opinion, producing a change of morals' which will render France 'truly free', when 'truth' will 'give life … real magnanimity', when justice will 'place equality on a stable seat', and when 'private virtue' will 'become the guarantee of patriotism'. Government, she concludes, will be perfected when citizens are virtuous.

Wollstonecraft's train of thought here moves swiftly beyond the images of property, both standing and fallen, with which it began, into a realm of more explicitly political thought which pulls towards abstractions – truth, freedom, justice, equality. Such abstractions though, by virtue of her very invocation of them, are unlocated and unlocatable, homeless and disembodied, caught in a much-desired future which is yet to arrive. Equality and all its fellows lack a 'stable seat'. But although the chapter ends on this anticipatory note, somewhere between hope and despair, something of

147

an answer as to where such virtues might be housed has already been suggested in the penultimate paragraph's account of 'smiling' nature presenting to the imagination, as it contemplates the empty gardens of Versailles, 'materials to build farms, and hospitable mansions, where, without raising idle admiration, that gladness will reign, which opens the heart to benevolence, and that industry, which renders innocent pleasure sweet'. The power of such a vision has 'broken the charm' which 'the palace of the great king' would otherwise inspire, enabling 'only pity' to be prompted in the onlooker.[2] This is a vision which replaces not only one kind of property (the palace) for another (the farm and the hospitable home), but which rewrites too the affective qualities which each prompts from the viewer: 'gladness', 'benevolence', and 'innocent pleasure' replace the 'charm' of 'idle admiration'. If the possible futures sought by the abstractions of political thought are eventually articulated, somewhat belatedly, in the chapter's very final sentences, the forms or embodiment which they lack have already here been presented to the imagination by beneficent nature. Whilst philosophical despair emerges as the keynote of the chapter's final cadences, pity lurks as an alternative, would the imagination only attend to the possibilities which nature depicts.

Wollstonecraft's 'pensive wanderer' anticipates the melancholy traveller depicted in her next publication, *A Short Residence in Sweden, Norway and Denmark* (1796), a work rarely read in relation to the *View*, despite the brief period of only two years between their publication. Properties of various kinds, from primitive huts to hospitable family homes, from prosperous farms to the houses of merchants and sailors, are among the objects on which Wollstonecraft trains her 'philosophic eye', as well as her Romantic sensibility, in that work, together with the social formations and economic behaviours (the family, the household, relations between parents and children, or masters and servants; agriculture, commerce, trade, consumption) which they suggest. In this concern with property in different forms, and the affective response which it prompts, Wollstonecraft engages with a central preoccupation of eighteenth-century political economic and moral thought. Property was conceptually fundamental to contemporary political economy: the natural jurisprudence tradition of the seventeenth century, from which political economy grew, had made property and its defence the basis of the nation state; security of property was fundamental to the generation of wealth which political economy theorised. Property might take many forms, including land, the products of work, and rights of ownership; most troublingly, it might include enslaved persons, whether those sold into enforced labour in plantation economies,

Property in Political Economy 149

or wives who, as Maria in *The Wrongs of Woman* reflects, are 'as much man's property as his horse, or his ass'.[3]

Domestic property in particular looms large in political economy's imaginary, so that property's primary, ur-form often appears to be the hut, cottage, cabin, or house.[4] The conjectural history offered in Jean-Jacques Rousseau's *Discourse on the Origin and Foundations of Inequality Among Men* (1755), for instance, identifies the 'age of the cabins', or the move from a nomadic, solitary, savage state to that of social settlements, as crucial in tipping natural man into modernity's property order, a moment as formative for humankind's moral character and affective behaviour as it is for its political organisation. From another perspective, domestic property, and the comfort and convenience which it might offer, does important rhetorical work in exemplifying the gains of commercial society, by contrast with a 'savage' state, in Adam Smith's comparison of the 'accommodation of the most common artificer or day-labourer' and the domestic arrangements of 'many an African king', at the end of the first chapter of his *The Wealth of Nations* (1776).[5] As these two examples show, from the foremost critic of commercial modernity and its most sophisticated theorist, the figure of property, especially in its domestic form, encapsulates and condenses some of the ambivalences and difficulties at the heart of late eighteenth-century commercial modernity. Not least among these are property's association, even among thinkers (including Rousseau and Wollstonecraft) who acknowledge the 'sacred right to property', with some of the most troubling and seemingly unavoidable, even necessary features of contemporary human behaviour. This chapter explores how all of this is in play when Wollstonecraft pays attention, as she so often does, to property and the behaviours and sentiments it prompts, and it suggests that it is through what might be termed her 'property imaginary' that she both critiques the contemporary political economic order and tries to imagine an alternative to it.[6]

These preoccupations are already present in Wollstonecraft's contemplation of the silent and empty Versailles, monument to the property and political order of the pre-Revolutionary age. The topos of the decline of court and monarchical power, and the property organisation with which it is associated, returns in the final chapter of the *View*, where Wollstonecraft elaborates how changing political structures will in turn produce geosocial transformation. Should 'a republican government be consolidated', she suggests, Paris itself will 'rapidly crumble into decay', as its 'rise and splendour' are owing 'chiefly, if not entirely, to the old system of government'; meanwhile, 'as the charms of solitary reflection and agricultural recreations are felt, the people, by leaving the villages and cities, will give a new complexion to the face of the country – and we may then look for a turn of mind more solid, principles more fixed, and a conduct more consistent and virtuous'.[7] It is clear that the abandoned Versailles in the earlier passage stands synecdochically for the collapse not just of the royal court, but of a whole political and economic order, and the forms of living, from cities through to lifestyles, behaviours and morals, which it sustained. In anticipating a 'new order of things' which will follow, Wollstonecraft shares with many thinkers of her time a sense that, after a long century of warfare in Europe and beyond, political and economic structures must be reorganised to enable a more peaceful, perhaps more equitable and virtuous society. Alongside the 'pity' prompted at Versailles then, 'a conduct more … virtuous' must also be rescued from the collapsed and abandoned structures of monarchical corruption and luxury.

The scene at Versailles stages the end of one form of political order by placing the solitary 'pensive wanderer' in stark relief against its ruin. Anticipating the crumbling of Paris into decay, Wollstonecraft suggests that 'it is not likely that the disparting structure will ever again rest securely on it's (*sic*) basis' but the rifts or schisms depicted at Versailles pertain not to the building but to the visitor, who is presented less as a unified self than as dismembered into fragmented parts: the 'solitary foot' which mounts the stair; the 'eye' which 'traverses the void'; the 'fleeting shadow' briefly visible in the 'long glasses' on the walls; the 'bosom' which receives a 'melancholy moral' from the 'frozen lesson of experience'; the 'breath' clogged by the 'chill' air; the 'oppressed heart' which 'seeks relief in the garden'.[8] Although the 'dampness of destruction' properly belongs to the building, it is as though it is the self, recipient of the 'frozen lesson of experience', who is required to rescue and reconstitute itself. The same recovery of the desolate, outcast self, returned to its constituent, pre-social parts following, in its case, rejection by the society it inhabits, is narrated in Rousseau's *Reveries of the Solitary Walker* (1782), with which Wollstonecraft's *Short Residence* was deeply influenced, and which explores similar themes of exile, isolation, abandonment and (perhaps partial) self-recovery. If Rousseau's *Discourse on Inequality* analysed the failings of eighteenth-century commercial society through a conjectural history of progress in which the origin of property marked the fall of the human character in modernity, so Wollstonecraft's Versailles scene sketches the reverse: the end of one instantiation of political-economic order, symbolised by the palace, and the end, too, of the particular constitution of human personhood and community which it required and sustained. The crucial

Domestic Property in Political Economy 151

question is what remains and what will follow it. In the *View*'s final chapter, Wollstonecraft anticipates the arrival of a 'new order of things', but the implication of *A Short Residence* is that any such rebuilding pertains less to property forms than to the individual self and her relation with the larger social whole, a recasting which will come at the cost of the self's near-dissolution. As this chapter will show, a journey which begins in the empty palace of Versailles thus continues in the forests, roads, and settlements described in *A Short Residence*, where Wollstonecraft continues to grapple with alternative possible futures for commercial modernity, as well as the question of her relation to it.

Domestic Property in Eighteenth-Century Political Economy

Smith's comparison of the 'accommodation' of the labourer with that of 'many an African king', in the opening chapter of *Wealth of Nations*, is just one of many instances in which the domestic house, its comforts and conveniences, figure in the argument and imaginary of eighteenth-century political economic writing. In this particular example, Smith evokes the difference between the living standards of the poor European worker and that of 'many an African king' to make a very particular defence of commercial modernity: not that it provides equally for all, nor that it is without its poor, but that it offers them better material living conditions than a pre- or non-commercial society can provide, even for (as he suspects, in a moment of anthropological fantasy) the African 'king'.[9] The economic system that his work will go on to describe is thus defended from the outset on the grounds of material, domestic provision, including in part the domestic 'conveniences' which, for Rousseau in the *Discourse on Inequality*, are the focus of marked invective, described as 'hardly necessary' and even as the cause of mankind's 'degeneration'.[10] The tendency of Smithian political economy towards abstractions (including value, wealth, labour, and circulation) often pulls it away from consideration of the concrete particularities to which it attends at the start of *Wealth* (details evoked include the labourer's coat, his linen shirt, his kitchen utensils, furniture and even his glass window); but nevertheless, the household and its various objects remain in Smith's rhetorical toolkit and are deployed periodically in his writing, as we shall see.

The presence of the house at the outset of *The Wealth of Nations* is a reminder of the domestic origins of political economy itself, in the knowledge of household management. Rousseau's article on 'Economy' for the *Encyclopedie* (also published in 1755 as his *Discourse on Political Economy*) states that the word 'Economy' derived from the Greek *oikos* for 'house', and *nomos*, for 'law', the term later being extended to refer to the government of the state, and distinguished, as 'political economy', from 'private or domestic economy'. Although Rousseau states that 'there will always be an enormous difference between domestic government ... and civil government', he makes repeated use of a comparison between the two in his discussion.[11] Rousseau's article predates the emergence of physiocracy by the so-called 'economists' in the 1760s, usually identified as the origin of modern political economy, but nevertheless an idealised image of the household at Clarens, in *Julie, ou la Nouvelle Héloïse* (1761) provided a focus for what Céline Spector has suggested is Rousseau's alternative political economy, with its agricultural self-sufficiency and natural abundance creating the conditions for moral virtue and social harmony.[12] Rousseau's commitment to viewing economic provision and the material conditions of life through the lens of the household could be seen as a resistance to the more abstracting tendencies of other political economic visions, as it ensures that human well-being and comfort are kept centre stage, whilst wealth is defined not in monetary terms but as a surplus of resources over needs.[13] In Rousseau's political economy, the household, as both a unit of material provision and a moral and social community, signals an acceptance of the institution of private property but mitigates its frequent effects in generating inequality, inaugurating rank, and separating the classes. Wollstonecraft's interest in the household and its associated social formations, in both the *View* and *Short Residence*, can arguably also be read from this perspective. Like Rousseau, who uses letters from Julie's former tutor, Saint-Preux, to describe the Clarens 'domain', Wollstonecraft also chooses the epistolary mode to present her observations of household economies in *Short Residence*: a form which, since Montesquieu's *Persian Letters* (1721), had long been used to address the nature and organisation of European society.[14] Like Montesquieu, whose work Wollstonecraft knew and admired, *Short Residence* uses the letters of an outsider to comment on social organisation and customs in countries foreign to the traveller.[15] Where the *Persian Letters* include story, fable, anecdote, and observation, and Saint-Preux's letters on Clarens are largely descriptive however, Wollstonecraft adapts the epistolary form to give space to individual experience and the lyric voice, thus placing subjective feeling alongside more impersonal observation and elevating happiness as an evaluative measure of what is seen.

In early eighteenth-century economic writing, the house is often used to address the question of wealth distribution, or what Bernard Mandeville, in *Fable of the Bees* (1714), provocatively describes as the 'public benefit'

Domestic Property in Political Economy

of the 'private vice' of luxurious consumption. Mandeville's famous bee-hive is replaced in Alexander Pope's 'Epistle to Burlington' (1731), with the rich man's villa, expenditure on which, whilst an expression of his self-regard, nevertheless has unintended distributive benefits: hence the Mandevillean paradox of his 'Charitable Vanity'.[16] The same idea, that the 'refinement' of 'conveniency' in the 'dress, … table, … houses and … furniture' of the rich constitutes 'the only means that can correct the unequal distribution of property' is present in Edward Gibbon's *Decline and Fall of the Roman Empire* (1776–1789).[17] In such writing, material domestic accoutrements become interpretable through the lens of what, by the late 1770s, is presented as the economic system. But even Smith's *The Wealth of Nations* used the household as an explanatory tool. Its illustration of the distinction between productive and unproductive labour, for instance, demotes the economic importance of the rich man at the heart of a luxurious household, who is waited on by a bevy of servants, by comparing him unfavourably to the capitalist investor: '[a] man grows rich by employing a multitude of manufacturers: He grows poor, by maintaining a multitude of menial servants'.[18] As we saw in Chapter 2, the image of the rich householder did not disappear from political economic discourse, however: Edmund Burke's *Reflections on the Revolution in France* (1790) redeployed the familiar argument about the economic role of the rich landowner to defend the monasteries from the National Assembly's predations. At the same time, as Donald Winch has noted, Burke's defence of the role of the idle rich in maintaining the 'great wheel' of circulation 'strategically dropped' Smith's important distinction between productive and unproductive labour in order to defend wealthy establishments.[19] Despite its strategic evasions, Burke's argument no doubt gained weight by drawing on the century-long deployment of the rich household as the primary example of the providential organisation of the relationship between wealth and poverty, and thus too of social and economic order.

Domestic property also played a role in the visual spectacle of modern commercial society. For both Rousseau and Smith, the visual economy of property – the way it is at the heart of the acts of looking, and of being looked at – is fundamental to the forming and shaping of human nature in commercial modernity, especially in terms of its moral and behavioural consequences. Rousseau's *Discourse on Inequality* offers a conjectural history of a shift from a pre-social, solitary, state in which 'savage man' led a 'roving, vagabond' life with no 'huts, houses, property of any kind' to the 'age of cabins', in which huts are built, families begin to live together, and property is instituted, together with familial affection, social bonds, and sexual difference.[20] Not only do men at this point start acquiring conveniences, 'the first yoke they unwittingly imposed on themselves', but '[e]ach person began to gaze on the others and to want to be gazed on himself'. The formation of judgements of value, beauty, and importance leads to the desire for 'public esteem', a 'burning desire to be talked about' and 'greed for distinction'.[21] Here for Rousseau is the crucial feature of the human character under modernity's property order: a dependence on the judgement and opinion of others which means that '[i]t was soon to one's advantage to be other than one actually was. Being and appearing became two quite different things'; thus 'everything is reduced to appearances, everything comes to be sham and put on – honour and friendship, virtue'.[22] Thus, whilst the 'savage lives within himself; the social man, outside himself, lives only in the opinion of others and it is, so to speak, from their judgement alone that he gets the sense of his own existence'; '[a]ll these evils are the first effects of property'.[23] It is an account which shows, as Rousseau concludes, how 'the soul and the human passions change their nature' and how a society of sham, façade, and artifice arises inexorably from the first institution of property.[24] Thus, for Rousseau, one central problem of property society is what Spector terms its proliferating 'pathologies of recognition'.[25] Smith's account of how the rich man – his example is Louis XIV – sits at the heart of a social network of gazes of admiration, which Wollstonecraft adapted to describe women's objectified status as objects of male attention in the *Vindication of the Rights of Woman*, owes much to Rousseau's analysis. With their identities dependent on and constructed through the gazes of others – caught, in Wollstonecraft's analysis, in a web of desire, vanity, and self-regard – women thus exemplify the problematic of identity in the visual economy of modernity's property order.[26]

Rousseau also informs the story of the poor man's son in Smith's *The Theory of Moral Sentiments*, who, as we saw in Chapter 3, so admires the 'condition of the rich' and their conveniences that he 'finds the cottage of his father too small for his accommodation, and fancies he should be lodged more at his ease in a palace'.[27] This 'fancy' is soon revealed to be a drive powerful enough to sustain the poor man's son's lifetime of labour; generalised as a principle of human nature, it is shown to stimulate and sustain all economic activity in general. Smith's account of the poor man's son's life of labour echoes Rousseau's description, at the end of the *Discourse*, of the 'ever-busy civilized man', who, in contrast to the 'peace and freedom' of the 'savage', 'sweats, scurries about, and constantly frets in search of ever more laborious occupations; he toils until death, and even hastens toward his grave in getting ready to live'. Like Smith's poor

Domestic Property in Political Economy

man's son, he 'pays court to great men he loathes and rich men he holds in contempt; he spares nothing to gain the honour of serving them'.[28] But where for Rousseau, the contrast between 'savage' and 'civilized man' illustrates the loss of freedom, inequality, and corruption entailed by property, Smith's account recoups the benefits of the 'deception' of nature which, causing us to be 'charmed with the beauty of the accommodation which reigns in the palaces and oeconomy of the great', 'rouses and keeps in motion the industry of mankind'.[29] Whilst Rousseau and Smith agree that the visual presence of property in modernity strongly influences human behaviour, Smith suggests that what, at an individual level, is a tragic 'fall' into the deceptive lure of property offers larger benefits in building and sustaining the human civilisation which is able to clothe, house, and feed its members.

Smith also differs from Rousseau in the precise nature of the affect which for him is prompted by looking at the property of others. If, in Rousseau, the onlooker is precipitated into a tsunami of feeling, involving vanity, self-regard, and the desire for the esteem of others, Smith identifies what he claimed was a love of the beauty of the machinery or system which delivers convenience as, he states, underlying our response to the possessions of the rich. This principle, on which he placed great weight, as ultimately stimulating all economic activity and civilisational growth, is presented explicitly in terms of an affective response to domestic property, in the first three examples with which Smith illustrates it. 'When we visit the palaces of the great', he asserts, 'we cannot help conceiving the satisfaction we should enjoy if we ourselves were the masters, and were possessed of so much artful and ingeniously contrived accommodation' he asserts.[30] Refining on Hume, who had suggested that it was the 'utility' provided by such arrangements that pleased us, Smith suggests that it is not the 'very end' delivered by it, but 'the exact adjustment of the means for attaining' that conveniency which ultimately moves us: the beauty and 'fitness' of the arrangement of things which will deliver it. That this is an aesthetic sentiment, an appreciation of a very particular species of beauty, is shown by invoking (again) the example of the house: '[t]he conveniency of a house gives pleasure to the spectator' just as much, he says, as 'its regularity'.[31] And the principle is illustrated with a further domestic example of disordered chairs, previously discussed in Chapter 3. Entering a room to find its chairs disordered, a person will go to the labour of arranging them properly, against the wall, to gain the 'conveniency' of leaving the floor 'free and disengaged', before sitting down on one of them, a tale which for Smith illustrates the labour which we will undertake to gain 'that arrangement of things' which 'promotes' conveniency, rather than the resulting conveniency (sitting on a chair) itself.[32] So convinced is Smith of the power of our appreciation of the 'arrangement of things' which delivers convenience that, later on in *The Theory of Moral Sentiments*, he suggests that those who advise their nation's legislators should describe 'the great system' by which 'all the wheels of the machine of government' might enable its subjects to be 'better lodged … better clothed … [and] better fed', rather than simply invoking that endpoint in itself, which 'will commonly make no great impression'.[33] Seemingly, the aesthetic appeal of an abstracted system is more compelling than the practical necessity of providing for material needs.

At work in the first two instances of Smith's exposition of our love of conveniency is a principle central to the larger edifice of Smith's moral theory: sympathy. Thus, our capacity to 'enter by sympathy into the sentiments of the master' enables us to take vicarious pleasure in the objects and houses which he owns.[34] And it is through this capacity for sympathy with others that Smith seeks to reform and reconfigure the visual economy of commercial society as set out by Rousseau; to rewrite the inevitable network of mutual evaluative looks which exist between social subjects from what in Rousseau are, in Spector's description, varieties of 'pathology' to a morally beneficially operation. *The Theory of Moral Sentiments* sets out the process through which, by looking at others, judging their behaviour, but also and reciprocally, perceiving their moral judgements of our behaviour, a complex economy of visual exchange between social actors establishes moral judgement, standards, and values. Although socially formed, these are internalised through the development of an interior 'impartial spectator'; individual moral self-consciousness, the moral 'self', is thus constructed through dialogic visual exchange of sentiments. Smith worried, however, that our propensity to admire the rich threatened to skew the carefully balanced moral geometry of society's visual field, a tendency which he attempted to address in revisions to the last edition of the *Theory* in 1790.[35] Given the importance placed on the act of looking at others in Smith's moral theory and understanding ourselves in turn as objects for their gaze, the implications of this prejudice in favour of the rich are serious: a corruption of the very moral sentiments by which he hoped the more rebarbative passions of commercial society might be restrained. Rousseau's troubling analysis of the effects of property on human behaviour, morality, and community – on the human personality itself – risked remaining unanswered.

As Michael McKeon notes, Smith deploys a metaphor of domestication to describe the process of 'bringing home' to ourselves the sentiments of others.[36] Indeed, Smith's metaphor leads him to describe this process as one

Domestic Property in Political Economy

which figures our social peers themselves as the very objects, the domestic conveniences, that the poor man might admire in the houses of the rich, for other people become mirrors, the 'only looking-glass by which we can … scrutinize the propriety of our own conduct'.[37] The 'bringing home' to our private selves – the domestication – of the publically available sentiments of others also reverses the move from the domestic to the public, which is embedded in the term 'political economy'. As McKeon observes, such comparison of personal sentiments with those of others to arrive at moral judgement is the corollary, in the field of moral or social psychology, of the role of the market in establishing value in the field of economic exchange.[38] Thus, both the psychology described in *The Theory of Moral Sentiments* and political economy itself are means of 'reconciling individual and society, particular and general', terms reconciled too in the various iterations of the image of the household whose history we have been tracing.[39] The much-celebrated capacity of the house to mediate distributively between individual and society, between rich men's desires and the lives of poor dependents, is thus part of the genealogy or prehistory of political economy's figure of the market, although political economy's preferred image for such a function became that of the invisible hand. To think about the household, and the relations it embodies and symbolises, as Wollstonecraft does, is thus also to open up such terms, and such relations, between individuals and the social whole, anew; potentially even to turn them inside out, as in Rousseau's staging of a resistance to political economy through a return, in his account of Clarens, to the economy of the household.

Unlike many other eighteenth-century women writers, Wollstonecraft did not write a novel centred on the domestic household, but the trace of these debates, and the imagery of houses and other forms of domestic property in which they are articulated, is nevertheless present in her non-fictional writing, as the remainder of this chapter explores. The absence, in Wollstonecraft's oeuvre, of a domestic novel may be significant: the familial household is most likely in her writing to be a space of oppression and neglect, as it is for the eponymous protagonist in the early novel *Mary*, or of sexual abuse, as it is for Jemima in *The Wrongs of Woman*. Indeed, in Wollstonecraft's fiction, the house and the family group it contains figure most often as that from which to escape, as it is for Mary, who flees to nature, to Ann, and then to Portugal; for Maria, who seeks to escape both her family of origin and, later, her disastrous marriage to Venables; for Jemima the jailor, whose stony-faced appearance signals the repression of all the affective sentiments supposedly fostered in the family unit of the house. The short-lived household that Maria and Darnford set up temporarily

158   Property in Political Economy

following their escape from prison is no more successful as a solution to the 'wrongs' of women, although critics are often more optimistic about the all-female household, of Maria, her daughter, and Jemima, as signalled in one of the possible endings of this unfinished novel. Wollstonecraft is alert, too, to the consequences for women of the status of the family property as inheritable, or not, by them: the initial neglect of Mary follows directly from her exclusion from the line of inheritance, during the lifetime of her brother, just as much as her coercion into a loveless marriage to secure the family property after her brother's death, is a consequence of her new legal identity as heiress. In neither situation, it is clear, does property equate with happiness for women. The woman who conforms most obediently to the female role in this property order, Mary's mother Eliza, is reduced to a 'machine', a 'nothing', neglectful of her daughter whilst lavishing affection on her dogs, passive in the face of her husband's infidelity, and brought eventually to a death-bed at which she locks her daughter into the same fate by marrying her to a neighbouring property owner's son, in a chilling conjunction of marriage and female death.[40] As we have seen, on her visit to the desolate Versailles, Wollstonecraft fails to see herself reflected in the 'long glasses' still hanging on the palace walls, which show only her 'fleeting shadow', an uncanny non-reflection which speaks to the impossibility of her measuring, as Smithian moral theory would invite her, the relationship between self and the social order represented by Versailles. In Smith's theory, the 'bringing home' to ourselves of the sentiments of others can take place even in their absence, through the work of the imagination, even in the limit case of sympathy with the dead. The Versailles scene, turning as it does on the possibility, and pathos, of imagining the lives of those who were there and are now absent, invites consideration through precisely such a Smithian lens, yet its reflective mirrors don't work, and Wollstonecraft's visitor remains unseen. Women's place, the possibility of their identity or selfhood, in the existing property order, Wollstonecraft seems to suggest, lies somewhere between these two gothic, impossible choices: the deathly lock of the marriage ring or the non-identity of the ghostly shadow, reflecting only a fleeting escape which struggles to find substantial form.

The Critique of Convenience: Domesticity, the 'Art of Living', and Comfort

Wollstonecraft's fiction continues a critique of the implications for women of the property order of commercial society, which, as Chapter 3 showed, her second *Vindication* had already got well under way. We return to her

Domesticity, the 'Art of Living', and Comfort 159

fiction again in Chapter 6. But another version of that critique, which is often worked out through Wollstonecraft's observations on the physical manifestation of property – in buildings of various kinds, and their inhabitants and manners – is present in her non-fictional writing, especially her *View of the French Revolution* and her *Letters Written During a Short Residence in Sweden, Norway and Denmark*. Wandering around the empty Versailles, the Wollstonecraftian persona in the former work experiences not a Smithian sympathy with the sentiments of those who would once have enjoyed its conveniences, but the more unexpected feeling of pity, a sentiment which for Rousseau is felt by 'natural' man, and so precedes the social order of commercial modernity. Here, perhaps, is a sign of Wollstonecraft's desire to escape a Smithian narrative of inevitable sympathy with the sentiments of property owners, a story to which the aspirational desires and motivation of labour in political economy are so closely tied. The 'charm' once presented by the 'abode of magnificence' is 'broken'; her 'pity' thus signals a critique of the values and attitudes embodied in political economy's existing property order. It is quickly followed, too, by a vision of an alternative form of social organisation which 'nature' presents to the imagination: farms and hospitable homes, for industry and 'gladness', benevolence, and 'innocent pleasures', a vision which was shared by many of Wollstonecraft's radical fellow thinkers.[41] This movement, between recognition of the failings of what exists, and visions, occasionally realised, of what might be, recurs repeatedly too, on Wollstonecraft's Scandinavian travels, as described in *Short Residence*.

One of the hopeful signs of progress mentioned by Wollstonecraft in the *View*'s final chapter, among the general 'advancement of science and reason', is the emergence of 'original compositions' in Germany which employ the judgement to 'estimate the value of things'.[42] Repeatedly for Wollstonecraft, property stages the question of value: of how to value, of what is valued, of conflicting forms of value. In *Wealth of Nations*, the bible of how value-as-wealth is generated through labour, Smith finds space to concede the worth of a lesser form of value, art, and ornament, exemplified through the noble house: 'Noble palaces, magnificent villas, great collections of books, statues, pictures, and other curiosities, are frequently both an ornament and an honour, not only to the neighbourhood, but to the whole country to which they belong. Versailles is an ornament and honour to France, Stowe and Wilton to England'.[43] Whilst acknowledged, however, such values are clearly subsidiary to Smith's focus on the main business of generating national wealth. Like Smith, for whom the regularity of a building, as well as its 'conveniency', was part of its beauty,

160   Property in Political Economy

Wollstonecraft can also appreciate symmetry in buildings as a touchstone for beauty.[44] Her *Hints* for an unwritten further volume of the *Vindication of the Rights of Woman* note that 'Grecian buildings are graceful – they fill the mind with all those pleasing emotions, which elegance and beauty never fail to excite in a cultivated mind – utility and grace strike us in unison – the mind is satisfied – things appear just what they ought to be: a calm satisfaction is felt'.[45]

In Smith, the aesthetic value of the beauty of a noble house receives only a passing nod en route to the larger project of establishing value via the market. In Wollstonecraft, by contrast, aesthetic judgement is deployed to discriminate between what is and isn't pleasing in built properties, and thereby to critique the physical manifestations of political economy's own valoration of convenience. If, in Smith, convenience is ultimately an aesthetic quality, pulling on the passions to motivate labour, Wollstonecraft flips this, offering a critique on the aesthetic grounds of the world that convenience has built. Thus, exploring, in *Short Residence*, two noble houses near Gothenburg, Wollstonecraft is 'delighted' with 'the hand of taste' evident in the 'improved land' of the first, but condemns the 'abortions of vanity' embodied by the second, whilst conceding, in conventional style, how its construction would have beneficially employed and 'improved' the local labourers.[46] In Christiana, however, Wollstonecraft finds the '[l]arge square wooden houses offend the eye', combining size with 'poverty of conception' which 'only a commercial spirit could give'. She links them to what she calls the 'absurd ... argument of convenience', which she criticises for the poverty of its conception: 'Who would labour for wealth, if it were to procure nothing but conveniencies?'[47] The way in which the Christiana houses make visible the values of Smithian political economy founded on convenience enables Wollstonecraft to critique its inadequacies precisely via the ugliness of its material manifestation: the houses embody the rebarbative and reductive values of the pursuit of wealth. This mobilisation of aesthetic critique is not only a rejection of a culture of wealth and property manifested in desirable buildings but also a refusal of the possibility, theorised by Smith, of sympathetic identification with the possessions of the rich. Rather than demoting the question of beauty then, it is by contrast elevated to critique that which seems to Wollstonecraft to embody all the ills of a political economy of 'convenience'. Wollstonecraft's commitment to material beauty, to sensory pleasure and taste, thus counters the demotion of beauty to a lesser plane of value in political economic writing, or even to an invisible abstraction, as in the 'great system' of 'all the wheels of the machine of government' through an appeal to which Smith advised

Domesticity, the 'Art of Living', and Comfort

that legislators might be brought to concern themselves in the interests of their country.[48] Whatever the beauty of that invisible system might be, Wollstonecraft makes clear that its material manifestation eschews any acknowledgement of the need for beauty, sidelining the human experience of pleasure, taste, and self-improvement. And if, as she says, the 'graces of architecture ... ought to keep pace with the refining manners of a people', the Christiana houses suggest that under the reign of 'commercial spirit', human nature itself suffers. As in the *View*'s account of Versailles, an alternative vision is offered within the same letter, as Wollstonecraft recalls the 'very picturesque' cottages and farms she has seen in the remote Norwegian countryside, and relates accounts she has heard of the 'substantial farmers' of north Norway, whose 'independence and virtue' carry her 'back to the fables of the golden age': 'affluence without vice; cultivation of mind, without depravity of heart; with "ever smiling liberty"'. Although she admits she 'wants faith' in such scenes apparently 'sketched by a fairy pencil', the allure of a moderately prosperous, comfortable, and independent life, achieved away from the depravities and 'meanness' of commerce, is undoubtedly very real.[49]

Wollstonecraft's quest for such alternative modes of existence was already under way in her *View of French Revolution*, where her attention to property, manners, and domestic habits was an integral part of her political economic analysis and critique. As she notes in a half-apology in that work's Advertisement, she has been unable to avoid 'entering into some desultory disquisitions' on 'descriptions of manners' which, although 'not strictly necessary to elucidate the events, are intimately connected with the main object'.[50] This analysis of French manners and character often proceeds through an attention to the domestic, even – perhaps especially – when that analysis points in two diametrically opposed directions. By and large, Wollstonecraft's account of the French is far from flattering. Because 'a variety of causes' have 'effeminated' their reason, the French 'may be considered as a nation of women', characterised in terms which recall her rebarbative description of the female sex in the *Vindication of the Rights of Woman*.[51] In that text, women are criticised for their failings in the domestic realm, where they amuse themselves with transient power play and trivial occupations, or else they flee from it to flit, 'helter-skelter' through London in their carriages.[52] Similarly devoted to present pleasures, the French 'sport away their time' without any plan for the future, as 'transient gusts of feeling prevent their forming firm resolves of reason'.[53] Whilst they have refined the senses, their 'susceptibility of temper' leaves 'no time for reflection' or judgements;

their 'effusions of mind' are 'violent' but 'transitory', and benevolence evaporates in 'sudden gusts of sympathy'.[54] It is this association with the feminine, perhaps, which leads Wollstonecraft to express the national character through an unusual attention to the domestic interior: '[i]ndolently restless, they make the elegant furniture of their rooms, like their houses, voluptuously handy'.[55] If Smith's chairs are evidence of a willingness to defer pleasure and undertake labour to gain convenience, effort is short-circuited in Wollstonecraft's reading of the domestic scene, where accoutrements are always already degraded and luxurious. Not simply property, but even the organisation of domestic interiors, is a measure of character, and character weakness: a sign of restlessness, transient attention, and the voluptuous pursuit of pleasure.

This damning analysis does not apply to all those whom Wollstonecraft observed in France, however; there are a 'rational few', often living in the provinces rather than the capital, who have 'really learned the true art of living', a mode again expressed as a style of domestic living. It consists in 'giving that degree of elegance to domestic intercourse, which, prohibiting gross familiarity, alone can render permanent the family affections, whence all the social virtues spring'.[56] This domestic happiness consists in an affectionate 'urbanity of behaviour' in the family, civility and friendship between husband and wife, parents and children, and affability to servants; in mothers attending to the education of their children, in hospitable openness to neighbours, and in the leisurely pursuit of taste and knowledge. Such scenes, in which the different manners of women in particular are noted, recall Rousseau's depiction of the ideal community of Clarens; the 'gladness' which is 'spread ... around' recalls its brief glimpse in Wollstonecraft's vision in the Versailles gardens of an alternative social order. But Wollstonecraft's account of this 'art of living' gains a wider historical significance by appearing at the end of a mini-history of human progress from the 'savage state' to the arts, property, and warfare of modern times. With government ensuring 'the security of our persons and property', an alternative to an age of war should be found through the pursuit of domestic happiness, which Wollstonecraft thus casts as the proper expression or culmination of human society itself:

> domestic felicity has given a mild lustre to human happiness superior to the false glory of sanguinary devastation, or magnificent robberies. Our fields and vineyards have thus gradually become the principal objects of our care – and it is from this general sentiment governing the opinion of the civilized part of the world, that we are enabled to contemplate, with some degree of certainty, the approaching age of peace.[57]

Domesticity, the 'Art of Living', and Comfort

In contrast with the analysis of the *Discourse on Inequality*, a book which Wollstonecraft nevertheless described as 'admirable', the rise of property does not have to be understood as giving inevitable rise to a society of vanity, aggression, competition, and selfishness; rather, the domestic offers an alternative sphere for the cultivation of human happiness and virtue, and alternative objects to be 'the principal objects of our care'.[58] The 'fields and vineyards' evoked here suggest that for Wollstonecraft, this is predominantly an agrarian, pastoral vision, an impression reinforced by the periodic assertion, in the *View*, of the superiority of living in the country – even on the land – to city living. This is a vision pursued in her next work, the *Short Residence*, where however it is also intercut with recurring anxieties about the potential stupor of country life. For the Wollstonecraft of the *View*, however, agrarian life offers a compelling alternative to the lifestyle and manners of commercial modernity, especially if domestic comfort, rather than luxurious and 'voluptuous' convenience, predominates.

Comfort, indeed, is one of the most important words in Wollstonecraft's political economic lexicon, which, whilst apparently innocuous and so easily overlooked, is deployed both in an analysis of the failings of the French *ancien régime*, and in an account of an ideal political economy. The 'comfort and independence of the people' is the 'most important end of society', she asserts; the 'comforts of life' are the 'just reward of industry' which should be attended to by legislators who should seek to secure and extend the 'comforts of its citizens'.[59] The 'duty' of the politician, indeed, is to 'not sacrifice any present comfort to a prospect of future perfection or happiness', and part of the tragedy of the French enthusiasm for revolution is that its rush for change threatens to 'destroy', instead of 'promoting … the comfort of those unfortunate beings, who are under their dominion'.[60] Recognition of how 'intimately their own comfort was connected with that of others' is one of the markers of mankind's progression from a 'savage' to social state, and political understanding itself grows from 'the interest [man] takes in the business of his fellow-men' to 'the comfort, misery, and happiness of the nation to which he belongs'.[61] The new 'science of politics and finance', whose early shoots Wollstonecraft welcomes, would appear to be a continuation or expression of that enquiry, measuring as it does the 'comforts', as well as the 'wants, maladies, … happiness, and misery' of the people.[62] The repeated deployment of the concept of 'comfort' in the chapter of *View* on political economic matters shows how central it is in Wollstonecraft's conception of such concerns. Necker's vague plans on the deficit are condemned as pernicious to both public credit and 'private comfort', and a discussion of currency notes that precious metals, whilst used as the standard measure of value, are 'necessary to our comfort' whilst paper money risks rising prices and so 'all the comforts of life, will bear a higher price'.[63] Elsewhere, pre-revolutionary taxes and customs are criticised for causing people to live hand to mouth, unable and unencouraged, to 'store up comforts' for the future.[64] It is clear that the consequences for the 'comfort' of the people – as opposed, say, to the wealth of the nation – are the gauge against which political economic actions should be measured.

A political economic vocabulary founded on comfort is also connected to a critique of the existing mode of 'civilization', where wealth has become 'more desirable than either talents or virtue', where 'inequality' reigns, and the rich 'tyrannize' over the poor.[65] In France, this proper focus on comforts has been disrupted, in part by a skewed economic development which focuses on the luxury of the upper classes, serving which makes 'machines' of the lower classes:

> Whilst pleasure was the sole object of living among the higher orders of society, it was the business of the lower to give life to their joys, and convenience to their luxury. This cast-like division, by destroying all strength of character in the former, and debasing the latter to machines, taught frenchmen (*sic*) to be more ingenious in their contrivances for pleasure and show, than the men of any other country; whilst, with respect to the abridgment of labour in the mechanic arts, or to promote the comfort of common life, they were far behind.[66]

Here, the pursuit of 'contrivances' for the wealthy – those which, in 'voluptuously handy' form, were earlier linked to the degeneracy of the effeminised urban rich – is explicitly opposed to the more proper object of 'the comforts of common life'. The 'aggrandisement' of courts has sacrificed 'the convenience and comfort of men' in favour of 'the ostentatious display of pomp and ridiculous pageantry'; extravagance rather than 'domestic virtue and happiness' has been practiced.[67] In a final, damning judgement, it is thus telling for Wollstonecraft that the French 'have no word in their vocabulary to express *comfort* – that state of existence, in which reason renders serene and useful the days, which passion would only cheat with flying dreams of happiness'. The French 'had never, in fact, acquired an idea of that independent, comfortable situation, in which contentment is sought rather than happiness; because the slaves of pleasure or power can be roused only by lively emotions and extravagant hopes'. Comfort is linked to a certain affective state, a contentment sometimes also called 'gladness', praise of which recurs in Wollstonecraft's writing. If at times it is sentimentalised and unattainably idealised, it nevertheless contrasts with the more dubious pursuit of pleasure and voluptuous sensation associated with wealth and luxury.

From one perspective, Wollstonecraft's remarks here re-echo Rousseau's attack on a political economy focused on urban manufacturing at the expense of the agricultural countryside. In this respect, her valoration of 'comfort' had already been answered in Smith's demonstration that a political economy open to manufacture, trade, and foreign commerce was the best way of providing for the needs, and comforts, of a nation's population. A Rousseauian political economy, such as he outlines in his advice to Corsica, closed off from foreign trade, and with embargoes on luxury consumption, would jeopardise economic growth and risk stagnation and poverty.[68] But Wollstonecraft is looking beyond an economic argument to one about the effects of different economic lifestyles on the human personality and quality of life. At stake is the question of what kind of life we might lead, and what kind of person we might be able to be, in each economic regime. This was a problem she was not alone in addressing: Smith too shared these concerns, as did his fellow Scot Adam Ferguson, in his *Essay in the History of Civil Society* (1767). But if Smith suggested education as a counter to the mental atrophy of workers under the division of labour, and Ferguson looked to the militia to revive a martial spirit lacking in a modern commercial age, Wollstonecraft addressed the problem at root. It was our 'manner of living', she believed, 'the occupations and habits of life', as well as our education, which 'in a great measure' informs our 'energy of thinking'.[69] From this, it followed that it was from the acquisition of different habits and manners, attained through living differently, that some alternative to commercial society might be attained, and the potential of the human personality realised. The problem, of course, was that in the Enlightenment conjectural history which informed her thinking, manners were a function of an era's socioeconomic 'stage'; Wollstonecraft thus risked being caught in a vicious circle whereby commerce formed manners which constrained and inhibited the possibility of human improvement which depended in turn on a change of manners. In her *Vindication of the Rights of Woman*, she had looked to a 'revolution' in female manners to break out of this bind, but the more thorough political revolution in France which she had just witnessed demonstrated the complexity of these problems. Whilst on the one hand, it clarified for her a vision of an alternative political, economic, and social settlement, centred on the alternative 'true art of living', on the other, it prompted her to advocate for gradual change as a surer way to achieve progress.

166 Property in Political Economy

In the last paragraph of her *View*, Wollstonecraft evokes the 'philosophical eye' which 'looks into the nature and weighs the consequences of human actions': it alone will be able to 'discern the cause' of the tumultuous political events such as she has related.[70] It is a figure which draws directly on Smith's own presentation of the privileged gaze of the philosopher, who, in a society governed by the division of labour, alone has the 'leisure and inclination to examine the occupations of other people'. Smith recognised that the 'acute and comprehensive' understandings of such people would be of no larger social good unless 'those few ... happen to be placed in some very particular situations' where 'their great abilities' might contribute to 'the good government or happiness of their society'.[71] Such a position sounds by no means a foregone conclusion. These questions of the viewing subject, of his or her relation to society, and of the destination or reception of their insights are replayed in Wollstonecraft's next work, which also investigates the very formation of subjects in the property order of modernity. It was perhaps by retracing the origin of the constitution of the human personality in the visual economy of property that some way out of history's bind might be found.

Property in *A Short Residence*: Thoughts
'Attached to the Idea of Home'

Wollstonecraft's *Letters Written During A Short Residence in Sweden, Norway and Denmark* (1796), despite being written soon after the *Historical View of the French Revolution*, is rarely considered alongside that work. *Short Residence* continues the earlier text's interest in property and the habits of domesticity as measurable signs of socio-political organisation, but its attention to property is more complex. The material embodiment of comfort hailed in the *View* is frequently depicted as idealised and unattainable, and the advances of a corrupt commercial age – the 'tyranny of wealth' which commands, everywhere, 'too much respect' – are more clearly depicted.[72] Where *View* offered occasional bursts of optimism founded on a more-or-less sustained faith in gradual improvement through rational enlightenment, *Short Residence* offers an ongoing battle with a melancholic perception of human society in the commercial age, leavened by moments of sublime transcendence or visions of beauty. It is these, rather than a route forward to progress through education and enlightenment, which offer periodic, if temporary, promises of release from the conditions and constraints of the historical moment. In *Short Residence*, the historical problem of commercial modernity, of which property is a

Property in *A Short Residence*   167

visible sign, thus proves to be intertwined with questions of the self: of human formation, of the human personality, and especially of its capacities for self-transcendence; meanwhile literary form emerges as an alternative property mode through which such questions can be framed, and the narrative of selfhood in the commercial age might be recast.

We have already seen how Wollstonecraft critiques a culture of wealth which is embodied in the material assets of buildings: both those, like the houses of Christiana, which illustrate the ugliness of political economy's principle of convenience, and those, like Versailles, which embody the property order's culture of display. Where alterative values are sketched, these are associated with comfort, domesticity, independence, and sufficiency. The 'straight road of observation' of Wollstonecraft's Scandinavian travels enables her to attend to innumerable variants of the home, read as signs of 'the increasing … happiness of the kingdoms' through which she passes.[73] From her first letter, thoughts 'attached to the idea of home' are 'mingled with reflections respecting the state of society I had been contemplating'; the domestic properties associated with such reflections include the 'wretched hut' and the comfortable farmhouse; the merchant's house near Gothenburg, the 'stupid kind of sadness' of the house of the Danish ambassador to London, and the empty palaces and mansions which symbolise a hoped-for decline of aristocratic and courtly power.[74] Each example offers its own instantiation of a mode of human existence, whether the 'true art of living' or otherwise.

As we saw in the previous section, Wollstonecraft can scarcely believe reports of the independent, virtuous farmers of north Norway, whose affluence, liberty, and 'cultivation of mind' take her back 'to the fables of the golden age'.[75] But she sees with her own eyes 'the sweetest picture of a harvest home I had ever beheld!': a 'little girl' mounted on a 'shaggy horse', her father walking at the side of the hay cart, carrying a child, and followed by a boy labouring with a fork to stop the harvested 'sheaves' from falling. Her 'eyes followed them to a cottage' and an 'involuntary sigh' whispers to her heart 'that I envied the mother'.[76] This 'sweetest picture' recalls similar cottage scenes viewed by Rousseau in his *Reveries of the Solitary Walker*, with whose sentiments Wollstonecraft's text is deeply imbued. Stopping on his walks to watch village workers 'repairing their flails, or women in their doorways with their children', Rousseau reports that '[t]here was something about this sight that touched my heart'; like Wollstonecraft, 'I felt myself sighing', although unlike her it is 'without knowing why'.[77] For both writers, the affective tug of such scenes derives from their status as irredeemable outsiders: the attractions of cottage life lie in part in its image of a wholesome social unit, the possibility of rectifying the alienation from the social body which both writers feel. But whereas Rousseau writes as a social outcast following the rejection of his writings by the authorities, what debars Wollstonecraft from participating in such scenes is at once both more personal and more structural. Certainly, her own 'babe' may 'never experience a father's care of tenderness', given her estrangement from Imlay, but equally the cottage mother, seen 'preparing their pottage', reminds Wollstonecraft how much she dislikes cooking. The alluring modesty and comfort of cottage domesticity, so akin to the rural 'arts of living' praised in *View*, runs intolerably, insufferably, against her personal taste, and perhaps something more. The double move, to and from the lure of such scenes, staged a number of times in *Short Residence*, marks a particular problem: of Wollstonecraft (or her persona) being at odds or out of step with her own time, and this is given an almost literal expression through the question of how or where she might house herself, of feeling homeless in relation to the different forms of home (for instance, the urban home or the rural cottage) which might be available to her.

Wollstonecraft and Rousseau were of course far from alone in the attraction they felt for the modest, cottage life. As I have explored in detail elsewhere, the cottage and its related image, of the farm or rural homestead, sheltering virtuous, independent citizens in a society characterised by moderate wealth and relative equality, recurs in a particular tradition of mid-to-late eighteenth-century philosophical and economic thinking, a tradition with which Wollstonecraft was deeply engaged.[78] Richard Price's praise for the 'simple manners' of the 'independent and hardy yeomanry' of Connecticut in his *Observations on the Importance of the American Revolution* (1784) evidenced his belief that the 'happiest state of man is the middle state between the savage and the refined ... between the wild and the luxurious', and Crèvecoeur's *Letters from an American Farmer* (1782) offered a beguiling picture of an American landscape characterised by a 'pleasing uniformity of decent competence', so different from a Europe where the 'hostile castle and the haughty mansion' contrasted with 'the clay-built hut and miserable cabin'.[79] Rousseau's *Social Contract* linked equality with moderation and suggested that the ideal state for humanity was moderate wealth, gentle government, simple manners, and commerce serving happiness. In the mid-1790s, the cottage was everywhere in literary culture: for Johnson's *Analytical Review*, Wollstonecraft herself reviewed (with characteristic acerbity) *The Cottage of Friendship, Juliet: or, The Cottager*, and *Christmas in a Cottage*; her review of Brissot's American travels mentions the neat cottages which contribute to the 'smiling aspect'

Property in *A Short Residence* 169

of 'industry and content' in the 'solitary wilds' between Boston and New York.[80] This omnipresence, sign of an unresolved cultural yearning, marked the difficulty of realising the vision of comfortable sufficiency that Price and Crèvecoeur had articulated. As Gregory Claeys has observed, the desire for a virtuous, simple, egalitarian society, often associated with an agricultural basis, was for many at odds with the pull of cultural progress, associated with commercial society, its refinements, and arts, a quandary expressed in *Short Residence*'s oscillation between the competing attractions of country and city.[81] Ultimately, however, for Wollstonecraft, a return to the cottage threatened indolence, stupidity, and torpor for the modern self. Stupidity – becoming, in the words of Smith himself, 'as stupid and ignorant as it is possible for a human creature to become' – was also recognised as the fate of the labouring poor under the repetitive and mindless regime of the division of labour.[82] To escape stupidity thus represented something of a historical problem, and a circular one. Wollstonecraft herself, despite her praise for Rousseau's 'admirable' *Discourse on Inequality*, refers sarcastically to his 'golden age of stupidity'; in *The Wrongs of Woman*, Darnford, reporting on his sojourn in America, describes how he built himself a house on the land in good settler style, but was driven from it by a longing for 'more elegant society, to hear what was passing in the world, and to do something better than vegetate with the animals'.[83] Much as she is drawn to the country, in the *Short Residence*, Wollstonecraft associates it with the '*inertia* of reason' and reflects a number of times on her need for the stimulation of city life, an urge clearly at odds with her distaste for the ugliness of Christiana, or, later, the devotion to money-making she finds in Hamburg.[84]

The ideal of the cottage thus marked a historical problem: what it means to inhabit commercial society and what must be left behind. Such leaving behind of the simple country life is the foundational story of the stadial history through which Wollstonecraft and her contemporaries understood commercial modernity. Montesquieu's parable of the Troglodytes, in his hugely influential *Persian Letters*, suggested that the virtuous agricultural stage of early human history inevitably gave way to alternative forms in the face of humankind's desire for wealth and political hierarchy; Rousseau's *Discourse on Inequality* also offered a powerful account of humanity's tragic but inevitable fall into property and modernity.[85] Even Smith acknowledged our 'predilection' for the 'charms' of country life whilst arguing that specialisation and the division of labour better enabled market society to provide for the needs of the people.[86] But Wollstonecraft's return to commercial society's primal scene offers a significant variation on these founding myths. For her, there is no return to an idealised pastoral existence not because of the irrefutable call of wealth, a competitive social vanity, or the pursuit of ever more refined material conveniences: rather it is because pastoral 'inertia' does not offer what is needed for the 'improvement of the heart' and the 'understanding'.[87] The attraction of cottage life certainly marks a resistance to the promises and costs of progress and a yearning for a simpler existence – an expression of unease in relation to one's contemporaneity, a temporal dislocation or disavowal which marks a feeling of homelessness within one's current time. But to turn down the lure of the cottage, as Darnford and Wollstonecraft both do, voices a conviction about the needs, and potential improvement, of the human subject in modernity. The unattainability of the cottage life is thus the impossibility of ceasing to be a modern subject: to be suddenly content stirring pottage, or vegetating with the animals; to no longer require the mental stimulation of taste, thought, and educated company. The dilemma, of course, is that such requirements are associated with the very embodiment of commercial modernity, the 'elegant' world of the city, whose attractions might also shade into more voluptuous or degraded ones. To address all this, in *Short Residence*, Wollstonecraft reconsiders the individual's relation to her history, to explore how the resources of modern subjectivity and interiority, of taste and feeling, might be brought to bear on the problem of such dislocated inhabiting of one's time. Also involved, given the centrality of property in accounts of modernity, is a reconsideration of property's role in forming the human person – of individuation through property – and a reformulation of the relation of the individual to the social whole. The problem of how to inhabit one's time thus involves dismantling a story which yokes the modern self to property, and articulating an alternative account founded on the possibility of 'improvement of the heart' and 'understanding' which is at odds with political economy's narrative of the self in commercial modernity. It is this that the conditions of displacement of her Scandinavian travels enable Wollstonecraft to consider.

Individuation and Sympathy in *A Short Residence*

As we saw earlier in this chapter, Rousseau and Smith both link the institution of property with the emergence of society: with affective and social bonds, community formation, and ultimately law and government. At the same time, for both property is also associated with individuation: with the emergence of self-consciousness and a sense of individual difference from others. Rousseau's conjectural narrative describes the shift

Individuation and Sympathy in A Short Residence   171

from the 'savage' state to modernity as marked by the emergence of self-awareness: the savage who lives in a solitary state in an abundant nature has no need of others, and therefore 'lives in himself'; but the 'man of society' depends on others, desires their gaze and approval, and so lives 'out of himself'. His self-recognition, dependent on recognition by others, is thus a state of self-alienation. In Smith's more benign account of the operation of the social gaze in property society, individual moral self-awareness is again achieved through receiving and assimilating the gazes of others, but Rousseau's account of a pressing need for the esteem of others, which can lead to vanity, competition, war, and revenge, is softened into a force for self-moderation and a desire for moral approval. For Smith, the 'natural man' who has not been in society has no sense of his moral self until he acquires this through reading in the faces of others how they are reacting to him. Both Smith and Rousseau offer conjectural accounts by which the contemporary social world, defined by modernity's property order, can be understood in contrast to a hypothesised alternative mode of human life which, it is postulated, may have preceded it. Their accounts of the individual subject, the modern self, are thus historical as well as conjectural: an explanation of the human personality as it appears in the property order of the commercial age.

These themes in Rousseau and Smith – the historical stages of human progress, marked by different property relations and forms of social organisation; the subjection of the individual to the gaze of others; the formation of social bonds and of self-alienation – are all present, and reworked in *A Short Residence*, which reworks too the story of the formation of the self in relation to property and the property order. From the outset, the text's narrating subject has a complex relation to the context of her historical formation: she is a fully-formed modern subject, a product of her time who enacts both philosophical observation and affective response, yet she is also separated, even alienated from her formative origins by virtue of a geographical displacement which appears to send her not only to another place, but to another historical time. In this text, the Wollstonecraftian persona is geographically but also, as it were, temporally displaced from modernity by what she understands as the rudimentary, even backward nature of the settlements she first encounters on landing in Sweden. First disembarking on Scandinavia's foreign shore, Wollstonecraft reports, is like arriving at the beginning of a new world, among men 'who remain so near the brute creation', where life seems 'congealed' at the 'source', and the inhabitants of a 'wretched hut' are '[s]carcely human' and nearly unintelligible.[88] The stage is set for a new mode of historical enquiry into human society as, over the course of her travels, this temporally displaced subject repeatedly views, reviews, and even participates in numerous 'tableaus' (a word Rousseau deploys to describe the ideal domestic scene of Clarens in *Julie*) of domesticity of various kinds. Such household scenes, where differing manners and modes of domesticity are on display, enable her to continue to revolve the questions about manners and the 'art of living' which she has brought with her from France: to reflect on the situations of wives and daughters, the manners of men, the relations of masters and servants, husbands and wives, and the different lives and morals of farmers, sailors and merchants, the educated and the uneducated. But here, questions about the possible progress of human society, and the growth of commerce, are staged in a context where both the consequences of that growth and what preceded it can be seen, in a vision which sweeps from the 'broken spirit' and misery of wretched poverty of the peasants in Sweden, to the economic and material improvement promised in the 'grand proof' of human industry, to an anticipatory, and melancholic mourning for humankind in a future when such improvements have reached their furthest extent, and the planet can no longer support them.[89] Along the way, she warns against the 'tyranny of wealth', bemoans the narrow sentiments of money-getters, and measures the costs and gains of 'progress' through fancy, reflection, and reverie.

These concerns, whilst potentially abstract, are never staged in a purely theoretical way; rather they emerge experientially, through the reflections and observations of the narrator, whose interior experience and repeated absorptions in reverie are as much part of what is being depicted and explored in this text as the external world: self-reflection and social knowledge, self-experience and external experience, go hand in hand. The persistence of Wollstonecraft's inquiry into the different social forms of human existence represents a significant difference from Rousseau's *Reveries of the Solitary Walker*, which nevertheless is an important intertext for her. Where *Reveries* stages Rousseau's withdrawal from the social world of human relations and celebrates his 'complete renunciation of the world' and 'great fondness for solitude', Wollstonecraft's travels represent a new mode of engagement with human society.[90] For Rousseau, who 'in the shade of a forest', seems to himself to be 'forgotten, free, and undisturbed, as if I no longer had any enemies', it is as though the retreat of the *Reveries* removes him from the problems of social life to the simpler forest existence akin to that of natural man. But if Rousseau seeks 'to escape as far as possible the memory of men', Wollstonecraft borrows from the inquiry into the self which Rousseau had modelled, but combines this with an

Individuation and Sympathy in A Short Residence   173

exploration of the nature and variable forms of human society itself, and the self's relation to it.[91]

Central to this exploration in *Short Residence* is the 'dialogic' exchange of the gaze which for both Rousseau and Smith forms social bonds and enables the individual to come into relation with society and to know him or herself. The text repeatedly puts this in play to revisit the story of the formation of the individual through self-consciousness in relation to others and the relation of that individual to the social order of modernity. Yet the play of this formative social gaze takes multiple forms or perspectives, to disturb and make more complex the story told by Rousseau and Smith. On the one hand, Wollstonecraft is, as it were, natural man, brought into society, recipient of the gazes of others, for whom she represents something not previously seen, as for those who are astonished to see a lone female traveller, or who comment that she asks '*men's questions*'.[92] At the same time, Wollstonecraft is the consciously framed philosophical observer, travelling on the 'straight road of observation', attentive to 'my favourite subject of contemplation, the future improvement of the world', whilst also casting herself in the third person, as she admits at the outset, as 'the little hero of each tale'.[93] Thus, in *Short Residence*, the individual subject, divorced from society, set down in its ruins, as it were, at the start of the world, traces something of a reverse of the conjectural history of human progress offered in Smith or Rousseau: the modern subject, the spectator of others, instead of being produced through social interaction with her surroundings, is instead transposed back in time, to view with sympathy and feeling a range of different social establishments, and to judge them appropriately. This geo-temporal transposition recasts what is, precisely, hypothetical or theoretical in conjectural history or moral philosophy, so that any knowledge achieved is arrived at through the gaze of the sympathetic spectator, transposed back through time to different stages of human progress. If, for Smith, our judgements are formed by our social surroundings, and our values are formed by and shared with our peers, in *Short Residence*, travel, as both geographical and historical displacement, enables the transhistorical testing of the self and its relation to different social forms. Thus, one form of political economy might be measured against others (including political economy in Rousseau's deliberately retrograde sense of household management), and modern commercial society submitted to the tests of social judgement and moral sentiments, as well as of taste and feeling. At the same time, the self, undergoing the constant, receptive experience of travel and observation, reveals its multivalent capacity to absorb and assimilate, register, and test the import of what is seen and felt, equally able to respond to the beauty of a young girl's face or the deathliness of Scandinavian pine forests, as to recall details of taxes and customs duties in the countries through which she travels.

The narrative persona's explorations and observations, measurements and reflections, are enacted through the text's characteristic movement, a restless oscillation between the interior self and the exterior world, between subjective experience and social judgement: a movement which echoes that of the sympathetic spectator described in Smith's moral theory. The philosophical 'eye' deployed by Wollstonecraft thus incorporates too the eye of the sympathetic onlooker: she is both an outside observer and a social participant, an object of other people's gaze. McKeon has described the continual exchange or crossing between self and world which is theorised in *The Theory of Moral Sentiments* as offering a form of knowledge which is also a social psychology and an ethics.[94] Wollstonecraft's philosophical understanding of the world and its 'future improvement' is thus a mode of knowledge which is social in two senses: it is arrived at by (in McKeon's words) a 'social dialectic' between subject and external world, and it understands the historicity and socially situated nature of the viewing subject. Similarly, the narratorial persona's interior landscapes and subjective experiences are repeatedly juxtaposed and intermingled with the external scenes through which she travels. The extent of this mixing transcends the 'social dialectic' of visual and affective exchange outlined in *The Theory of Moral Sentiments*, which enables not only social harmony but also 'self-knowledge: we know ourselves only as we sympathetically internalise the social other'.[95] In Smith's words, the self-knowledge acquired in this process is of 'the real littleness of ourselves', learned by 'introjecting' into ourselves the view of us that others have.[96] Smith thus explains how self-knowledge, the 'importance and difficulty' of which is commented on by Rousseau (perhaps surprisingly), in the Preface to *Discourse on Inequality*, might be acquired in commercial modernity.[97] The self-knowledge which Rousseau attempts in the *Reveries* (a text which he described as an appendix to the revolutionary experiment in self-knowledge of his *Confessions*) comes less via social dialectic and more via introspection, social withdrawal, and reverie.[98] Wollstonecraft's mode of self-knowledge in *Short Residence* has elements of both Rousseauian introspection and Smithian introjection. She repeatedly moves between inner and outer, from introversion to external engagement; her reveries or transports take place in the midst of her observations of different instantiations of human society, juxtaposing the Smithian subject's experience of the external world with a depiction of the interior realms such as those attended to by Rousseau's

Individuation and Sympathy in *A Short Residence*   175

solitary walker. Such moments of transport, too, often enact a movement of contemplation on the nature of the self and her relation with material externality, or with others – even, at times, when such preoccupations appear to have been abandoned. In the process, the Smithian story about the relationship of the self to the social order which forms him – the question of individuation – is both pursued and recast.

The presence of such concerns is announced from the very first letter, which stages a crisis in the relation of the self to the social whole, as Wollstonecraft lies awake reflecting 'on the idea of home' and 'the state of society I had been contemplating that evening', thoughts which prompt tears to fall onto the check of her sleeping daughter. 'What … is this active principle which keeps me awake?' Wollstonecraft continues, '[w]hat are these imperious sympathies' which 'made me feel more alive than usual?' Past moods of melancholy and misanthropy, she reflects, have caused her to consider 'myself as a particle broken off from the grand mass of mankind … alone, till some involuntary sympathetic emotion, like the attraction of adhesion, made me feel that I was still a part of a mighty whole, from which I could not sever myself'.[99] As in Smith, sympathy is the foundational social bond, but here it is akin to a material principle, 'involuntary' and 'imperious', somehow greater than the subject whom it overcomes and whose mood it transforms, whose very limits and boundaries it rewrites. Similar reflections on his state of social exile appear in Rousseau's first walk in the *Reveries*, but whilst, like Wollstonecraft, his 'soul remains active', his 'heart has been stripped of all worldly affections': no 'involuntary' sympathy arrives to reconnect 'particle' to the 'grand mass'.[100] The pleasures of his still-persisting, still-active soul are staged a little later in the text, when Rousseau describes lying in a drifting boat, lost for 'hours at a time' in a 'thousand vague but delightful reveries', but ultimately the delight of such hours is the god-like happiness of self-sufficiency: '[w]hat does one enjoy in such a situation? Nothing external to the self, nothing but oneself and one's own existence: as long as this state lasts, one is self-sufficient like God. The feeling of existence stripped of all other affections is in itself a precious feeling of contentment and peace'.[101] In Wordsworth's *Prelude*, too, the boat will be a vehicle for arriving at a complex self-awareness, but when Wollstonecraft similarly drifts in a boat off the shore near Tonsberg, she experiences not the divine self-sufficiency of the self but both its fragility and a resistance to its finitude:

> I cannot bear to think of being no more – of losing myself – though existence is often but a painful consciousness of misery; nay, it appears to me impossible that I should cease to exist, or that this active, restless spirit, equally alive to joy and sorrow, should only be organised dust – ready to fly

176 Property in Political Economy

> abroad the moment the spring snaps, or the spark goes out which kept it together. Surely something resides in this heart that is not perishable, and life is more than a dream.[102]

As in the early passage in Letter 1, the emotional stress experienced by the self only reinforces Wollstonecraft's sense of being more than she is: but where the earlier passage turned to a material image – the 'involuntary' force of adhesion – to relay the 'something more', here it is the inverse, a necessary assumption of something beyond the material life of 'organised dust'. The 'active, restless' turning from material to immaterial language marks a persistent urge to penetrate the mysteries of human existence: the nature of social bonds, the boundaries between self and others, a resistance to the merely material existence of the solitary self.

In this and similar moments, Wollstonecraft evokes and retreads a whole strand of eighteenth-century moral philosophy, into the nature of human subject and moral and social feeling, to which Smith and Rousseau had both contributed. But where Rousseau resolves such questions through retreat to the happiness of a solitary state, and Smith achieves social harmony through each individual learning his 'real littleness', Wollstonecraft allows her insistence on the 'something' more than isolated individualism to reverberate through her text, to sit alongside its larger questions about the purpose of human community, the destiny of 'progress', and the nature of commercial modernity itself. The same 'active, restless spirit', the persistent more-than-material 'something' will reject the beautiful inertia of cottage life and will be deployed to critique the 'chase after wealth' viewed in the merchants of Hamburg, where, in the 'strange machine' of human nature, the love of 'humanity' is sacrificed to self-interest and business.[103] If, as Michael Igantieff describes, market society is a 'society of strangers, of mediated and indirect social relations', where, famously, provision is made via the invisible hand of the market rather than the 'benevolence of the butcher, the brewer, or the baker', Wollstonecraft insists on the persistence of an alternative form of intersubjectivity, a social bond whose capaciousness does not proscribe a capacity for critique.[104] Sympathy, the inevitable 'attraction of adhesion', is notably withheld from the 'embruted' possessors of '[m]ushroom fortunes' derived from 'extensive' commercial speculations.[105]

The social bond of sympathy, thrown into relief by such periodic crises in *Short Residence*, is far from being Wollstonecraft's innovation (and, as the text's few moments of irrecoverable despair bear witness, it is not always available, despite its apparently 'imperious' powers). The very first sentence of *The Theory of Moral Sentiments* asserted the self-evidence of

Individuation and Sympathy in A Short Residence   177

'some principles' in man's nature which, '[h]ow selfish soever' he may be supposed, 'interest him in the fortune of others'; the *Discourse on Inequality* claimed the existence of a sympathy-like '*amour propre*' between beings in the 'savage' state. In Smith and Rousseau, however, sympathy is tied to a story of the property order, or progression to it: Smith's claim of a fundamental social interest in human nature is the first step in a theory of social and moral cohesion which seeks to counter the divisive effects of a society founded on property ownership; in Rousseau, *amour propre* gives way to '*amour soi*', or self-love, with the institution of private property. That sympathy (usually, although not always) persists even in the context of Wollstonecraft's alienated and dislocated state, detached and removed from the context of her social formation, makes a powerful case for its existence not simply as a product of history, time, and culture but as transcendent, detached from such contexts. It is both residue, what remains of the self when detached from the context of its social formation, and also, importantly, what one always has: the 'honest sympathy of nature' is found even among the unexpectedly hospitable peasants of the pre-social wilds of the shores of Sweden.[106] In one sense, this confirms Smith's claim that it is a primary, natural instinct, but what in Smith is a necessary first supposition on which the whole apparatus of his theory is built is stated much more powerfully in Wollstonecraft, and allowed far more extensive range. *Short Residence* detaches the principle of sympathy and the whole apparatus of its operation from the specific context of commercial society and renders its reach and potential far more extensive, whilst at the same time mobilising it, where necessary (as with the critique of the principle of convenience signalled by the ugly Christiana houses), to oppose and counter the values on which commercial society is built. In so doing, the question of individuation, as well as of social connection, is radically detached from the context of property through which it has previously been understood.

Transcendent, transhistorical sympathy, which constitutes just one example of the affective powers of the individual subject explored in *A Short Residence*, thus enables a dismantling of the modern subject's relation to property. In Wollstonecraft's text, the modern subject is not produced through the property order but displaced from it; sympathy becomes freewheeling and unfixed, a principle of social bond detached from social context, and human affection or 'adhesion' is freed from association with any particular mode of politico-social order. This radically cuts the genealogical connection by which existing accounts of human sentiment tie it to a story, in both Smith and Rousseau, of origin and progression, a

Property in Political Economy

narrative in which the property order of modernity is destination. Smith's worry, addressed in his additions to the 1790 edition of *The Theory of Moral Sentiments*, that sympathy for the rich skewed the operation of the moral sentiments, makes manifest his attention to such contexts. By contrast, in *A Short Residence*, by virtue of Wollstonecraft's temporal and geographic displacement, sympathy transcends any material condition of its formation, underlined by its presence even at times of alienation or isolation which can verge on the suicidal, and in states of propertylessness, homelessness, and exile from human community. Equally, the imagination which in Smith mediates between inner and other, self and world, self-interest and social judgement, but often, in McKeon's words, works to internalise the 'public view', in Wollstonecraft instead enables the transcendence, in fleeting moments of sublime transport, of both self and world: a transcendence which is also a splitting of the self between material embodiment and immaterial transport.[107] Viewed as the apotheosis of the self through her imaginative, affective powers, such transports do not resolve the question of the subject's relation to the material world, but they express or transmute alienation into the form of aesthetic and imaginative power. Such transitory realisation of subjective powers offers a powerful rebuff to the shrinking of the self – the 'narrow enclosing of the self in one task' – prescribed by the division of labour, and refuses the narrative of the self's relation to the social whole (alienated, inert, stupefied, dependent) offered by political economy.[108] Importantly too, as we shall now see, aesthetic vision gives the subject a voice independent from the property order, in literary form.

'Desultory Letters'

For all its insights into the shortcomings of commercial society, *Short Residence* cannot resolve many of the questions it raises, nor reintegrate the alienated self to whom it gives voice. Its penultimate letter pulls no punches in condemning the 'whirlpool of gain', as 'dishonourable as gambling', in which the 'interests of nations are bartered by speculating merchants' through 'artful trains of corruptions'. Here is the 'mean machinery' which lurks behind the scenes of 'what are vulgarly termed great affairs', whose 'depredations' on 'human life' are likened to a 'swarm of locusts', and far exceed those of the earlier age of the 'sword'.[109] The text ends on a note of weariness: a disinclination for further 'rambles' and constant scene-changing; the fleeing of the 'spirit of observation'; a vision of the 'insignificant' cliffs of Dover, bathetic in comparison with those of Sweden and Norway; and aimless wandering around 'dirty' Dover simply to 'kill time'.[110] 'Take, O world! thy much indebted tear!' Wollstonecraft repeats from Edward Young's *Night Thoughts*: as much a jab at a world engulfed in commerce as a description of personal misery.[111] Signing off the final letter with her name, 'Mary', she reminds her reader of the epistolary nature of her writing, a form loose and flexible enough to contain the extraordinary variety of her observations, as well as to communicate enough of the narrator's own interiority to beguile its readers.[112] Ultimately, it is through the letter form that the self is sketched, conveyed, and individuated: through which a self not defined by, or against, property comes into being.

For Rousseau, the age of property was inaugurated with an act of enclosure: 'the first man who, having enclosed a piece of land, thought of saying, "This is mine", and came across people simple enough to believe him'.[113] Although he admits that such a scene could only take place if the *idea* of property had already arisen, Rousseau's image of fencing off land depicts property as a demarcation and separation of what is owned from what is not, what is private from what is held in common. This is a model of property which the literary form of the letter fundamentally troubles. By opening itself out to the reader, the letter initiates dialogue; it is the sign and enactment of an exchange; it exists in order to share, not in order to fence off or keep out. Letters inhabit an interstitial space, a betweenness, the gap of possible communication between persons, and as such they have a peculiarly ambivalent relation to property. If left unshared, and retained in the possession of its author, the letter fails to fulfil its communicatory purpose; if possession and ownership transfer to the recipient, here is a property form, originating wholly in the labour of another, which may be obtained through no act of exchange or transaction, or perhaps even will. As John Brewer has commented, the personal letter thus raises 'fundamental questions about literary property'.[114] Wollstonecraft's chosen form for *Short Residence* thus in itself poses the question of ownership and places the question of property centre stage. The multiple further ambivalences of the text (its disclosure of personal experience whose apparent specificity of reference remains nevertheless veiled; the anonymity of its addressee and, until the last page, of its speaker; its occupation of a generic space between travelogue, memoir, personal journal and autobiography; its reliance on, yet nondisclosure of, the motivating purpose of Wollstonecraft's journey) generate further ambiguities. Among Wollstonecraft's first acts of authorship was the compilation of anthologies which, as Brewer notes, were themselves innovative forms of literary property.[115] It is wholly appropriate that in *A Short Residence*, she uses the letter form, a literary form which so troubles conventional notions of property, and which redraws the boundaries between what is private and what is publically shared, to reconsider the place of the subject in a world defined by property, and to reorient the subject's relation to property order itself.

As noted earlier in this chapter, the letter form in the hands of Montesquieu inaugurated the dominant narrative of commercial modernity, the puzzle with which Wollstonecraft wrestles in *A Short Residence*, as throughout her work. In his later 'Reflections on *The Persian Letters*' (1754), Montesquieu explained his formal choice: 'in using the letter form, in which neither the choice of characters, nor the subjects discussed, have to fit in with any pre-conceived intentions or plans, the author has taken advantage of the fact that he can include philosophy, politics, and moral discourse ... and can connect everything together with a secret chain which remains, as it were, invisible'.[116] Like a novel, the emergent cultural form of eighteenth-century commercial modernity, the *Persian Letters* cloaks an overarching order or narrative with apparent variety, difference, and plurality; unlike the anthology, which also collects together variety and difference, its defining ordering principles are not made overt to the reader. Montesquieu's image of the 'secret chain' echoes that of Samuel Johnson's near-contemporaneous evocation, in *The Adventurer* in 1753, of the 'secret concatenation' which 'links together' members of the human community.[117] It also anticipates Smith's invisible hand, which, as we saw in an earlier section, replaces the profligate spending of the rich man as political economy's preferred figure for the unintended and beneficial distributive effects through which market society provides for its members, binding a 'society of strangers' together through the 'mediated and indirect' relations of the market.[118] Like the disparate parts of Montesquieu's letter sequence, *Short Residence* similarly yokes apparently disconnected particulars and multiple themes with a secret, invisible chain of connection. As with the *Persian Letters*, it includes 'philosophy, politics ... moral discourse' and more, whilst mimicking the world of commercial modernity itself in its commitment to the variety of plural experiences which are collected and organised, in this case, through the eye and pen of the observing subject. In this case, then, it is the writing subject who provides the principle of connection and order, although she does this through the letter form which, posing the puzzle of the 'secret chain', plays with the gaps and spaces of unseen connections. In an early reflection on the nature of philosophical inquiry, in his prized essay on the 'History of Astronomy' which, unlike other discarded works, he kept throughout his life, Smith makes much of the gaps between observed phenomena, spaces bridged by

'*Desultory Letters*'

the connective leaps of the philosopher's imagination, as well as making use, like Montesquieu, of the image of the connective 'chain'.[119] The gaps between observed particulars which for Smith are addressed by the privileged insight of the philosopher, become, in the literary form of the letters, available to all Wollstonecraft's readers.

The form of *A Short Residence* owes much too to Rousseau's *Reveries*, which, presented in a series of letter-like 'Walks', offered Wollstonecraft a model for loose, personal, unstructured writing. In his account of his method, Rousseau explains his chosen mode as the formal corollary of his project of self-revelation, self-inquiry, and self-consciousness:

> These pages will in fact be merely a shapeless account of my reveries. They will often be about me, because a reflective solitary man necessarily thinks about himself a lot. What is more, all the strange ideas which come into my head as I walk will also find their place here. I shall say what I have thought just as it came to me and with as little connection as yesterday's ideas have with those of tomorrow. But a new awareness of my character and my temperament will nevertheless result from an awareness of the feelings and thoughts which feed my mind day by day in the strange state in which I find myself.[120]

As Rousseau progresses, he compares his project to the 'sort of experiments that physicists perform on air to analyse its composition day by day. I shall apply the barometer to my soul, and these experiments, conducted well and repeated time and time again, might yield results as reliable as theirs'. At the same time, he will not attempt to reduce his experiments to 'a system'; rather, writing only for himself, his words will 'double my existence' by enabling him, in later years, to 'live with myself in another age, as if living with a younger friend'.[121] An alternative expression of this loose, aimlessness, self-meditation is floating in the drifting boat as described above, a passage echoed pretty exactly in Wollstonecraft although, as we have seen, with markedly different import. In Rousseau, the self is the 'secret concatenation' between the different parts of his writing, and the splitting of his experience into different 'walks' and episodes enables him to understand, record, and re-experience himself as a connected person, a 'younger friend', seen through various perspectives as though through different angles of light. In Wollstonecraft, the loose 'experiment' of writing does not resolve itself into a record of the self in such a self-contained way: although in part this is what is achieved, there is a strong impression too of 'something getting', or remaining 'free'.[122] Rousseau's self-experiment, his multiple moments of viewing himself, recalls Smith's unitary model of the subject in *The Theory of Moral Sentiments*, who works to assimilate all his various perceptions into a relatively unified position of moral judgement and value, represented by the 'impartial spectator', the 'man within the breast', an internalised 'other' like Rousseau's 'younger friend'. In Wollstonecraft, by contrast, the gaze of the writing subject is diffracted into different directions, externally as well as internally focused, rendering the gaze dialogic, the speaker multivocal and complex. Rather than remembering the subject, the possibilities of dissolution, disappearance, and death often press themselves into consciousness, as with her thoughts of the fragility of existence discussed earlier, or her response to the sight of preserved bodies in Tonsberg: 'Life, what art thou? Where goes this breath? this I, so much alive?'.[123] Even decaying pine forests suggest the thought that 'death, under every form, appears to me like something getting free', a slipping away into 'I know not what element' as the speaker herself appears to do, as she signs off at the end of the correspondence.[124] Undoubtedly, the self is offered as one point of organising principle, one element of the 'secret chain' in *A Short Residence*, but it is a self open to its own limits and finitude, shot through with a sense of the boundedness of human life and an urge to transcend or escape it. If, according to Rousseau's *Discourse*, freedom pertains to existence prior to individuation by property, the Wollstonecraftian persona asks how and whether freedom is possible after it. This is a text where the self never comes home, and is always on the road; where material embodiment is only one level of 'conscious being', and where the writing of experience as ongoingness, like that of travel, or of the correspondence itself, means that the self is never completed or fenced off like a defined object of property.[125] Not only Wollstonecraft's chosen literary form, but her very writing of the self, troubles the bounded and finite culture of property and accumulation which she inhabits and traverses.

In Smithian political economy, individuals, and the differences which exist between them, are the very origin of property society, as those differences prompt acts of exchange from which all benefit. A 'difference of talents' enables expression of 'the general disposition to truck, barter, and exchange'; thus 'every man may purchase whatever part of the produce of other men's talents he has occasion for', and the market emerges as the expression of social connection.[126] As we saw earlier, despite the insights of his specialised work, the philosopher may be unable to contribute to this social marketplace of the talents: as Smith comments, unless they 'happen to be placed in some very particular situations', philosophers risk contributing 'very little to the good government or happiness of their society'.[127] This observation in *The Wealth of Nations* undercuts the recommendation

'Desultory Letters'

in the earlier *The Theory of Moral Sentiments* (again as we saw above) that philosophers might best advise legislators to best provide for their subjects by describing to them the 'great system' by which 'the wheels of the machine of government' might serve that end.[128] The 'secret connections' which the philosopher postulates as existing between things, in the work of the philosophical imagination, risk being of no benefit to the 'good government or happiness' of society. Here, as Ignatieff has commented, is a structural weakness in market society which lacks 'the means to know its own general interest as such – hence its unique vulnerability to faction and conflict among economic interests'.[129] In a society ruled by the division of labour, who can attend to the connection between its parts?

One answer to this problem is suggested by Montesquieu. As well as describing how the different concerns of his *Persian Letters* were linked together with a 'secret chain', he noted that '[n]othing pleased' his readers more than finding the work 'unexpectedly a sort of novel', one whose pleasures included characters giving 'a description of their present state' and 'communicat[ing] emotion' alongside those other matters, 'philosophy, politics, and moral discourse'.[130] Literary form, then, resolves the philosopher's problem of station and makes his contemplation of an 'infinite variety of objects', and his imaginative labour of connection, available to the reading public. Like the philosopher as described by Smith, Montesquieu's readers might exercise 'their minds in endless comparisons and combinations', to render 'their understandings, in an extraordinary degree, both acute and comprehensive' by viewing the 'infinite variety of objects' present in society. Against political economy's bridging of individual difference via transactional exchange, the novel offers a broader vision of social cohesion through the imaginative, emotional, and aesthetic pleasures of discovering 'secret chains' of connection; against the market's 'society of strangers', the novel offers the deep pleasures of knowing the self.[131] Offering 'improvement' of the 'heart' and 'understanding', it counters the tendencies to stupidity and ignorance innate in commercial modernity, and in addressing, as it often does, the sympathies of its readers, it invites them to enact affective connection. Literary form, which, as a mode of textual comportment or conduct, might perhaps be considered as manners in writing, thus promises to continue the 'revolution in manners' for which Wollstonecraft has earlier called. In *Short Residence* too, the novel-like letters enable their readers to share the 'philosophical observations' of its author, tracing the links in its 'secret chain', whilst experiencing too the novelistic pleasure of communicated emotion, the self's fluctuating 'present states' revealed. The ambiguous literary form of the correspondence thus offers a knowledge which is the property of both all and of no-one, made available in the public form of printed text, of literary object, but privately consumed. If, in Ignatieff's words, property is the 'progressive individuation of the means of subsistence', literary property participates in the sharing of talents facilitated by 'truck, barter or exchange' to offer its readers 'something' more than itself, perhaps 'something getting free'.[132]

Montesquieu's description of the novel as presenting a variety of observed particulars mixed with philosophical, political, and moral discourse, and the pleasurable description of subjectivity and states of emotion, is a suggestive one. It makes a case for the novel as sharing with – or perhaps taking over from – philosophy the role of describing and understanding the world, and especially seeking the connections which link disparate appearances and seemingly unlinked phenomena. In this reading, the novel asks its readers to seek for the 'secret chain' which yokes and explains the world they live in, whilst offering too the affective pleasure of communicated states of subjectivity and the temporal, structural pleasure of experiencing 'beginning, development, and ending'.[133] All of this might explain why Wollstonecraft, who famously attacked the novel in her *Vindication of the Rights of Woman*, turned to fiction in what would be the final, unfinished work of her career, finding there a form capable of attending to the concrete particulars of the lives of her protagonists in order to reveal larger truths about the world forged by political economy and the experience of female sensibility in it. As Chapter 6 shows, the work enabled Wollstonecraft to show the deep effects on female lives of a world governed by property, speculation, and the pursuit of wealth, in a 'secret chain' which yokes its oddly distanced and disparate scenes of action together. But whereas Smith's invisible hand describes pseudo-providential distributive acts which provide and sustain, in Wollstonecraft, the secret chain is the interlinked oppressions of modernity's property order and its gender system. At the same time, as we shall see, in exploring the role of dialogue, exchange, and communication, in a fiction made up of a community of sympathetic listeners and which addresses itself similarly to the sympathies of its readers, Wollstonecraft foregrounds a principle of affective connection, whose social force offers a promise of reckoning with, and perhaps countering, political economy's 'society of strangers'.

CHAPTER 6

Credit and Credulity
Political Economy, Gender, and the
Sentiments in The Wrongs of Woman

I have rather endeavoured to pourtray (sic) passions than manners.

The sentiments I have embodied.[1]

Wollstonecraft's final major work, her novel *The Wrongs of Woman, or, Maria,* was left unfinished at her death in September 1797. Published as a 'fragment' the following year by her bereaved husband, William Godwin, his introductory note suggests the work is a sketch of what, had it been completed, 'would perhaps have given a new impulse to the manners of a world'. As it stands, *Wrongs* offers 'melancholy delight' to 'minds of taste and imagination' which find pleasure in contemplating the 'unfinished productions of genius'. The work is thus presented as inviting a very particular 'sentiment' of mournful appreciation by those best able to judge 'talents' with 'the greatest accuracy and discrimination'.[2] Writing here becomes a literary relic, an object for taste, and a peculiar species of pleasure, for those capable of such appreciation.

Wollstonecraft's own prefatory note – itself, Godwin relates, incomplete but 'worth preserving' – situates the work in relation to the passions in a markedly different way. Contrary to Godwin, Wollstonecraft asserts that she has sought to portray 'passions', not 'manners', specifically to show the 'misery' felt by women which is caused by the 'partial laws and customs of society'. If any improvement might be made to the 'manners of a world', as Godwin suggests, it would be through attending to the tales of such passions. The passions thus underlie or precede the manners on which much of her earlier writing has focused: they are where the effects of manners are felt, where their wrongs are experienced, and where an argument for change must begin. This commitment to affect as the ground of experience brings with it in turn a reformation of literary method. Rejecting (as her early fiction, *Mary* had too) the unreal models of female characters offered by other novelists, Wollstonecraft chose instead to 'embody' the sentiments, to create the tale of 'woman', rather than an imagined individual, and to 'restrain' her fancy so that the 'invention of the story' told the tale of female 'misery and oppression'. At the same time, she rejects the anticipated criticism that the work is merely the result of her own bad feelings: the 'abortion of a distempered fancy, or the strong delineations of a wounded heart'. Where for Godwin, the literary work is a manifestation of 'genius' to be appreciated by 'taste', for Wollstonecraft, the object of attention is the lived affective experience of a 'woman of sensibility' who is forced to 'renounce all the humanizing affections' and suffer degradation of 'the mind'. Whilst she agrees that the 'delineation of finer sensations … constitutes the merit of our best novels', it is clear that any such depiction serves the larger purpose of showing the consequences, for a woman's 'taste', her 'perception of grace and refinement of sentiment', of the 'matrimonial despotism' depicted in her novel.[3] Although it is not spelled out, such degradation of female capacity for feeling, under the conditions depicted in her novel, points to the limits of women's participation in the sentimental approbation of genius sketched out in Godwin's ostensibly gender-neutral account. Before women are able to appreciate objects of taste and before the novel can be approached as such by them, more fundamental concerns need to be addressed.

The passions and sentiments, then, are the grounds on which what would be Wollstonecraft's final account of 'things as they are' (to use Godwin's original title for his 1794 novel, *Caleb Williams*) would rest: the means through which she would show the consequences of existing 'laws and customs of society' and trace the links between established social and political oppressions to the lived experience of individual lives. Less a record of lost genius, an object for contemplation by connoisseurs of taste, her novel stages passion, in its many forms, to uncover the affective experience of female lives in late eighteenth-century commercial society. Such a return to the passions as the grounds for examining commercial modernity is apt, for, as we have seen in earlier chapters, political economy itself stemmed from a theory of human nature which newly emphasised the individual's experience of the world less through rational processes than through desires, sensations, and feeling. Indeed, in one reading, political economy can be seen as one of a number of attempts to harness and regulate the potentially wayward impulses in humankind: to make social, as well as economic, sense of a human nature whose passions are both destabilising and powerful. In his recent account of the historical and epistemological formation of modernity, Clifford Siskin has suggested that, through the mid- and late eighteenth century, political economy was 'a primary site for the totalizing and rationalizing of the social'.[4] Wollstonecraft's turn to the literary genre – the novel – which attends to the relation between social structures and human feeling shows a determination to place passions and sentiments centre stage. Yoking a narrative of female feeling – of affective events and episodes which often involve constraint, degradation, renunciation, even abandonment – to the material, legal, and economic, structures which follow from political economy's systematisation of social lives shows how the 'misery' and 'oppression' of women are one of its outcomes.

Political Economy and Belief in Crisis: Credit and Credulity

The relation between the affective, the social, and the political economic was thrown starkly into relief by events on a national scale, even as Wollstonecraft was working on her novel. In February 1797, worries about a shortage of coin, perhaps prompted by hoarding due to fears of an imminent invasion, caused William Pitt and the Directors of the Bank of England to prohibit the Bank from issuing specie in cash payments until further notice, an order which became law in May 1797 and whose provisions, although initially proposed as a temporary measure, remained in place for the next twenty four years.[5] The Bank's suspension of cash payments produced a political crisis in which it became clear how much the nation's economic system depended on and was sustained by investments of belief and affect – a relation represented in gendered terms both in parliamentary debate and print satire. In many ways, the Bank's move simply consolidated the use of numerous instruments of credit (bills of exchange, bank notes, and paper money) which had been in widespread circulation in Britain and beyond for well over a century.[6] But the withdrawal of the guarantee to convert paper money into specie appeared as a broken promise, rupturing the sustaining forms of agreement and belief on which the economy, and economic actors, depended. Given the close links between the Bank of England and the government (the Bank had been founded a century earlier to provide state-backed loans to fund military activity), this was a rupture too in the unspoken contracts which existed between subjects and government. Robert Mitchell has suggested that in periodic moments of crisis and financial panic, systems of state finance become 'visible *as* a "system"' that connects people 'to one another through affective bonds of belief, "Opinion", and desire'.[7] 1797 was precisely such a moment: a crisis through which the affective bonds which constitute forms of governmentality are revealed. All this was underway just as Wollstonecraft worked on a novel which revealed the cost to women, measured in affective experience, of the larger social, economic, material, and legal systems to which they were bound.

As commentators in and beyond Parliament weighed in on the implications of the Bank Restriction Act, it was to the nature of credit itself – that entity which was at once economically fundamental, yet also curiously intangible and elusive – that they often returned. The crisis not only made evident the extent to which Britain's economy operated on credit: it offered a dizzying image of an economy in which credit circulated endlessly, without reconversion into the reassuringly material form of gold. It thus posed the question of what exactly credit was, if not backed by, or convertible into, metal assets. By removing the fiction, sustained by belief, that credit was a temporary replacement for some more solid form of value, it made it possible to ask quite what it was that was sustaining the nation's economic activity (and hence the social and political life which depended on it). Credit was defined, on the one hand, through a technical and abstracted language of political economy, as when Pitt referred to paper money simply as a 'circulating medium' or 'medium of exchange', and on the other, through the symbolic and gendered language used to describe, even personify, credit over the course of the preceding century, including by supporters of the Whig mercantile regime seeking to familiarise public opinion with a credit economy.[8] Lord Shelburne's assertion that a gentleman should 'shudder at the scene of the attack' on the 'delicate frame of public credit' thus repeated a long tradition of moralised and sexualised rhetoric which placed a personified and feminised credit, the object of chivalric gentlemanly attention, at the heart of Britain's new identity as a commercial nation.[9] Pitt's Act thus became an attack on the 'morals of the constitution', which undermined the 'sacred reverence for that most delicate and indefinite thing, called public credit'.[10] Such sexual logic, in which 'delicate credit' was dependent on gentlemanly propriety, but vulnerable to its predations, was made explicit in Richard Brinsley Sheridan's personification of the Bank as an elderly lady nearly seduced by Pitt, a characterisation which inspired James Gillray's famous image of the 'Political Ravishment' of Old Lady of Threadneedle Street (Figure 6.1). Meanwhile, Lord Grey's description of credit as 'an edifice reared by the hand of simplicity, upon the basis of truth', obtained through 'belief' not 'admiration', and 'confidence' not 'power', further elaborated credit's perceived moral foundations.[11] Such assertions enabled Charles James Fox to describe the suspension of payments as an act of fraud, which precipitated a widespread crisis of belief: in the Bank, in Pitt, and in Parliament itself.

Political Economy and Belief in Crisis 189

Figure 6.1 James Gillray, 'Political-Ravishment, or, The Old Lady of Threadneedle Street in Danger!'

Credit, he implied, was foundational to political and moral relations, in the investments of belief which bound subjects to governmentality.[12] For Pitt to refer to credit, in neutral language, as a 'circulating medium', was thus to sidestep a whole set of deeply rooted assumptions about the bonds of belief which sustained not only Britain's economy but also its polity, and even its morality. His linguistic move marked an attempted shift in the whole discourse of politics and government, in which the relations of subjects to each other, to their government and the nation, had long been understood. What Fox attacked as Pitt's questionable 'new terms' thus signalled an attempt to replace an older, gendered, and sexualised Whig discourse of political, economic, and social order, with political economy and its abstract, technical terminology. The debate over the Bank Restriction Act, as well as staging a crisis in the forms of belief fundamental to liberal governmentality, thus also enacted a struggle over the authority of the new discourse of political economy and its account of relations between government and subjects.[13]

Both sides of this debate, ongoing as Wollstonecraft worked on her 'troublesome' novel, were likely to have been anathema to her.[14] Where political economic language used technical terms to erase notions of political community, Whig political discourse could only express social bonds in sexualised terms whose basis would appear, to her eyes, entirely objectionable. The necessary bonds of belief through whose circulation society inheres, however, remained, and demanded expression. It is precisely these questions of belief and credit, of proper and improper forms of social relation and morality, of broken bonds and financial impropriety, and of the forms of affective connection which should, and perhaps might, exist between persons in the system of society, which are at the heart of Wollstonecraft's unfinished novel.

One strand of this concern can be traced through the story of the novel's protagonist, Maria, whose leading characteristic is the 'extreme credulity' which she shares with her romantically minded uncle, part of whose fortune, given to Maria at her marriage, funds the questionable 'speculations' of Maria's husband Venables. Credulity is linked too to the novel's persistent preoccupation with the work of fancy, imagination, and speculation: terms which have usually been approached by literary critics in the context of Romanticism's interest in the imagination as a creative capacity. But it is also possible to consider how Maria's credulity, her vulnerability to the alluring, perhaps deceptive visions offered by the 'magic lamp' of her imagination, identifies her as a descendant of Lady Credit, the allegorical personification at the heart of the elaborate cultural work which, earlier in the century, smoothed the path to acceptance of the new Whig credit economy.[15] Read this way, Maria, like Lady Credit, marks the question of the relationship of affect to the world of economic activity inhabited by her husband, and suggested by his name; but unlike Lady Credit, Maria is exiled from that world rather than being harnessed by it, or serving as its symbolic figurehead.[16] Wollstonecraft's figure of female credulity thus revisits the Whig trope of feminised and personified credit to investigate and destabilise it, but she also complicates the figure of inconstant, fickle, female feeling both to trace the causes of female credulity in Maria's upbringing in the gendered social unit of the family, and to move beyond it to depict more assured forms of feeling in the sympathy and sensibility which eventually emerge as the basis for new forms of social bond.[17] As the novel opens, Maria is imprisoned, forcibly removed from the sphere of public life to a space which is the gothic 'other' to the throne room at the heart of government in which Lady Credit is often presented. Re-echoing with the sounds of Maria's fellow incarcerated, the 'mansion of despair' is also suggestive of the destabilised mind itself, whose vulnerability to 'gusts' of feeling Wollstonecraft had earlier traced in her second *Vindication*.[18] As such, it is the binary 'other' to the male world of rationality and action, and of exchange under the sign of credit. Maria's forced displacement ensures that the illegal financial acts of her husband, Venables, which exploit existing credit systems, can continue without interruption, in an inversion of the ritualistic centrality of Lady Credit to mercantile activity in the allegories of Addison and Defoe. Equally, as Maria's narrative later reveals, the chivalric wooing, the careful attention lavished on Lady Credit in the latter, has been overturned in Venables' attempt to prostitute Maria to his creditor to stave off repaying his debts.

To view the 'woman of sensibility' whose story is announced in Wollstonecraft's Preface as in some way a descendant or relation of the figure of 'extreme credulity' embodied by Lady Credit in the early eighteenth century is to illuminate how Wollstonecraft's radically new envisaging of fiction doesn't just rewrite the usual courtship and marriage plots of so many eighteenth-century novels, it also recasts the economic romances such stories so often contained. It underlines how the question of female feeling has accompanied, and disturbed, commercial society from its outset, as both extrinsic but also somehow necessary to it. As such, *The Wrongs of Woman* can be viewed as a text which repeatedly demonstrates, and troubles, the mutual imbrication of financial and sexual economies in the late eighteenth-century commercial society to which the early-century Whig settlement gave birth. It therefore continues, and focuses, the preoccupation with political economy's 'rationalization' of the social which, as we have seen in previous chapters, runs across Wollstonecraft's work. As Gillian Russell has commented, public credit at this time had long been represented as an inconstant woman to be 'tamed by the rational masculine subject', a representation which replays, and genders, the ongoing relationship between emotion and regulation which, as Jon Mee has shown, was fundamental to thinking about the place of affect in polite society in eighteenth-century moral and political philosophy.[19] But, by tracing a different route for credulity (an affect closely related to the enthusiasm on which Mee focuses) to that of regulation, or education, or containment, Wollstonecraft resists telling the tale traced by Russell in which the 'irrational, dizzily speculative' feminine is the binary 'other' to masculine rationality. Her attention to credulity, and its opposite, prudence, unpicks the story of credit which sustains contemporary political economy, and indeed informs the whole affective model of personhood associated with commercial society.[20] At the same time, credulity, or a capacity for belief, finds a formal home in the novel genre which was to be Wollstonecraft's last weapon with which to engage the political economic 'truths' of her time.

Wollstonecraft's tale of 'a woman of sensibility' is thus, among the many different and competing iterations of 'sensibility' in her time, an account of how one particular kind of sensibility, its formation and expression, is a deliberate counter to the forms of feeling on which, according to political economy, commercial modernity rests. In commercial society's founding tales from Smith onwards, sensibility, as a marked capacity (often excessive) for feeling, was feminised and domesticated, relegated to the home as 'unfit for the world' as Smith would have it, whilst her more worldly brother, prudence, brought home the bacon.[21] Any account, therefore, of the 'wrongs' suffered by a 'woman of sensibility' would need to address too the gendered story of affect offered by political economy. *The Wrongs of Woman* shows how Wollstonecraft recognised that, in order to rewrite the late eighteenth-century's received account of gender, the story of credit and belief would need retelling too. Political economy's narrative of feeling, of the forms of feeling which are allowed and disallowed – those whose effects are allowed to flourish in shared social and political life, and those which must remain at home – runs parallel to, and is deeply imbricated with, the account of gender with which Wollstonecraft had long been at war. Her story of the woman of sensibility thus rewrites the affective economy of credit on which political economy rests and reimagines the system of gender which it perpetuates.[22]

Thus, although presented initially as a fault, Maria's credulity – a term defined by Samuel Johnson as both 'easiness of belief' and 'readiness of credit' – ultimately provides a route to the experience, self-reflection, and self-education which Wollstonecraft so valued as a means of social and political reform. This is the means whereby *The Wrongs of Woman* critiques the account of the moral sentiments which for Smith underpin and produce political economy, a critique which rejects a Smithian valoration of prudence in favour of a more wide-ranging, if at times mistaken, capacity for affirmation and belief. Prudence was central too to parliamentary defences of credit, as well as being linked to 'proper' notions of female conduct, as Sheridan's depiction of the Old Lady of Threadneedle Street's inexcusable '*faux pas*' reminds us. Depicting prudence, instead, as weak-spirited and too easily counterfeited, Wollstonecraft searches for an alternative formulation of relations between morality and commercial society: between affect and money. In all this, the questions and issues which were fundamental to the parliamentary debates on credit were reconsidered in the register of novelistic discourse. *The Wrongs of Woman* ultimately rejects both a regime of credit founded on a chivalrous model of sexual relations and the amorality of political economy, to instead mobilise an alternative economy of social feeling, which can reform a selfish and sexualised commercial economy based on self-interest. In the process, this novel about credulity remodels what credit might be, and what it is that might be circulated to social advantage. It also, by addressing such concerns within the socially shared literary form of the novel, contests the separation of economic issues, and their related terms, into a distinct area of technical knowledge. The ability of the novel form to circulate as an object of shared knowledge which stimulates the generation and circulation of readerly sentiments – its association with the powers of circulation on which Godwin insisted as he defended his decision to publish the novel's 'fragments' following Wollstonecraft's death – also explains Wollstonecraft's return to the novel form which she had famously disparaged in her earlier *Vindication of the Rights of Woman*.

The 'History of the Human Mind': Prudence, Credulity, and Belief

Early on in *The Wrongs of Woman*, Wollstonecraft brings together her two soon-to-be-lovers, Maria and Darnford, and the jailor, Jemima, to present a triptych of their personal autobiographies, which, in overlapping and divergent ways, offers a stark and critical account of the behaviours and passions of late eighteenth-century society. In particular, Darnford's tale, which links inherited wealth to sexual, social, and financial dissipation, offers a condensed version of the critique of eighteenth-century commercial society which Wollstonecraft had already set out in her two *Vindications*. Darnford's parents, people of fashion united in an arranged marriage, exemplify the dissipation of the upper classes attacked too in Wollstonecraft's early novel *Mary*; Darnford's inheritance, following his parents' death, is squandered in similar financial and sexual excess. Emigration to America offers a fleeting possibility of an escape, but there Darnford witnesses how America, seated on 'her bags of dollars', has also been corrupted, her pioneer spirit having 'now turned into commercial speculations'. The national character, Darnford observes, 'exhibited a phenomenon in the history of the human mind – a head enthusiastically enterprising, with cold selfishness of heart'.[23] Darnford's insights are notably divorced from any moral self-regulation, however. On return from America, he resumes his hedonistic lifestyle, only briefly interrupted by his incarceration and liaison with Maria; his later inheritance of a second fortune enables his resumption of further sexual and financial dissipation. Darnford's tale exemplifies how moral failings – failings of character, feeling, belief, and sentiment – flourish in a commercial culture allied, on both sides of the Atlantic, to inherited wealth and 'selfish' enterprise. It is not enough simply to be hostile to commerce: Darnford asserts, readily enough, that he 'detested commerce'. Rather, the crucial question is how the 'history of the human mind' might be rewritten to point in a different direction, so that the 'cold selfishness of heart' on which credit culture rests might be reformed at the very root. It is precisely such reformation of feeling in Maria, and Jemima too, which the rest of the novel traces.

As we have seen in previous chapters, the dominant late eighteenth-century 'history of human mind' was written by the same Scottish philosophers who also theorised political economy. Their account of commercial society was underpinned by a science of man, or theory of human nature, in which belief, credit, and credulity loomed large, whether to inform David Hume's account of the role of passions in his sceptical critique of reason, or, in the form of sympathy and the moral sentiments, which Adam Smith harnessed into a fully-elaborated description of moral, and eventually economic, behaviour. When Pitt and others used a putatively neutral political economic vocabulary in parliamentary debates over the Bank Restriction Act, they contributed to the establishment of political economy as a distinct area of technical knowledge quite separate from the moral philosophy and jurisprudence which Smith had taught at Glasgow University. And once established as a university discipline from the early nineteenth century, political economy became a knowledge practice quite separated from social, ethical, psychological, and affective concerns. In its Smithian origins, however, the moral and the economic were closely linked, as is apparent when the role of prudence and credit in Smithian philosophy is traced. Prudence, belief, and credulity as presented in both *The Theory of Moral Sentiments* (1759) and *The Wealth of Nations* (1776) illuminate the theory of personhood, and the regulation of feeling, elaborated in the account of human nature from which political economy stems.

The development of Smith's thinking about prudence is a good illustration of the relation of the moral thinking of *The Theory of Moral Sentiments* to the economic thought of the later *The Wealth of Nations*. In the earlier text, prudence is a central part of Smith's moral system, proclaimed as a virtue despite its strong associations with utility, industry, and self-advancement. Combined with benevolence and justice, Smith claims that it makes the most perfect virtue, but he also devotes considerable space to elaborating how the prudent man's attention to his health, wealth, rank, and reputation can, when yoked to industry and propriety, produce multiple rewards: 'wealth, and power, and honours of every kind', Smith asserts, are the 'natural consequences of prudence, industry, and application'; it is through prudence and its associated qualities of industry, frugality, and even parsimony that men of 'inferior rank' raise themselves to public notice, even in the face of the 'jealousy' and 'resentment' of 'all those who were born their superiors'.[24] In *The Theory of Moral Sentiments*, then, prudence is a virtue, even if it is 'of all the virtues that which is most useful to the individual', but *The Wealth of Nations* extends this analysis to emphasise the economic implications of the good judgement, self-command, and reason in which prudence consists.[25] In *The Wealth of Nations*, prudence becomes a quality, even the touchstone, of economic sense and judgement; and given what the *Theory* observes is our approval of the prudent man, prudence is also the basis of the credit which an economic actor might get from others. Prudence, then, is fundamental to the behaviour of individual economic actors, both, as its relation to credit implies, where that behaviour is the object of judgement by others, and in its relation to the pursuit of self-interest. Even the division of labour itself, Smith conjectures, was 'naturally introduced by the prudence of individuals'.[26]

The centrality of prudence to the economic system is perhaps most evident in Smith's observation that the circulation of paper notes – in the 'great wheel' of circulation – is only possible where there is trust in the prudence of the banker:

> When the people of any particular country have such confidence in the fortune, probity, and prudence of a particular banker, as to believe that he is always ready to pay upon demand such of his promissory notes as are likely to be at any time presented to him; those notes come to have the same currency as gold and silver money, from the confidence that such money can at any time be had for them.[27]

This description of how belief in the prudence of the banker underwrites the circulation of money makes evident how the refusal to exchange paper for gold, as instituted by the Bank Restriction Act, constituted a crisis in credit. It also underlines how, in Smith's eyes, the operation of the economic system is underwritten by a system of faith and belief. Wollstonecraft, for her part, when discussing paper money in her *View of French Revolution*, comments that it is in the nature of the 'spirit of commerce' to extend it beyond what should be its proper limits: a suggestion that the system of belief and prudence which for Smith should regulate paper money would give way under the pressures of the 'spirit of commerce'.[28]

But whilst Smith extends prudence from being a virtue in *The Theory of Moral Sentiments* into the quality which motivates and underwrites the economic system itself in *The Wealth of Nations*, his treatment of credulity, perhaps the flipside of prudence, differs markedly between the two texts. In the first, Smith admits that credulousness is natural to us, a childlike quality which is difficult to suppress entirely even as adults:

> There seems to be in young children an instinctive disposition to believe whatever they are told. [...] Their credulity ... is excessive, and it requires long and much experience of the falsehood of mankind to reduce them to a reasonable degree of diffidence and distrust. In grown-up people the degrees of credulity are, no doubt, very different. The wisest and most experienced are generally the least credulous. But the man scarce lives who is not more credulous than he ought to be, and who does not, upon many occasions, give credit to tales, which not only turn out to be perfectly false, but which a very moderate degree of reflection and attention might have taught him could not well be true. The natural disposition is always to believe. It is acquired wisdom and experience only that teach incredulity, and they very seldom teach it enough. The wisest and most cautious of us all frequently gives credit to stories which he himself is afterwards both ashamed and astonished that he could possibly think of believing.[29]

But credulity is mentioned only once in *The Wealth of Nations*, in an aside defending established religion as a means to restrain alternative 'ghostly practitioners' from preying on the 'credulity' of the population.[30] At the same time, Smith's account in the *Theory* of the horrors of not being believed emphasises how much we want to be in credit with others:

> It is always mortifying not to be believed, and it is doubly so when we suspect that it is because we are supposed to be unworthy of belief and capable of seriously and wilfully deceiving. To tell a man that he lies, is of all affronts the most mortal. But whoever seriously and wilfully deceives is necessarily conscious to himself that he merits this affront, that he does not deserve to be believed, and that he forfeits all title to that sort of credit from which alone he can derive any sort of ease, comfort, or satisfaction in the society of his equals. The man who had the misfortune to imagine that nobody believed a single word he said, would feel himself the outcast of human society, would dread the very thought of going into it, or of presenting himself before it, and could scarce fail, I think, to die of despair.[31]

Smith's imagined scene of the man 'outcast' from human society because 'nobody believed a single word he said' anticipates Godwin's *Caleb Williams*, which explores both how central bonds of belief are to sociality, and how readily such beliefs can be manipulated or corroded by power. (It also attacks as 'barbarous prudence' the excessive devotion to his self-image of Caleb's nemesis, Falkland).[32] But even in Smith, the extreme desire to be in credit with others, combined with the fundamental credulousness of human nature, suggests a fault in the affective system founded on prudence which otherwise sustains Smith's political economy. If, as the passage continues, even in 'the most cautious the disposition to believe is apt to prevail over that to doubt and distrust', we are likely to believe too easily in the prudence of others, thereby short-circuiting the system of moral and economic judgement which prudence is supposed to uphold.

From this perspective, Smith's extensive attention to prudence in the *Theory* looks like an attempt to insert a fail-safe into an affective economy in which human nature doubly conspires for credit readily to be given by the credulous. This repression of our powers of, and desire for, belief is all the more striking given the importance of sympathy (a form of belief in others) in Scottish moral philosophy, and especially given the extensive attention given to belief, and its powers over reason and the passions, by Smith's close friend David Hume. From this perspective, the *Theory* appears a self-contradictory book, which both insists on the work necessary to sustain others' belief in ourselves even whilst insisting, from its first sentence, on our fundamental fellow-feeling for others. From the perspective of *The Wealth of Nations*, meanwhile, it is as though Smith doesn't want to risk undermining the importance (both moral and economic) of being believed in, and being creditable, by admitting how credulous we all are: how freely available and ready to circulate belief is, how readily credit is actually given, and how easily it might circulate. This account of the treatment of credulity and belief in Smith suggests that *The Wrongs of Woman* might be read as addressing some of the following questions: what might a moral economy of the credulous look like? What would happen if our powers of belief were not restrained, for instance, by prudence or propriety? And what would it mean to free ourselves from the necessity of others' belief in us, so that, in place of Smith's yoking of prudence and industry to personal advancement and enrichment, the powers of belief inform a renewed circulation of social sentiments?

We saw above how, in Smith's account, trust in the banker sustains the circulation of paper money, and prudence and belief underwrite and assure economic activity to the benefit of all. But the fragility of a circulatory system sustained by affect is betrayed later, when the circulation of paper money is described as 'suspended upon Daedalian wings'.[33] The use of paper money, Smith argues, stimulates economic activity, by enabling banks' otherwise 'dead stock' of gold and silver to circulate. But when commerce and industry are 'suspended upon the Daedalian wings of paper money', they are less secure than when they 'travel about upon the solid ground of gold and silver', being especially liable to accidents and misuses from which 'no prudence ... can guard them'. As well as banks over-issuing paper money, abuses include 'fatal circles' of merchants drawing and redrawing bills of exchange in 'fictitious payments', or the fraudulent use of accommodation bills, which Venables uses in *The Wrongs of Woman*.[34] Smith's image of Daedalian wings, which he describes as a 'violent' metaphor, asks us to perceive the belief which sustains circulation as potentially flimsy and fragile, echoing the fear present in the *Theory*'s observation of human credulousness. But Daedalian wings might also be understood differently, to recast the significance of the belief which they signify. In mythic accounts of Daedalus, his wings are used to escape from the tower in which he is imprisoned by the King of Crete in order that his knowledge is not circulated. As well as signifying Daedalus's inventiveness as craftsman, artist, and innovator, his wings thus also figure the power of his belief in material form to effect escape, to resist the obstructive operation of power, and to assert the possibility of artistic creation in the service of the circulation of knowledge. Daedalian wings occur too, in a failed attempt to escape the happy valley, in one of Wollstonecraft's favourite novels, Samuel Johnson's *Rasselas* (1759), a text which addresses the 'credulity' of its readers in its very first sentence and which she references late on in *The Wrongs of Woman*. If in *Rasselas*, as in the Greek myth, the Daedalian wings fail, it is nevertheless on the wings of belief – fostered by sympathy, nurtured through the collective sharing of personal testimony, and a willingness to invest credence in the words of others – that Maria, Jemima, and Darnford escape their own imprisonment from oppressive power in Wollstonecraft's novel.

Passions and Prudence in the *Vindication of the Rights of Woman*: A 'Natural Course of Things'

As we shall see, Wollstonecraft's treatment of prudence and credulity in *The Wrongs of Woman* constitutes a direct critique of the Smithian affective economy. The lines of this attack were already present in remarks on education in Chapter 5 of the *Vindication of the Rights of Woman* which, whilst ostensibly responding to Lord Chesterfield's advice letters to his son, also address other, unnamed men who have 'coolly seen mankind through the medium of books'.[35] In her engagement with the 'unmanly, immoral system' of Chesterfield, Wollstonecraft counters as an over-reliance on precept and prudence by insisting on the value of learning from experience, even where mistakes may occur, for the passions are the 'winds of life'.[36] Her defence of youthful feeling, of youth as a time of feeling, and her

Passions and Prudence

rejection of 'dry caution', maps out a position elaborated in her depiction of Maria in the later fiction, where 'youthful ebullitions of animal spirits and instinctive feelings' mature, despite 'worldly mischances', into the 'enlarged social feeling' of humanity.[37]

At the heart of Wollstonecraft's argument is a recognition that feelings and habits, not principles, are the foundation from which people act. From this, it follows that the work of education is to allow 'natural youthful ardour' to flourish, as it is from this that 'not only great talents, but great virtues', even 'vigorous exertions of genius or benevolence' will flow.[38] This means that Chesterfield's recommendation, that young people should acquire an 'early knowledge of the world', is misguided, for this 'turns to poison the generous juices which should mount with vigour in the youthful frame, inspiring warm affections and great resolves', an observation which Maria repeats, near verbatim, in *The Wrongs of Woman*.[39] A youth formed by instruction and precepts, by contrast, renders the heart not merely cool, but hard. Instead, reading will produce 'speculative knowledge' and 'natural reflections', and whilst this means that a young person will 'enter the world with warm' and perhaps 'erroneous expectations … this appears to be the course of nature' which should be followed: 'for every thing … there is a season'.[40] All this is risked if young people are shown the world 'as it is': instead of being given a 'hasty unnatural knowledge of the world', they should be allowed to gradually discover both its imperfections and its virtues.[41] In comments which point to her own youthful friendship with Fanny Blood, depicted in *Mary* as the protagonist's intense relationship with Ann, Wollstonecraft defends the 'enthusiastic attachment' of a young person who deifies the 'beloved object' in a first friendship.[42] Although 'mistaken', the attachment is harmless, and might lead to higher sentiments, as indeed it does for the unnamed spirit, in Chapter 3 of the early fiction *Cave of Fancy* (1787), who learns to look beyond a romantic infatuation with the unattainable object of a married man to religious feeling.

Setting out her argument, Wollstonecraft deploys organic comparisons with the natural world to counter Chesterfield's 'system'. Just as trees over time are able to grow, develop roots, and survive a storm, so too should the mind similarly be allowed to mature from youth through experience: 'every thing' is 'in a progressive state'.[43] This perspective enables her to return to the scene of the insights of old age which in Smith's tale of the poor man's son in his *The Theory of Moral Sentiments* sees the old man realising that his life's exertions towards achieving the conveniences of the rich have been worthless. Wollstonecraft agrees that we realise in age that 'all that is done under the sun in vanity', but asserts that, if the insight of age is shared with the young, to 'prudently' guard against 'the common casualties of life', this would be to replace 'the nobler fruit of piety and experience' which would otherwise be attained, with the mere 'wisdom of the world'.[44] Indeed, it would be to interfere with 'the natural course of things': a phrase which, as we saw in Chapter 2, is used by both Smith and Burke to describe the economic system set out in *The Wealth of Nations*. In Smith, as we saw in Chapter 3, the history of the human mind through life progresses from desire and aspiration to effort and disillusionment, but in the philosopher's eyes, the despair of age weighs little against the realisation that each life's work is the means through which civilisation is built and human progress is made. Wollstonecraft's perspective is different: whilst she shares Smith's sense of the stadial nature of life, the 'natural course of things' should have a different outcome: experience should enable attention on worldly things to be replaced with 'piety'.

Wollstonecraft's differences from Smith are crystallised in the *Vindication*'s attack on the Smithian virtue of prudence – a quality which 'early in life' is, she claims 'but the cautious craft of ignorant self-love' – and which culminates by associating prudence with the pursuit of 'ease and prosperity on earth', eclipsing any attention to the soul.[45] In a 'circle of life and death' which is untroubled by any sense of 'futurity', 'moderation' is 'supreme wisdom': prudence would 'procure the greatest portion of happiness' and 'knowledge beyond the conveniences of life' would be 'a curse'. But in what she terms a 'vegetable life', the passions, the 'powers of the soul' would be of 'little use' and would likely only 'disturb our animal enjoyments'. In such an existence, whilst 'the letter of the law' would be adhered to, few would 'rise much above the common standard' or 'aim at attaining great virtues'. That we are raised above such a 'prudent' perspective through our passions means that 'the regulation of the passions is not, always, wisdom', a point reinforced with the observation that men often have 'superior judgement, and more fortitude than women' as 'they give freer scope to the grand passions, and by more frequently going astray enlarge their minds'.[46] By exercising their reason, they fix on stable principles through the 'force of their passions', even if nourished by 'false views of life'; in a Rasselasian image to which she returns in *The Wrongs of Woman*, they are 'permitted to overleap the boundary that secures content'. Another literary reference, to Swift's *Gulliver's Travels*, shows how the bestial passions of the Yahoos, and the passionless rationality of the Houyhnhnms are equally undesirable. If 'generous feeling' is dampened by the 'cold hand of circumspection', we would be left only with 'selfish prudence and reason just rising above instinct'; rather, fostering the passions encourages the 'habit of reflection' and offers self-knowledge and the growth of reason.[47] Given that passions constitute the 'common stream' which runs through our natures, they cannot be escaped; experience, as Rousseau asserts, is necessary to cultivate reason, understanding, and sensibility. The value of experience as a route to knowledge appears again in what reads as a veiled reference to Smith's impartial spectator: 'the world cannot be seen by an unmoved spectator; we must mix in the throng and feel as men feel, before we can judge of their feelings'.[48] From experience comes reflection, and hence virtue will be founded on the 'the clear conviction of reason' not 'the impulse of the heart', and morality will rest on a rock 'against which the storms of passion vainly beat'.[49]

Perhaps unconsciously, Godwin echoed Wollstonecraft's image of the rock in his *Memoirs of the author of 'The Rights of Woman'*, putting it to quite different effect when he described her in the midst of her affair with Imlay as 'like a serpent upon a rock' appearing with the 'brilliancy, the sleekness, and the elastic activity of its happiest age'.[50] As his deletion of the sentence in the second edition of the *Memoirs* suggests, the image, with its emphasis on physical being and sexual satiation, conveys an entirely different attitude to the passions than Wollstonecraft's rock image would suggest. Behind her engagement with Chesterfield and the other unnamed moral writers is a reorientation of the relationship to affect, but not an indulgence of it: a recognition that emotional experience must be the basis of an education which moves through youthful enthusiasm to reflection and rational growth. Feeling is here released from a regulatory hold not in order to flow in unconstrained freedom but rather as the experiential basis for cultivating the reflection and reason through which virtue is attained. Wollstonecraft's vision of organic moral growth through affective experience thus avoids the binary of wild, Rousseauvian nature opposed to culture and civilization, or of sensibility versus reason, but rather understands, as Maria puts it, the 'culture of the heart' as necessarily accompanied by that of 'an improving mind'.[51]

The Wrongs of Woman and the History of the Passions: Prudence, Credulity, and Sensibility

In *The Wrongs of Woman*, Wollstonecraft returns to these themes, attacking prudence as often a superficial deception and tracing a history of the passions from youthful credulity to mature social feeling. Unfinished though the work is, Wollstonecraft adds a further element to her ongoing critique of commercial modernity by linking financial corruption to affective failings, and she begins to sketch out a means for affective reform. In America, Darnford had witnessed a 'phenomenon in the history of the human mind': the 'head enthusiastically enterprising, with cold selfishness of heart'.[52] The story of Maria's husband, George Venables, and his father, Venables senior, enables Wollstonecraft to personalise this 'phenomenon', to 'embody' the sentiments, as she put it in her preface. By showing the 'history' of such sentiments in George Venables' upbringing and formation, she yokes her attack on the moral failings underlying commercial society with her earlier attention to the role of education in the formation of character; the history of Maria's sentiments, by contrast, points in a different direction.

Wollstonecraft had already condemned, in her *View of the French Revolution*, the merchant who 'enters into speculation so closely bordering on fraudulence, that common straight forward minds can scarcely distinguish the devious art of selling any thing for a price far beyond that necessary to ensure a just profit'.[53] Her account of the Venables offers a more extended critique of commercial and moral fraud, which attends to affective formation. Venables senior, who makes a brief appearance in the narrative, is a merchant who exemplifies Smithian values, following a 'prudential plan' in business and engaging only in 'narrow ... and cautious speculation'.[54] It is not a good sign, however, that the unremitting care with which he attends to business ruins his health and brings about his death. His son George, whilst apparently sharing his father's creditable character, uses this as a 'mask' behind which his 'habits of libertinism' are concealed from his 'commercial connections'.[55] Prudence, which oils the wheels of a Smithian economy, is easily counterfeited, its fakery a threat not only to commerce, but in the moral and sexual spheres too. Venables' 'reputation of being attentive to business' explicitly informs Maria's uncle's approval of their marriage, 'for habits of order in business would, he conceived, extend to the regulation of the affections in domestic life'.[56] Venables' 'mask' of prudence is thus a significant factor in a marriage which will consign Maria to financial and sexual exploitation. Writing to her daughter with the wisdom of hindsight, Maria notes that Venables' reputation for prudence was won simply by maintaining silence in her uncle's company, apart from an occasional question or deferential remark. Compared with the 'youthful ebullitions' stemming from the 'animal spirits' of other young people, this proved effective in building Venables' reputation, but, in terms which echo Wollstonecraft's analysis in the *Vindication*, Maria observes that there is a troubling absence of passion in Venables and his like: 'these prudent young men want all the fire necessary to ferment their

The Wrongs of Woman *and the History of the Passions*   203

faculties, and are characterized as wise, only because they are not foolish'. George's silence is not prudence but 'sheer barrenness of mind, and want of imagination'.[57] In his discussion of the 'influence of belief' in his *Treatise of Human Nature*, Hume had used similar language to argue that a 'ferment of the blood and spirits' is capable of so disordering the imagination as to make it impossible to distinguish 'betwixt truth and falsehood'.[58] Maria's critique inverts Hume's worry about 'the influence of belief' to present the opposite danger: an absence of the very passions which even for Hume give 'vigour' to our mental functioning.[59]

In place of the 'fire' which might 'ferment' his faculties, Venables displays only a 'gambling desire to start suddenly into riches'.[60] To that end, he obtains money by 'violating the laws of his country' and by forging Maria's signature, but his 'despicable speculation' also involves accommodation bills, fraudulent versions of credit instruments widely used by traders.[61] Venables' practice of drawing and redrawing bills is described by Smith as being used by 'chimerical projectors' to raise money which they can never hope to repay, drawing creditors into a 'fatal circle' which might ultimately result in the failure of banks.[62] Such fraudsters exploit the difficulty of distinguishing between 'a real and a fictitious bill of exchange' – one which reflects an actual business transaction and one which doesn't. In the context of local or regional business transactions, knowledge of the credit-worthiness of individual actors might be secure, but Venables is able to operate beyond the purview of a prudence which Smith hoped would secure economic transactions, exploiting a serious faultline in commercial practice and exposing the flawed security of prudence on which commerce was founded.[63]

The vulnerability of the credit on which much economic activity depended had of course long been recognised: it was in part the cause for the numerous writings on credit in which Lady Credit herself featured. Wollstonecraft's innovation is to link the economic fragility of credit to its effects in the social and sexual spheres, in a text about the woman of sensibility. She does this by showing how Venables' main object of speculation is Maria herself. Her dowry of £5,000 is used by Venables to fund various unsuccessful projects, before Maria herself is further mined as an economic, and in a disturbing continuity, sexual asset, by her husband, in his quest for further sums and loans. Speculation is thus linked not only with financial fraud, but also personal or sexual fraud, as Venables tries to trick Maria into sexual relations with one of his creditors, in a scene which rewrites, in starker and more shocking form, Gilray's image of the Pitt's assault on the Old Lady of Threadneedle Street. Like the Bank of England, whose propriety should be assured by gentlemanly credit practices, Maria is the female object of male financial and sexual depredation, no longer protected but instead asset-raided. The parallel enables Wollstonecraft to expose the flipside to the chivalrous defence of delicate, feminine credit lauded in Parliament, by demonstrating the intertwined nature of financial and sexual exploitation, in a culture where women are not extrinsic to commercial society but objects of exchange within it, on whose sexual value men attempt to capitalise. Meanwhile, hampered by credulity and the social expectations which the *Vindication* has already outlined, women are ill-equipped to make judgements about the behaviour and character of others, and instead of acting with prudence, fall back on its empty shell, propriety. Even that, as Maria's fate shows, cannot protect them from determined assault.

From all this, it follows that commercial, sexual, and social reform must happen together, so it is only appropriate that Maria's eventual rejection of 'prudence', and what she terms 'little concerns', occurs at the moment of the sexual consummation of her relationship with Darnford. From this sentimental revolution eventually stems a transformation of credulity into a wide-ranging capacity for belief and affirmation. Already enacted by Maria, Darnford, and Jemima's sympathetic listening to each other's personal testimonies, and repeated in Wollstonecraft's readers' own acts of reading, sympathetic belief, a new kind of credit, eventually finds a wider horizon in a moment of apotheosis which indicates how further social transformation might be founded.

Maria's relationship with Darnford – itself perhaps a 'little concern' – is short-lived, but it is part of a sentimental regeneration in Maria which soon moves beyond the narrow confines of the sexual to a more expansive social engagement. Such a refiguring of what credulity might become is perhaps surprising in a text whose opening scenes clearly present the dangers of overindulged fancy. Wollstonecraft herself observed, when attacking Burke in her first *Vindication*, that enthusiasm, a close relative of credulity, can too easily tip into madness; excessive, enthusiastic, belief had long been associated with women in particular. Yet Wollstonecraft's description of Maria's ability to 'trust without sufficient reason' – given, with provoking irony, at the moment of her sexual consummation with Darnford – throws such dangers to the wind:

> There was one peculiarity in Maria's mind: she was more anxious not to deceive, than to guard against deception; and had rather trust without sufficient reason, than be for ever the prey of doubt. Besides, what are we, when the mind has, from reflection, a certain kind of elevation, which exalts the contemplation above the little concerns of prudence! We see what we wish, and make a world of our own...[64]

The Wrongs of Woman *and the History of the Passions* 205

In an apparent *volte face* with the text's initial exposition, it appears that Maria's tendency to 'extreme credulity' may point a route beyond the difficulties in which prudence too easily gets bogged down: difficulties of judgement, doubt, and deception. Credulity might not be a quality to be restrained, but one whose energy, like the 'animal spirits' of the ebullient young people mentioned earlier, might be a 'fire' to 'ferment the faculties', and raise the mind beyond 'little concerns'. It was precisely a failure of such spirit which Darnford identified in his account of how the energy of the American pioneers had morphed into 'commercial speculations' carried out 'with cold selfishness of heart'. The 'peculiarity of Maria's mind', her willingness to 'trust without sufficient reason', revalues, in socially positive ways, the credulity which Smith saw as natural to the human condition, and as persisting into adulthood despite the regulatory processes of education and the moral self-surveillance outlined in *The Theory of Moral Sentiments*. If for Smith there is a need to reign in the tendency to believe which for him is both a mark of the child and a natural condition of humanity, *The Wrongs of Woman* essays a refiguration of credulity to point to forms of belief which might reform social, sexual, and financial circulation itself. And if Smith's adult is vulnerable to the eruptions of childish fantasies, against which he must always be on his guard, Wollstonecraft places her faith instead in the process of maturation, by which feelings might become, as the *Vindication* puts it, a kind of 'rock'. Where Smith's valoration of prudence in the *Theory* condenses into the praxis of self-interest in *The Wealth of Nations*, we shall see that Maria's credulity – in line with the *Vindication*'s advice to allow passions to mature through experience – eventually opens out into a discovery of the 'substantial happiness' of 'social pleasure' produced through a flowering of the 'real affections of life', comparable to the unfettered pleasure of 'roving through nature at large'. Such a 'state of mind' is only brought to an end with the release of the 'dogs of law', in the form of the adultery case against Darnford, which makes clear both the need for larger social reforms and the difficulty of realising them.

If Maria's trust in Darnford ultimately proves a failed investment, it is nevertheless a route to other forms of social reconnection. Jemima's witnessing of the relationship also plays a part in her parallel emotional regrowth. And, just as Maria's credulity enables the later flowering of more extensive and substantial social feeling, it is notable that both Maria and her uncle (whose benevolent impulses are strongly marked by what Wollstonecraft describes as a kind of petrified romantic feeling) attempt to use money, otherwise strongly associated in the text with corrupt financial transactions, to ameliorate social relations and enact social justice. In this, Maria presents a contrast with other female figures who in various ways are presented as resisting economic circulation: whether Gilray's 'Old Lady of Threadneedle Street', fending off Pitt's attack; or America seated cold-heartedly, in Darnford's depiction, on her bags of dollars; or even Jemima, Maria's jailor, who hoards her wages in an act presented as the only way she might escape the cycles of exploitation in which she herself circulates as an object. Like Jemima, Maria is associated with sexual, social, and monetary circulation, passing from father to uncle to husband to lover, in a way which illustrates the transactional nature of social relations, and the sexualised nature of financial ones. But Maria is also an active financial agent, causing money to circulate, often for socially benevolent ends: whether raising charity for the destitute Peggy, supporting Venables' illegitimate child, establishing her siblings in financially secure positions, or paying Jemima's wages; she also pays household bills from her own pocket, and is the guardian of her daughter's inheritance from her uncle on his death.[65] Admittedly, it is also her money, originating from her uncle, which funds Venables' 'despicable speculations', but nevertheless, the two figures (Maria and her uncle) who attempt to circulate money in positive ways are both marked by forms of 'romantic' feeling – in contrast with Venables' calculating, speculating, prudence. At the same time, money is clearly an imperfect means by which to circulate social feeling. Venables' sole act of charity, a contribution for Peggy, is a calculated, counterfeit gesture designed to manipulate Maria's perception of him; the fact that it is his own father's rent collector who is the immediate cause of Peggy's distress only underlines the empty performativity of the act. As the hidden motivation of Venables' charitable donation suggests, Maria is able to be effective in this particular 'project of usefulness' in part due to the effects of her youth and beauty: 'my eloquence was in my complexion, the blush of seventeen'.[66] As shown too by the unwanted kiss Maria receives from the attorney to whom she pleads on Peggy's behalf, female benevolence remains vulnerable to, and dependent on, the men whose sexual predations constitute their own 'projects'.

The 'Real Affections of Life'

Maria's capacity for social feeling is set out in a little commented-on paragraph from the penultimate chapter of *The Wrongs of Woman*, which follows her escape from the madhouse:

The real affections of life, when they are allowed to burst forth, are buds pregnant with joy and all the sweet emotions of the soul; yet they branch out with wild ease, unlike the artificial forms of felicity, sketched by an imagination painfully alive. The substantial happiness, which enlarges and civilizes the mind, may be compared to the pleasure experienced in roving through nature at large, inhaling the sweet gale natural to the clime; while the reveries of a feverish imagination continually sport themselves in gardens full of aromatic shrubs, which cloy while they delight, and weaken the sense of pleasure they gratify. The heaven of fancy, below or beyond the stars, in this life, or in those ever-smiling regions surrounded by the unmarked ocean of futurity, have an insipid uniformity which palls. Poets have imagined scenes of bliss; but, fencing out sorrow, all the extatic (*sic*) emotions of the soul, and even its grandeur, seem to be equally excluded. We dose (*sic*) over the unruffled lake, and long to scale the rocks which fence the happy valley of contentment, though serpents hiss in the pathless deserts, and danger lurks in the unexplored wiles. Maria found herself more indulgent as she was happier, and discovered virtues, in characters, she had before disregarded, while chasing the phantoms of elegance and excellence, which sported in the meteors that exhale in the marshes of misfortune. The heart is often shut by romance against social pleasure; and, fostering a sickly sensibility, grows callous to the soft touches of humanity.[67]

As she does elsewhere, Wollstonecraft describes affective states with the language of the natural world, giving 'wiles' (tricks, dangers, or deceptions) material form, to 'lurk' as features of the landscape. The 'pathless desert' inhabited by serpents recalls the barren setting of her early fictional fragment, the *Cave of Fancy*, whilst the 'happy valley of contentment' references Johnson's *Rasselas*, to which the opening paragraph of *Cave of Fancy* had also alluded. The contrast between artificial or imagined scenes, and natural ones, recalls the prefatory Advertisement to *Mary*, whose attack on the usual representations of women in fiction also contrasts 'insipid', measured steps on the 'beaten track' with authentic 'rambles' in nature; the opposition between artifice and originary experience underpins the late essay 'On Poetry' too.[68] Such density of reference, combined with the wrought language and elevated register, points to the importance of the thoughts being sketched here, and the persistence of Wollstonecraft's preoccupation with them, as well as something of Wollstonecraft's aims in relation to fiction itself, especially with regard to female feeling, and female lives.

The unmistakable reference to *Rasselas* foregrounds Wollstonecraft's concern with credulity, as shared with that text. At its outset, *Rasselas* presents itself as a cautionary tale on the dangers of credulity, addressing '[y]e who listen with credulity to the whispers of fancy, and peruse with eagerness the phantoms of hope'.[69] Given fiction's dependence on readerly belief, acknowledged in Johnson's *Rambler* essay on fiction, which states that we require scenes that we can 'credit', it is a curious warning.[70] The first paragraph of *Cave of Fancy* similarly warns against a 'life lost in desultory wishes'.[71] But where Rasselas's extended journey from the happy valley offers no clear resolution – in its conclusion, 'nothing is concluded' – and *Cave of Fancy* points past the 'delusion of the imagination' to suggest that '[e]arthly love leads to heavenly', Maria finds happiness in the 'real affections of life', the pleasures not of romantic but of social happiness.[72] The rejection of the 'heaven of fancy', the 'scenes of bliss' sketched by poets, suggests that full weight should be given to the 'real' of Maria's 'real affections'. Her happiness has been arrived at by overleaping the boundaries of the 'happy valley of contentment', as the *Vindication* had shown that men, but not women do; to stay in the bounds of contentment is as stupefying as cottage life. The sage Sagestus in *Cave of Fancy* also 'overleaped the boundary prescribed to human knowledge'; the fact that he gives his name to his adoptive daughter suggests that she too will repeat such transgressive feats.[73] Maria has arrived at the 'happiness' of social connection not on what 'On Poetry' calls the 'silken wings of fancy', but through navigating the 'pathless deserts' of 'real' experience, alert to the 'soft touches of humanity': an experience traced too, if vicariously, by the young Segesta as she listens to the tale of educative spirit in the *Cave of Fancy*'s last chapter.

Karen O'Brien has suggested that throughout her writing, Wollstonecraft was 'struggling to define and bring into being a stage of society beyond the stage of commerce'; this passage suggests that allowing the 'real affections of life' to 'burst forth' is a means to that end.[74] These, perhaps, are the Daedalian wings on which the happy valley might be escaped, in what is nevertheless a difficult enterprise: 'danger lurks in the unexplored wiles'. As Wollstonecraft's highly metaphorical writing suggests, even naming such 'real' forms of affect is tricky, although distinguishing them, in a familiar move, from 'sickly sensibility' is a start.[75] Rather than becoming bound down in such difficulties, Wollstonecraft's imagery does suggestive work, asserting the proper 'roving ... at large' of the affective female subject, the branching out of 'wild ease'. Where 'sickly sensibility' suggests enclosure in the claustrophobic bubble of romance, connection with others is emphasised in such 'roving': Maria finds herself able to appreciate 'virtues' in others which she might otherwise have overlooked. In the 'social pleasure' of such humanity, Wollstonecraft recasts the fraught, slippery, and overworked discourse around female feeling to locate it firmly in the world and to emphasise its emancipatory, experiential pleasures.[76] In releasing feeling to found and constitute social connection, she resists Smith's confinement of female feeling to the home, as in *The Theory of Moral Sentiments*, where humanity, 'the virtue of a woman', 'consists merely in the exquisite fellow-feeling' of a spectator, which, whilst agreeable, is 'unfit for the world' and is in part described through its lack of other qualities: it requires 'no self-denial, no self-command, no great exertion of the sense of propriety'.[77] Smith contrasts humanity with the masculine quality of generosity, the examples of which are located in the public, active world: an ambitious man ceding to another an office at which he had long aimed; the soldier sacrificing his life; Brutus defending the Roman republic even against his own sons.[78] The 'unbounded attachment' seemingly lauded in Maria's 'roving through nature' is distinct from the 'dissolving' tenderness which Godwin suggests characterises readers' responses to the *Short Residence*; and it differs too from the 'gusts' of sensibility which blow women off course as described by Wollstonecraft in the second *Vindication*.[79] Locating the 'real affections of life' in a metaphorical natural landscape of experience contests women's exclusion from public life, whilst the image of existence as 'roving through nature at large' resists the very categories of public and private used since Smith to enforce a gender divide, and still operative, if complexly, in today's historiographical literature on eighteenth-century female lives.[80]

As Pamela Clemit has noted, many radical writers in the 1790s, inspired by Rousseau, looked to the affections to inspire social or political change.[81] Even the most 'dangerous' affect, enthusiasm, as Jon Mee remarks, if contained within the confines of literary culture, could be viewed as 'a means of returning an alienated society to values that were seen as more essentially human'.[82] The potential of particular forms of affect to enlarge 'the sphere of our happiness', in the philosopher's words, can also be traced to Hume's essay 'Of the Delicacy of Taste and Passion', which discussed how, whilst extravagant passions were liable to take the individual beyond prudent bounds, 'taste' focused on cultural objects could provide a safer form of pleasure.[83] In Hume, this distinction between objects of taste and life (objects of passion) marks a fear of emotional extravagance or excess which is self-protective: whilst passion can cause misery and disrupt happiness, 'delicacy of taste' contains and regulates emotional excess by providing a safe outlet for affective experience. The availability to taste of particular categories of aesthetic objects to do such work helps to preserve the rest of experience from the dangerous eruptions of affect to which humanity is all too susceptible. Wollstonecraft's assertion of the 'real affections of life' rejects such a separation by demanding that the 'enlarged sphere of our happiness' is located not just in the realm of cultural objects, but in the social exchange of existence itself. She thus refuses what would come to be considered as the separate sphere of the aesthetic as a privileged arena for enacting happiness, and frees our capacity for happiness to 'roam' at will in the world. That the aesthetic would also come to be distinguished from the economic, a separation articulated by the distinction between different forms of value (beauty and pleasure versus use), gives additional significance to Wollstonecraft's refusal to compartmentalise and segregate different areas of human experience.

What new forms of social relation and community might be founded on the 'real affections of life'? The 'merely ... habitable' buildings which Maria views from her window at the start of *The Wrongs of Woman* suggests that these are urgently needed.[84] One possibility is indicated by the temporary community constituted by Maria, Jemima, and Darnford as they share their life stories with each other, modelling the sympathetic reception of personal narrative which Wollstonecraft asks of her readers; another is suggested in the later triangle of Jemima, Maria, and her daughter, which, in pointed rejection of the social norm of marriage, is sketched in one possible ending of the text.[85] A community founded on sympathetic feeling, whether of readers or listeners, offers a different model of society from that founded on the rational exchanges of civil society's public sphere, which constituted one eighteenth-century self-image. As discussed in Chapter 3, eighteenth-century civil society was also property society: its foundation on property excluded most women and many men, and its rationality was, Terry Eagleton claims, 'articulable only by those with the social interests which property generates'.[86] To recognise the rationality of the public sphere as the expressive mode of property society is to recognise the oppositional potential of affect in commercial society. Daniel White has demonstrated that, for dissenters such as Joseph Priestley, John Aiken, or Anna Letitia Barbauld, sensibility and other forms of 'humane' feeling were deployed to achieve an accommodation with commercial society: taste and feeling would, in Priestley's account, restrain, regulate, and reform the more extreme, rebarbative effects of commercial society.[87] Godwin's *Enquirer* similarly hoped that polite refinement would regulate and reform, an aspiration echoing too in Godwin's presentation of *The Wrongs of Woman* as potentially giving 'a new impulse to the manners of a world'.[88] But to place the 'real affections of life' centre stage as the basis of the primary exchanges which constitute social existence goes further than this. It is to assert humane feeling not as a secondary means of regulating the acquisitive and aspirational impulses on which commercial society depends, but as itself a fundamental, constitutive social structure: feeling is not a secondary, delayed, regulatory force which lags behind the energy of commerce and softens the oppressions and inequalities of property, but is itself an originary mode of engagement with the materiality of the world and its people. In terms of the opposition to which Wollstonecraft returns repeatedly in her writing, this is to regard the commercial world as fake and artificial, and the world of 'real affection' as the nature in which to 'rove'. As well as rejecting the Smithian confinement of female 'humanity' to the home, this version of 'real affection' refuses too the Smithian repression and regulation of forms of affect (credulity, belief, passion more broadly) which are necessitated in the turn to commerce, to public life, and to adulthood. Instead, 'real affection' is cast as constituting the fundamental and primary mode of existing in and engaging with the world.

Wollstonecraft's assertion of 'real affections' thus strongly challenges a political economy whose account of human feeling pins human lives – cut through with wants, desires, aspirations – into the shape of their economic existence. By engaging with political economy at its affective foundations, Wollstonecraft reorients the relation of human subjects to their feelings and traces new stories and social outcomes. Maria's rejection of 'little concerns', her enjoyment of fleeting social pleasures, counters Smith's narrative of material acquisition (as in the tale of the poor man's son, for whom desire is contained under the sign of property) with an alternative narrative of affective spontaneity, of immediate, not delayed, pleasure, and of pleasure, too, achieved in ways other than through material acquisition of alienated objects.[89] Where pleasure in Wollstonecraft *is* object-oriented, feeling is exercised in relations with the natural world or in social connection, not in the man-made world of goods. Even if at times swayed by the 'chimerical' imagination, feeling can also be its own object – unlike in Smith's instrumental positioning of feeling as being goal-oriented, a motivation or stimulus to something: a 'spring' towards labour or acquisition. Given that Smith turns to feelings to explain how and why humans do things, affect is always yoked to a teleological narrative. As sketched by Wollstonecraft, whether in her remarks on fiction or on poetry, or as embodied all too briefly by Maria, affect is potentially or actually anti-teleological, as suggested by its characteristic movement of 'wandering' and 'roving'. It may thus be capable of reorienting an energy geared towards progress, development, improvement, and wealth, all located in the future, and finding instead present sufficiency and satiety. Unbounded 'roving' in nature may thus provide an alternative means of accessing the contentment marked elsewhere in Wollstonecraft's writings by the more ambivalent sign of the modestly sufficient cottage.

In line with Wollstonecraft's choice of literary form for what was to be her last major work, perhaps it is the novel itself which best expresses this mobility of feeling, of feeling freed to roam at will, to perhaps be credulous, and to bud forth with wild ease. The novel, after all, especially in the form of Wollstonecraft's affective history of a 'woman of sensibility', explores states of mind and episodes of feeling, and rouses those of its readers. Something of this is anticipated, perhaps unintentionally, in *Rasselas*. In the description of the joys of winged flight given by the artist – 'with what pleasure a philosopher, furnished with winds ... would see the earth, and all it's *(sic)* inhabitants' – it is almost as though the invention being described is that of the pre-eminent literary flight mechanism, the novel itself, which, as we saw at the end of the previous chapter, was praised by Montesquieu a few years before the publication of *Rasselas* as opening new forms of vision and connective insights to its reader.[90] In *Rasselas*, however, the art of flying is enacted only on condition that it is not shared; the 'art shall not be divulged' as it may enable others to invade the happy valley, and states of bounded contentment might be breached.[91] In the event, as with the original myth of Daedalus, the attempt at flight fails; perhaps the warning against credulity at the text's opening has been too fully ingested.[92] Having the 'strength to believe' is, by contrast, reiterated a number of times in *Cave of Fancy*. The absence of belief in Sagesta's mother, who had no 'courage to form an opinion of her own', is lamented; Sagesta herself is commanded by her adoptive father to 'ever trust to the first impression', especially in distinguishing between affected social virtues and real ones; a third, unnamed male character, is suggested to have been someone able to silence those 'who doubted' because lacking the 'strength to believe'.[93] The capacity for belief, of course, perhaps more so than the Godwinian taste, is required of the novel reader, but it is not limited to that object: Maria's feelings, roused by her readings in books loaned by Darnford, soon seek expression beyond the literary object.[94] Maria's reading releases feeling to become a transformative social force, as perhaps Wollstonecraft hoped would be the case for her readers too. The feeling associated with the literary object is not contained there, but circulates – roves – more widely. If the regulation of credulity is required by Smithian political economy, the novel's dependence on credulity is necessary for reformative, transformative feeling to circulate, in a metaphor which, ironically, replicates the circulatory movement of the economy itself.

We saw earlier how, whilst *The Wrongs of Woman* is in part about male exploitation of different kinds of credit, Maria puts money to benevolent ends. Money is a potent emblem of her capacity for credulity: George's donation of a guinea for a charitable cause seals Maria's feelings for him: the 'magic touch' of the coin 'invested' him 'with more than mortal beauty'.[95] Maria's eyes are later 'opened': experience, as the *Vindication* asserts, brings reflection and maturity, whilst not stifling humanity and generous feeling.[96] The financially circulatory role which Maria plays throughout the text might be regarded as just one expression of her capacity for social connection as celebrated in the passage we have been reading. Her generosity contrasts with Smith's claim that 'the fair-sex, who have commonly much more tenderness than ours, have seldom so much generosity. That women rarely make considerable donations, is an observation of the civil law'.[97] Maria's ability to unite generosity and humanity explodes Smith's attempt to differentiate, and gender, these qualities; the monetary expression of her generosity, as a mark of social feeling, counters too his attempt to exclude such unprudent acts from the world of commerce and exchange, to separate social feeling from economic enterprise, to exclude the enthusiasm of youth from the experience of age.

As noted above, Wollstonecraft's late essay 'On Poetry' returns to the opposed qualities of artifice and 'real' experience which she had long explored in her writing. Here the familiar opposition between the artificial and the authentic is elaborated by further distinguishing between fake and real feeling; between immediacy and spontaneity as against labour, memory, and rational cognition. As in her earlier writings, Wollstonecraft's late exercise in aesthetic theory valorates feeling, authenticity, originality, fancy, and sensation, and it downgrades instruction, precept, copying, and rules. In her *Vindication of the Rights of Men*, Wollstonecraft had exploited a well-established link between poetry and excessive feeling in her attack on Burke: his 'fine phrensy', like the 'enthusiasm of genius', was thinly divided from madness.[98] 'On Poetry', by contrast, encounters a different problem: not excess of feeling but its suppression and weakness, an underdevelopment associated with the modern commercial era itself, where books are a 'hot-bed in which artificial fruits are produced' and where 'luxury' has made 'calm sensations' unsatisfying even for the 'moderate pursuer of artificial pleasures'.[99] As Daniel White has noted, the figure of the poet has a reforming role to play here: he is presented as a moderating and unifying force, capable of blending 'fire of enthusiasm' but 'enlarged by thought'.[100] Just one year after the publication of Wollstonecraft's essay, Wordsworth too would celebrate the poet's ability to recollect passion in tranquillity, in the Preface to the *Lyrical Ballads*, but the more such regulatory, moderating capacities were associated with the poet, the more they risked removal, into more rarefied literary air, from the arena of commercial society itself. Wollstonecraft's essay moves beyond its discussion of the poet, however, to note that 'gross minds are only to be moved by forcible representations', and that the 'thoughtless' must be roused by 'objects ... calculated to produce tumultuous emotion'.[101] As well as a critique of the failure or corruption of affective response in 'the present state of society', such words arguably point beyond the efforts of the poet to the methods required by her own objectives as a reforming novelist.

Located as she is in the 'merely ... habitable' structures of commercial society, mixing 'in the throng', as Wollstonecraft recommends in the second *Vindication*, Maria, the woman of sensibility whose 'humanizing affections' are under siege as she navigates a world full of 'wiles', performs a role arguably comparable to that of the poet, blending passion and originary experience, enthusiasm and reflection, but continuing to 'rove through nature at large'.[102] Such 'roving' recasts the figure of circulatory exchange central to political economy, just as the novel, as an alternative site for imagining social existence, counters political economy's claim to 'rationalise the social'. Yoking the figure of female feeling to that of circulatory 'roving', Wollstonecraft finds a means to regulate her potential excesses, to expose her to the education of experience, yet also to release her socially beneficial effects, whilst resisting political economy's value-less account of circulation as simply the accumulated transactions of the 'medium of exchange'. That Maria ultimately runs up against a legal institution whose representative, the judge, thrice rejects the possibility of 'letting women plead their feelings' and calls her incarceration a 'prudent measure', only underlines the need for reform, and the limits of rational discourse to achieve it.[103] At the same time, the figure of circulation is linked, in the prefatory notes written by both Godwin and Wollstonecraft to the fates both of women and of the novel itself. Wollstonecraft's assertion that nothing can be worse for a woman than to be 'bound ... for life' to such a man as Venables claims for women the emancipatory possibility of circulation; and Godwin asserts for the unfinished novel text itself (elsewhere described as a 'project of public interest') the same possibility of a circulation which will establish the text's value, as well as improve the 'manners' of the world.[104] It is only fitting, after all, that fiction, itself an instrument of credit, dependent on a readerly capacity for belief, should not be turned against credulity, but rather mobilise its powers to reform the world in which it circulates.

Conclusion
Imagination, Futurity, and the Value of Things

> I anticipated the future improvement of the world, and observed how much man has still to do to obtain of the earth all it could yield […] Imagination went still farther, and pictured the state of man when the earth could no longer support him. Whither was he to flee from universal famine? Do not smile; I really became distressed for these fellow creatures yet unborn.

> *

> I stretched out my hand to eternity, bounding over the dark speck of life to come.

> *

> Futurity, what has thou not to give to those who know that there is such a thing as happiness![1]

In each of these moments from her *Short Residence in Sweden, Norway and Denmark*, Wollstonecraft addresses the future: whether her own or that of humankind; whether perceptible or hidden in veils of time; whether anticipating happiness or in a deep despair that makes her feel that 'death under every form, appears to me like something getting free'.[2] In the third epigraph, as often in the *Short Residence*, Wollstonecraft uses the rhetorical device of apostrophe, described by Anahid Nersessian as constituting a specific 'relational bearing' which brings a 'sustained attention' to 'things it can't even see or can't expect to look back'; apostrophe looks 'to the world … as the thing it cannot explain and with which it can only partially communicate'.[3] One of the effects of this 'one-sided attention' is to enable lyric subjectivity to become indeterminate: to allow the solitary subject to speak beyond the historical present to address other, as yet unlived, temporal frames. Although, writing as she is in summer 1796, it is only one year since Wollstonecraft completed her last major work, in which she casts the 'philosophic eye' of the historian on the early events of the French Revolution, here her relationship with time, as well as with human community, is itself recast, as her very choice of genre and modes of speech indicate. Even the act of observing the cascade near Fredericstadt in Norway – an 'always varying, still the same, torrent' – opens out to the future, as, stimulated by the 'tumultuous emotions' which 'this sublime object excited', an 'equal activity' is produced in Wollstonecraft's mind and she stretches out her 'hand to eternity' to grasp 'at immortality', as though impelled by what, in the first of these letters, she describes as an 'imperious' and 'involuntary sympathy', whose 'attraction of adhesion' which makes her feel part of a 'mighty whole'.[4] The 'sublime' cascade which prompts this move thus denotes not simply the 'impetuous dashing of the rebounding torrent' but the equally unceasing 'current of [her] thoughts'. If, in her first letter, Wollstonecraft reflects on the involuntary sympathies which bind her to others in the present, by the Fredericstadt cascade, the compulsion is directed 'to eternity', dissolving the temporal distance which would divide the Wollstonecraft of 1796 from, for instance, her readers today, just as the distinction between her thoughts and the 'dashing of the rebounding torrent' is also dissolved. If Wollstonecraft reaches towards the future here, how might we, her future readers, receive her? Sylvana Tomaselli has observed that Wollstonecraft is reinvented by each age for the needs and purposes of their own time.[5] What Wollstonecraft do we need for ours? How, more specifically, given the concerns of this book, might an understanding of Wollstonecraft's engagement with the political economy of her time inform the political and economic debates and challenges of our moment, and our future?

These are big questions, and ones which have many possible answers given that we live in an era of multiple global stresses and crises, on many fronts, including geopolitical, economic, and democratic.[6] Whilst, clearly, investigating such a breadth of concerns lies beyond the purview of this book, we might echo Wollstonecraft's willingness, whilst gazing into the cascade, to let her thoughts flow in a similarly unrestrained 'current', and reflect on the differences between the political economy of Wollstonecraft's day and the economics of our own time, and especially what such differences mean in terms of equipping us to think our futurity, as Wollstonecraft does. Tomaselli notes that eighteenth-century political economy was in part a 'science' of balancing the needs of the present with those of the future; it thus 'sought to speak about tomorrows, the long-term consequences of the endeavor to satisfy today's desires'.[7] Such an endeavour is arguably absent from today's economics in its orthodox forms, given that, as is widely

Conclusion 217

recognised, our planet's future is imperilled by a climate catastrophe which is a direct consequence of our existing economic systems and paradigms, with their extractive logics of productivity and growth driven by fossil fuels: a 'futurity' in some sense recognised in Wollstonecraft's anticipation of how 'the future improvement of the world' might lead to a point where 'the earth could no longer support' its future inhabitants.[8] The limitations of mainstream economics in this context are evident for instance in Geoffrey West's observation that concepts such as energy, entropy, and metabolism, which are central to any understanding to the future of life on the planet, 'have not found their way into mainstream economics', even whilst, ironically, economics 'is almost entirely structured according to metaphors from nineteenth-century energy physics', and especially the 'static physics model of equilibrium'.[9]

How did we get here, from Wollstonecraft's time? How and why is the economic thinking of our day so different from the burgeoning political economy of hers? Tim Rogan's recent study of the moral critique of capitalism attempted by twentieth-century economic thinkers Karl Polyani, E. P. Thompson and R. H. Trelawny, *The Moral Economists*, offers one way of answering these questions. In particular, Rogan shows how Polyani's search for an alternative account of the 'human personality' from that of the 'economic man' at the centre of liberal individualism took him back to Smith, from where he traced the history of post-Smithian economic thought through to the early twentieth century. Polyani identified Smith as a 'moral economist of a kind', and proposed that a 'declension into economism began *after* the publication of *The Wealth of Nations*'.[10] The 'humanistic foundations' of political economy were thus eroded after Smith, starting with Malthus and Ricardo, as economic maxims beyond moral rules emerged.[11] The naturalistic turn (which modelled human nature as site of supposedly natural drives and behaviours) further extruded moral thought from economics, and the stage was set for nineteenth-century utilitarian reasoning, which eliminated 'every passion and motivation other than the appetite for pecuniary gain from the understanding of social life'.[12] By 1836, John Stuart Mill could define political economy as a science approaching persons 'solely as beings who desire to possess wealth', and as perfected by the 'entire abstraction of every other human passion or motive', although he also argued that its conclusions 'are only true conditionally'.[13] By the end of the nineteenth century, economics had 'adopted the metaphors and techniques of physics', in particular energy physics and the 'dominant metaphorical referent' of the engine.[14] If, in the late nineteenth- and early twentieth centuries, economists analysed the forces of 'equilibrium and disequilibrium in specific markets and industries', another set of models further intrenched economic rationalism in the mid-twentieth century, as modernist concepts of system, structure, and organisation took hold across the social sciences.[15] By the 1930s and 1940s, the concept of 'the economy', defined as the 'integrated system of exchange of a specific nation', became the object of economics as a modern social science, and GDP was invented, a measure still at the heart of national economic policy despite the metric's failure to measure quality of life or societal well-being.[16]

This brief history helps to explain what economics is today, as a discipline and knowledge practice, as well as what it is not. As Joanna Rostek has described, economics is a social science which models market behaviour; it is suspicious of embedded values of individuals or social groups; it encourages its students to distinguish what is 'positivist and rationalist' from individual, subjective, or social value.[17] Moral questions tend to be sidelined, whilst 'economic' ones are foregrounded; economics thus obscures its own values by presenting them as value-neutral. Thus, as Julie Nelson suggests, '[m]orality is left to the humanists, while mainstream economists pursue "objective" study based on an assumed analogy between economic "laws" … and the "laws" of physical science'. As Mariana Mazzucato comments, economics measures 'the price of everything and the value of nothing'.[18] Such omissions lay the discipline open to critique, motivated precisely by the values and perspectives it excludes, and such critiques abound.[19] In Nitasha Kaul's words, '[i]t is instructive to note what is the outside of neoclassical stories about the economy: women, nonmarketable ideas/objects, the environment, history, emotions, nonreductive, nonformalizable, nonmeasurable elements of comprehension'.[20] Also excluded is any sense of its own history as a discipline, as Iain Hampsher-Monk has noted.[21] To reform, then, economics arguably needs to look outside itself. In his call for economists to learn 'lessons from Romanticism', Richard Bronk argues that 'successful explanations of the behaviour of economic agents … need to take as much account of the roles played by imagination and sentiment as of those played by deductive reasoning and optimisation calculations'; he argues too that economics' commitment to a single 'holistic explanatory system or set of synthetic models' needs to be modified by the realisation that 'only fragmentary insight is ultimately possible'.[22] Nicholas Maxwell's contrasting of 'wisdom-inquiry' from 'knowledge-inquiry' is instructive here: whereas the latter 'demands that emotions, desires, values, human ideals and aspirations, philosophies of life be excluded from the intellectual domain of inquiry, wisdom-inquiry requires that they be included'.[23]

Conclusion

In terms of what is central to economics, and what is excluded from it, Mazzucato's observation, that many women scholars 'have put life at the centre of the economy, not the economy at the centre of life', is instructive.[24] Her citing of Hannah Arendt on the public life, *vita active*; Elinor Ostrom on community creation via the commons; Kate Raworth's circular economy; and others on transformative finance, value creation, and green transition shows how some female economists have urged the primacy of human life and worked for an economics which serves humanity, rather than the other way around.[25] From the point of view of where Wollstonecraft started from, as this book has shown, we have in some ways come full circle, in the attempt to return what Rogan terms a 'displaced humanism' to economic thinking.[26] Given what this book has demonstrated, such figures should be seen as having an important predecessor in Wollstonecraft, situated as she was just at the hinge point before the bedding down of certain economic attitudes and orthodoxies – later to be described as 'economism' – which she battled to hold off, and against which she sought to defend alternative values, and alternative ways of thinking and writing.[27]

I want to use the figure of 'displaced humanism' to return to Wollstonecraft's *Short Residence*, to inquire further into what might be enabled or performed by the imagination from which Bronk suggests today's economics has much to learn. Displaced humanism, or humanity, is a good description of the thematic concerns of this deeply fraught text, written on what for Wollstonecraft were the geographical margins of the 'improved' civilisation of late Enlightenment Europe, whose ideals, in any case, were fracturing as the events of the French Revolution unfolded. Dislocated as she is from her home country, from the heart of Europe, from her collapsing relationship with Imlay, and perhaps too from the political beliefs which sustained – just – the hard-won optimism of the *Historical and Moral Review of the French Revolution*, of all Wollstonecraft's texts, this is where displacement, on all these levels, is explored most fully. Displacement as both mood and ontological experience is evident in Wollstonecraft's sense of disconnection from human community, from a 'world' which 'has disgusted me' and 'friends' who 'have proved unkind'; and she confesses that she has often 'considered myself as a particle broken off from the grand mass of mankind'.[28] Elsewhere, it appears to her that 'death, under every form, appears to me like something getting free – to expand in I know not what element'; she is only diverted from this most extreme form of displacement, into death, by the presence of the cascade or 'cataract', which, as we saw above, enables her to reach out in thought

220   Conclusion

'to eternity'.[29] Caught between death and futurity, for Wollstonecraft, it is only imaginative freedom of thought that enables the burdens of existence to be tolerated: only imagination, in some form, which can mediate and make liveable otherwise unendurable states of displacement.

A little earlier in the text, another imaginative reaching forward through the currents of time occurs as Wollstonecraft voyages along Norway's 'wild coast':

> I anticipated the future improvement of the world, and observed how much man has still to do to obtain of the earth all it could yield. I even carried my speculations so far as to advance a million or two of years to the moment when the earth would perhaps be so perfectly cultivated, and so completely peopled, as to render it necessary to inhabit every spot – yes, these bleak shores. Imagination went still farther, and pictured the state of man when the earth could no longer support him. Whither was he to flee from universal famine? Do not smile; I really became distressed for these fellow creatures yet unborn.[30]

Here is an alternative form of displacement than the alienation from the 'grand mass of mankind' discussed above: not the unwilled fragmentation of the individual from the social whole, but its opposite, imaginatively mediated transport from a specifically inhabited time and place to affective communion with an absent, 'yet unborn' human community. This imaginative transcendence of the self unfolds various prospects of 'futurity', of land in states both of 'improvement' and exhaustion; and it enables forms of fellow-feeling with 'these fellow creatures yet unborn'. In Smith's *The Theory of Moral Sentiment*, our capacity to experience sympathy with the dead illustrates how fellow-feeling even operates in limit cases, beyond the line dividing the living from the dead.[31] Relatedly, Judith Butler has observed how grievability, 'attributed to living creatures', marks 'their value'.[32] Wollstonecraft's projective sympathy with the starving future inhabitants of the earth inverts the temporal direction of Smith's test case, from those no longer alive to those yet to live, and does so to assert community with them; to assert, in Butler's terms, their grievability and hence their worth. Evident in the scene is how the imagination is a power of transgression beyond limits of time, place, and subjective life – 'the imagination went still farther'; it is also a power of cohesion, marked by the affective response of 'distress' through which the bonds of the human community are felt even across temporal distance, and even (given that it is the imagination which enables all this) in the absence of rational knowledge.

The sympathetic imagination pictures what is yet to come; it secures the affective bonds in which human community coheres, and by which it values, even beyond the bounds of time and place. Imagination, the figure or movement of displacement, of going out of oneself, mediates the experience which defines 'humanity': fellow-feeling with those beyond oneself. Defined both as a capacity for fellow-feeling, and as the name for our species, humanity is unthinkable without the self-displacement of the sympathetic imagination: to be human involves the capacity to be displaced from the self, as manifested through feeling, distress, or otherwise. That same movement of self-dispossession enables the act of valuing evident in grief: as Butler states, grief shows how we are 'implicated in lives that are not our own', a 'sphere of dispossession' which exposes our 'primary sociality', and which is 'fundamental' to who we are.[33] Such moves recall the 'negative epistemology' of the ethics required to underwrite environmental policy today, which must address 'future persons' not 'our present self-interest', hypothetical beings, not actual ones, the 'form of a life' rather than 'some specific living thing'.[34] If, as John Whale says, Wollstonecraft argues for a 'moral version' of political economy, here is an ethics which does more than oppose the self-interest on which political economy is founded, but which can go 'still farther' to anticipate not simply the lives of others, but their possible futures too.[35] For Smith, political economy's central concern is provisioning the populace (its first object is to provide 'a plentiful revenue or subsistence for the people, or more properly to enable them to provide such a revenue or subsistence for themselves').[36] Wollstonecraft's imaginative move here shows how political economy's account of 'improvements' is bounded by the limits of existing planetary resources. Extending 'future improvements' to their limit point, Wollstonecraft thinks a future beyond political economy's bounds, and reveals its incapacity to do so too. By the same token, if political economy's purpose is to provision the people, what Wollstonecraft views here is its endpoint: both where it is heading and where it will fail.

For some critics, the repeated staging of scenes of imaginative transport in *Short Residence* suggests a reading of the text in the context of eighteenth-century aesthetic theory, for instance, as a critique of 'disinterested contemplation'.[37] But explicit geopolitical and ecological concerns present in Wollstonecraft's contemplation of the 'future improvement of the world' suggest that the imagination might equally be understood as the instrument of, or capacity for, a more than aesthetic experience: it points to the operation of what might be termed an economic or environmental imagination, one as 'proleptically ecological' as, for Jonathan Kramnick, eighteenth-century locodescriptive writing is.[38] For imaginatively at stake here is not just community with future inhabitants of earth, but relations with the planet itself, its land, and finite resources, traced through 'improvement' (or extractive exploitation) to 'perfect cultivation' and beyond, to the exhaustion of planetary resources. If fellow-feeling with others enacts the shared bond of membership in human community, there is a third party in that relationship, the planet itself: a relationship recognised in today's environmentalist thought as the fundamental ethic of humans' co-community with land.[39] Ecofeminist readings of *Short Residence*, by attending to those moments in the text where Wollstonecraft finds imaginative communion with spring water, or the sea, or jellyfish, thus see them as dissolving a problematic dualism of mankind versus nature, and enacting an alternative imaginative and reciprocal relation with the materiality of the world through an ecological consciousness.[40] If the imagination is an 'adhesive' force in such instances, it shows the cleaving of the human not only to the 'mass of mankind' but to that too of the material natural world; it suggests the centrality of imagination in thinking through that relation in all its implications, including in both 'improved' and catastrophic versions of futurity. If, as noted earlier, the exclusion from 'mainstream economics' of concepts such as energy, entropy, and metabolism which are central to any understanding of the future of life on the planet means that economics cannot plot a future beyond the depletion of energy and other resources, such absences do not constrain Wollstonecraft's imagination.[41] Wollstonecraft's proleptic imagination, indeed, has multiple imaginative capacities – to reach out 'to eternity'; to bind itself in affective community with the material world; to mediate the affective bonds through which we value – which might usefully supplement and reinvigorate the narrowly focused economic thought of today.

Imagination can free us, then, in this reading, into new modes of thinking in which our futurity might be grasped. But imagination can also constrain and imprison: a situation to which, for Wollstonecraft, writing, in all its resources, must be applied. In particular for Wollstonecraft, imagination has been captured, even corrupted, by commercial society; as the Whig theorists of Lady Credit realised, far from being excluded from the realm of economic activity, imagination is in fact at its heart. Commerce, Wollstonecraft observes in *Short Residence*, 'wears out the most scared principles of humanity and rectitude', and the seductions of imagination are central to such erosion.[42] In her 'Letter on the Character of the French Nation', the imagination is a 'wanton' who, 'with her artful coquetry, lures us forward, and makes us run over a rough road, pushing aside every obstacle merely to catch a disappointment'. Here is the same deception of human nature into desire for wealth, consumer conveniences, and comfort

Conclusion 223

which Smith sketched in his tale of the poor man's son. As Wollstonecraft tells the tale, it is the sterner reason which must be recovered, for 'the wants of reason are very few, and, were we to consider dispassionately the real value of most things, we should probably rest satisfied with simple gratification of our physical necessities, and be content with negative goodness'.[43] Arriving at such dispassionate realisation of 'real value', however, is precisely the problem, given the capturing of reason by the feminine allurements of imagination. In *Short Residence*, the drama of reason's struggle against imagination is recast in the 'noble forests' and 'wild coasts' of Norway, where imagination's capacity to reach forward into the future enables it to take different forms. If the 'wanton imagination' of commercial society is devoted to self-interest, advancement, and pleasure, displaced from such objects, the imagination operates differently, able to consider, in its meditations of humanity's future, or its relation with the material world, the 'real value of most things'. Such contemplation suggests ways a 'displaced humanism' might return to economic thought, through a movement which involves fellow-feeling with others: precisely the opposite of the self-interest enshrined at the heart of orthodox economisms, and exactly the 'elementary solidarities' between individuals which, in Rogan's account, twentieth-century moral economists sought to mobilise against capitalism's atomised conception of the individual.[44] Although not named in Kaul's list, quoted above, of what is excluded from contemporary economics, the imaginative, alongside the affective, the feminine, and the social, sits outside the rational world of economics or the construction of economic man driven by self-interest. Wollstonecraft shows both how the imagination is at the heart of economic desire and action, and how, in a reformed operation, it might enable us to consider the 'real value of most things'. If, as Tomaselli has commented, the problems of commercial society ultimately required 'a new order of self-understanding', the imagination, so central to the mechanisms and drives of commercial society, must surely be central to such self-revisioning.[45]

Wollstonecraft returns to the question of value at the end of her *Historical and Moral View of the French Revolution*, a text written shortly after the 'Letter on the Character of the French Nation' and which continues many of its themes, as well as addressing the role of writing in bringing about reform. Reviewing the factors which both enabled and hindered the growth of political knowledge, she notes how in France it 'had long been the fashion to talk of liberty, and to dispute on hypothetical and logical points of political economy'. Whilst 'gleams of truth' were thus disseminated, 'demagogues' flourished at a time of 'taste for sheer declamation',

224   Conclusion

and the French language itself, through the 'pomp of diction' and 'oratorial flourishes', enabled the production of a 'singular fund of superficial knowledge, caught in the tumult of pleasure from the shallow stream of conversation'.[46] By contrast, she observes how the emergence of new forms of 'original composition' in Germany, replacing 'laborious erudition' which merely elucidated 'ancient writers', enabled the estimation of 'the value of things'.[47] Superficial, fashionable speech contrasts with original writing which articulates value: a privileging of writing's potential to reveal, reform, renew, and rouse, which is repeated in her last published work, the essay 'On Poetry' of April 1797. Such compositions, perhaps, show how a 'political system more simple' than those of existing governments would 'check' their 'follies', as she speculates in the *View*'s final page.[48] Sweeping though her remarks are, it is clear what is at stake for Wollstonecraft in the work of late Enlightenment print culture, including in her own decade-long career: the capacity to distinguish what is of 'value' from what is not, to contribute to the pulling down of the old, and the construction of the improved. Her distinction between French and German knowledge cultures turns precisely on their respective capacities to contribute to such ends, and her own repeated turn to the generically varied tools of contemporary print culture signals her own deep interest in the role of writing less as a means to systematise her beliefs into abstractions and principles and more for its communicative power and potential effects. An attempt to organise her writing into systematic principles and positions is thus fundamentally at odds with what her writing is, how it works, what it seeks to do. Something of this is perhaps suggested by Wollstonecraft's unrooted, displaced, mobile location throughout the *Short Residence*: she is a wanderer, a traveller on rough seas, navigating dangerously around rocks hidden beneath the surface. It is in precisely such moments of precarity, jeopardy, and isolation that she finds her voice, and the power of that voice stems from its ability to speak despite and across such contexts.

Notes

Introduction

1 *SND*, p.343.
2 See R. M. Janes, 'On the Reception of Mary Wollstonecraft's *A Vindication of the Rights of Woman*', *Journal of the History of Ideas* 39:2 (1978), 293–302 (p.294).
3 Sylvana Tomaselli, 'Political Economy: The Desire and Needs of Present and Future Generations', in *Inventing Human Science: Eighteenth-Century Domains* eds. Christopher Fox, Roy Porter, and Robert Wokler (University of California Press, 1995), pp.292–322 (pp.295–96).
4 Michel Foucault, *The Order of Things* (Routledge, 1970), pp.166–67.
5 See Donald Winch, 'Political Economy', in *Oxford Companion to the Romantic Age,* ed. Iain McCalman (Oxford University Press, 2001), pp.311–19 (p.312).
6 Richard Whatmore claims that eighteenth-century political economy 'was the archetypal science of reform, premised on the unavoidability of commercial society as an element of human progress': see 'Burke on Political Economy', in *The Cambridge Companion to Edmund Burke*, eds. David Dwan and David Dwan (Cambridge University Press, 2012), pp.80–91 (p.81).
7 Turgot, Letter to Price, 22 March 1778. Published with Mirabeau's *Considerations on the Cinncinati*, English translation 1785, p.156. See Chapter 4 below.
8 Tomaselli, 'Political Economy', p.310.
9 *WN*, vol. 1, p.312. I prefer to use contemporaneous terminology: so 'commercial society' rather than 'capitalism' or 'liberal society'. For the difference of commercial society from capitalism, see Michael Sonenscher, *Capitalism: The Story Behind the Word* (Princeton University Press, 2022); for liberalism as a later development, see Winch, 'Political Economy', p.319.
10 Saree Makdisi, *William Blake and the Impossible History of the 1790s* (University of Chicago Press, 2003), p.85; Clifford Siskin, *System: The Shaping of Modern Knowledge* (MIT Press, 2016), p.163; James Thompson, *Models of Value: Eighteenth-Century Political Economy and the Novel* (Duke University Press, 1996), p.27.
11 Quoted in Nicholas Phillipson, *Adam Smith: An Enlightened Life* (Allen Lane, 2010), p.1.

226   *Notes to pages 4–11*

12 See Stedman Jones, *An End to Poverty*, p.226. For an illuminating account of
    key markers of disciplinarity, see Robin Valenza, *Literature, Language and the
    Rise of the Intellectual Disciplines in Britain 1680–1820* (Cambridge University
    Press, 2009) pp.5–7.

13 Dugald Stewart, 'Account of the Life and Writings of Adam Smith, L.L.D',
    in *EPS*, p.309. See also Emma Rothschild, *Economic Sentiments* (Harvard
    University Press, 2001).

14 Matthew Sangster, *Living as an Author in the Romantic Period* (Palgrave, 2021),
    p.14, pp.42–3.

15 For the engagement of Romantic thinkers with the 'spirit of commerce'
    from Malthus onwards, see Philip Connell's *Romanticism, Economics and the
    Question of 'Culture'* (Oxford University Press, 2001).

16 *HMV*, p.183, p.231.

17 On the difference of political economy from economics see Richard Bronk,
    The Romantic Economist (Cambridge University Press, 2009), pp.9–10. For
    a history of the bifurcation of eighteenth-century moral philosophy into a
    political economic discourse oriented around use-value, and an alternative dis-
    course oriented to aesthetics and affect, see John Guillory, *Cultural Capital*
    (University of Chicago Press, 1995).

18 Wollstonecraft's relation to Smith has received relatively little commentary,
    but see Carol Kay, 'Canon, Ideology and Gender: Mary Wollstonecraft's
    Critique of Adam Smith' *New Political Science* 7:1 (1986), 63–76, and Barbara
    Taylor, *Mary Wollstonecraft and the Feminist Imagination* (Cambridge
    University Press, 2003), p.158, p.161 and p.172.

19 *VRW*, pp.127–28, p.205.

20 Ibid., p.205.

21 *HMV*, p.233.

22 Ibid., p.234.

23 Ibid., pp.233–34.

24 *WN*, vol. 2, p.782.

25 *WN*, vol. 1, p.145; *HMV*, p.233. See also *WN*, vol. 1, p.84.

26 Rothschild, *Economic Sentiments*, pp.67–8.

27 *WW*, p.181.

28 Thomas Carlyle, 'Occasional Discourse on the Negro Question', *Fraser's
    Magazine for Town and Country*, 40 (February 1849), 527–39 (536). Often
    taken to be Carlyle's response to Malthus, the phrase 'Dismal Science' was in
    fact coined in the context of the debate on the reintroduction of slavery, to
    depict a world governed by the rule of supply and demand.

29 *HMV*, p.235. For a discussion of Smith's use of the self-healing, self-preserving
    language of nature, see my 'System and Subject in Adam Smith's Political
    Economy: Nature, Vitalism, and Bioeconomic Life', in *Systems of Life:
    Biopolitics, Economics and Literature on the Cusp of Modernity* eds. Richard A.
    Barney and Warren Montag (Fordham University Press, 2019), 93–114. For
    Smith's discussion of the philosophical eye, see 'The Principles which Lead
    and Direct Philosophical Enquiries', in *EPS*.

Notes to pages 11–14 227

30 Makdisi, *William Blake*, p.83.
31 William Godwin proposed 'romance' as the best means to understand 'the machine of society' and direct it 'to its best purpose' in his essay 'On History and Romance' (1797). See Miranda Burgess, *British Fiction and the Production of Social Order 1740–1830* (Cambridge University Press, 2000), p.8.
32 Letter to Everina Wollstonecraft, 1787. *The Collected Letters of Mary Wollstonecraft* ed. Janet Todd (Columbia University Press, 2003), p.139.
33 Janet Todd 'Prefatory Note', *Works*, vol. 7, p.14.
34 For a full account of Johnson and his circle, see Daisy Hay, *Dinner with Joseph Johnson* (Chatto and Windus, 2022).
35 Wollstonecraft, *Collected Letters* ed. Todd, p.314; Mary A. Favret, *Romantic Correspondence: Women, Politics and the Fiction of Letters* (Cambridge University Press, 2008), p.128.
36 Favret, *Romantic Correspondence*, p.97, quoting Ralph Wardle, *Mary Wollstonecraft: A Critical Biography* (University of Nebraska Press, 1951), p.256.
37 *SND*, p.296.
38 'On Poetry', *Works*, vol. 7, pp.7–11 (p.7).
39 For Smith's claim that the labour of 'men of letters', even if noble, valuable, and 'useful', but 'produces nothing which could afterwards purchase or procure an equal quantity of labour', see *WN*, vol. 1, p.331. For an alternative account of the social role of the writer, see the discussion of David Williams on 'genius' in Sangster, *Living as an Author*, p.190.
40 Stephen C. Behrendt, *British Women Poets and the Romantic Writing Community* (Johns Hopkins University Press, 2009), p.5.
41 In many ways, Wollstonecraft doesn't 'fit' Sangster's model of a Romantic author, for instance, see *Living as an Author*, pp.13–49.
42 See Burgess, *British Fiction,* p.131. For anxiety about women in the public intellectual sphere and efforts to displace them, see Sangster, *Living as an Author*, p.32.
43 For the relative low status and low remuneration of such forms of writing, compared with poetry and fiction, see Sangster, *Living as an Author*, p.29.
44 Sangster, *Living as an Author*, p.19.
45 On systems in this period, see David Simpson, *Romanticism, Nationalism and the Revolt against Theory* (University of Chicago Press, 1993).
46 On the conjectural history of women, see Tomaselli, 'Political Economy', p.293.
47 Wollstonecraft's admiration of Montesquieu is evident in a reference to his *Persian Letters* in the *Analytical Review*: see *Works*, vol.7, p.341.
48 Taylor's *Mary Wollstonecraft and the Feminist Imagination* devotes one chapter to a consideration of Wollstonecraft and commerce, many observations from which are taken up and pursed more fully in this book. The chapter on Wollstonecraft in Karen O'Brien's *Women and Enlightenment in Eighteenth-Century Britain* (Cambridge University Press, 2009) discusses her engagement with Scottish Enlightenment thought on the history of manners. Jane Rendall's work on Wollstonecraft's history writing also valuably emphasises

228   *Notes to page 15*

the Scottish philosophical context: see '"The grand causes which combine to carry mankind forward": Wollstonecraft, History and Revolution', *Women's Writing* 4.2 (1997): 155–72. Carol Kay's discussion of Wollstonecraft's response to Smith in 'Canon, Ideology and Gender' focuses on Smith's *The Theory of Moral Sentiments* and makes little reference to his political economy. Susan Ferguson's account of Wollstonecraft references Smith but approaches her work via the anachronistic terms 'liberalism' and 'socialism': see 'The Radical Ideas of Mary Wollstonecraft', *Canadian Journal of Political Science* 32:3 (Sept 1999), 427–50. Nancy E. Johnson and Paul Keen's recent valuable collection, *Mary Wollstonecraft in Context* (Cambridge University Press, 2020), offers insightful essays on many of Wollstonecraft's historical and cultural contexts, including philosophical frameworks, legal contexts, and political theory, but nothing specifically on her engagement with political economy.

49 Kay, 'Canon, Ideology, and Gender', p.63. Following the recovery of her work by feminist literary critics from the 1970s, there is now a substantial body of analysis exploring Wollstonecraft in the context of eighteenth-century gender, sensibility and the imagination, and the ideology and cultures of gender. Two examples of the best work in this vast field are Mary Poovey's *The Proper Lady and the Woman Writer* (University of Chicago Press, 1984), which explores Wollstonecraft's negotiation of contemporary gender ideologies, and Claudia L. Johnson's *Equivocal Beings: Politics, Gender, and Sentimentality in the 1790s* (University of Chicago Press, 1995), which situates Wollstonecraft in the politics of sensibility of the 1790s. Wollstonecraft has also received renewed attention recently from political theorists and philosophers: see Virginia Sapiro, *A Vindication of Political Virtue* (University of Chicago Press, 1992); Eileen Hunt Botting, *Family Feuds: Wollstonecraft, Burke, and Rousseau on the Transformation of the Family* (State University of New York Press, 2006) and *Wollstonecraft, Mill and Women's Human Rights* (Yale University Press, 2016); and *The Social and Political Philosophy of Mary Wollstonecraft* eds. Sandrine Bergès and Alan Coffee (Oxford University Press, 2016).

50 At the same time, my understanding of the nature of political economic discourse, and its relationship to other areas of philosophical inquiry in the eighteenth century, is greatly indebted to work in this area by intellectual historians, including: Istvan Hont and Michael Ignatieff's edited collection, *Wealth and Virtue: The Shaping of Political Economy in the Scottish Enlightenment* (Cambridge University Press, 1983); Donald Winch's *Riches and Poverty: An Intellectual History of Political Economy in Britain, 1750–1834* (Cambridge University Press, 1996); Gareth Stedman Jones's *An End to Poverty?* (Profile, 2004); Michael Sonenscher's *Before the Deluge: Public Debt, Inequality and the Intellectual Origins of the French Revolution* (Princeton University Press, 2007); and Richard Whatmore's *Against War and Empire Geneva, Britain and France in the Eighteenth Century* (Yale University Press, 2012). Wollstonecraft, however, whilst gaining an occasion mention, rarely makes more than a cameo appearance in these writings, despite often being a member of the circle of thinkers discussed.

Notes to pages 15–26

51 For the period's understanding of digression as a 'legitimate expository mode', see Johnson, *Equivocal Beings*, p.26. On *copia* or elaboration in classical rhetoric, see Mary Poovey, *The Genres of the Credit Economy: Mediating Value in Eighteenth- and Nineteenth-Century Britain* (Chicago, 2008), p.98. On conversation, see Jon Mee, *Conversable Worlds: Literature, Contention and Community 1762–1830* (Oxford, 2011).

52 See Clifford Siskin, *System: The Shaping of Modern Knowledge* (MIT Press, 2016); David Simpson, *Romanticism, Nationalism and the Revolt against Theory* (University of Chicago Press, 1993).

53 For Babeuf, see Taylor, *Feminist Imagination*, p.173.

54 For a study of Wollstonecraft as philosopher and novelist, see Deborah Weiss, *The Female Philosopher and Her Afterlives* (Palgrave Macmillan, 2107), pp.51–85.

55 Ralph Cohen, 'History and Genre', *New Literary History* 17:2 (1986), 203–18; *Transformations of a Genre* (Palgrave Macmillan, 2021).

56 Elizabeth Wingrove, 'Getting Intimate with Wollstonecraft in the Republic of Letters', *Political Theory* 33:3 (June 2005) 344–69 (p.356); *VRW* p.76. Examples of innovation in print culture in this period include, for instance, the literary culture of dissent; experimental life-writing; and the periodical project of the *Analytical Review* itself. See, respectively: Daniel E. White, *Early Romanticism and Religious Dissent* (Cambridge University Press, 2006); Julie Murray, 'Mary Hays and the Forms of Life', *Studies in Romanticism* 52 (2013), 61–84; and Wingrove, 'Getting Intimate'.

57 Poovey highlights early Wollstonecraft's compulsive abstraction away from feeling in *Proper Lady*; Cora Kaplan, in a classic essay, indites her for importing into feminism Rousseau's model of excess female feeling: see 'Wild Nights' in *Sea Changes: Essays on Culture and Feminism* (Verso, 1986). Simon Swift considers the opposition of reason and feeling, in 'Mary Wollstonecraft and the "Reserve of Reason"', *Studies in Romanticism* 45:1 (2006), 3–24.

58 *VRM*, p.53, and compare Hint no. 30 in Wollstonecraft's notes for a second, unwritten, part of *VRW*: *Works*, vol. 5, p.276.

59 See White, *Early Romanticism*, p.114.

60 White, *Early Romanticism*, p.110.

61 *SND,* p.343.

62 Ibid., p.309.

1 Political Economy and Commercial Society in the 1790s

1 See *AR* 27:6 (June 1798), 655; *AR* 13:1 (May 1792), 119–20; *AR* 22:2 (Aug 1795), 224 and *AR* 22:3 (Sept 1795), 332–33.

2 For Johnson and his circle, see Daisy Hay, *Dinner with Joseph Johnson* (Chatto & Windus, 2022).

3 See Janet Todd 'Prefatory Note', *Works*, vol. 7 pp.14–8; Gerald P. Tyson, *Joseph Johnson: A Liberal Publisher* (University of Iowa Press, 1979), pp.103–4.

4 See *AR* 22:3 (Sept 1795), 324.

5 *WN*, vol. 1, p.428.

230 *Notes to pages 26–28*

6 See Donald Winch, *Riches and Poverty: An Intellectual History of Political Economy in Britain, 1750–1834* (Cambridge University Press, 1996), p.21.

7 *WN*, vol. 1, p.428; Winch, *Riches*, p.21. For a full account of Smith's philosophical project, see Nicholas Philipson, *Adam Smith: An Enlightened Life* (Penguin, 2011).

8 Winch, *Riches*, p.164.

9 Ibid., p.165, p.163.

10 James Thompson, *Models of Value: Eighteenth-century Political Economy and the Novel* (Duke University Press, 1996), p.27.

11 The classic essay collection, *Wealth and Virtue: The Shaping of Political Economy in the Scottish Enlightenment* eds. Istvan Hont and Michael Ignatieff (Cambridge University Press, 1983), marks the origin of much of this phase of important work.

12 For one study that shows how economic thinking was embedded in other discourses, including literary ones, see Joanna Rostek, *Women's Economic Thought in the Romantic Age* (Routledge, 2021).

13 Gareth Stedman Jones, *An End to Poverty? A Historical Debate* (Profile, 2004), p.226.

14 Stedman Jones, *End to Poverty?* p.9.

15 For Burke and Paine's contrasting use of Smith, see Winch, *Riches*, pp.127–36. Godwin and Coleridge were among the radical voices rejecting a society founded on private property.

16 See Winch, *Riches*, pp.169–70, and Emma Rothschild, *Economic Sentiments: Adam Smith, Condorcet and the Enlightenment* (Harvard University Press, 2001), pp.57–61. For an extended study of Smith's sceptical and 'speculative' epistemology, see Richard Adelman, *Doubtful Knowledge: Scepticism and the Birth of Political Economy* (forthcoming).

17 Winch, *Riches*, p.326, n.9, and pp.326–27.

18 Greg Claeys, 'The French Revolution Debate and British Political Thought', *History of Political Thought* 11:1 (Spring 1990), 59–80.

19 See John Bugg, 'How Radical Was Joseph Johnson and Why Does Radicalism Matter', *Studies in Romanticism* 57:2 (2018) 173–343. For different strands of progressive thought in this period, from rational dissent to 'artisan radicalism', see Jon Mee, *Dangerous Enthusiasm: William Blake and the Culture of Radicalism in the 1790s* (Clarendon Press, 1992), pp.220–23. Tyson's biography of Johnson describes him as a 'liberal' publisher.

20 Helen Braithwaite, *Romanticism, Publishing and Dissent: Joseph Johnson and the Cause of Liberty* (Palgrave Macmillan, 2003), pp.168–69.

21 Braithwaite, *Romanticism, Publishing and Dissent*, p.158, p.160; Tyson, *Joseph Johnson* p.162. On Johnson's trial, see also Susan Oliver, 'Silencing Joseph Johnson and the *Analytical Review*', *The Wordsworth Circle*, 40: 2–3 (2009), 96–102. On Johnson and the *Analytical Review*, see also special issues of *The Wordsworth Circle*, 40: 2–3 (2009) and *The Wordsworth Circle*, 33:3 (Summer 2002). Johnson's circle included William Blake, Henry Fuseli, William Godwin, and many others: see Hays, *Dinner with Joseph Johnson*.

Notes to pages 29–31

22 Tyson, *Joseph Johnson*, pp.93–6; Braithwaite, *Romanticism, Publishing and Dissent*, pp.87–90. Daniel E. White describes Johnson as the 'London agent' for the Warrington dissenting academy: see *Early Romanticism and Religious Dissent* (Cambridge University Press, 2006), p.24.

23 See White, *Early Romanticism*, esp. p.14.

24 White, *Early Romanticism*, p.11, p.17. Gregory Claeys, 'Virtuous Commerce and Free Theology: Political Economy and the Dissenting Academies 1750–1800', *History of Political Thought*, 20:1 (Spring 1999) 141–72.

25 Christie, letter to John Nichols, quoted in Tyson, *Joseph Johnson*, p.97. See also 'To the Public', *AR* 1:1 (May 1788), i.

26 Many of the *Analytical Review*'s liberal, educated middle-class readers were indeed dissenters: Braithwaite, *Romanticism, Publishing and Dissent*, p.86. For a full account of the literary and political public spheres in the late eighteenth century, including the role of the *Analytical Review*, see Paul Keen, *The Crisis of Literature in the 1790s* (Cambridge University Press, 1999), esp. chap 1.

27 Little scholarly attention has been paid to the *Analytical Review*'s coverage of commerce or political economy – concerns absent in Braithwaite's description of its politics, quoted above – despite the journal's recognised links to the commercial interests of the professional middle classes. Bugg's reassessment of the politics of Johnson's publishing practice also omits mention of any political economic work published by Johnson, other than Malthus's 1798 *Essay on the Principle of Population*.

28 Listed subjects are: theology and morality; philosophy; mathematics; medicine and related; natural history and agriculture; trade and politics; law, history, and topography; biography; poetry and criticism; drama and romances; and miscellaneous. See Tyson, *Joseph Johnson*, pp.101–2.

29 *AR* 23:6 (June 1796), 594–99.

30 *AR* 25:1 (Jan 1797), 97–8 and *AR* 23: 3 (March 1796), 297–99.

31 *AR* 9:3 (March 1791), 257–76. Percival was a leading dissenter; his work appeared in the *Memoirs of the Literary and Philosophical Society of Manchester*, an organisation instituted at Percival's house which had founded the Manchester New College in 1783 after the closure of the Warrington dissenting academy. See White, *Early Romanticism*, pp.28–9.

32 *AR* 17:2 (Oct 1793), 210–13 (210).

33 *WN*, p.428.

34 *AR* 21:2 (Feb 1795), 155–65.

35 Ibid., 146–55 (153).

36 Present, for instance, in the review of Sir Frederic Morton Eden's *State of the Poor*, *AR* 25:4 (April 1797) 353–62 (354–55).

37 *AR* 21:2 (Feb 1795), 156.

38 *AR* 26:6 (Dec 1797), 623; review of *Essays Political, Economical and Philosophical* by Benjamin, Count of Rumford, *AR* 26:1 (July 1797) 11–26.

39 *AR* 23:6 (June 1796) 594–99 (595).

40 Ibid., 595, 596–97.

41 *SND*, p.343.

232   *Notes to pages 32–35*

42 *HMV*, p.183.

43 *AR* 26:3 (Sept 1797), 302–3 (302).

44 *AR* 25:6 (June 1799), 635–36.

45 Winch, *Riches*, p.23. Malthus's was admittedly an iconoclastic work, offering a riposte to Ricardo and other political economic thinkers. Political economy's closeness to morality was asserted too by Adam Smith's leading follower in France, Jean-Baptiste Say, for whom a 'good treatise on political economy must be the first book of morality': see Stedman Jones, *End to Poverty?*, p.128.

46 See Oliver, 'Silencing Joseph Johnson', p.96.

47 Cox and Galperin, 95.

48 Bugg, 'How Radical Was Joseph Johnson?', p.188.

49 *AR* 27:3 (March 1798), 304–6; *AR* 26:1 (July 1797), 78–9 and *AR* 25:6 (June 1797), 584–90 (587).

50 See John Brewer: *Sinews of Power: War, Money and the English State 1688–1783* (1989).

51 *VRW*, p.216. On anxieties about national debt, see Richard Whatmore, *Against War and Empire: Geneva, Britain and France in the Eighteenth Century* (Yale University Press, 2012) and Peter de Bolla, *The Discourse of the Sublime: Readings in History, Aesthetics and the Subject* (Basil Blackwell, 1989), Chapter 4 'The Discourse of Debt'. For anxieties about debt in pre-revolutionary France, see Michael Sonenscher, *Before the Deluge: Public Debt, Inequality and the Intellectual Origins of the French Revolution* (Princeton University Press, 2007).

52 Rousseau was the 'clearest expositor of a jeremiad view of the prospects for commercial states small and large': see Whatmore, *Against Empire*, p.54. David Hume, 'Of public credit', in *Essays: Moral, Political and Literary*, ed. Eugene F. Miller (Liberty Fund, 1987), pp.349–65 (pp.360–61). For Hume's concerns about national bankruptcy, see J. G. A. Pocock 'Hume and the American Revolution: The Dying Thoughts of a North Briton', in *Virtue, Commerce, History: Essays on Political Thought and History* (Cambridge University Press, 1985), pp.125–42. Smith argued that growth would help address the debt burden, but nevertheless suggested that Britain should adapt itself to the 'real mediocrity' of her circumstances: see Winch, *Riches*, pp.116–17, p.132.

53 The full title of the work is: *The Political Progress of Britain; or, an impartial History of Abuses in the Government of the British Empire, in Europe, Asia and America. From 1688 to the present.* No author is given, although a postscript is signed by James Thomason Callender. See *AR* 22:2 (Aug 1795), 203–5.

54 *AR* 27:3 (March 1798), 304.

55 *AR* 23:2 (February 1796), 193–97 (193). Morgan, a Unitarian, shared his uncle's politics and socialised with Horne Tooke and Thomas Paine.

56 Ibid., 196. On the Imperial loans, see Karl F. Helleiner, *The Imperial Loans: A Study in Financial and Diplomatic History* (Clarendon Press, 1965).

57 Ibid., 193–94.

58 *AR* 23: 3 (March 1796), 297–99 (299).

59 *AR* 26:1 (July 1797), 78–9. Patje thought that only the interest, not the principal, of the loan might be repaid in this way. VRM, p.57.

Notes to pages 35–41 233

60 *AR* 26:1 (July 1797), 79. Italics in original.
61 *AR* 22:3 (Sept 1795), 289–92. For a review of Part 1, see *AR* 12:4 (April 1792), 452–60. Barlow was also a friend of Paine. In 1790, Barlow had promised to take Wollstonecraft's brother to America to gain farming experience and acquire land, a plan which Paine agreed would meet with success, but which was derailed by the Barlows' instead visiting France. See Janet Todd, *Mary Wollstonecraft: A Revolutionary Life* (Weidenfeld and Nicholson, 2000), pp.190–91, p.210, p.213.
62 *AR* 22:3 (Sept 1795), 289.
63 Ibid., 292.
64 *AR* 28:1 (July 1798), 107–12 (109).
65 Ibid., 135.
66 Ibid., 109.
67 Ibid., 110.
68 Ibid., 112, 110.
69 See Winch, *Riches*, pp.129–31.
70 See Richard Whatmore, *Against Empire*, esp. pp.182–89; see also *Commerce and Peace in the Enlightenment*, eds. Béla Kapossy, Isaac Nakhimovsky, and Richard Whatmore (Cambridge, 2018) and Isaac Nakhimovsky, 'The "Ignominious Fall of the European Commonwealth": Gentz, Hauterive, and the Armed Neutrality of 1800' in *Trade and War: The Neutrality of Commerce in the Interstate System*, ed. Koen Stapelbroek (Helsinki Collegium for Advanced Studies, 2011), pp.177–90. I am also grateful to Christopher Brooke for sight of his unpublished manuscript, 'The Idea of a European Union'.
71 See Winch, *Riches*, pp.102–3, p.130.
72 *AR* 25:4 (April 1797), 353–62 (353). Italics in the original.
73 The review of Eden's work begins in *AR* 25:3 (March 1797) 229–38 and continues in *AR* 25:6 (June 1797), 584–90.
74 See Stedman Jones, *End to Poverty?* p.44.
75 *AR* 26:3 (Sept 1797), 302–3.
76 Ibid., 328–47.
77 Ibid., 244; *AR* 25:6 (June 1797), 584–90 (587–88); VRM, p.57.
78 *AR* 16:4 (Aug 1793), 388–404 (402).
79 Winch, *Riches*, p.258; for Godwin on property, see also Stedman Jones, *End to Poverty?* p.96.
80 *AR* 21:4 (April 1795), 374–82 (375–76).
81 *AR*, 26:3 (Sept 1797), 239, 240–41.
82 *AR* 26:3 (Sept 1797), 302–3.
83 See Winch, *Riches*, pp.57–89 for a discussion of *WN* as the 'culmination' of the eighteenth-century debate on luxury, and for the claim of a broader switch from a discourse on luxury and the moral corruptions of commerce, to one on wealth and virtue.
84 *AR* 26:3 (Sept 1797), 239–40. Italics in the original.
85 *SND*, p.269.

86 White, *Early Romanticism*, pp.124–25, pp.80–2. Barbauld's piece appears in J. and A. L. Aikins' *Miscellaneous Pieces in Prose* (London, 1773). Aikin's *Description of the Country from Thirty to Forty Miles round Manchester* is warmly reviewed in *AR* 22:5 (November 1795), 449–57.

87 *AR* 23:6 (June 1796), 594–99. Canals and channels are also figures deployed in Smith's *WN*.

88 *SND*, pp.316–17.

89 For Parliamentary debates on the poor, see Winch, *Riches*, pp.198–220. Pitt's Poor Law Bill was debated in 1796 but not passed. For a discussion of the use of statistics, including by Burke and Young, in relation to other forms of representation, see Frans de Bruyn, 'From Georgic Poetry to Statistics and Graphs: Eighteenth-Century Representations and the "State" of British Society', *Yale Journal of Criticism* 17: 1 (2004), 107–39.

90 *AR* 26:3 (Sept 1797), 243.

91 *AR* 23:6 (June 1796), 594; *AR* 25:4 (April 1797), 353–62 (353–56).

92 Ibid., 594–95; *AR* 26:3 (Sept 1797), 303.

93 *AR* 14:4 (Dec 1792), 366–76.

94 Ibid., 376.

95 *WN*, vol. 1, p.380. See Winch, *Riches*, p.114.

96 Richard Price, *Observations on the Importance of the American Revolution* (1785) in *Political Writings* ed. D. O. Thomas (Cambridge University Press), pp.116–51 (p.148). See also Winch, *Riches*, pp.152–54.

97 Price, *Observations on the American Revolution*, p.145.

98 *AR* 1:1 (May 1788), v, vi.

99 Jon Mee, *Conversable Worlds: Literature, Contention and Community 1762–1830* (Oxford, 2011). On the importance of conversation and sociability for Johnson himself and as the context for *AR*, see p.145.

100 See Tyson, *Joseph Johnson*, p.97.

101 For a discussion of the problems identifying Wollstonecraft's reviews, see Todd, 'Prefatory Note'.

102 See *Works*, vol. 7, 'Index of Books Reviewed', pp.487–502. For Wollstonecraft's curt review of the biography of Paine, see pp.395–96; for its author's attack on Paine and correspondence with Smith, see Winch, *Riches*, p.155; for Wollstonecraft's review of Brissot, see *Works*, vol. 7, pp.390–93.

103 *Works*, vol. 7, pp.441–42 (p.442).

104 For more on Wollstonecraft's reviews, see the editors' 'Prefatory Note' in *Works*, vol.7, pp.14–8.

105 For 'trash', see 'Prefactory Note', *Works*, vol.7, p.15.

106 Miranda Burgess, *British Fiction and the Production of Social Order 1740–1830* (Cambridge, 2000), p.1.

107 William Godwin, 'On History and Romance' (1797): see Burgess, *British Fiction*, p.8.

108 For a discussion of McCulloch, see Mary Poovey, *A History of The Modern Fact: Problems of Knowledge in the Sciences of Wealth and Society* (Chicago, 1998), pp.295–306.

2 The Engagement with Burke

1 *VRM*, p.37.

2 Ibid., p.5.

3 Phrase coined in Marilyn Butler, *Burke, Paine, Godwin and the Revolution Controversy* (Cambridge University Press, 1984), and repeated, for instance, by Barbara Taylor, *Mary Wollstonecraft and the Feminist Imagination* (Cambridge University Press, 2003) p.145, p.149.

4 See Wollstonecraft's review of Price's sermon, in *Works*, vol. 7, pp.185–87 (p.187).

5 See Frederick Dreyer, 'The Genesis of Burke's *Reflections*', *The Journal of Modern History* 50:1 (1978), 462–79 (463), and, for instance, Greg Claeys, in 'Utopianism, Property, and the French Revolution Debate in Britain' in *Utopias and the Millennium* eds. Krishan Kumar and Stephen Bann (Reaktion Books, 1993) pp.46–62 (p.51) and Claudia Johnson, *Equivocal Beings: Politics, Gender and Sentimentality in the 1790s* (University of Chicago Press, 1995), p.25. On the origins of Burke's *Reflections*, see also F. P. Lock, *Burke's Reflection on the Revolution in France* (George Allen & Unwin, 1985), pp.31–61.

6 Taylor, *Feminist Imagination*, p.147.

7 Burke, Letter to Calonne, 25 October 1790, *Correspondence of Burke* vol. 6, p.141.

8 Donald Winch, *Riches and Poverty: An Intellectual History of Political Economy in Britain, 1750–1834* (Cambridge University Press, 1996), p.134. See also Richard Whatmore, 'Burke on Political Economy' in *The Cambridge Companion to Edmund Burke*, eds. David Dwan and Christopher J. Insole (Cambridge University Press, 2021), pp.80–91.

9 Edmund Burke, Letter to Philip Francis, 20 February 1790, in *The Correspondence of Edmund Burke*, ed. Thomas W. Copeland, 10 vols, vol. 6, eds. Alfred Cobban and Robert A. Smith (Cambridge University Press and University of Chicago Press, 1967), pp.91–2. On attempts by the Shelburne circle to develop free trade as an alternative to British foreign policy caught in the grip of mercantilism and war, see Richard Whatmore, *Against War and Empire: Geneva, Britain and France in the Eighteenth Century* (Yale University Press, 2012) esp. pp.182–89; see also Caroline Robbins, *The Eighteenth-Century Commonwealthman* (Harvard University Press, 1961), p.346. Price himself by no means an uncritical proponent of commerce however, warning the new American republic of its moral dangers. J. G. A. Pocock suggests Shelburne's patronage of radical intellectuals caused him to be associated with reform, hence 'one of the most powerful motives' behind the *Reflections*. See Pocock, introduction to Edmund Burke, *Reflections on the Revolution in France*, ed. J. G. A. Pocock (Hackett, 1987), pp.vii–xlviii (p.xxiv).

10 Burke, 'Letter to the Sheriffs of Bristol' (1777), quoted in Dreyer, 'Genesis', 467. See also Richard Price, *Observations on the Nature of Civil Liberty* (1776) in Price, *Political Writings*, ed. D. O. Thomas (Cambridge University Press, 1991), pp.20–75 (p.26). For a discussion of Price's *Observations* and Burke's longstanding enmity with Price, see Robbins, *Eighteenth-Century Commonwealthman*, pp.336–41, p.345.

236 *Notes to pages 52–56*

11 Barbauld, 'Against Inconsistency in our Expectations' (1773), quoted in Harriet Guest, *Small Change: Women, Learning, Patriotism, 1750–1810* (University of Chicago Press, 2000), p.285. Wollstonecraft praises this as 'an excellent essay' in *VRW*, p.184.

12 For Mary Poovey's description of *VRM* as a 'political disquisition' see her *The Proper Lady and the Woman Writer* (Chicago University Press, 1984), pp.56–7.

13 For a full account of Macaulay and her influence on Wollstonecraft, see Karen O'Brien, *Women and Enlightenment in Eighteenth-Century Britain* (Cambridge University Press, 2009), pp.173–80. See also Guest, *Small Change*, p.196, p.271.

14 Catharine Macaulay, *Letters on Education: With Observations on Religious and Metaphysical Subjects* (Cambridge University Press, 2014) p.271. For Wollstonecraft's review, see *Works*, vol. 7, 309–22 (315).

15 J. G. A. Pocock, 'The Political Economy of Burke's Analysis of the French Revolution', in his *Virtue, Commerce, History* (Cambridge University Press, 1985), pp.193–212.

16 Pocock, 'Political Economy of Burke', p.194.

17 For earlier struggles to defend and extend British liberties in this period, see Linda Colley, 'Radical Patriotism in Eighteenth-Century England', in *Patriotism: The Making and Unmaking of British National Identity, vol.1: History and Politics*, ed. Raphael Samuel (Routledge, 1989), pp.169–87 and Robbins, *Eighteenth-Century Commonwealthman*, pp.356–77.

18 *VRM*, p.37.

19 *Reflections*, p.140.

20 Ibid., p.372, p.271.

21 *AR* 25:4 (April 1797), pp.353–62 (p.353).

22 *VRW* p.76; Paul Hamilton, *Metaromanticism* (University of Chicago Press, 2003) p.157.

23 Janet Todd, *Mary Wollstonecraft: An Annotated Bibliography* (Garland, 1976, repr. Routledge, 2013) p.2. For other critical deprecations of the *Vindication*, as well as its gradual reassessment, see Claudia Johnson, *Equivocal Beings*, p.26, who also discusses the period's understanding of digression as a 'legitimate expository mode'. On the use of *copia* or elaboration in classical rhetoric, see Mary Poovey, *The Genres of the Credit Economy: Mediating Value in Eighteenth- and Nineteenth-Century Britain* (University of Chicago Press, 2008), p.98. Burke explicitly valued the looseness of his writing mode: 'I beg leave to throw out my thoughts, and express my feelings, just as they arise in my mind, with very little attention to formal method', *Reflections*, p.92. For further comment on the generic looseness of these texts, see Catherine Packham, 'Genre and the Mediation of Political Economy in Edmund Burke's *Reflections on the Revolution in France* and Mary Wollstonecraft's *A Vindication of the Rights of Men*', *The Eighteenth Century: Theory and Interpretation*, 60:3 (Autumn 2019), 249–68.

24 Burke, *Observations on a Late Publication Intituled The Present State of the Nation* (1769), quoted in *Correspondence of Burke*, vol. 6, p.10, note 2. For the context of this remark, see Whatmore, 'Burke on Political Economy'.

25 *Reflections*, p.232.

Notes to pages 56–61 237

26 *Reflections*, p.234.

27 Ibid., pp.235–36.

28 *WN*, vol. 1 pp.22–3.

29 See Adam Smith, 'The Principles which Lead and Direct Philosophical Enquiries; Illustrated by the History of Astronomy', in *EPS*, pp.31–105. For a discussion, see my 'Feigning Fictions: Imagination, Hypothesis and Philosophical Writing in the Scottish Enlightenment', *Eighteenth Century: Theory and Interpretation* 48:2 (2007), 149–71.

30 Burke, Letter to Philip Francis, 20 February 1790, *Correspondence of Edmund Burke*, vol. 6, p.89.

31 John Barrell, 'The Public Prospect and the Private View: The Politics of Taste in Eighteenth-century Britain' in *Landscape, Natural Beauty and the Arts*, eds. S. Kemal and I. Gaskell (Cambridge University Press, 1993), pp.81–102.

32 Horace Walpole, Letter to Mary Berry, December 1790. Quoted in Susan Wiseman, 'Catharine Macaulay: History, Republicanism and the Public Sphere', in *Women, Writing and the Public Sphere, 1700–1830*, eds. Elizabeth Eger, Charlotte Grant, Clíona Ó Gallchoir and Penny Warburton (Cambridge University Press, 2001), pp.181–99 (p.181). Macaulay, one of the 'Amazonians' named by Walpole, was known as a so-called 'city Whig', named for a supposedly metropolitan radicalism. See Guest, *Small Change*, p.265.

33 *WN*, vol. 1, p.428.

34 *VRM*, p.57.

35 Ibid., p.58. The fate of the poor who are 'shamefully left a prey to the ignorant and the interested' in public hospitals are the focus of a long footnote in Wollstonecraft's review of Macaulay's *Letters on Education*, in the *AR* in November 1790. The note draws on the observations of 'a friend of the writer' who has frequently visited the hospitals; it responds to Macaulay's remarks on the abuse of public charities. See Wollstonecraft, *Works*, vol. 7, p.316.

36 *VRM*, pp.57–8.

37 Ibid., p.58. For a discussion of the 'enormous ingenuity' with which Wollstonecraft capitalises on the rhetorical and affective models of late-eighteenth century print culture, and this passage in particular, see Elizabeth Wingrove, 'Getting Intimate with Wollstonecraft in the Republic of Letters', *Political Theory* 33:3 (June 2005) 344–69 (357–58).

38 Althusser, 'Contradiction and Over-determination', in *For Marx*, quoted in James Thompson, *Models of Value: Eighteenth-Century Political Economy and the Novel* (Durham, 1996), pp.6–7, emphasis as in original.

39 Thompson, *Models of Value*, p.7.

40 For more on description and knowledge in the late eighteenth century, see *Regimes of Description: In the Archive of the Eighteenth Century* eds. John Bender and Michael Marrinan (Stanford University Press, 2005).

41 *VRM*, p.18.

42 *VRW*, p.256, and see the 'Advertisement' to *Mary*, p.5 and 'Author's Preface', *WW*, p.83.

43 *VRM*, p.56. Emphasis as in the original.

238   *Notes to pages 61–68*

44 *VRM*, p.57.

45 Interestingly, Macaulay also highlights 'mendicants' in her response to Burke: those in Paris are 'even more numerous, if possible, than those who infest and disgrace our capital'. See Catharine Macaulay, *Observations on the Reflections of the Right Hon. Edmund Burke, on the Revolution in France, in a Letter to the Right Hon. the Earl of Stanhope* (1790), p.35. As we will see in Chapter 4, Wollstonecraft would return to the political significance of monks: see *HMV*, p.51.

46 Dreyer, 'Genesis', p.462.

47 *Reflections*, p.170, p.126.

48 Macaulay, *Observations on the Reflections of the Right Hon. Edmund Burke*, pp.32–3.

49 *Reflections*, p.234: 'I believe the difference in the form of the two governments to be among the causes of this advantage of the side of England'.

50 My argument is this and the next section draws in part from my article 'Genre and the Mediation of Political Economy in Edmund Burke's *Reflections on the Revolution in France* and Mary Wollstonecraft's *A Vindication of the Rights of Men*', *Eighteenth Century: Theory and Interpretation*, 60:3 (Autumn 2019), 249–68.

51 Jane Burke to William Burke, 21 March 1791, in *Correspondence of Edmund Burke*, vol. 6, p.239; see also Pocock, Introduction to Burke's *Reflections*, p.xl.

52 *Reflections*, p.372.

53 *Vindication*, p.55.

54 See Macaulay, *Observations on the Reflections of the Right Hon. Edmund Burke*, p.44.

55 *Reflections*, p.270.

56 Ibid., p.271. There is a fascinating echo of this passage in Victor Frankenstein's description of himself, whilst labouring on the body of his creature prior to its animation, as 'like on doomed by slavery to toil in the mines, or any other unwholesome trade'. See Mary Shelley, *Frankenstein* (Oxford University Press, 2008), p.38.

57 Howard Caygill, *The Art of Judgement* (Oxford, 1989), p.101, quoted in John Guillory, *Capital Culture: The Problem of Literary Canon Formation* (Chicago University Press, 1993), p.312.

58 This unpreserved manuscript is quoted in Dugald Stewart's 'Account of the Life and Writings of Adam Smith, L.L.D', in *EPS*, p.322.

59 *WN*, vol. 1, p.289, p.291.

60 Smith, *Lectures on Jurisprudence* ed. R. L. Meek, D. D. Raphael and Peter Stein (Oxford University Press, 1978) p.341. This passage is discussed in Corey Robin, 'Edmund Burke and the Problem of Value', *Raritan* 36:1 (Summer 2016), 82–106 (98).

61 Robin, 'Burke and Value', 99 (quoting Burke).

62 Gary Kelly, *Revolutionary Feminism: The Mind and Career of Mary Wollstonecraft* (Macmillan, 1992).

63 *VRM*, p.52.

64 Macaulay, *Letters on Education* (1790), quoted in Wollstonecraft review, *Analytical Review* November 1790, in *Works*, vol.7 p.315. Macaulay's words

Notes to pages 68–77 239

here would seem to counter Harriet Guest's reading of Macaulay as a 'female Brutus', the founder of Rome who sacrificed his two sons who had conspired against the republic, and therefore as one who 'values liberty more than natural affection'. See Guest, *Small Change*, p.250, and for Macaulay's rejection of the 'stoicism of the first Brutus', see Wiseman, 'Catharine Macaulay', pp.185–86.

65 *VRM*, p.53, emphasis in the original.

66 *VRM*, p.60. Wollstonecraft later commented, in relation to Louis XIV's reported delight in torturing animals, that 'death seems to be the sport' not of gods but 'kings'. See *HMV*, p.74.

67 Frans de Bruyn, *The Literary Genres of Edmund Burke* (Oxford University Press, 1996), p.192. Wollstonecraft also references Hamlet three times in *VRM*, alongside quotations too from *Richard III* and *A Midsummer Night's Dream*. See VRM, p.37, p.45, p.55, p.43 and p.29, respectively.

68 Ronald Paulson, *Representations of Revolution, 1789–1820* (Yale University Press, 1983), p.48.

69 Guillory, *Cultural Capital*, p.302

70 Robin, 'Burke and Value' p.84.

71 Thompson, *Models of Value*, pp.17–8.

72 *Reflections*, p.136, p.274, p.120.

73 Ibid., p.169.

74 *VRM*, p.15. In a related vein, Wollstonecraft later condemned the French for the theatricality of their character: see *HMV*, p.25.

75 *Don Dismallo Running the Literary Gantlet*, 1790, last in a series of three attacking Burke as the Quixotic knight Don Dismallo, is discussed briefly by Harriet Guest in *Small Change*, p.225.

76 *VRM*, p.45.

77 'On Poetry', *Works*, vol. 7, pp.7–11.

78 Macaulay, *Observations on the Reflections of the Right Hon. Edmund Burke*, p.7.

79 *VRM*, 'Advertisement', p.5.

80 Ibid., p.5.

81 *VRM*, p.53. Wollstonecraft was still considering these matters when compiling her 'Hints' for the second, unwritten, part of *VRW*: see Hint no. 30 in 'Hints', *Works*, vol. 5, p.276.

82 *VRM*, p.16.

83 Ibid., p.53.

3 Property, Passions, and Manners

1 *VRM*, p.5.

2 William Godwin, *Memoirs of the Author of A Vindication of the Rights of Woman*, ed. Richard Holmes (Penguin, 1987) p.229.

3 See Frederick Dreyer, 'The Genesis of Burke's *Reflections*', *Journal of Modern History* 50:3 (1978), 462–79.

240   *Notes to pages 77–81*

4 For 'first of a new genus', see Wollstonecraft's letter to her sister Everina, 7 November 1787, in *The Collected Letters of Mary Wollstonecraft*, ed. Janet Todd (Columbia University Press, 2003), p.139. That the *Vindication* was written by a woman was only evident from the second edition. For the republic of letters in the 1790s, see Paul Keen, *The Crisis of Literature in the 1790s* (Cambridge University Press, 1999).

5 See Jürgen Habermas, *The Structural Transformation of the Public Sphere*, trans. T. Burger and F. Lawrence (MIT Press, 1989). For a modification of Habermas's thesis to suggest 'multiple' and 'overlapping' public spheres, see Craig Calhoun, ed. *Habermas and the Public Sphere* (MIT Press, 1992), p.37; for a discussion of women and the public sphere, see *Women, Writing and the Public Sphere 1700–1830,* eds. Elizabeth Eger, Charlotte Grant, Clíona Ó Gallchoir and Penny Warburton (Cambridge University Press, 2001), pp.7–9.

6 Terry Eagleton, *The Function of Criticism: From The Spectator to Post-Structuralism* (Verso, 1984), p.26, pp.16–7; see also Daniel E. White, *Early Romanticism and Religious Dissent* (Cambridge University Press, 2006), p.123.

7 For the transformation of the public sphere in 1790s, see White, *Early Romanticism*, and Keen, *Crisis of Literature.*

8 Keen describes the considerable suspicion by conservatives of literary and political public spheres which they suspected as being used to promote the particular interests of the reformist and professional middle classes. For discussion of Burke's opposition to 'political men of Letters', see Keen, *Crisis of Literature*, pp.43–4.

9 *VRM*, p.40.

10 I draw here on Clifford Siskin's account of professionalism in his *The Work of Writing: Literature and Social Change in Britain, 1700–1830* (Johns Hopkins University Press, 1998), pp.103–29. For Wollstonecraft's claim that her knowledge of human nature enables her to discover 'extenuating circumstances' in Burke, see *VRM*, pp.7–8.

11 *VRM*, p.9.

12 Ibid., p.49, p.39, p.47.

13 *VRW*, p.105.

14 *VRM*, pp.14–5.

15 Ibid., p.10.

16 Ibid., p.17.

17 Catharine Macaulay, *Observations on the reflections of the Right Hon. Edmund Burke, on the Revolution in France* (London, 1790), p.19.

18 *VRM*, p.19, p.58, p.57.

19 Ibid., p.9, p.59, p.58, p.21, p.40.

20 Ibid., p.17, p.22, p.58.

21 Ibid., p.51, p.57, p.56.

22 Ibid., p.9.

23 Ibid., pp.47–8.

24 Ibid., p.49, pp.45–6.

Notes to pages 82–86 241

25 As Lena Halldenius notes, the phrase the 'demon of property' is borrowed from Rousseau. See 'Mary Wollstonecraft's Feminist Critique of Property: On Becoming a Thief from Principle', *Hypatia* 29:4 (2014), 942–57 (943).

26 *VRM*, pp.22–3.

27 *Mary*, p.20.

28 *VRM*, p.24, p.23.

29 Ibid., p.24, p.10.

30 Ibid., p.23.

31 Ibid., p.48.

32 Ibid., p.48. Smith uses a language of 'channels' throughout *WN*, as well as in the early (1755) manuscript which set out his arguments in brief. See Adam Smith, unpreserved manuscript, quoted in Dugald Stewart, 'Account of the Life and Writings of Adam Smith, LL.D', in *EPS*, p.322.

33 *VRM*, pp.19–20.

34 Ibid., p.16.

35 See, *inter alia*, Miranda Burgess, *British Fiction and the Production of the Social Order 1740–1830* (Cambridge University Press, 2000), pp.130–35; Claudia L. Johnson, *Equivocal Beings: Politics, Gender, and Sentimentality in the 1790s* (University of Chicago Press, 1995), pp.26–9; Mitzi Myers, 'Politics from the Outside: Mary Wollstonecraft's First *Vindication*', *Studies in Eighteenth-Century Culture* 6 (1977), 113–32; Barbara Taylor, *Mary Wollstonecraft and the Feminist Imagination* (Cambridge University Press, 2003), p.64ff; and Sylvana Tomaselli, 'A Vindication of the Rights of Men', in *The Wollstonecraftian Mind* ed. Sandrine Bergès, Eileen Hunt Botting, and Alan Coffee (Routledge, 2019).

36 See Elizabeth Wingrove, 'Getting Intimate with Wollstonecraft in the Republic of Letters', *Political Theory* 33:3 (2005), 344–69.

37 For a discussion of another kind of idleness, contemplative meditation, in Wollstonecraft, see Richard Adelman, *Idleness, Contemplation, and the Aesthetic, 1750–1830* (Cambridge University Press, 2011).

38 *Reflections*, p.270.

39 David Hume, 'Of Public Credit' in *Essays: Moral, Political and Literary*, ed. Eugene F. Miller (Liberty Fund, 1985), pp.349–65 (p.355, pp.357–58). See also J. G. A. Pocock, 'The Political Economy of Burke's *Reflections on the Revolution in France*' in *Virtue, Commerce, History* (Cambridge University Press, 1985) pp.193–212.

40 Corey Robin, 'Edmund Burke and the Problem of Value', *Raritan* 36:1 (2016), 82–106 (104).

41 David Hume, *A Treatise of Human Nature* ed. P. H. Nidditch (Clarendon Press, 1978), p.413.

42 David Hume, *Essays Moral, Political and Literary* ed. Eugene Millar (Liberty Fund, 1985), p.146. Italics in original.

43 Smith, *TMS*, p.180. This paragraph draws on an argument made in my article, 'Domesticity, Objects and Idleness: Mary Wollstonecraft and Political Economy', *Women's Writing* 19:4 (2012), 544–62 (550–51).

44 *TMS*, p.180.

242 *Notes to pages 86–92*

45 See Smith, *WN*, pp.673–74, p.343; see also pp.466–67, p.473, p.496, p.604. For a full discussion of Smith's theorisation of the economic subject, see my 'System and Subject in Adam Smith's Political Economy: Nature, Vitalism, and Bioeconomic Life', in *Systems of Life: Biopolitics, Economics and Literature on the Cusp of Modernity*, eds. Richard A. Barney and Warren Montag (Fordham University Press, 2019), pp.93–113.

46 *VRW*, p.93.

47 *VRM*, p.42.

48 *VRW* p.93. See also Chapter 9 for more on the social effects of rank.

49 *Mary*, p.7; *VRW*, p.112.

50 *VRM*, p.42. For Wollstonecraft as advocate of bourgeois meritocracy, see Gary Kelly, *Revolutionary Feminism: The Mind and Career of Mary Wollstonecraft* (Macmillan, 1992). For Wollstonecraft's sense of the moral value of labour, see Lena Halldenius 'Mary Wollstonecraft's Feminist Critique of Property: On Becoming a Thief from Principle', *Hypatia* 29:4 (2014), 942–57 (948).

51 *VRM*, p.24. For a discussion of Smith's account of value as rooted in labour, see Robin, 'Burke and Value', 97–8. According to Robin, for Smith labour is as much a 'universal measure of value' as it is 'a marker of our common humanity' (98).

52 *VRM*, p.57.

53 *VRW*, p.8. For a comparable argument about a 'meritocracy of mental energy', see Jon P. Klancher, *The Making of English Reading Audiences, 1790–1832* (University of Wisconsin Press, 1987), p.41.

54 *Reflections*, p.271.

55 *VRM*, p.16.

56 Wollstonecraft's recognition of the importance of the passions is contrary to what Saree Makdisi argues is an 'Orientalist hostility' to the passions. See Saree Makdisi, *William Blake and the Impossible History of the 1790s* (University of Chicago Press, 2003), pp.44–5.

57 *VRM*, p.16.

58 Ibid., p.19.

59 Ibid., pp.19–20.

60 Ibid., p.33. 'Phlogiston' was thought to be present in all combustible materials; its existence was soon to be disproved through Lavoisier's discovery of oxygen.

61 *VRM*, p.19, p.53.

62 This is a recurring theme in *VRW*.

63 *VRM*, p.53.

64 Ibid., p.31.

65 Ibid., p.33. Italics in the original.

66 Ibid., p.46.

67 Ibid., pp.16–17.

68 Ibid., p.82.

69 *Reflections*, Pocock, 'Political economy of Burke', p.206.

70 Quote is from Pocock, 'Political Economy', p.203.

Notes to pages 92–95

71 Sylvana Tomaselli correctly notes that the first *Vindication* is often eclipsed by a focus on the gender analysis offered by the second: see *Wollstonecraft: Philosophy, Passion, and Politics* (Princeton University Press, 2021), pp.2–3, p.9. In *Women and Enlightenment in Eighteenth-Century Britain*, Karen O'Brien offers only a very brief account of *VRM*. Whilst she suggests that its 'diagnosis of modern manners' is more fully developed in *VRW*, her argument that Wollstonecraft's reading of Macaulay's *Letters of Education* (1790) was a key event informing the second text tends to de-emphasise any continuity between the two *Vindications* (pp.181–83).

72 *VRW*, p.73.

73 *VRM* p.10. The particular analytic significance of manners in this context is to be distinguished from the broader movement for a moral reform of manners of the 1780s, as described by Joanna Innes: see 'Politics and Morals: The Reformation of Manners Movement in Later Eighteenth-Century England', in *The Transformation of Political Culture: England and Germany in the Late Eighteenth Century* ed. Eckhart Hellmuth (Oxford University Press, 1990), pp.57–118.

74 *VRW*, p.265. For an account of Burke's use of the phrase 'revolution in manners' in *Reflections*, see Pocock, 'Political economy of Burke'.

75 Conjectural history offered a stadial view of the development and progress of human society, which it traced through four successive stages of development, culminating in the commercial stage. See O'Brien, *Women and Enlightenment*, pp.31–2.

76 *VRW*, p.73.

77 For discussion of this tradition, see Sylvana Tomaselli, 'The Enlightenment Debate on Women', *History Workshop Journal* 20:1 (1985), 101–24.

78 Wollstonecraft's mobilisation of virtue for its larger reformative effects is thus distinct from what Dana Harrington describes as the emergence of a separate domestic moral sphere to compensate for the corruptions of commerce: see her 'Gender, Commerce, and the Transformation of Virtue in Eighteenth-Century Britain', *Rhetoric Society Quarterly*, 31:3 (2001), 33–52 (45).

79 It is notable that Wollstonecraft refers to other writers for and about women, including conduct writers, as specifically addressing 'female education and manners': *VRW*, p.91.

80 The problem gives its name to a classic collection of essays on eighteenth-century political economy: *Wealth and Virtue: The Shaping of Political Economy in the Scottish Enlightenment*, eds. Istvan Hont and Michael Igantieff (Cambridge University Press 1986). See also Pocock, 'Political economy of Burke', pp.195–96.

81 See O'Brien, *Women and Enlightenment*, p.182.

82 See, for example, *VRW*, p.210; *WN*, pp.673–74.

83 'Against Inconsistency in Our Expectations', in *Anna Letitia Barbauld: Selected Poetry and Prose* ed. William McCarthy and Elizabeth Kraft (Ontario: Broadview, 2002), pp.186–94; *VRW*, p.184.

84 *VRW*, p.82.

85 *VRM*, p.87.
86 *VRW*, p.216.
87 Ibid., p.82.
88 Ibid., p.212.
89 See O'Brien, *Women and Enlightenment*, p.182. Relatedly, Harriet Guest discusses the problem of the lack of both a moral and professional language to 'articulate female virtue' in commercial society, in *Small Change: Women, Learning and Patriotism, 1750–1810* (University of Chicago Press, 2000), pp.286–87.
90 *VRW*, p.83.
91 Ibid., p.212.
92 Ibid., p.99, p.84.
93 Ibid., p.84.
94 Ibid., p.178.
95 Ibid., pp.177–78. The reference is to Ecclesiasticus 1:14: 'all the works that are done under the sun … [are] vanity and vexation of spirit'.
96 *TMS*, pp.181–83.
97 Jean-Jacques Rousseau, *Discourse on the Origin of Inequality*, trans. Franklin Philip (Oxford University Press, 1994), pp.83–4. This passage, which Smith quoted at length, is one of three which Smith included in his discussion of the *Discourse* in his letter to the *Edinburgh Review* of 1756. See *EPS*, pp.242–54 (pp.253–54).
98 *TMS*, p.183.
99 Ibid., p.181, p.183; *VRW*, p.82.
100 *VRW*, p.99, p.83.
101 *TMS*, pp.181–82.
102 *VRW*, p.180.
103 Ibid., p.180. A similar image recurs in Wollstonecraft's next work, her *Historical and Moral View of the French Revolution*, where Louis XVI's purported taste for torturing animals causes her to comment that 'death seems to be the sport of kings'. See *HMV*, p.74.
104 *VRW*, p.84.
105 Ibid., p.179. This is discussed further in Chapter 6 below.
106 *VRW*, p.178.
107 Ibid., p.179.
108 Ibid., pp.179.
109 Ibid., p.181.
110 For a discussion of how the political economy of Smith and Hume originates in their accounts of human nature, character, and behaviour, see Miranda Burgess, *British Fiction and the Production of Social Order 1740–1830* (Cambridge University Press, 2000), pp.14–21.
111 *VRW*, p.215; similarly, 'Public spirit must be nurtured by private virtue', p.210. Wollstonecraft's address to the 'legislator' recalls Smith's definition of political economy as a 'branch of the science of the legislator', *WN* i, p.428.
112 *VRW*, p.215.

113 Ibid., p.125.

114 Ibid., p.90.

115 Ibid., p.120.

116 Ibid., p.217.

117 Ibid., p.109.

118 Joseph Addison, [Allegory of Public Credit], *The Spectator* 3, 3 March 1711. Defoe's allegory of Credit, daughter of Prudence, appears in his *Review* of 1710. See Paula R. Backscheider 'Defoe's Lady Credit', *Huntington Library Quarterly* 44:2 (Spring 1981), 89–100.

119 Defoe's Moll Flanders and Roxana, early eighteenth-century reincarnations of the mythical figure of 'Fortuna', are just two examples; for more, see Edward Copeland, *Women Writing about Money* (Cambridge University Press, 1995).

120 See 'Of the Rise and Progress of the Arts and Science', in David Hume, *Essays: Moral, Political and Literary* ed. Eugene F. Miller (Liberty Fund, 1985), pp.111–37.

121 Guest, *Small Change*, p.279.

122 For anxiety about gender in the 1790s, see Claudia Johnson, *Equivocal Beings: Politics, Gender, and Sentimentality in the 1790s* (University of Chicago Press, 1995).

123 Adela Pinch, *Strange Fits of Passion: Epistemologies of Emotion, Hume to Austen* (Stanford University Press, 1996), p.22.

124 Pinch, *Strange Fits,* p.24.

125 *VRW*, p.112–13, p.218.

126 Ibid., p.215.

127 Ibid., p.215.

128 Ibid., p.104, p.266.

129 Ibid., p.211.

130 Ibid., p.218.

131 Ibid., p.215, 211.

132 Ibid., p.211.

133 Ibid., p.214.

134 Ibid., p.216.

135 Ibid., p.124.

136 Ibid., p.155.

137 Ibid., p.205.

138 Ibid., p.212.

139 Ibid., pp.123–24, p.211.

140 Ibid., p.207, 215, p.112.

141 Ibid., p.199.

142 Ibid., pp.211–12.

143 Ibid., p.225.

144 Ibid., pp.112–13.

145 Ibid., p.225.

146 Ibid., p.249.

147 Ibid., p.217.

246 *Notes to pages 108–15*

148 Ibid., p.218.
149 Ibid., pp.218–19.
150 Ibid., p.212.
151 Ibid., p.219.
152 Pocock, 'Political economy of Burke', p.195.
153 *VRW*, p.120
154 Ibid., p.126.
155 *VRW*, p.123. For a discussion of the differences between modern feminism and late eighteenth-century 'rights of women' debates, see Karen Offen, 'Was Mary Wollstonecraft a feminist? A Contextual Re-reading of *A Vindication of the Rights of Woman* 1792–1992' in *Quilting a New Canon: Stitching Women's Words*, ed. Uma Parameswaran (Black Women and Women of Colour Press, Sept 1996), pp.3–24.
156 *VRW*, p.90.
157 For a full account of the role of Wollstonecraft's faith in her thinking, see Taylor, *Feminist Imagination*.
158 *VRW*, p.105.
159 Ibid., p.106, p.124, p.91.
160 Ibid., p.90, p.114.
161 Ibid., p.68.
162 Ibid., p.68.
163 Ibid., p.215.
164 Ibid., p.210.
165 *VRW*, p.106.

4 Political Economy in Revolution

1 Janet Todd, *Mary Wollstonecraft: A Revolutionary Life* (Weidenfeld and Nicholson, 2000), p.155.
2 Karen Offen, 'Was Mary Wollstonecraft A Feminist? A Contextual Re-reading of *A Vindication of the Rights of Woman* 1792–1992', pp.3–24 in *Quilting a New Canon: Stitching Women's Words*, ed. Uma Parameswaran (Black Women and Women of Colour Press, 1996), p.6.
3 Offen, 'Contexual Re-reading', p.7.
4 For an account of arguments from Tallyrand and others for establishing the assignats, see Florin Aftalion, *The French Revolution: An Economic Interpretation* (Cambridge University Press, 1990), pp.61–5.
5 See Richard Whatmore, *Against War and Empire: Geneva, Britain and France in the Eighteenth Century* (Yale University Press, 2012), pp.202–3; pp.245–46, p.248. For the crisis of the assignats from October 1791 onwards, see Aftalion, *French Revolution*, p.109.
6 See Aftalion, *French Revolution*, p.39, p.37.
7 For discussion of *HMV*, see Harriet Devine Jump, '"The cool eye of observation": Mary Wollstonecraft and the French Revolution' in *Revolution in Writing: British literary responses to the French Revolution*, ed. Kelvin Everest

Notes to pages 115–19 247

(Open University Press, 1991) pp.101–20, and Vivien Jones, 'Women Writing Revolution: Narratives of History and Sexuality in Wollstonecraft and Williams', in *Beyond Romanticism* eds. John Whale and Stephen Copley (Routledge, 1992), pp.178–99.

8 Todd, *Life*, p.240.

9 Christie was often in Paris on business between October 1789 and August 1793: see Helen Braithwaite, *Romanticism, Publishing and Dissent: Joseph Johnson and the Cause of Liberty* (Palgrave Macmillan, 2003) p.94. For Turnbull Forbes, see Todd, *Life*, p.210.

10 For Christie's connection with Turnbull, Forbes and Co, which lasted at least until autumn 1793, see the letter of Thomas Paine's in Clio Rickman*, Life of Paine* (London 1819), pp.238–49. For Wollstonecraft drawing bills through the firm, see *Shelley and His Circle 1773–1822* (1961) pp.121–23, pp.128–30.

11 *HMV*, p.217.

12 See Savi Munjal, 'He Drinks the Knowledge in Greedy Haste': Tasting History Through James Gillray's Political Prints. *AIC* 11 (1: 2013), pp.39–64 (p.39, p.48).

13 For debates over the grain trade from the 1740s on, see Michael Sonenscher, 'Property, Community and Citizenship', in *The Cambridge History of Eighteenth-Century Political Thought* eds. Mark Goldie and Robert Wokler (Cambridge, 2006), pp.465–94 (p.466).

14 *HMV*, p.132.

15 Ibid., p.19.

16 On the history of physiocracy, see T. J. Hochstrasser, 'Physiocracy and the Politics of Laissez-faire', in *Cambridge History of Eighteenth-Century Political Thought* ed. Mark Goldie and Robert Wokler (Cambridge University Press, 2006), pp.419–42.

17 In a classic essay, Istvan Hont and Michael Ignatieff locate *The Wealth of Nations* precisely within this debate about subsistence, community, and justice, and suggest that political economy's founding text was a 'scandal' in its suggestion that the market mechanism could best provide for all. See 'Needs and Justice in the *Wealth of Nations*', in *Wealth and Virtue: The Shaping of Political Economy in the Scottish Enlightenment* eds. Istvan Hont and Michael Ignatieff (Cambridge University Press, 1983), pp.1–44.

18 Emma Rothschild, *Economic Sentiments: Adam Smith, Condorcet, and the Enlightenment* (Harvard University Press, 2001), p.72.

19 Turgot is also praised as excelling in the science of political economy in *AR* 21:2 (February 1795), pp.153–55.

20 See Rothschild, *Economic Sentiments,* pp.72–86.

21 *HMV*, p.19.

22 Ibid., p.225. Wollstonecraft's praise runs exactly counter to Burke's characterisation of the *Encyclopédie* as a 'literary cabal' of 'political Men of Letters' formed for the 'destruction of the Christian religion', which deliberately cultivated 'the monied interest' of 'Turgot and almost all the people of the finance'. See Edmund Burke, *Reflections*, p.211, p.213.

248   *Notes to pages 119–24*

23 *HMV*, p.226.
24 Ibid., p.226. Earlier in her discussion, Wollstonecraft had attacked the 'vexatious impediments thrown in the way of trade, by barriers and monopolies', and the 'clogs on husbandry' which means that agriculture is 'continually dampened by … various restrictions' and 'an invincible impediment was thrown in the way of agricultural improvement': see *HMV*, p.54, p.50. And a footnote contrasting the open commerce of London with the intrigues dogging the provisioning of Paris, she notes that the 'wealth of the nation' depends on London's relatively unconstrained 'intercourse': *HMV*, pp.92–3.
25 For a detailed account of the various measures and reforms taken in relation to the grain trade over the period 1789–1799, see Aftalion, *French Revolution*.
26 Rothschild, *Economic Sentiments*, p.60.
27 See Rothschild, *Economic Sentiments*, pp.57–9.
28 Morrellet's translation of Smith was not published: see Whatmore, *Against Empire*, p.186, p.341 n.50.
29 *Mémoires de L'Abbé Morellet*, quoted in Rothschild, *Economic Sentiments* pp.60–1.
30 Robert Darnton, *Gens de lettres, Gens du Livre*, quoted in Rothschild, *Economic Sentiments*, n.59, p.274.
31 *HMV*, p.225.
32 William Godwin, *Memoirs of the Author of 'The Rights of Woman'*, in Mary Wollstonecraft and William Godwin, *A Short Residence in Sweden and Memoirs of the Author of 'The Rights of Woman'* ed. Richard Holmes (Penguin, 1987), p.244.
33 Whatmore, *Against Empire*, p.182–89. I am indebted to this work throughout this and the next section.
34 For Dugald Stewart's account of Smith and Turgot's shared opinions on 'the most essential points of political economy', see 'Account of the Life and Writings of Adam Smith', in *EPS*, p.304.
35 Whatmore, *Against Empire*, p.186. For an account of Smith's conversations with Shelburne, see Ian Simpson Ross, *The Life of Adam Smith* (Oxford, 2010), p.188.
36 Whatmore, *Against Empire*, p.181, p.13.
37 Ibid., p.187, p.181.
38 Ibid., p.340 n.32, p.185
39 Ibid., p.185.
40 *Discourse on the Love of Our Country* in *Richard Price: Political Writings* ed. D. O. Thomas (Cambridge, 1991) pp.176–96 (p.181–82).
41 *HMV*, p.183.
42 Béla Kapossy, Isaac Nakhimovsky, and Richard Whatmore, 'Introduction: Power, Prosperity and Peace in Enlightenment Thought', in *Commerce and Peace in the Enlightenment* eds. Béla Kapossy, Isaac Nakhimovsky, and Richard Whatmore (Cambridge University Press, 2017), p.1; Whatmore, *Against Empire*, p.192.
43 Whatmore, *Against Empire*, p.195.

Notes to pages 124–29

44 Ibid.
45 Turgot, Letter to Price, 22 March 1778. Published with Mirabeau's *Considerations on the Cinncinati*, English translation 1785, p.162, p.164.
46 Turgot, Letter to Price, p.155, p.156.
47 See *Gilbert Imlay: Citizen of the World*, by Wil Verhoeven (Pickering & Chatto, 2008), p.200.
48 *SND*, p.342. Todd is mistaken in identifying Wollstonecraft's dinner companion as John Dickenson, an error also made in Richard Holmes' Penguin edition of this work.
49 Review of Brissot's *Nouveau Voyage Dans Les Etats-Unies de L'Amerique Septentrionale, fait en 1788. Travels in the United States of North America*, in *Works*, vol. 7, pp.390–93 (p.391).
50 Stedman Jones, *End to Poverty*, p.123.
51 Whatmore, *Against Empire*; Stedman Jones, *End of Poverty*, p.121.
52 Brissot, *Life of J. P. Brissot, Written by Himself* (1794), quoted in *AR* 18:4 (April 1794), 374–78 (p.374). In fact, Brissot's father was a restauranteur in Chartres. See Frederick A. de Luna, 'The Dean Street Style of Revolution: J.-P. Brissot, Jeune Philosophe', *French Historical Studies* 17:1 (Spring 1991), 159–90 (162). Wollstonecraft also reviewed David Williams's *Lectures on Education* for the *Analytical* too; Brissot, who met Williams in London whilst trying to establish a Lycée and Assembly in 1783–1784, described Williams's plans for educational reform as a manifesto for teaching of republican manners: see Whatmore, *Against Empire*, p.232. For Brissot's activities in London, see Simon Burrows, 'The Innocence of Jacques-Pierre Brissot', *The Historical Journal* 46:4 (2003), 843–71.
53 Brissot confessed that his ideas had, before meeting Clavière, been 'rather French': see Whatmore, *Against Empire*, p.14.
54 Whatmore, *Against Empire*, p.212.
55 Ibid., p.225.
56 The second edition of 1791, translated as 'Considerations on the Relative Situation of France and the United States: shewing the importance of the American Revolution to the welfare of France: giving also an account of their productions, and the reciprocal advantages which may be drawn from their commercial connexions', attributed authorship to both Brissot and Clavière.
57 See Richard Whatmore, 'Commerce, Constitutions, and the Manners of a Nation: Etienne Clavière's Revolutionary Political Economy, 1788–93', *History of European Ideas* (22: 5–6), 351–68 (p.353).
58 Whatmore, *Against Empire*, pp.242–43. As Verhoeven reports, silver melted into bars was later used as payment for goods imported into France by Barlow and Imlay; Wollstonecraft oversaw its loading onto the *Maria and Margarethe*, the ship which later went missing with its precious cargo, and whose pursuit later took her to Scandinavia. See Verhoeven, pp.191–94.
59 For a discussion of *De La France*, see Whatmore, *Against Empire*, pp.212–13.
60 Whatmore, *Against Empire*, p.214.
61 Ibid., p.349 n.172.

250   *Notes to pages 129–35*

62 *HMV*, p.6.
63 Wollstonecraft, 'Letter on the Present Character of the French Nation', in *Works*, Vol. 6, pp.443–46.
64 I draw here on the account offered in Todd, *Life*, pp.210–15.
65 Todd, *Life*, p.215.
66 Helen Braithwaite, *Romanticism, Publishing and Dissent: Joseph Johnson and the Cause of Liberty* (Palgrave Macmillan, 2003) p.94; Verhoeven, *Imlay*, p.150–51.
67 Todd, *Life*, p.210, p.215.
68 Gary Kelly, *Revolutionary Feminism* (Macmillan, 1992), p.166.
69 Arthur Young describes the prevalence of discussions on such topics, prompted by newspaper reports and political debates, in his *Travels in France During the Years 1787, 1788 and 1789*, 2 vols (London, 1794). See, for instance, vol. 1, p.625.
70 Todd, *Life*, p.215.
71 Wollstonecraft, *Letters to Imlay*, in *Works*, vol. 6, p.388, p.373. Wollstonecraft's complaint in July 1794, in relation to Imlay's trading activity, that 'the government is perpetually throwing impediments in the way of business' is less well known. *The Collected Letters of Mary Wollstonecraft* ed. Janet Todd (Columbia University Press, 2003), p.255.
72 For a detailed account of Imlay's involvement in the Louisiana scheme, see Verhoeven, *Imlay*, pp.151–57. For Barlow and Louisiana, see p.159 and p.155.
73 See Verhoeven, Imlay, pp.160–61; pp.170–75. See also Mary A. Favret, *Romantic Correspondence: Women, Politics and the Fiction of Letters* (Cambridge University Press, 2008), pp.97–8.
74 Verhoeven, *Imlay*, p.166–67.
75 Ibid., p.169.
76 *AR*, 18:2 (February 1794), p.220; 18:4 (April 1794), pp.374–78 (p.374), review of the *Life of J. P. Brissot Written by himself* (1794); *AR* 22:2 (Aug 1795), pp.137–45 (p.142, p.144). Williams is referring to Algernon Sidney, William Russell, and John Hampden.
77 Verhoeven, *Imlay*, p.96. For full discussion of Imlay's publications, see Chapters 5 and 6 in the same valuable study. Although alert to Imlay's 'geopolitical vision', Verhoeven's broad characterisation of Imlay's texts and the contemporaneous literature on America as either Jacobin or anti-Jacobin does not capture the specific nature of the Girondin political ideology with which I am concerned here. Thus, whilst noting the influence of Crèvecoeur's *Letters from an American Farmer*, Verhoeven characterises that influence as a 'European cultural heritage of transatlantic pastoralism and agrarian primitivism' (p.96) without addressing the political discourse and projects with which that vision, and as mentioned above, Crèvecoeur himself, was associated.
78 See Verhoeven, *Imlay*, pp.162–65.
79 Verhoeven notes that Barlow was worth $120,000 by 1796, having been virtually destitute a few years earlier. See *Imlay*, p.169.
80 *HMV*, p.184.
81 Ibid., p.7.

Notes to pages 135–41

82 Ibid., p.144.

83 Ibid., p.181.

84 Ibid., p.180, 181.

85 Ibid., p.183.

86 Ibid., p.183.

87 Ibid., p.113. A similar historical narrative is offered in the first chapter of *VRW*.

88 See Burrows, 'Innocence of Brissot', p.870. Wollstonecraft is undecided as to the rumours of court manipulation of bread supplies: at times such shortages are dismissed as manifesting the 'inventive mistrust of the nation', but she also accuses the Duke of Orleans of involvement in such plots: see *HMV*, pp.128–30, p.199.

89 *HMV*, p.196. The remainder of this section and the next draw in part on discussion previously published in my article, '"The common grievance of the revolution": Bread, the Grain Trade, and Political Economy in Wollstonecraft's *View of the French Revolution*', *European Romantic Review* 25:6 (2014), 705–22.

90 *HMV*, p.210.

91 Ibid., p.196.

92 Ibid., p.196.

93 Ibid., p.181.

94 Ibid., p.213. For Wollstonecraft's participation in a Scottish tradition of philosophical history, including her knowledge of progressive histories of 'improvement by John Millar and William Robertson, see Jane Rendell, '"The grand causes which combine to carry mankind forward": Wollstonecraft, History and Revolution', *Women's Writing* 4.2 (1997): 155–72.

95 See J. G. A. Pocock, 'Edmund Burke and the Redefinition of Enthusiasm: The Context as Counter-Revolution', in *The French Revolution and the Creation of Modern Political Culture* eds. François Furet and Mona Ozouf (Pergamon, 1989), pp.19–36 (p.20).

96 'British and Foreign History; for the Year 1790. Chapter 1. France', *The New Annual Register, or General Repository of History, Politics, and Literature, for the Year 1790*. (London, 1791), pp.3–32 (p.49). This account also offers a much less dignified account of Maillard's speech, as well as one less focused on provision of subsistence: Maillard is interrupted by the women, 'inveighs' against aristocrats for causing bread shortages, and complains of insults to the national cockade. For a discussion of the difference of Wollstonecraft's history from the *New Annual Register*'s 'constitutional Whiggism', see Karen O'Brien, *Women and Enlightenment in Eighteenth-Century Britain* (Cambridge University Press, 2009), pp.192–93.

97 See 'The Moral Economy of the English Crowd in the Eighteenth Century' and 'The Moral Economy Reviewed', in E. P. Thompson, *Customs in Common* (Merlin, 1991), pp.185–351.

98 See for instance, Gary Kelly, *Revolutionary Feminism*, p.165, and Joan Landes, *Women and the Public Sphere in the Age of the French Revolution* (Cornell University Press, 1988), pp.148–51.

252   *Notes to pages 141–49*

99 For a full account of popular protest in eighteenth-century Britain, including food riots, see Adrian Randall, *Riotous Assemblies: Popular Protest in Hanoverian England* (Oxford University Press, 2006).

100 The free domestic circulation of grain was halted in May 1793, under mob pressure, and with the fall of the Girondins. A uniform 'maximum' price for grain was established across all France in September 1793. A free grain trade was re-established in June 1797. See Aftalion, *French Revolution*, p.134, p.149, p.171.

101 *HMV*, p.202; 'British and Foreign History; for the Year 1791. Chapter 2. State of Paris after the Capture of the Bastille', *The New Annual Register, or General Repository of History, Politics, and Literature, for the Year 1791* (London 1792), pp.25–61 (p.49).

102 On this, see Donald Winch, *Riches and Poverty: An Intellectual History of Political Economy in Britain, 1750–1834* (Cambridge University Press, 1996), pp.198–220.

103 See Sandra Sherman, '*The Wealth of Nations* in the 1790s', *Studies in Eighteenth-Century Culture* 34 (2005), 81–96, and Rothschild, *Economic Sentiments*, pp.52–71.

104 *HMV*, p.183.

105 *WN*, vol. 2, p.782.

106 *HMV*, p.234.

107 Ibid., p.230.

108 Ibid., pp.233–34.

109 Ibid., p.233.

110 Ibid., p.233.

111 Gilbert Imlay, *A Topographical Description of the Western Territory of North America* (London, 1797), p.216.

112 Wollstonecraft does observe that 'notes … which are issued by a state before it's (sic) government is well established, will certainly be depreciated', gold and silver will 'vanish' and prices will rise. But this is phrased as a general truth, not a particular comment on the assignats. *HMV*, p.182.

113 *HMV*, p.231.

114 Ibid., p.231.

115 Ibid., p.234. 'Lazy friars' is, for Wollstonecraft, an unusually mild description; elsewhere she refers to monks as 'canker-worms', 'leeches of the kingdom', and the 'idols of the ignorant'. See *HMV*, p.51 and *Reflections*, p.271.

116 *HMV*, p.6.

5 Property in Political Economy

1 *HMV,* p.84.

2 Ibid., pp.84–5.

3 *WW*, p.149. For women as property and as slaves, see Lena Halldenius, 'Mary Wollstonecraft's Feminist Critique of Property: On Becoming a

Thief from Principle', *Hypatia* 29:4 (2014), 942–57 and Alan Coffee, 'Mary Wollstonecraft, Freedom and the Enduring Power of Social Domination', *European Journal of Political Theory* 12:2 (2013), 116–35; for property and slavery, see Laura Brace, *The Politics of Slavery* (Edinburgh University Press, 2018). For a survey of the theme of property in Wollstonecraft, see Virginia Sapiro, *A Vindication of Political Virtue: The Political Theory of Mary Wollstonecraft* (University of Chicago Press, 1992), pp.89–100.

4 For a valuable collection of perspective on property in this period, see *Early Modern Conceptions of Property* eds. John Brewer and Susan Staves (Routledge, 1995).

5 *WN*, vol.1, pp.22–4.

6 For an alternative account of Wollstonecraft's thinking on property, which attends to her difference from a Lockean rights tradition, see Halldenius, 'Feminist Critique of Property'.

7 *HMV*, p.229.

8 Ibid., pp.84–5.

9 *WN*, p.24.

10 Jean-Jacques Rousseau, *Discourse on the Origin of Inequality* trans. Frankin Philip (Oxford University Press, 1994) p.32, p.31.

11 Jean-Jacques Rousseau, 'Discourse on Political Economy' in *The Social Contract*, trans. Christopher Betts (Oxford University Press 1994), p.3.

12 Céline Spector, *Rousseau* (Polity, 2019), pp.153–54. For a discussion of Clarens, see also Jimena Hurtado, 'Jean-Jacques Rousseau: économie politique, philosophie économique et justice', *Revue de philosophie économique* 11:2 (2010), 69–101.

13 Spector, *Rousseau*, p.154.

14 Other examples of the letter form being used for reflections on political and socioeconomic matters include Rousseau's *Letters Written from the Mountain* (1764), a response to Jean-Robert's Tronchin's *Letters Written from the Country* (1763) and their fellow Genevan Jean-Andre Deluc's *Lettres physiques et morales, sur les montagnes et sur l'histoire de la terre et de l'homme* (published in one volume in 1778, and later in six volumes in 1779–1780), which Richard Whatmore describes as reading like a sentimental novel. See Whatmore, *Against War and Empire: Geneva, Britain and France in the Eighteenth Century* (Yale University Press, 2012) p.138.

15 For Wollstonecraft's praise of the wit, sagacity, and profundity of Montesquieu's *Letters*, see *Works*, vol. 7, p.341.

16 Alexander Pope, 'Epistle to Burlington' l.172, in *Alexander Pope: The Major Works*, ed. Pat Rogers (Oxford University Press, 2008), p.249. For a discussion, see Jonathan Sheehan and Dror Wahrmann, *Invisible Hands: Self-Organization and the Eighteenth Century* (Chicago University Press, 2015), pp.8–9.

17 Quoted in Donald Winch, *Riches and Poverty: An Intellectual History of Political Economy in Britain, 1750–1834* (Cambridge University Press, 1996), pp.65–6.

18 *WN*, Vol. 1, p.330. On frugality in Smith, see Winch, *Riches and Poverty*, pp.76–80.

19 Winch, *Riches and Poverty*, p.216. For discussion of Burke on the monasteries, see Richard Bourke, *Empire & Revolution: The Political Life of Edmund Burke* (Princeton University Press, 2015), pp.734–35.

20 Rousseau, *Inequality*, p.38, pp.58–9; Spector, *Rousseau*, p.33.

21 Ibid., p.80.

22 Ibid., p.65, p.84.

23 Ibid., p.84, p.66.

24 Ibid., p.85.

25 Spector, *Rousseau*, p.30.

26 For more discussion of gender in commercial society, especially with regard to object relations, see my article '"Domesticity, Object and Idleness": Mary Wollstonecraft and Political Economy', *Women's Writing* 19:4 (2012), pp.544–62, which offers an earlier exposition of some of the argument in this section.

27 *TMS*, p.181.

28 Rousseau, *Inequality*, pp.83–4. This is one of three passages which Smith quotes in his rather disparaging discussion of the *Discourse on Inequality* in his 'Letter to the *Edinburgh Review*' of 1756. See *EPS*, p.242–54.

29 *TMS*, p.183.

30 Ibid., p.179.

31 Ibid., p.179.

32 Ibid., p.180.

33 Ibid., p.186.

34 Ibid., p.179.

35 See Winch, *Riches and Poverty*, p.74, and *TMS*, pp.61–6, added to the final edition. For a discussion of *TMS* in terms of geometry, see Matthew Wickman, *Literature After Euclid: The Geometric Imagination in the Long Scottish Enlightenment* (University of Pennsylvania Press, 2016).

36 Michael McKeon, *The Secret History of Domesticity: Public, Private, and the Divisions of Knowledge* (Johns Hopkins University Press, 2005), p.377; *TMS*, p.107.

37 *TMS*, p.112.

38 McKeon, *Secret History*, p.380, p.794 n.115.

39 Ibid., p.380.

40 *Mary*, p.7, p.20.

41 *TMS*, p.85.

42 *HMV*, p.227. Wollstonecraft's editors suggest that she may have had works by Kant (including the *Critique of Pure Reason*, 1781), Goethe and Schiller in mind.

43 *WN*, p.347; see also Winch, *Riches and Poverty*, p.79. Smith also notes that expenditure on such 'durable commodities' represents a stock which will retain some value in contrast to expenditure on food, servants and animals.

44 *TMS*, p.179.

Notes to pages 160–67

45 Wollstonecraft, 'Hints. [Chiefly designed to have been incorporated in the Second Part of the Vindication of the Rights of Woman.]', in *Works* vol. 5, pp.275–76. Compare *TMS*, p.179.

46 *SND*, pp.256–57. The editors note that the second property is Gunnebo House, owned by Scottish merchant John Hall.

47 *SND*, p.307.

48 *TMS*, p.186.

49 *SND*, pp.307–9.

50 *HMV*, p.5.

51 Ibid., p.121.

52 *VRW*, p.217.

53 *HMV*, p.75, p.122.

54 Ibid., p.213.

55 Ibid., p.121.

56 Ibid., pp.147–48.

57 Ibid., p.147.

58 Ibid., p.61.

59 Ibid., p.231, p.20, p.182.

60 Ibid., p.154, p.45.

61 Ibid., p.21, p.223.

62 Ibid., p.183.

63 Ibid., p.180, p.182.

64 Ibid., p.50.

65 Ibid. p.46.

66 Ibid., pp.230–31.

67 Ibid., p.233.

68 See *WN*, pp.686–87; Michael Igantieff, *The Needs of Strangers* (Hogarth Press, 1984), p.118; Winch, *Riches and Poverty* p.72.

69 *HMV*, p.231.

70 Ibid., p.235.

71 *WN*, p.783.

72 *SND*, p.309, p.296.

73 Ibid., p.326, p.346. My discussion in this paragraph draws on an argument already published in 'Mary Wollstoncraft's Cottage Economics: Property, Political Economy, and the European Future', *ELH* 84 (2017), 453–74 (p.461, p.469). Among many other critical discussions of *SND*, see Mary A. Favret, 'Travelling with Mary Wollstonecraft' in *The Cambridge Companion to Mary Wollstonecraft* ed. Claudia L. Johnson (Cambridge University Press, 2002), 214–17 and Ingrid Horrocks, *Women Wanderers and the Writing of Mobility, 1784–1814* (Cambridge University Press, 2017), pp.140–68.

74 *SND*, p.248, p.244, p.257, p.285, pp.328–29.

75 Ibid., p.307–9.

76 Ibid., p.315.

77 Jean-Jacques Rousseau, 'Ninth Walk', *Reveries of the Solitary Walker* trans. Russell Goulbourne (Oxford, 2011), p.104. For discussion of another resonant

256   *Notes to pages 168–75*

cottage scene, in Wollstonecraft's *Vindication of the Rights of Woman*, see Packham, 'Cottage Economics', pp.462–63.

78 For a full discussion, see Packham, 'Cottage Economics'.

79 Richard Price, 'Observations on the Importance of the American Revolution' in *Richard Price: Political Writings*, ed. D. O. Thomas (Cambridge: Cambridge University Press, 1991), p.145; J. Hector St John de Crèvecœur, *Letters from an American Farmer*, ed. Susan Manning (Oxford University Press, 1997) p.41.

80 For Wollstonecraft's reviews, see *Works*, vol. 7 p.174, p.92, p.225; p.392. John Barrell discusses the representation of the cottage in the 1790s in his chapter 'Cottage Politics' in *The Spirit of Despotism: Invasions of Privacy in the 1790s* (Oxford, 2006) pp.210–46. His examples include Charlotte Smith's *Marchmont* (1794), in which the hero is caught between desire for a cottage retreat and anticipation of its undesirable 'stagnation', and John Thelwall's short essay on cottages in his *The Peripatetic* (1793). For Wollstonecraft's review of *Marchmont*, see *Works* vol.7, pp.485–86.

81 See Gregory Claeys, 'Virtuous Commerce and Free Theology: Political Economy and the Dissenting Academies 1750–1800', *History of Political Thought* 20:1 (1999), 141–72 (167). Claeys is referring here particularly to Godwin and his circle.

82 *WN*, p.782. Smith also noted that ignorance was a problem for the landlord class too: see p.265.

83 *SND*, p.288; *WW*, p.102.

84 Ibid., p.284 (italics in original). See also pp.256–57.

85 For Montesquieu's influence in the Scottish Enlightenment, see Richard B. Sher, 'From Troglodytes to Americans: Montesquieu and the Scottish Enlightenment on Liberty, Virtue, and Commerce', in David Wootton ed. *Republicanism, Liberty and Commercial Society 1649–1776* (Stanford University Press, 1994) pp.368–402.

86 See *WN*, p.378, and Winch, *Riches and Poverty*, p.84.

87 *SND*, p.284, p.256.

88 Ibid., p.245, p.262, p.244.

89 Ibid., pp.316–17, pp.294–95.

90 Rousseau, *Reveries*, p.24. W. G. Sebald considers this passage in his essay on Rousseau in his *A Place in the Country* trans. Jo Catling (Hamish Hamilton, 2013).

91 Rousseau, *Reveries*, p.79.

92 *SND*, p.248.

93 Ibid., p.326, p.338; p.241.

94 McKeon, *Secret History*, pp.376–78.

95 Ibid., p.378.

96 *TMS*, p.137; McKeon, *Secret History*, p.379.

97 Rousseau, *Inequality*, p.14.

98 Rousseau, *Reveries*, p.8.

99 *SND*, pp.248–49.

Notes to pages 175–84

100 Rousseau, *Reveries*, p.8.
101 Ibid., p.52, p.56.
102 *SND*, p.281.
103 Ibid., p.342.
104 Michael Igantieff, *Needs of Strangers*, p.119; *WN*, p.27.
105 *SND*, p.340.
106 Ibid., p.246.
107 McKeon, *Secret History*, p.378.
108 Ignatieff, *Needs of Strangers*, p.119.
109 *SND*, p.344.
110 Ibid., p.345.
111 Ibid., p.344.
112 William Godwin famously described the text as able to 'make a man in love with its author': see his *Memoirs of the Author of a 'Vindication of the Rights of Woman'*, in Mary Wollstonecraft and William Godwin, *A Short Residence in Sweden and Memoirs*, ed. Richard Holmes (Penguin, 1987), p.249.
113 Rousseau, *Inequality*, p.55.
114 John Brewer, 'Introduction', *Early Modern Property*, p.9.
115 Brewer, *Early Modern Property*, p.10.
116 Montesquieu, 'Some Reflections on The Persian Letters', in *Persian Letters* trans. C. J. Betts (Penguin, 1993) p.283. For a discussion, see Sheehan and Wahrman, *Invisible Hands*, pp.3–4.
117 *The Adventurer*, 67, 26 June 1753; see Donald Winch, *Riches and Poverty*, p.57.
118 Ignatieff, *Needs of Strangers*, p.119.
119 Smith, 'The Principles which Lead and Direct Philosophical Enquiries; Illustrated by the History of Astronomy', in *EPS*, pp.33–105.
120 Rousseau, *Reveries*, p.8.
121 Ibid., p.9.
122 *SND*, p.311.
123 Ibid., p.279.
124 Ibid., p.311.
125 Ibid., p.311.
126 *WN*, pp.29–30.
127 Ibid., p.783.
128 *TMS*, p.186.
129 Ignatieff, *Needs of Strangers*, p.120.
130 Montesquieu, 'Some Reflections', p.283.
131 Catherine Gallagher discusses fiction's 'character-effect' and the 'relief of knowability' it offers readers in 'The Rise of Fictionality', in *The Novel* ed. Franco Moretti [2 vols], Vol. 1 (Princeton UP 2006), pp.336–63 (pp.356–57).
132 Ignatieff, *Needs of Strangers*, p.111.
133 Montesquieu, 'Some Reflections', p.283.

258   *Notes to pages 185–88*

6 Credit and Credulity

1 Author's Preface, *WW*, p.83.
2 Preface, *WW*, p.81.
3 Author's Preface, *WW*, pp.83–4.
4 Clifford Siskin, *System: The Shaping of Modern Knowledge* (MIT Press, 2016), p.163.
5 Other discussions of the Bank Restriction Act by literary critics include Matthew Rowlinson, *Real Money and Romanticism* (Cambridge University Press, 2010), pp.50–3 and Mary Poovey, *Genres of the Credit Economy* (University of Chicago Press, 2008) for whom it provides an approach to the broken promises in Jane Austen's *Pride and Prejudice* (pp.369–72); for a response, see Alexander Dick, *Romanticism and the Gold Standard* (Palgrave, 2013), pp.154–55.
6 On the history of bills and paper money, which originated in the bills used by merchants and traders to conduct business overseas without carrying bulky and insecure amounts of coin with them, see Poovey, *Credit Economy*. On the widespread use of credit by businessmen in eighteenth-century England, see Julian Hoppit, 'The Use and Abuse of Credit in Eighteenth-century England', in *Business Life and Public Policy* eds. Neil McKendrick and R. B. Outhwaite (Cambridge University Press, 1986), pp.64–78. Those least used to paper money were hardest hit by the Restriction: see Rowlinson, *Real Money*, pp.51–2.
7 Robert Mitchell, *Sympathy and the State in the Romantic Era: Systems, State Finance, and the Shadows of Futurity* (Routledge, 2007), p.5.
8 Writings on credit included: Daniel Defoe's *An Essay upon Publick Credit* (1710) and his essays on credit in his review (1706–1711); essays by Joseph Addison and Richard Steele in *The Spectator*; and Charles Davenant, who warned that 'Of all beings that have existence only in the minds of men, nothing is more fantastical and nice than Credit; it is never to be forced; it hangs upon opinion; it depends upon our passions of hope and fear; it comes many times unsought for, and often goes away without reason, and when once lost, is hardly to be recovered': *Discourses on the Public Revenue, and on the Trade of England* (1698), quoted in Hoppitt, 'Use and Abuse of Credit', p.78. Extensive commentary on the cultural representation of credit includes: Paula Backscheider, 'Defoe's Lady Credit'. *Huntingdon Library Quarterly* 44 (1981), 89–100; Terry Mulcaire, 'Public Credit, or the Feminization of Virtue in the Marketplace', *PMLA* 114:5 (1999), 1029–42; John F. O'Brien, 'The Character of Credit: Defoe's Lady Credit, The Fortunate Mistress, and the Resources of Inconsistency in Early Eighteenth-Century Britain', *ELH* 63: 3 (1996), 603–31; and Simon Schaffer, 'Defoe's Natural Philosophy and the Worlds of Credit' in *Nature Transfigured: Science and Literature 1700–1900* eds. John Christie and Sally Shuttleworth (Manchester University Press, 1989) pp.13–44.
9 *Parliamentary History (Hansard)* February 1797, vol. 32, 1564.
10 Ibid., vol. 33, 57 and vol. 32, 1564.

11 Ibid., vol. 33, 549.
12 For a discussion of the relation between credit and liberal governmentality from the early eighteenth century, see Mary Poovey, *A History of the Modern Fact* (University of Chicago Press, 1998), p.147, pp.157–69.
13 See Patrick Brantlinger's claim, in *Fictions of State: Culture and Credit in Britain, 1694–1994* (Cornell University Press, 1996) that the 1797 banking crisis and its aftermath contributed to emergence of 'political economy' as a widely acknowledged social science (p.111).
14 Janet Todd, *Mary Wollstonecraft: A Revolutionary Life* (Weidenfeld and Nicholson, 2000), p.426.
15 *WW*, p.105.
16 The *Oxford English Dictionary* lists 'venable' as a rare usage for 'vendible', or 'capable of being vended or sold'.
17 For a variation on the theme of credit's vulnerability, in which the precariousness is attributed not to a feminised credit but to the merchant, see Richard Steele, 'Glory, Reputation and Credit in the World of Fame', *The Spectator* no. 218 (9 November 1711).
18 *WW*, p.85; *VRW*, p.129.
19 Gillian Russell 'Faro's Daughters', *Eighteenth Century Studies* 33:4 (2000), 497; Jon Mee, *Romanticism, Enthusiasm and Regulation* (Oxford University Press, 2005).
20 Russell, 'Faro's Daughters', p.500.
21 *TMS*, p.40. See Harriet Guest, *Unbounded Attachment* (Oxford University Press, 2013), pp.4–5.
22 For a related but slightly different argument, see Miranda Burgess's claim that sensibility is a 'shared regulatory standard uniting social and economic exchange': see *British Fiction and the Production of Social Order, 1740–1830*, p.23.
23 *WW*, p.101.
24 *TMS*, p.167; pp.54–6.
25 Ibid., p.189.
26 *WN* vol. 2, p.697. The valoration of prudence as an economic virtue goes back at least to the early eighteenth century: see Mary Poovey, A *History of the Modern Fact*, p.144 for a discussion of Steele's account, in *The Spectator* for 19 September 1711, of Sir Andrew Freeport's defence of merchants' accounting practices as 'prudent'. Anna Letitia Barbauld describes prudence as 'jealous and worldly-minded' and associates it with the acquisition of wealth in her essay 'Against Inconsistency in our Expectations', (1773), which Wollstonecraft praised in *VRW*. See *Anna Letitia Barbauld: Selected Poetry and Prose* ed. William McCarthy and Elizabeth Kraft (Ontario: Broadview, 2002), pp.186–94 (p.188).
27 *WN* vol. 1, p.292.
28 *HMV*, p.182.
29 *TMS*, pp.335–36.
30 *WN*, vol. 2. p.791. This sole instance however hints towards the widespread fear of 'enthusiasm' in many Enlightenment thinkers. Hume commented that

260   *Notes to pages 196–203*

'quacks and projectors' are more readily believed when they offer 'magnificent pretentions' than more moderate ones. See David Hume, *A Treatise of Human Nature* ed. L. A. Selby-Bigge (Clarendon Press, 1978), p.120.

31 *TMS*, p.336.

32 William Godwin, *Caleb Williams* (Oxford University Press, 1970), p.305.

33 *WN*, vol. 1. p.321.

34 Ibid., vol. 1. p.315. Examples discussed by Smith include the then recent failure of Ayr bank and John Law's infamous Mississippi scheme. Hume had been much more sceptical about possibilities of paper money (See his essays 'Of Money' and on 'Balance of Trade').

35 *VRW*, p.179.

36 Ibid., p.175, p.178.

37 Ibid., p.176.

38 Ibid., p.176.

39 Ibid., p.175. 'How quickly is the so much vaunted milkiness of nature turned into gall, by an intercourse with the world, if more generous juices do not sustain the vital source of virtue' Maria notes in *WW*, p.137.

40 *VRW*, pp.175–76.

41 Ibid., pp.176–77.

42 Ibid., p.177.

43 Ibid., p.177.

44 Ibid., p.178.

45 Ibid., p.182.

46 Ibid., pp.178–79.

47 Ibid., p.181.

48 Ibid., p.181

49 Ibid., p.183.

50 William Godwin, *Memoirs of the Author of* A Vindication of the Rights of Woman, ed. Richard Holmes (Penguin, 1987), p.242.

51 *WW*, p.116.

52 Ibid., p.101.

53 *HMV*, p.233. She also attacks commercial speculation in her *SND*.

54 *WW*, p.127.

55 Ibid., p 127.

56 Ibid., p.134.

57 Ibid., p.134.

58 Hume, *Treatise*, p.123. This is the section where Hume calls poets 'liars by profession' and attempts to maintain a difference between dangerous beliefs of the imagination (chimeras) and others.

59 As Hoppit notes, Smith (in *WN*) also feared a lack of prudence in young men, whose economic dealings were marked by too much hope and not enough fear. See Hoppit, 'Use and Abuse of Credit', p.72.

60 *WW*, p.138.

61 Ibid., p.151, p.175. The OED defines an accommodation bill as 'a bill not representing or originating in an actual commercial transaction, but for the

Notes to pages 203–209

purpose of raising money on credit'. See also Mary Poovey's discussion of accommodation bills, and bills of exchange generally, in *Genres of the Credit Economy*, p.36ff.

62 *WN*, p.316, p.315.

63 See Hoppit, 'Uses and Abuses of Credit'. The issue of *AR* for December 1796 also describes the process of conmen setting up as merchants, getting goods on credit, and exploiting bills of credit to defraud others.

64 *WW*, p.173.

65 According to the economic historian Hannah Barker, it was unusual for a woman to act as sole trustee for a child's inheritance: is Wollstonecraft attempting to imagine a new operation of the law here? See Barker, *Family and Business during the Industrial Revolution* (Oxford University Press, 2017), p.69.

66 *WW*, p.130.

67 Ibid., pp.176–77. The development from erotic love to a more universal benevolence recurs elsewhere in Wollstonecraft and is influenced by Rousseau: see, for instance, Laura Kirkley's illuminating reading of *Mary* in *Mary Wollstonecraft: Cosmopolitan* (Edinburgh University Press, 2022), pp.44–7.

68 *Mary*, p.5.

69 Samuel Johnson, *The History of Rasselas, Prince of Abissinia* (Oxford University Press, 1988), p.1.

70 Samuel Johnson, *Rambler* no 4 (31 March 1750), pp.27–36. This requirement for fiction to be creditable is at odds with Johnson's view that the purpose of that fiction is to shape the beliefs of unformed youth: his readers are thus at once deemed capable of determining what can be credited, and in need of the very tutelage in belief that fiction provides.

71 *Cave of Fancy*, in *Works* vol. 1, p.191.

72 *Rasselas*, p.122; *Cave of Fancy*, p.206.

73 *Cave of Fancy*, p.191.

74 Karen O'Brien, *Women and Enlightenment in Eighteenth-Century Britain* (Cambridge University Press, 2009), p.200.

75 In one of her reviews, Wollstonecraft notes that 'pleasures arising from taste and feeling' as well as being 'complex and accidental' are 'almost incommunicable'; in another, on Gilpin, she notes that ideas which are merely 'excited' rather than 'represented' are more 'acceptable' to the 'mind in which they are raised'. See *Works* vol. 7, p.161, p.387.

76 For the instability of sensibility, see Markman Ellis, *Politics of Sensibility* (Cambridge University Press, 1996), p.7; for the 'extraordinary volatility of notions of sensibility', see Harriet Guest, *Small Change* (University of Chicago Press, 2000), p.291.

77 *TMS*, p.190, p.40, p.191. See Guest, *Unbounded Attachment*, pp.4–5.

78 *TMS*, pp.191–92.

79 'Unbounded attachment' is Godwin's description of Wollstonecraft: see Guest, *Unbounded Attachment,* p.5, and see p.7 in the same work for the observation that 'Godwin suggests Wollstonecraft's *Short Residence* enacts on its readers by "dissolv[ing] us in tenderness"; *VRW,* p.129.

80 On this, see Guest, *Small Change*, pp.1–13. See Guest, *Unbounded Attachment*, p.3, for the claim that sensibility enabled women's writing to accomplish the 'transition from the private or intimate to the general or social'.

81 Pamela Clemit, Introduction, in William Godwin, *Memoirs of the Author of 'A Vindication of the Rights of Woman'* (Broadview, 2001), p.23.

82 Jon Mee, *Dangerous Enthusiasm* (Clarendon Press, 1992), p.25.

83 See Hume 'On the Delicacy of Taste and Passion', in *Essays Moral, Political, Literary* ed. Eugene F. Miller (Liberty Fund, 1985); see also Adela Pinch, *Strange Fits of Passion* (Stanford University Press, 1996), pp.51–3.

84 *WW*, p.86.

85 Similarly, Sylvana Tomaselli points out that Wollstonecraft located the origins of society and sociability in the 'long stories' told by elders to their 'listening progeny'. See Tomaselli, *Wollstonecraft: Philosophy, Passion and Politics* (Princeton University Press, 2021), p.131–32; *HMV*, p.146.

86 Terry Eagleton, *The Function of Criticism: From the Spectator to Post-Structuralism* (Verso, 1984), p.26, pp.16–7. See Guest, *Small Change* pp.5–6 for a subtle and suggestive discussion of women's relation to rational exchanges of civil society.

87 Daniel E. White, *Early Romanticism and Religious Dissent* (Cambridge University Press, 2006); see also Gregory Claeys, 'Virtuous Commerce and Free Theology: Political Economy and the Dissenting Academies 1750–1800', *History of Political Thought* 20:1 (Spring 1999), 141–72.

88 White, *Early Romanticism*, p.110; Preface, *WW*, p.81.

89 For his discussion of Wollstonecraft's 'affective spontaneity', see White, *Early Romanticism*, p.114.

90 Johnson, *Rasselas*, p.15.

91 Ibid., p.16.

92 Ibid., p.1.

93 *Cave of Fancy* in *Works* vol. 1, p.199, p.195.

94 On 'fictionality' as a historically and culturally specific capacity for belief which enabled the rise of the novel, see Catherine Gallagher, 'The Rise of Fictionality', in *The Novel* ed. Franco Moretti [2 vols], Vol. 1 (Princeton University Press, 2006), pp.336–63.

95 *WW*, p.131.

96 Ibid., p.137.

97 *TMS*, p.190.

98 *VRM*, p.29.

99 'On Poetry', in *Works*, vol. 7, p.9, p.11.

100 Daniel White, *Early Romanticism*, p.116–18. As Sylvana Tomaselli has noted, remarks on history painting given tangentially in *VRM* also turn on the relation between imitation and inspiration: see Tomaselli, *Wollstonecraft: Philosophy, Passion, and Politics* (Princeton University Press, 2021), p.26.

101 'On Poetry', p.10.

102 *VRW*, p.181.

103 *WW*, p.181.

104 Ibid., p.83, p.81.

Notes to pages 215–18   263

Conclusion

1 *SND*, pp.294–95, p.311, p.249.
2 Ibid., p.311.
3 Anahid Nersessian, *The Calamity Form: On Poetry and Social Life* (University of Chicago Press, 2020), p.135.
4 *SND*, p.311, pp.248–49.
5 Sylvana Tomaselli, *Wollstonecraft: Philosophy, Passion, and Politics* (Princeton University Press, 2021), p.210. Sometimes this reinvention takes surprising forms, as in Virginia Woolf's celebration of Wollstonecraft: her 'face, at once so resolute and so dreamy, so sensual and so intelligent, and beautiful into the bargain with its great coils of hair and … large bright eyes … the most expressive [Southey] had ever seen'. From *Nation and Athenaeum*, 5 October 1929; see *Virginia Woolf: Women and Writing* ed. Michèle Barrett (The Women's Press, 1979), pp.99.
6 For one survey, whose title conveys much, see Helen Thompson, *Disorder: Hard Times for the Twenty-First Century* (Oxford University Press, 2022).
7 Sylvana Tomaselli, 'Political Economy: The Desire and Needs of Present and Future Generations' in *Inventing Human Science: Eighteenth-Century Domains,* eds. Christopher Fox, Roy Porter, and Robert Wokler (University of California Press, 1995), pp.292–322 (p.313).
8 For calls for alternative economic models, whether green growth, post-growth, or steady-state, as well as the need to realign our economic system with social and planetary good, see, for instance, Andreas Malm, *Fossil Capital* (Verso, 2015), Tim Jackson *Post Growth: Life after Capitalism* (Polity, 2021), and Ann Pettifor, *The Case for the Green New Deal* (Verso, 2019).
9 Geoffrey West, *Scale: The Universal Laws of Life and Death in Organisms, Cities and Companies* (Weidenfeld and Nicolson, 2017), p.238; Richard Bronk, *The Romantic Economist* (Cambridge University Press, 2009), p.24, drawing on Philip Mirowski, *More Heat than Light* (Cambridge University Press, 1989).
10 Tim Rogan, *The Moral Economists: R. H. Tawney, Karl Polanyi, E. P. Thompson* (Princeton University Press, 2017), p.57.
11 Rogan, *Moral Economists*, p.88.
12 Ibid., p.88, p.91.
13 Quoted in Rogan, *Moral Economists*, p.79; John Stuart Mill, *Autobiography* (Penguin, 1989), p.178; quoted in Bronk, *Romantic Economist,* p.54.
14 Bronk, *Romantic Economist*, p.10, p.24; Hunter Heyck, *Age of System: Understanding the Development of Modern Social Science* (Johns Hopkins University Press, 2015), p.12.
15 Heyck, *System*, p.6, pp.3–6.
16 Ibid., pp.5–6; Kate Raworth, *Doughnut Economics* (Penguin, 2017), pp.35–40; Amit Kapoor and Bibek Debroy, 'GDP Is Not a Measure of Human Well-Being', *Harvard Business Review* (4 October 2019), https://hbr.org/2019/10/gdp-is-not-a-measure-of-human-well-being. The critique of GDP is hardly new, being a feature of Robert Kennedy's 1968 campaign for the US Presidency: see Jackson, *Post Growth*, pp.1–16.

264   *Notes to pages 218–20*

17 Joanna Rostek, *Women's Economic Thought in the Romantic Age* (Routledge, 2021), p.58.

18 Julie Nelson, 'How Did "the Moral" Get Split from "the Economic"?' in *Toward a Feminist Philosophy of Economics* eds. Drucilla Barker and Edith Kuiper (Routledge, 2003), pp.134–41 (p.135); Mariana Mazzucato, 'What If Our Economy Valued What Matters?', www.project-syndicate.org/commentary/valuing-health-for-all-new-metrics-for-economic-policy-and-progress-by-mariana-mazzucato-2022-03, accessed 9 March 2022.

19 From a potentially vast literature of economists critical of economics, see Diane Coyle, *Cogs and Monsters: What Economics Is, and What It Should Be* (Princeton University Press, 2021); Robert Skidelsky, *What's Wrong With Economics* (Yale University Press, 2020); *Rethinking Capitalism* eds. Michael Jacobs and Mariana Mazzucato (Wiley-Blackwell, 2016) collects essays by leading economists on the need to rethink current economic orthodoxies; Kate Raworth, *Doughnut Economics: Seven Ways to Think Like a 21st Century Economist* (Random House, 2018) argues for a new economics to respond to the challenges of our time. For pressure to reform economics as it is taught in universities, see *Economics, Education and Unlearning: Economics Education at the University of Manchester*, Post-Crash Economics Society (PCES), April 2014, accessed 28 September 2020, www.post-crasheconomics.com/download/778r. See also Richard Adelman and Catherine Packham, 'The Formation of Political Economy as a Knowledge Practice' in *Political Economy, Literature & the Formation of Knowledge, 1720–1850* eds. Adelman and Packham (Routledge, 2018), pp.1–21.

20 Nitasha Kaul, 'The Anxious Identities we inhabit: Post'isms and Economic Understanding', in *Toward a Feminist Philosophy of Economics*, pp.194–210 (p.203).

21 Iain Hampsher-Monk, 'Edmund Burke, Political Economy, and the Market', *Cosmos + Taxis* (2021), 9: 9–10, 10–8 (p.11).

22 Bronk, *Romantic Economist*, pp.xiii–xv; see pp.7–8 for his account of responses to such criticisms from within the discipline.

23 Nicholas Maxwell, 'From Knowledge to Wisdom: The Need for an Academic Revolution', in Ronald Barnett and Nicholas Maxwell eds. *Wisdom in the University* (Routledge, 2008), pp.1–20 (p.14). For a measured defence of economics as a collection of models, see Dani Rodrik, *Economics Rules* (Oxford University Press, 2015).

24 Mariana Mazzucato, *Mission Economy* (Penguin, 2021), p.211.

25 Mazzucato, *Mission Economy*, p.211.

26 Rogan, *Moral Economists*, p.87.

27 For 'economism', see Richard Norgaard, 'The Church of Economism and Its Discontents', December 2015, https://greattransition.org/publication/the-church-of-economism-and-its-discontents, accessed 20 February 2022.

28 *SND*, pp.248–49.

29 Ibid., pp.310–11.

30 Ibid., pp.294–95.

31 *TMS*, pp.12–3.
32 Judith Butler, *The Force of Nonviolence: An Ethico-Political Bind* (Verso, 2020), p.59.
33 Judith Butler, *Precarious Life: The Powers of Mourning and Justice* (Verso, 2004), p.28.
34 Nersessian, *Calamity Form*, p.54.
35 John Whale, *Imagination Under Pressure* (Cambridge University Press, 2000) p.187.
36 *WN*, vol. 1, p.428.
37 Elizabeth A. Bohls, *Women Travel Writers and the Language of Aesthetics, 1716–1818* (Cambridge University Press, 1995), p.151.
38 Nersessian, *Calamity Form*, p.142, and see Jonathan Kramnick, *Paper Minds: Literature and the Ecology of Consciousness* (University of Chicago Press, 2018), p.83.
39 Barbara K. Seeber, 'Mary Wollstonecraft: "Systemiz[ing] Oppression": Feminism, Nature and Animals', in Peter F. Cannavo, J. H. H, Lane et al. eds., *Engaging Nature: Environmentalism and the Political Theory Canon* (MIT Press, 2014), pp.173–88 (p.174). See also Enit Karafili Steiner, 'Mood, Provisionality, and Planetarity in Mary Wollstonecraft's *A Short Residence in Sweden, Norway, and Denmark*', *Criticism* 61:1 (2019), 27–50.
40 Seeber, 'Systemiz[ing] Oppression', p.175, pp.182–83.
41 West, *Scale*, p.238.
42 *SND*, p.304.
43 *Works*, vol. 6, p.445.
44 Rogan, *Moral Economists*, p.200, p.85.
45 Tomaselli, *Wollstonecraft*, p.128.
46 *HMV*, p.228.
47 Ibid., p.227.
48 Ibid., p.235.

Bibliography

Periodicals

Analytical Review
Parliamentary History (Hansard)
The Adventurer
The New Annual Register, or General Repository of History, Politics, and Literature
The Rambler
The Spectator

Other Primary and Secondary Sources

Adelman, Richard. *Idleness, Contemplation, and the Aesthetic, 1750–1830* (Cambridge University Press, 2011).

Adelman, Richard. and Packham, Catherine. 'The Formation of Political Economy as a Knowledge Practice', in *Political Economy, Literature and the Formation of Knowledge, 1720–1850* eds. Richard Adelman and Catherine Packham (Routledge 2018), pp.1–21.

Aftalion, Florin. *The French Revolution: An Economic Interpretation* (Cambridge University Press, 1990).

Aikin, John and Aikin, Anna Laetitia *Miscellaneous Pieces in Prose* (London, 1773).

Backscheider, Paula R. 'Defoe's Lady Credit', *Huntington Library Quarterly* 44:2 (Spring, 1981), 89–100.

Barbauld, Anna Letitia. 'Against Inconsistency in Our Expectations' in *Anna Letitia Barbauld: Selected Poetry and Prose* eds. William McCarthy and Elizabeth Kraft (Ontario: Broadview, 2002), pp.186–94.

Barker, Hannah. *Family and Business during the Industrial Revolution* (Oxford University Press, 2017).

Barrell, John. 'The Public Prospect and the Private View: The Politics of Taste in Eighteenth-Century Britain' in *Landscape, Natural Beauty and the Arts* eds. Salim Kemal and Ivan Gaskell (Cambridge University Press, 1993), pp.81–102.

Barrell, John. *The Spirit of Despotism: Invasions of Privacy in the 1790s* (Oxford University Press, 2006).

Bibliography

267

Barrett, Michèle, ed. *Virginia Woolf: Women and Writing* (The Women's Press, 1979).

Behrendt, Stephen C. *British Women Poets and the Romantic Writing Community* (Johns Hopkins University Press, 2009).

Bender, John and Michael, Marrinan, eds. *Regimes of Description: in the Archive of the Eighteenth Century* (Stanford University Press, 2005).

Bergès, Sandrine and Coffee, Alan, eds. *The Social and Political Philosophy of Mary Wollstonecraft* (Oxford University Press, 2016).

Black, R.D. Collison. 'Ingram, Robert Acklom', *ODNB*, 2004.

Bohls, Elizabeth A. *Women Travel Writers and the Language of Aesthetics, 1716–1818* (Cambridge University Press, 1995).

Botting, Eileen Hunt. *Family Feuds: Wollstonecraft, Burke, and Rousseau on the Transformation of the Family* (State University of New York Press, 2006).

Botting, Eileen Hunt. *Wollstonecraft, Mill and Women's Human Rights* (Yale University Press, 2016).

Botting, Eileen Hunt, ed. *Portraits of Wollstonecraft* (Bloomsbury, 2021).

Bourke, Richard. *Empire & Revolution: The Political Life of Edmund Burke* (Princeton University Press, 2015).

Brace, Laura. *The Politics of Slavery* (Edinburgh University Press, 2018).

Braithwaite, Helen. *Romanticism, Publishing and Dissent: Joseph Johnson and the Cause of Liberty* (Palgrave Macmillan, 2003).

Brantlinger, Patrick. *Fictions of State: Culture and Credit in Britain, 1694–1994* (Cornell University Press, 1996).

Brewer, John. *Sinews of Power: War, Money and the English State 1688–1783* (Routledge, 1989).

Brewer, John and Staves, Susan, eds. *Early Modern Conceptions of Property* (Routledge, 1995).

Bronk, Richard. *The Romantic Economist* (Cambridge University Press, 2009).

Bugg, John. 'How Radical Was Joseph Johnson and Why Does Radicalism Matter', *Studies in Romanticism* 57:2 (2018), 173–343.

Burgess, Miranda. *British Fiction and the Production of Social Order 1740–1830* (Cambridge University Press, 2000).

Burke, Edmund. *The Correspondence of Edmund Burke* eds. Thomas W. Copeland, Alfred Cobban and Robert A. Smith 10 vols, vol. 6 (Cambridge University Press and University of Chicago Press, 1967).

Burke, Edmund. *Reflections on the Revolution in France* ed. Conor Cruise O'Brien (Penguin, 1968).

Burrows, Simon. 'The Innocence of Jacques-Pierre Brissot', *The Historical Journal* 46:4 (2003), 843–71.

Butler, Judith. *Precarious Life: The Powers of Mourning and Justice* (Verso, 2004).

Butler, Judith. *The Force of Nonviolence: An Ethico-Political Bind* (Verso, 2020).

Butler, Marilyn. *Burke, Paine, Godwin and the Revolution Controversy* (Cambridge University Press, 1984)

Calhoun, Craig, ed. *Habermas and the Public Sphere* (MIT Press, 1992).

Cameron, Kenneth N., ed. *Shelley and his Circle 1773–1822*, 2 vols. (Harvard University Press, 1961).

Bibliography

Carlyle, Thomas. 'Occasional Discourse on the Negro Question', *Fraser's Magazine for Town and Country* 40 (February 1849), 527–39.

Caygill, Howard. *The Art of Judgement* (Basil Blackwell, 1989).

Claeys, Gregory. 'The French Revolution Debate and British Political Thought', *History of Political Thought* 11:1 (Spring 1990), 59–80.

Claeys, Gregory. 'Utopianism, Property, and the French Revolution Debate in Britain' in *Utopias and the Millennium* eds. Krishan Kumar and Stephen Bann (Reaktion Books, 1993), pp.46–62.

Claeys, Gregory. 'Virtuous Commerce and Free Theology: Political Economy and the Dissenting Academies 1750–1800', *History of Political Thought* 20:1 (Spring 1999), 141–72.

Clemit, Pamela. 'Introduction', in *Memoirs of the Author of 'A Vindication of the Rights of Woman'* ed. William Godwin (Broadview, 2001), pp.11–36.

Coffee, Alan. 'Mary Wollstonecraft, Freedom and the Enduring Power of Social Domination', *European Journal of Political Theory* 12:2 (2013), 116–35.

Cohen, Ralph. 'History and Genre', *New Literary History* 17:2 (1986), 203–218.

Cohen, Ralph. *Transformations of a Genre* (Palgrave Macmillan, 2021).

Colley, Linda. 'Radical Patriotism in Eighteenth-Century England' in *Patriotism: The Making and Unmaking of British National Identity, vol.1: History and Politics* ed. Raphael Samuel (Routledge, 1989), 169–87.

Connell, Philip. *Romanticism, Economics and the Question of 'Culture'* (Oxford University Press, 2001).

Cox, Jeffrey N. and Galperin, William. 'Joseph Johnson' in *The Wordsworth Circle* 40:2–3 (Spring and Summer 2009), 93–5.

Coyle, Diane. *Cogs and Monsters: What Economics Is, and What It Should Be* (Princeton University Press, 2021).

Crèvecœur, J. Hector St John de. *Letters from an American Farmer* ed. Susan Manning (Oxford University Press, 1997).

de Bolla, Peter. *The Discourse of the Sublime: Readings in History, Aesthetics and the Subject* (Basil Blackwell, 1989).

de Bruyn, Frans. *The Literary Genres of Edmund Burke* (Oxford University Press, 1996).

de Bruyn, Frans 'From Georgic Poetry to Statistics and Graphs: Eighteenth-Century Representations and the "State" of British Society', *Yale Journal of Criticism* 17:1 (2004), 107–39.

de Luna, Frederick A. 'The Dean Street Style of Revolution: J.-P. Brissot, Jeune Philosophe', *French Historical Studies* 17:1 (Spring 1991), 159–90.

Dick, Alexander. *Romanticism and the Gold Standard* (Palgrave, 2013).

Dreyer, Frederick. 'The Genesis of Burke's *Reflections*', *Journal of Modern History* 50:3 (1978), 462–79.

Eagleton, Terry. *The Function of Criticism: From The Spectator to Post-Structuralism* (Verso, 1984).

Eger, Elizabeth, Charlotte Grant, Clíona Ó Gallchoir and Penny Warburton eds. *Women, Writing and the Public Sphere 1700–1830* (Cambridge University Press, 2001).

Bibliography

Ellis, Markman. *The Politics of Sensibility* (Cambridge University Press, 1996).

Favret, Mary A. 'Travelling with Mary Wollstonecraft' in *The Cambridge Companion to Mary Wollstonecraft* ed. Claudia L. Johnson (Cambridge University Press, 2002), 214–17.

Favret, Mary A. *Romantic Correspondence: Women, Politics and the Fiction of Letters* (Cambridge University Press, 2008).

Ferguson, Susan. 'The Radical Ideas of Mary Wollstonecraft', *Canadian Journal of Political Science* 32:3 (September 1999), 427–50.

Foucault, Michel. *The Order of Things: An Archaeology of the Human Sciences* (Routledge, 1989).

Gallagher, Catherine. 'The Rise of Fictionality' in *The Novel* ed. Franco Moretti, 2 vols, Vol. 1 (Princeton University Press, 2006), pp.336–63.

Gaull, Marilyn. 'Joseph Johnson: Webmaster', *The Wordsworth Circle* 40:2–3 (2009), 107–110.

Godwin, William. *Caleb Williams* (Oxford University Press, 1970).

Godwin, William. *Memoirs of the Author of 'The Rights of Woman'* in *A Short Residence in Sweden and Memoirs of the Author of 'The Rights of Woman'* eds. Richard Holmes, Mary Wollstonecraft and William Godwin (Penguin, 1987), pp.203–77.

Guest, Harriet. *Small Change: Women, Learning, Patriotism, 1750–1810* (University of Chicago Press, 2000).

Guest, Harriet. *Unbounded Attachment* (Oxford University Press, 2013).

Guillory, John. *Capital Culture: The Problem of Literary Canon Formation* (Chicago University Press, 1993).

Habermas, Jurgen. *The Structural Transformation of the Public Sphere* trans. T. Burger and F. Lawrence (MIT Press, 1989).

Halldenius, Lena. 'Mary Wollstonecraft's Feminist Critique of Property: On Becoming a Thief from Principle', *Hypatia* 29:4 (2014), 942–57.

Hamilton, Paul. *Metaromanticism* (University of Chicago Press, 2003).

Hampsher-Monk, Iain. 'Edmund Burke, Political Economy, and the Market', *Cosmos + Taxis* 9:9–10 (2021), 10–18.

Hay, Daisy. *Dinner With Joseph Johnson* (Chatto & Windus, 2022).

Helleiner, Karl F. *The Imperial Loans: A Study in Financial and Diplomatic History* (Clarendon Press, 1965).

Heyck, Hunter. *Age of System: Understanding the Development of Modern Social Science* (Johns Hopkins University Press, 2015).

Hochstrasser, T. J. 'Physiocracy and the Politics of Laissez-Faire' in *Cambridge History of Eighteenth-Century Political Thought* ed. Mark Goldie and Robert Wokler (Cambridge University Press, 1991), pp.419–42.

Hont, Istvan and Ignatieff, Michael, eds. *Wealth and Virtue: The Shaping of Political Economy in the Scottish Enlightenment* (Cambridge University Press, 1983).

Hoppit, Julian. 'The Use and Abuse of Credit in Eighteenth-Century England' in *Business Life and Public Policy* eds. Neil McKendrick and R. B. Outhwaite (Cambridge University Press, 1986), pp.64–78.

Bibliography

Horrocks, Ingrid. *Women Wanderers and the Writing of Mobility, 1784–1814* (Cambridge University Press, 2017), pp.140–68.

Hume, David. *A Treatise of Human Nature* eds. L. A. Selby-Bigge and P. H. Nidditch (Clarendon Press, 1978).

Hume, David. *Essays: Moral, Political, Literary* ed. Eugene F. Miller (Liberty Fund, 1985).

Hurtado, Jimena. 'Jean-Jacques Rousseau: économie politique, philosophie économique et justice', *Revue de philosophie économique* 11:2 (2010), 69–101.

Huzel, James P. 'Ruggles, Thomas', *ODNB*, 2004.

Igantieff, Michael. *The Needs of Strangers* (Hogarth Press, 1984).

Imlay, Gilbert. *A Topographical Description of the Western Territory of North America* (London, 1797).

Innes, Joanna. 'Politics and Morals: The Reformation of Manners Movement in Later Eighteenth-Century England' in *The Transformation of Political Culture: England and Germany in the Late Eighteenth Century* ed. Eckhart Hellmuth (Oxford University Press, 1990), pp.57–118.

Jackson, Tim. *Post Growth: Life after Capitalism* (Polity, 2021).

Jacobs, Michael and Mazzucato Mariana, eds. *Rethinking Capitalism* (Wiley-Blackwell, 2016).

Janes, R. M. 'On the Reception of Mary Wollstonecraft's *A Vindication of the Rights of Woman*', *Journal of the History of Ideas* 39:2 (1978), 293–302.

Johnson, Claudia L. *Equivocal Beings: Politics, Gender, and Sentimentality in the 1790s* (University of Chicago Press, 1995).

Johnson, Nancy E. and Keen, Paul, eds. *Mary Wollstonecraft in Context* (Cambridge University Press, 2020).

Johnson, Samuel, *The History of Rasselas, Prince of Abissinia* (Oxford University Press, 1988).

Jones, Vivien, 'Women Writing Revolution: Narratives of History and Sexuality in Wollstonecraft and Williams' in *Beyond Romanticism* eds. John Whale and Stephen Copley (Routledge, 1992), pp.178–99.

Jump, Harriet Devine. '"The Cool Eye of Observation": Mary Wollstonecraft and the French Revolution' in *Revolution in Writing: British Literary Responses to the French Revolution* ed. Kelvin Everest (Open University Press, 1991), pp.101–20.

Kaplan, Cora. *Sea Changes: Essays on Culture and Feminism* (Verso, 1986).

Kapoor, Amit and Debroy, Bibek. 'GDP Is Not a Measure of Human Well-Being', *Harvard Business Review* (4 October 2019), https://hbr.org/2019/10/gdp-is-not-a-measure-of-human-well-being.

Kapossy, Béla, Nakhimovsky, Isaac and Whatmore Richard eds. *Commerce and Peace in the Enlightenment* (Cambridge, 2017).

Kaul, Nitasha. 'The Anxious Identities We Inhabit: Post'isms and Economic Understanding' in *Toward A Feminist Philosophy of Economics* eds. Drucilla Barker and Edith Kuiper (Routledge, 2003), pp.194–210.

Kay, Carol. 'Canon, Ideology and Gender: Mary Wollstonecraft's Critique of Adam Smith' *New Political Science* 7:1 (1986), 63–76.

Keen, Paul. *The Crisis of Literature in the 1790s* (Cambridge University Press, 1999).

Bibliography

Kelly, Gary. *Revolutionary Feminism: The Mind and Career of Mary Wollstonecraft* (Macmillan, 1992).

Kirkley, Laura. *Mary Wollstonecraft: Cosmopolitan* (Edinburgh University Press, 2022).

Klancher, Jon P. *The Making of English Reading Audiences, 1790–1832* (University of Wisconsin Press, 1987).

Kramnick, Jonathan. *Paper Minds: Literature and the Ecology of Consciousness* (University of Chicago Press, 2018).

Landes, Joan. *Women and the Public Sphere in the Age of the French Revolution* (Cornell University Press, 1988).

Lock, F. P. *Burke's Reflection on the Revolution in France* (George Allen & Unwin, 1985).

Macaulay, Catharine. *Observations on the Reflections of the Right Hon. Edmund Burke, on the Revolution in France, in a Letter to the Right Hon. the Earl of Stanhope* (1790).

Macaulay, Catharine. *Letters on Education: With Observations on Religious and Metaphysical Subjects* (Cambridge University Press, 2014).

Makdisi, Saree. *William Blake and the Impossible History of the 1790s* (University of Chicago Press, 2003).

Malm, Andreas. *Fossil Capital* (Verso, 2015).

Maxwell, Nicholas. 'From Knowledge to Wisdom: The Need for an Academic Revolution' in *Wisdom in the University* eds. Ronald Barnett and Nicholas Maxwell (Routledge, 2008), pp.1–20.

Mazzucato, Mariana. *Mission Economy* (Penguin, 2021).

Mazzucato, Mariana. 'What If Our Economy Valued What Matters?', www.project-syndicate.org/commentary/valuing-health-for-all-new-metrics-for-economic-policy-and-progress-by-mariana-mazzucato-2022-03.

McKeon, Michael. *The Secret History of Domesticity: Public, Private, and the Divisions of Knowledge* (Johns Hopkins University Press, 2005).

Mee, Jon. *Dangerous Enthusiasm: William Blake and the Culture of Radicalism in the 1790s* (Clarendon Press, 1992).

Mee, Jon. *Romanticism, Enthusiasm and Regulation* (Oxford University Press, 2005).

Mee, Jon. *Conversable Worlds: Literature, Contention and Community 1762–1830* (Oxford, 2011).

Mitchell, Robert. *Sympathy and the State in the Romantic Era: System, State Finance, and the Shadows of Futurity* (Routledge, 2007).

Montesquieu, 'Some Reflections on *The Persian Letters*' in *Persian Letters* trans. C. J. Betts (Penguin, 1993).

Mulcaire, Terry. 'Public Credit, or the Feminization of Virtue in the Marketplace', *PMLA* 114:5 (1999), 1029–42.

Munjal, Savi. '"He Drinks the Knowledge in Greedy Haste": Tasting History Through James Gillray's Political Prints', *AIC* 11:1 (2013), 39–64.

Murray, Julie. 'Mary Hays and the Forms of Life', *Studies in Romanticism* 52 (2013), 61–84.

Myers, Mitzi. 'Politics from the Outside: Mary Wollstonecraft's First *Vindication*'. *Studies in Eighteenth-Century Culture* 6 (1977), 113–32.

Nakhimovsk, Isaac. 'The "Ignominious Fall of the European Commonwealth": Gentz, Hauterive, and the Armed Neutrality of 1800' in *Trade and War: The Neutrality of Commerce in the Interstate System* ed. Koen Stapelbroek (Helsinki Collegium for Advanced Studies, 2011), pp.177–90.

Nelson, Julie. 'How Did "The Moral" Get Split from "the Economic"?' in *Toward a Feminist Philosophy of Economics* eds. Drucilla Barker and Edith Kuiper (Routledge, 2003), pp.134–41.

Nersessian, Anahid. *The Calamity Form: On Poetry and Social Life* (University of Chicago Press, 2020).

Norgaard, Richard. 'The Church of Economism and its Discontents', December 2015, https://greattransition.org/publication/the-church-of-economism-and-its-discontents.

O'Brien, John F. 'The Character of Credit: Defoe's Lady Credit, The Fortunate Mistress, and the Resources of Inconsistency in Early Eighteenth-Century Britain', *ELH* 63:3 (1996), 603–31.

O'Brien, Karen. *Women and Enlightenment in Eighteenth-Century Britain* (Cambridge University Press, 2009).

Offen, Karen. 'Was Mary Wollstonecraft A Feminist? A Contextual Re-reading of *A Vindication of the Rights of Woman* 1792–1992' in *Quilting a New Canon: Stitching Women's Words*, ed. Uma Parameswaran (Black Women and Women of Colour Press, September 1996), pp.3–24.

Oliver, Susan. 'Silencing Joseph Johnson and the *Analytical Review*', *The Wordsworth Circle*, 40:2–3 (2009), 96–102.

Packham, Catherine. 'Feigning Fictions: Imagination, Hypothesis and Philosophical Writing in the Scottish Enlightenment', *Eighteenth Century: Theory and Interpretation* 48:2 (2007), 149–71.

Packham, Catherine. 'Domesticity, Object and Idleness': Mary Wollstonecraft and Political Economy', *Women's Writing* 19:4 (2012), 544–62.

Packham, Catherine. '"The Common Grievance of the Revolution": Bread, the Grain Trade, and Political Economy in Wollstonecraft's *View of the French Revolution*', *European Romantic Review* 25:6 (2014), 705–22.

Packham, Catherine. 'Mary Wollstoncraft's Cottage Economics: Property, Political Economy, and the European Future', *ELH* 84 (2017), 453–74.

Packham, Catherine. 'Genre and the Mediation of Political Economy in Edmund Burke's *Reflections on the Revolution in France* and Mary Wollstonecraft's *A Vindication of the Rights of Men*', *The Eighteenth Century: Theory and Interpretation* 60:3 (Autumn 2019), 249–68.

Packham, Catherine. 'System and Subject in Adam Smith's Political Economy: Nature, Vitalism, and Bioeconomic Life' in *Systems of Life: Biopolitics, Economics and Literature on the Cusp of Modernity* eds. Richard A. Barney and Warren Montag (Fordham University Press, 2019), pp.93–113.

Paulson, Ronald. *Representations of Revolution, 1789–1820* (Yale University Press, 1983).

Bibliography

Pettifor, Ann. *The Case for the Green New Deal* (Verso, 2019).

Philipson, Nicholas. *Adam Smith: An Enlightened Life* (Penguin, 2011).

Pinch, Adela. *Strange Fits of Passion: Epistemologies of Emotion, Hume to Austen* (Stanford University Press, 1996).

Pocock, J. G. A. *Virtue, Commerce, History: Essays on Political Thought and History* (Cambridge University Press, 1985).

Pocock, J. G. A. ed. 'Introduction to Edmund Burke' *Reflections on the Revolution in France* (Hackett, 1987), vii–xlviii.

Pocock, J. G. A. 'Edmund Burke and the Redefinition of Enthusiasm: The Context as Counter-Revolution' in *The French Revolution and the Creation of Modern Political Culture* eds. François Furet and Mona Ozouf (Pergamon, 1989), pp.19–36.

Poovey, Mary. *The Proper Lady and the Woman Writer* (University of Chicago Press, 1984).

Poovey, Mary. *A History of the Modern Fact: Problems of Knowledge in the Sciences of Wealth and Society* (University of Chicago Press, 1998).

Poovey, Mary. *Genres of the Credit Economy: Mediating Value in Eighteenth- and Nineteenth-Century Britain* (University of Chicago Press, 2008).

Pope, Alexander. *The Major Works*, ed. Pat Rogers (Oxford University Press, 2008).

Price, Richard. *Political Writings*, ed. D. O. Thomas (Cambridge University Press, 1991).

Randall, Adrian. *Riotous Assemblies: Popular Protest in Hanoverian England* (Oxford University Press, 2006).

Raworth, Kate. *Doughnut Economics: Seven Ways to Think Like a 21st Century Economist* (Random House, 2018).

Rendell, Jane. '"The Grand Causes Which Combine to Carry Mankind Forward": Wollstonecraft, History and Revolution', *Women's Writing* 4:2 (1997), 155–72.

Rickman, Clio. *Life of Paine* (London, 1819).

Robbins, Caroline. *The Eighteenth-Century Commonwealthman* (Harvard University Press, 1961).

Robin, Corey. 'Edmund Burke and the Problem of Value', *Raritan* 36:1 (Summer 2016), 82–106.

Rodrik, Dani. *Economics Rules* (Oxford University Press, 2015).

Rogan, Tim. *The Moral Economists: R. H. Tawney, Karl Polanyi, E. P. Thompson* (Princeton University Press, 2017).

Ross, Ian Simpson. *The Life of Adam Smith* (Oxford University Press, 2010).

Rostek, Joanna. *Women's Economic Thought in the Romantic Age* (Routledge, 2021).

Rothschild, Emma. *Economic Sentiments: Adam Smith, Condorcet and the Enlightenment* (Harvard University Press, 2001).

Rousseau, Jean-Jacques. *Discourse on the Origin of Inequality* trans. Franklin Philip (Oxford University Press, 1994), p.32, p.31.

Rousseau, Jean-Jacques. 'Discourse on Political Economy' in *The Social Contract*, trans. Christopher Betts (Oxford University Press 1994), pp.1–41.

Rousseau, Jean-Jacques. *Reveries of the Solitary Walker* trans. Russell Goulbourne (Oxford University Press, 2011).

Rowlinson, Matthew. *Real Money and Romanticism* (Cambridge University Press, 2010).

Russell, Gillian. 'Faro's Daughters', *Eighteenth Century Studies* 33:4 (2000), 481–505.

Sangster, Matthew. *Living as an Author in the Romantic Period* (Palgrave, 2021).

Sapiro, Virginia. *A Vindication of Political Virtue* (University of Chicago Press, 1992).

Schaffer, Simon. 'Defoe's Natural Philosophy and the Worlds of Credit' in *Nature Transfigured: Science and Literature 1700–1900* eds. John Christie and Sally Shuttleworth (Manchester University Press, 1989), pp.13–44.

Sebald, W. G. *A Place in the Country* trans. Jo Catling (Hamish Hamilton, 2013).

Seeber, Barbara K. 'Mary Wollstonecraft: "Systemiz[ing] Oppression": Feminism, Nature and Animals' in eds. Peter F. Cannavo, J. H, Lane et al. *Engaging Nature: Environmentalism and the Political Theory Canon* (MIT Press, 2014), pp.173–88.

Sheehan, Jonathan and Dror Wahrmann. *Invisible Hands: Self-Organization and the Eighteenth Century* (University of Chicago Press, 2015).

Shelley, Mary. *Frankenstein* (Oxford University Press, 2008).

Sher, Richard B. 'From Troglodytes to Americans: Montesquieu and the Scottish Enlightenment on Liberty, Virtue, and Commerce' in ed. David Wootton *Republicanism, Liberty and Commercial Society 1649–1776* (Stanford University Press, 1994), pp.368–402.

Sherman, Sandra. 'The Wealth of Nations in the 1790s', *Studies in Eighteenth-Century Culture* 34 (2005), 81–96.

Simpson, David. *Romanticism, Nationalism and the Revolt against Theory* (University of Chicago Press, 1993).

Siskin, Clifford. *The Work of Writing: Literature and Social Change in Britain, 1700–1830* (Johns Hopkins University Press, 1998).

Siskin, Clifford. *System: The Shaping of Modern Knowledge* (MIT Press, 2016).

Skidelsky, Robert. *What's Wrong with Economics* (Yale University Press, 2020).

Smith, Adam. *The Theory of Moral Sentiments* eds. D. D. Raphael and A. L. Macfie (Oxford University Press, 1976).

Smith, Adam. *Lectures on Jurisprudence* ed. R. L. Meek, D. D. Raphael and Peter Stein (Oxford University Press, 1978).

Smith, Adam. *An Inquiry into the Nature and Causes of the Wealth of Nations* ed. R. H. Campbell and A. S. Skinner, 2 vols. (Oxford University Press, 1979).

Smith, Adam. *Essays on Philosophical Subjects* ed. W. P. D. Wightman and J. C. Bryce (Oxford University Press, 1980).

Sonenscher, Michael. 'Property, Community and Citizenship' in *The Cambridge History of Eighteenth-Century Political Thought* eds. Mark Goldie and Robert Wokler (Cambridge, 2006), pp.465–94.

Sonenscher, Michael. *Before the Deluge: Public Debt, Inequality and the Intellectual Origins of the French Revolution* (Princeton University Press, 2007).

Sonenscher, Michael. *Capitalism: The Story Behind the Word* (Princeton University Press, 2022).

Bibliography

Spector, Céline. *Rousseau* (Polity, 2019).

Stedman Jones, Gareth. *An End to Poverty? A Historical Debate* (Profile, 2004).

Stewart, Dugald. 'Account of the Life and Writings of Adam Smith, LL.D' in *EPS*, p.322.

Swift, Simon. 'Mary Wollstonecraft and the "Reserve of Reason"', *Studies in Romanticism* 45:1 (2006), 3–24.

Taylor, Barbara. *Mary Wollstonecraft and the Feminist Imagination* (Cambridge University Press, 2003).

Thompson E. P. ed. 'The Moral Economy of the English Crowd in the Eighteenth Century' and 'The Moral Economy Reviewed' in *Customs in Common* (Merlin, 1991), pp.185–351.

Thompson, Helen. *Disorder: Hard Times for the Twenty-First Century* (Oxford University Press, 2022).

Thompson, James. *Models of Value: Eighteenth-Century Political Economy and the Novel* (Duke University Press, 1996).

Todd, Janet. *Mary Wollstonecraft: An Annotated Bibliography* (Garland, 1976, repr. Routledge, 2013).

Todd, Janet. *Mary Wollstonecraft: A Revolutionary Life* (Weidenfeld and Nicholson, 2000).

Todd, Janet, ed. *The Collected Letters of Mary Wollstonecraft* (Columbia University Press, 2003).

Tomaselli, Sylvana. 'The Enlightenment Debate on Women', *History Workshop Journal* 20:1 (1985), 101–24.

Tomaselli, Sylvana. 'Political Economy: The Desire and Needs of Present and Future Generations' in *Inventing Human Science: Eighteenth-Century Domains* eds. Christopher Fox, Roy Porter and Robert Wokler (University of California Press, 1995), pp.292–322.

Tomaselli, Sylvana. *Wollstonecraft: Philosophy, Passion, and Politics* (Princeton University Press, 2021).

Tyson, Gerald P. *Joseph Johnson: A Liberal Publisher* (University of Iowa Press, 1979).

Valenza, Robin. *Literature, Language and the Rise of the Intellectual Disciplines in Britain 1680–1820* (Cambridge University Press, 2009).

Verhoeven, Wil. *Gilbert Imlay: Citizen of the World* (Pickering & Chatto, 2008).

Weiss, Deborah. *The Female Philosopher and Her Afterlives* (Palgrave Macmillan, 2107).

West, Geoffrey. *Scale: The Universal Laws of Life and Death in Organisms, Cities and Companies* (Weidenfeld and Nicolson, 2017).

Whale, John. *Imagination Under Pressure* (Cambridge University Press, 2000).

Whatmore, Richard. 'Commerce, Constitutions, and the Manners of a Nation: Etienne Clavière's Revolutionary Political Economy, 1788–93', *History of European Ideas*, 22:5–6 (1996), 351–68.

Whatmore, Richard. *Against War and Empire: Geneva, Britain and France in the Eighteenth Century* (Yale University Press, 2012).

Bibliography

Whatmore, Richard. 'Burke on Political Economy' in *The Cambridge Companion to Edmund Burke* eds. David Dwan and Christopher J. Insole (Cambridge University Press, 2021), pp.80–91.

White, Daniel E. *Early Romanticism and Religious Dissent* (Cambridge University Press, 2006).

Wickman, Matthew. *Literature After Euclid: The Geometric Imagination in the Long Scottish Enlightenment* (University of Pennsylvania Press, 2016).

Winch, Donald. *Riches and Poverty: An Intellectual History of Political Economy in Britain, 1750–1834* (Cambridge University Press, 1996).

Winch, Donald. 'Political Economy' in *Oxford Companion to the Romantic Age* ed. Iain McCalman (Oxford University Press, 2001), pp.311–19.

Wingrove, Elizabeth 'Getting Intimate with Wollstonecraft in the Republic of Letters', *Political Theory* 33:3 (June 2005) 344–69.

Wiseman, Susan. 'Catharine Macaulay: History, Republicanism and the Public Sphere' in *Women, Writing and the Public Sphere, 1700–1830* eds. Elizabeth Eger, Charlotte Grant, Clíona Ó Gallchoir and Penny Warburton (Cambridge University Press, 2001), pp.181–99.

Wollstonecraft, Mary. *The Works of Mary Wollstonecraft* ed. Janet Todd and Marilyn Butler, 7 vols. (Pickering and Chatto, 1989).

Young, Arthur. *Travels in France During the Years 1787, 1788 and 1789*, 2 vols. (London, 1794).

Index

accommodation bills, 198, 203
Addison, Joseph, 105, 191
agrarianism, 14, 16, 43, 64, 115, 163, 168
Aikin, John, 42, 210
Althusser, Louis, 60
Analytical Review, 1, 5, 12, 20, 25–47, 50, 54, 93, 109, 115, 126, 131, 133
Arendt, Hannh, 219
assignats, 37, 62, 79, 112, 125, 128, 145, 246, 252
Austen, Jane, 87

Babeuf, Gracchus, 16
Bank Restriction Act (1797), The, 23, 187–89, 194, 195
Barbauld, Anna Laetitia, 42, 52, 210
'Against Inconsistency in Our Expectations', 94
Barlow, Joel, 22, 36, 45, 126, 132–34, 233, 249, 250
Barrell, John, 58
Behrendt, Stephen C., 13
Brissot, Jacques Pierre, 22, 46, 126–34, 168
Bronk, Richard, 218
Bruyn, Frans de, 69
Burgess, Miranda, 13, 48
Burke, Edmund, 4, 6, 21, 27, 31, 36, 37, 81, 88, 97, 100, 145
and idleness, 84
Letter to a Noble Lord, 85
Philosophical Enquiry into the Origin of Our Ideas of the Sublime and the Beautiful, 57, 83, 139
Reflections on the Revolution in France, 13, 16, 36, 39, 49–79, 85, 123, 142, 153
Butler, Judith, 220
Butler, Marilyn, 50

Carlyle, Thomas, 5
Caygill, Howard, 66
Chesterfield, Lord, 101
Christie, Thomas, 28, 29, 45, 115, 116, 131, 132, 142, 231, 247, 258
Claeys, Gregory, 28, 169

Clavière, Etienne, 113, 127–29, 133, 134, 136, 146, 249
Clemit, Pamela, 209
Cohen, Ralph, 17
Coleridge, Samuel Taylor, 5, 16, 28, 47, 116, 230
commercial society, 3, 4
affective and psychic conditions of, 18
emergence of, 94, 95
future of, 8, 20
and manners, 21, 92–95
and morality, 14
and passions, 95–104
and Scottish Enlightenment, 7
and women, 7, 22, 93, 104–11
Condorcet, Marquis de, 123, 127, 128, 131
conjectural history, 92, 93, 104, 149, 150, 165, 173
in Rousseau, 170
credit, system of, 80, 105, 187–89, 203. *See also* Lady Credit
credulity, 193–98
Crèvecœur, J. Hector St. John de, 125–27, 132, 145, 256
Letters from an American Farmer, 168

Darnton, Robert, 121
Defoe, Daniel, 105, 191
division of labour, 9, 43, 144, 146, 165, 169, 178, 183, 195

Eagleton, Terry, 77, 210
economics, 2
critiques of, 216–18
history of, 217–18
Eden Treaty, 38, 113, 122
Encyclopédie, 119, 121, 122

Favret, Mary, 12
Fénelon, François, 123, 124
Ferguson, Adam, 165
Foucault, Michel, 2
Fox, Charles James, 116, 188, 189, 225, 263

Franklin, Benjamin, 124
free trade, 8, 16, 22
  in grain, 112–46
Fuseli, Henry, 131

GDP, 218
Gibbon, Edward
  Decline and Fall of the Roman Empire, 153
Girondins, 8, 22, 114, 120, 122, 125–34
  fall of, 121, 125, 128
Godwin, William, 19, 45, 48, 121, 129, 185, 186,
    193, 196, 209, 210, 214, 227, 230, 233–35,
    239, 248, 256, 257, 260–62
  Memoirs of the Author of 'A Vindication of the
    Rights of Woman', 77, 201
  and property, 40
Gregory, John, 1
Guest, Harriet, 105
Guillory, John, 70

Habermas, Jurgen, 77
Hamilton, Paul, 58
happiness, 21, 31, 52, 54, 68–70, 74, 99, 162
  in Rousseau, 176
  science of public, 125
human nature, theories of, 3, 18, 68, 78, 84,
    89, 194
Hume, David, 7, 34, 40, 84, 87, 89, 91, 105, 155,
    194, 197
  'Of the Delicacy of Taste and Passion', 209
  and manners, 94, 99, 105
  'The Stoic', 85
  Treatise of Human Nature, 85, 203
  and utility, 155

idleness, 65, 87
  and property, 83–87
Ignatieff, Michael, 176, 183
imagination, 12, 21, 24, 62, 66, 74, 89, 90, 178
  and commercial society, 222, 223
  and futurity, 220–21
  and political economy, 55, 58
  and property, 91
Imlay, Gilbert, 11, 17, 22, 36, 44, 113, 115, 126,
    132, 134, 168, 201, 219, 249, 250, 252
  The Emigrants, 134
  Topographical Description of the Western
    Territory of North America, 133, 145

Jefferson, Thomas, 129
Johnson, Joseph, 1, 12, 113, 115. *See also Analytical*
  Review
  treason trial, 5, 28
Johnson, Samuel, 180
  Rasselas, 198, 207, 212

Kaul, Nitasha, 218
Kay, Carol, 14
Kelly, Gary, 67, 131
Kramnick, Jonathan, 221

Lady Credit, 105, 190, 191, 203, 222, 245, 258

Macaulay, Catharine, 1, 52, 63, 64, 68, 74, 79,
    80, 90, 236–40, 243
  Letters on Education, 52
Makdisi, Saree, 3, 11
Malthus, Thomas, 5, 27, 33, 217
  Principles of Political Economy, 33
Mandeville, Bernard, 94, 152
manners, 84, 87, 92–95, 115
  in commercial society, 79, 165
  and conjectural history, 104
  and women, 104–11
Mazzucato, Mariana, 218
McKeon, Michael, 156, 174, 178
Mee, Jon, 45, 191, 209
mercantilism, 38
Mill, J. S., 217
Mirabeau, Honoré Gabriel Ricqueti, Conte de,
    112, 124, 125, 127, 133, 135, 225, 249
Mitchell, Robert, 187
Montchrétien, Antoine de, 2
Montesquieu, Charles de Secondat, Baron de, 7,
    14, 34, 38, 123, 183–84, 212
  Persian Letters, 94, 152, 169, 180
  'Reflections on *The Persian Letters*', 180
moral economy, 114, 141
Morellet, abbé de, 121–23, 128
Munjal, Savi, 116
Myers, Mitzi, 18

national debt, 33–36
Necker, Jacques, 30, 56, 127, 135, 163
Nelson, Julie, 218
Nersessian, Anahid, 215

O'Brien, Karen, 96, 208

Paine, Thomas, 4, 27, 65, 46, 127, 128, 131, 142
  The Rights of Man, 38
paper money, 197
Paulson, Ronald, 69
physiocrats, 114, 117, 121, 122, 136, 145. *See also*
  Quesnay, François
Pinch, Adela, 105
Pitt, William, 4, 187, 194
Pocock, J. G. A., 52, 91, 109
political economy, 20
  and aesthetic value, 5, 159–61
  and civil society, 27, 60

Index

279

and comfort, 5, 163–66
as 'dead science', 5
definition of, 2, 59, 217
and disciplinarity, 18, 70, 194
and dissent, 29
eighteenth-century, 3
emergence of, 4, 26, 70, 85
and landscape writing, 62
and liberty, 53
and the novel, 183–84
Romantic critiques of, 6, 10
and science of wealth, 4
and tragedy, 61, 67, 69–75
versus economics, 216–17
and women, 14, 94
Polyani, Karl, 217
Pownall, Thomas, 3
Price, Richard, 3, 19, 29, 30, 34, 43, 46, 53, 61, 90, 128, 145
Discourse on the Love of our Country, 53–55, 123, 133, 136
Observations on the Importance of the American Revolution, 43, 124, 125, 127, 168
Observations on the Nature of Civil Liberty, 123, 124
and Shelburne, 38
Priestley, Joseph, 19, 29, 34, 38, 46, 51, 210
property, 14, 19, 21, 22, 33, 36
in *Analytical Review,* 36–39
and the 'art of living', 159–66
Burke's defence of, 65–67, 80
critique of, 53–55, 76–111
domestic, in political economy, 151–58
and literary form, 178–84
and manners, 54, 82, 92–95, 165
and personhood, 105–6, 158, 166, 167, 178, 182
in political economy, 147–84
in *Short Residence in Sweden, Norway and Denmark,* 166–70
system of, 63
and visual spectacle, 153–56, 171
and women, 88, 107–11, 158
prudence, 101, 192–98
in *Vindication of the Rights of Woman,* 198–201
in *Wrongs of Woman,* 201–6

Quesnay, François, 30, 117

Robin, Corey, 67, 70
Rogan, Tim, 217, 223
Rostek, Joanna, 218
Rothschild, Emma, 9, 118, 120
Rousseau, Jean-Jacques, 1, 6, 7, 16, 19, 22, 38, 40, 84, 97, 106, 112, 128, 156, 159, 162, 173, 174, 201

Discourse on the Origin of Inequality, 98, 149–51, 153–54, 163, 169, 174, 177, 182
Discourse on Political Economy, 26, 151
Emile, 34, 83
Julie, ou La Nouvelle Héloïse, 152, 172
Letter to d'Alembert on Spectacles, 75
and political economy, 165
and property, 179
Reveries of the Solitary Walker, 150, 167, 172, 174, 175, 182
The Social Contract, 168
Russell, Gillian, 191

Sangster, Matthew, 5, 13
sensibility, 19, 41, 68, 192, 209, 210
and Edmund Burke, 81
Shelburne, William Petty, Lord, 22, 38, 51, 122–24, 126, 127, 188, 235, 248
Sheridan, Richard Brinsley, 116, 188, 192
Siskin, Clifford, 3, 186
slave trade, 80, 106, 149
Smith, Adam, 1, 3, 4, 6, 22, 42, 82, 89, 94, 97, 102, 106, 114, 120, 122, 125, 143, 144, 173, 194
in *Analytical Review,* 30
and credulity, 198–201, 205
definition of political economy, 26, 59, 221
on European economic development, 43
'History of Astronomy', 180
invisible hand, 180, 184
on the labouring poor, 9
Lectures on Jurisprudence, 67
on mercantile behaviour, 9, 66
and the 'philosophical eye', 166
and the physiocrats, 118
and property, 40, 151–58, 170
and prudence, 194–98, 200
and sympathy, 177
Theory of Moral Sentiments, 7, 82, 85, 96, 98–101, 107, 130, 156, 174, 176, 178, 181, 194, 199, 209, 220
Wealth of Nations, 1, 3, 7, 9, 26, 38, 57, 66, 86, 95, 118, 123, 136, 149, 151, 153, 159, 182, 194
Smith, Charlotte, 47
Southey, Robert, 5
Spector, Celine, 152, 154, 156
stadial history, 7, 169
Steuart, James, 26
Stewart, Dugald, 4, 27, 120
sympathy, 176–78, 194, 220

Talleyrand, Charles Maurice de, 63, 112, 113, 122, 128
Thompson, E. P., 141, 217
Thompson, James, 3, 26, 70
Todd, Janet, 131

280   *Index*

Tomaselli, Sylvana, 2, 3, 216, 223
Trelawny, R. H., 217
Turgot, Anne Robert Jacques, 3, 25, 30, 113, 118–20, 122–26, 128, 225, 247–49

value, 70, 83, 87, 223
  and imagination, 223
  and property, 159
Verhoeven, Wil, 132, 134

Walpole, Horace, 58
Wardle, Ralph, 12
wealth, problem of, 95–104, 172
West, Geoffrey, 217
Whale, John, 221
Whatmore, Richard, 122, 124
White, Daniel, 18, 19, 42, 210, 213
Williams, Helen Maria, 121, 133
Winch, Donald, 26
Wollstonecraft, Mary
  Cave of Fancy, 18, 199, 207, 208, 212
  and debt, 11, 12
  early works, 13
  Hints [for a second part of *Vindication of the Rights of Woman*], 160

Historical and Moral View of the French Revolution, 8, 10, 12, 22, 30, 32, 96, 112–46, 147–51, 159–66, 195, 202, 223
'Letter on the Present Character of the French Nation', 129, 134, 222
Mary A Fiction, 11, 12, 18, 72, 82, 83, 87, 157, 185, 193, 199, 207
on the novel, 17, 61, 101, 157–58, 184, 193
'On Poetry', 12, 18, 72, 207, 213, 224
reviews in *Analytical,* 46, 52, 126, 133, 169
Short Residence in Sweden, Norway and Denmark, 12, 17, 22, 41, 42, 126, 139, 148–50, 152, 159–61, 163, 166–79, 215–16, 219–23
and Smith, Adam, 7–11
Vindication of the Rights of Men, 12, 13, 18, 21, 35, 38, 40, 49–55, 74–112, 204, 213
Vindication of the Rights of Woman, 1, 7–8, 12, 17, 21, 34, 54, 64, 68, 76–112, 134, 154, 161, 184
Wrongs of Woman The, 10–12, 17, 19, 23, 41, 48, 72, 88, 92, 101, 106, 149, 157, 169, 185–87
Wordsworth, William, 20, 213

Young, Arthur, 43
Young, Edward, 179

CAMBRIDGE STUDIES IN ROMANTICISM

General Editor
JAMES CHANDLER, University of Chicago

1. *Romantic Correspondence: Women, Politics and the Fiction of Letters*
   MARY A. FAVRET

2. *British Romantic Writers and the East: Anxieties of Empire*
   NIGEL LEASK

3. *Poetry as an Occupation and an Art in Britain, 1760–1830*
   PETER MURPHY

4. *Edmund Burke's Aesthetic Ideology: Language, Gender and Political Economy in Revolution*
   TOM FURNISS

5. *In the Theatre of Romanticism: Coleridge, Nationalism, Women*
   JULIE A. CARLSON

6. *Keats, Narrative and Audience*
   ANDREW BENNETT

7. *Romance and Revolution: Shelley and the Politics of a Genre*
   DAVID DUFF

8. *Literature, Education, and Romanticism: Reading as Social Practice, 1780–1832*
   ALAN RICHARDSON

9. *Women Writing about Money: Women's Fiction in England, 1790–1820*
   EDWARD COPELAND

10. *Shelley and the Revolution in Taste: The Body and the Natural World*
    TIMOTHY MORTON

11. *William Cobbett: The Politics of Style*
    LEONORA NATTRASS

12. *The Rise of Supernatural Fiction, 1762–1800*
    E. J. CLERY

13. *Women Travel Writers and the Language of Aesthetics, 1716–1818*
    ELIZABETH A. BOHLS

14. *Napoleon and English Romanticism*
    SIMON BAINBRIDGE

15. *Romantic Vagrancy: Wordsworth and the Simulation of Freedom*
    CELESTE LANGAN

16. *Wordsworth and the Geologists*
JOHN WYATT

17. *Wordsworth's Pope: A Study in Literary Historiography*
ROBERT J. GRIFFIN

18. *The Politics of Sensibility: Race, Gender and Commerce in the Sentimental Novel*
MARKMAN ELLIS

19. *Reading Daughters' Fictions, 1709–1834: Novels and Society from Manley to Edgeworth*
CAROLINE GONDA

20. *Romantic Identities: Varieties of Subjectivity, 1774–1830*
ANDREA K. HENDERSON

21. *Print Politics: The Press and Radical Opposition in Early Nineteenth-Century England*
KEVIN GILMARTIN

22. *Reinventing Allegory*
THERESA M. KELLEY

23. *British Satire and the Politics of Style, 1789–1832*
GARY DYER

24. *The Romantic Reformation: Religious Politics in English Literature, 1789–1824*
ROBERT M. RYAN

25. *De Quincey's Romanticism: Canonical Minority and the Forms of Transmission*
MARGARET RUSSETT

26. *Coleridge on Dreaming: Romanticism, Dreams and the Medical Imagination*
JENNIFER FORD

27. *Romantic Imperialism: Universal Empire and the Culture of Modernity*
SAREE MAKDISI

28. *Ideology and Utopia in the Poetry of William Blake*
NICHOLAS M. WILLIAMS

29. *Sexual Politics and the Romantic Author*
SONIA HOFKOSH

30. *Lyric and Labour in the Romantic Tradition*
ANNE JANOWITZ

31. *Poetry and Politics in the Cockney School: Keats, Shelley, Hunt and their Circle*
JEFFREY N. COX

32. *Rousseau, Robespierre and English Romanticism*
GREGORY DART

33. *Contesting the Gothic: Fiction, Genre and Cultural Conflict, 1764–1832*
JAMES WATT

34. *Romanticism, Aesthetics, and Nationalism*
DAVID ARAM KAISER

35. *Romantic Poets and the Culture of Posterity*
ANDREW BENNETT

36. *The Crisis of Literature in the 1790s: Print Culture and the Public Sphere*
PAUL KEEN

37. *Romantic Atheism: Poetry and Freethought, 1780–1830*
MARTIN PRIESTMAN

38. *Romanticism and Slave Narratives: Transatlantic Testimonies*
HELEN THOMAS

39. *Imagination under Pressure, 1789–1832: Aesthetics, Politics, and Utility*
JOHN WHALE

40. *Romanticism and the Gothic: Genre, Reception, and Canon Formation, 1790–1820*
MICHAEL GAMER

41. *Romanticism and the Human Sciences: Poetry, Population, and the Discourse of the Species*
MAUREEN N. MCLANE

42. *The Poetics of Spice: Romantic Consumerism and the Exotic*
TIMOTHY MORTON

43. *British Fiction and the Production of Social Order, 1740–1830*
MIRANDA J. BURGESS

44. *Women Writers and the English Nation in the 1790s*
ANGELA KEANE

45. *Literary Magazines and British Romanticism*
MARK PARKER

46. *Women, Nationalism and the Romantic Stage: Theatre and Politics in Britain, 1780–1800*
BETSY BOLTON

47. *British Romanticism and the Science of the Mind*
ALAN RICHARDSON

48. *The Anti-Jacobin Novel: British Conservatism and the French Revolution*
M. O. GRENBY

49. *Romantic Austen: Sexual Politics and the Literary Canon*
CLARA TUITE

50. *Byron and Romanticism*
JEROME MCGANN AND JAMES SODERHOLM

51. *The Romantic National Tale and the Question of Ireland*
INA FERRIS

52. *Byron, Poetics and History*
JANE STABLER

53. *Religion, Toleration, and British Writing, 1790–1830*
MARK CANUEL

54. *Fatal Women of Romanticism*
ADRIANA CRACIUN

55. *Knowledge and Indifference in English Romantic Prose*
TIM MILNES

56. *Mary Wollstonecraft and the Feminist Imagination*
BARBARA TAYLOR

57. *Romanticism, Maternity and the Body Politic*
JULIE KIPP

58. *Romanticism and Animal Rights*
DAVID PERKINS

59. *Georgic Modernity and British Romanticism: Poetry and the Mediation of History*
KEVIS GOODMAN

60. *Literature, Science and Exploration in the Romantic Era: Bodies of Knowledge*
TIMOTHY FULFORD, DEBBIE LEE, AND PETER J. KITSON

61. *Romantic Colonization and British Anti-Slavery*
DEIRDRE COLEMAN

62. *Anger, Revolution, and Romanticism*
ANDREW M. STAUFFER

63. *Shelley and the Revolutionary Sublime*
CIAN DUFFY

64. *Fictions and Fakes: Forging Romantic Authenticity, 1760–1845*
MARGARET RUSSETT

65. *Early Romanticism and Religious Dissent*
DANIEL E. WHITE

66. *The Invention of Evening: Perception and Time in Romantic Poetry*
CHRISTOPHER R. MILLER

67. *Wordsworth's Philosophic Song*
SIMON JARVIS

68. *Romanticism and the Rise of the Mass Public*
ANDREW FRANTA

69. *Writing against Revolution: Literary Conservatism in Britain, 1790–1832*
KEVIN GILMARTIN

70. *Women, Sociability and Theatre in Georgian London*
GILLIAN RUSSELL

71. *The Lake Poets and Professional Identity*
BRIAN GOLDBERG

72. *Wordsworth Writing*
ANDREW BENNETT

73. *Science and Sensation in Romantic Poetry*
NOEL JACKSON

74. *Advertising and Satirical Culture in the Romantic Period*
JOHN STRACHAN

75. *Romanticism and the Painful Pleasures of Modern Life*
ANDREA K. HENDERSON

76. *Balladeering, Minstrelsy, and the Making of British Romantic Poetry*
MAUREEN N. MCLANE

77. *Romanticism and Improvisation, 1750–1850*
ANGELA ESTERHAMMER

78. *Scotland and the Fictions of Geography: North Britain, 1760–1830*
PENNY FIELDING

79. *Wordsworth, Commodification and Social Concern: The Poetics of Modernity*
DAVID SIMPSON

80. *Sentimental Masculinity and the Rise of History, 1790–1890*
MIKE GOODE

81. *Fracture and Fragmentation in British Romanticism*
ALEXANDER REGIER

82. *Romanticism and Music Culture in Britain, 1770–1840: Virtue and Virtuosity*
GILLEN D'ARCY WOOD

83. *The Truth about Romanticism: Pragmatism and Idealism in Keats, Shelley, Coleridge*
TIM MILNES

84. *Blake's Gifts: Poetry and the Politics of Exchange*
SARAH HAGGARTY

85. *Real Money and Romanticism*
MATTHEW ROWLINSON

86. *Sentimental Literature and Anglo-Scottish Identity, 1745–1820*
JULIET SHIELDS

87. *Romantic Tragedies: The Dark Employments of Wordsworth, Coleridge, and Shelley*
REEVE PARKER

88. *Blake, Sexuality and Bourgeois Politeness*
SUSAN MATTHEWS

89. *Idleness, Contemplation and the Aesthetic*
RICHARD ADELMAN

90. *Shelley's Visual Imagination*
NANCY MOORE GOSLEE

91. *A Cultural History of the Irish Novel, 1790–1829*
CLAIRE CONNOLLY

92. *Literature, Commerce, and the Spectacle of Modernity, 1750–1800*
PAUL KEEN

93. *Romanticism and Childhood: The Infantilization of British Literary Culture*
ANN WEIRDA ROWLAND

94. *Metropolitan Art and Literature, 1810–1840: Cockney Adventures*
GREGORY DART

95. *Wordsworth and the Enlightenment Idea of Pleasure*
ROWAN BOYSON

96. *John Clare and Community*
JOHN GOODRIDGE

97. *The Romantic Crowd*
MARY FAIRCLOUGH

98. *Romantic Women Writers, Revolution and Prophecy*
ORIANNE SMITH

99. *Britain, France and the Gothic, 1764–1820*
ANGELA WRIGHT

100. *Transfiguring the Arts and Sciences*
JON KLANCHER

101. *Shelley and the Apprehension of Life*
ROSS WILSON

102. *Poetics of Character: Transatlantic Encounters 1700–1900*
SUSAN MANNING

103. *Romanticism and Caricature*
IAN HAYWOOD

104. *The Late Poetry of the Lake Poets: Romanticism Revised*
TIM FULFORD

105. *Forging Romantic China: Sino-British Cultural Exchange 1760–1840*
PETER J. KITSON

106. *Coleridge and the Philosophy of Poetic Form*
EWAN JAMES JONES

107. *Romanticism in the Shadow of War: Literary Culture in the Napoleonic War Years*
JEFFREY N. COX

108. *Slavery and the Politics of Place: Representing the Colonial Caribbean, 1770–1833*
ELIZABETH A. BOHLS

109. *The Orient and the Young Romantics*
ANDREW WARREN

110. *Lord Byron and Scandalous Celebrity*
CLARA TUITE

111. *Radical Orientalism: Rights, Reform, and Romanticism*
GERARD COHEN-VRIGNAUD

112. *Print, Publicity, and Popular Radicalism in the 1790s*
JON MEE

113. *Wordsworth and the Art of Philosophical Travel*
MARK OFFORD

114. *Romanticism, Self-Canonization, and the Business of Poetry*
MICHAEL GAMER

115. *Women Wanderers and the Writing of Mobility, 1784–1814*
INGRID HORROCKS

116. *Eighteen Hundred and Eleven: Poetry, Protest and Economic Crisis*
E. J. CLERY

117. *Urbanization and English Romantic Poetry*
STEPHEN TEDESCHI

118. *The Poetics of Decline in British Romanticism*
JONATHAN SACHS

119. *The Caribbean and the Medical Imagination, 1764–1834: Slavery, Disease and Colonial Modernity*
EMILY SENIOR

120. *Science, Form, and the Problem of Induction in British Romanticism*
DAHLIA PORTER

121. *Wordsworth and the Poetics of Air*
THOMAS H. FORD

122. *Romantic Art in Practice: Cultural Work and the Sister Arts, 1760–1820*
THORA BRYLOWE

123. *European Literatures in Britain, 1815–1832: Romantic Translations*
DIEGO SIGALIA

124. *Romanticism and Theatrical Experience: Kean, Hazlitt and Keats in the Age of Theatrical News*
JONATHAN MULROONEY

125. *The Romantic Tavern: Literature and Conviviality in the Age of Revolution*
IAN NEWMAN

126. *British Orientalisms, 1759–1835*
JAMES WATT

127. *Print and Performance in the 1820s: Improvisation, Speculation, Identity*
ANGELA ESTERHAMMER

128. *The Italian Idea: Anglo-Italian Radical Literary Culture, 1815–1823*
WILL BOWERS

129. *The Ephemeral Eighteenth Century: Print, Sociability, and the Cultures of Collecting*
GILLIAN RUSSELL

130. *Physical Disability in British Romantic Literature*
ESSAKA JOSHUA

131. *William Wordsworth, Second-Generation Romantic: Contesting Poetry after Waterloo*
JEFFREY COX

132. *Walter Scott and the Greening of Scotland: The Emergent Ecologies of a Nation*
SUSAN OLIVER

133. *Art, Science and the Body in Early Romanticism*
STEPHANIE O'ROURKE

134. *Honor, Romanticism, and the Hidden Value of Modernity*
JAMISON KANTOR

135. *Romanticism and the Biopolitics of Modern War Writing*
NEIL RAMSEY

136. *Jane Austen and Other Minds: Ordinary Language Philosophy in Literary Fiction*
ERIC REID LINDSTROM

137. *Orientation in European Romanticism: The Art of Falling Upwards*
PAUL HAMILTON

138. *Romanticism, Republicanism, and the Swiss Myth*
PATRICK VINCENT

139. *Coleridge and the Geometric Idiom: Walking with Euclid*
ANN C. COLLEY

140. *Late Romanticism and the End of Politics: Byron, Mary Shelley and the Last Men*
JOHN HAVARD

141. *Experimentalism in Wordsworth's Later Poetry: Dialogues with the Dead*
TIM FULFORD

142. *Romantic Fiction and Literary Excess in the Minerva Press Era*
HANNAH DOHERTY HUDSON

143. *Byron's Don Juan*
RICHARD CRONIN

144. *Sound and Sense in British Romanticism*
JAMES GRANDE AND CARMEL RAZ

145. *Wordsworth After War: Recovering Peace in the Later Poetry*
PHILIP SHAW

146. *Staël, Romanticism and Revolution*
JOHN CLAIBORNE ISBELL

147. *Romantic Epics and the Mission of Empire*
MATTHEW LEPORATI

148. Caricature and Realism in the Romantic Novel
OLIVIA FERGUSON

www.ingramcontent.com/pod-product-compliance
Ingram Content Group UK Ltd.
Pitfield, Milton Keynes, MK11 3LW, UK
UKHW030637171224
452390UK00008B/99